Introducing Sociology

Peter Worsley

Roy Fitzhenry, J. Clyde Mitchell,
D. H. J. Morgan, Valdo Pons, Bryan Roberts,
W. W. Sharrock, Robin Ward

Penguin Books

Penguin Books Ltd, Harmondsworth,
Middlesex, England
Penguin Books Inc., 7110 Ambassador Road,
Baltimore, Md 21207, U.S.A.
Penguin Books Australia Ltd,
Ringwood, Victoria, Australia

First published 1970
Copyright © Peter Worsley and contributors, 1970

Made and printed in Great Britain by
Cox & Wyman Ltd, London, Reading and Fakenham
Set in Monotype Times

Contents

Part Three

To our students

Acknowledgements

Our thanks are due to Penguin Education, and especially to Charles Clark and Richard Mabey for their unstinting help in arranging for the testing of the initial version of the text, and for much subsequent assistance and advice.

Secondly, we must thank our other colleagues, both teaching staff-members and postgraduates of Manchester University Department of Sociology and Social Anthropology, who helped us by using the first draft for teaching, and who relayed back to us the criticisms of students. D. R. Watson, M. A. Atkinson and E. C. Cuff also used the pilot text at Didsbury College of Education. David Jary and Joel Richman performed the same invaluable service at Manchester College of Commerce, and David Boulton at Mather College of Education, and Robin Ward also used the trial version in teaching extra-mural adult classes.

Alan Shuttleworth, Chris Pickvance and Colin Lacey also contributed to writing and criticism, while Pat Walters was the catalyst who made us undertake the operation.

Mrs Christine Hayes masterminded the complex work of co-ordination, together with Mrs Barbara Hulme. Mrs Marjorie Gray was responsible for the final stages of the operation.

Finally, my daughters, Deborah and Julia, numbered the pages.

Acknowledgement is made to the following for permission to use copyright material: Charles Schultz, *Peanuts* cartoon, to United Features Syndicate; lyric by Sammy Cahn, 'Love and Marriage', to Barton Music; Brian Jackson and Dennis Marsden, *Education and the Working Class*, to Routledge & Kegan Paul and Monthly Review Press; Colin Lacey, *Hightown Grammar: The School as a Social System*, to Manchester University Press; Tom Lehrer, 'Wernher von

Braun', *Tom Lehrer's Second Song Book*, to Crown Publishers and Elek Books; Conrad M. Arensberg and Solon T. Kimball, *Family and Community in Ireland*, to Harvard University Press.

Manchester, 1969   P.W.

Preface

This textbook is written by a group of sociologists in response to needs perceived by themselves as teachers, and by their students. Though there are good textbooks available, we have found even the best of them unsuitable for the use of those coming to sociology for the first time: the simpler ones tending to be too sketchy and to 'talk down' to the reader, the others attempting to cover too great a range of topics and societies. This book, however, although introductory, is not intended to be elementary, While we have striven to write it lucidly, we did not wish to over-simplify or to duck thorny issues of theory.

On the other hand, we have not attempted to emulate or replace the compendious 'blockbuster' type of textbook. This is an introductory textbook, not a summary of human knowledge. One crucial defect in these large textbooks is that as they tend to draw nearly all their illustrative material from the United States, they often seem rather parochial to non-Americans. This perhaps reflects the pre-eminence of American sociology rather than any narrowness of vision. Yet it seemed good to us to counteract this by making our endeavour as 'cross-cultural' as we could manage, so that other English-speaking readers, especially British, would find analyses of their own experience, and American readers would not lack appropriate analyses of other peoples' experience. While we draw on a good deal of British studies, we have inevitably used a great amount of the best American sociological literature.

More than this, we are part of a joint anthropology/sociology department in which the anthropology segment is the senior and the more distinguished. Hence in this book we move freely across the disciplines, and are always conscious that though we are addressing ourselves in the first place to students and to the general reader in English-speaking developed countries, we – and any intelligent reader

– must be constantly looking at our own society within the context of the rest of the contemporary world, including the communist societies and the 'Third World', as well as within the context of the variety of societies and the patterns of development that history has recorded. And we should always be attempting to apply the theoretical notions developed in one context to other, quite different, cultural situations.

Because we feel that it is vital to understand the relationship of sociology to society, the nature of sociological theorizing, and the logic and procedures sociologists use, we start the book with a consideration of these topics. Part One, therefore, deals with questions of theory and method, and should be read carefully, even though it may well be tempting to launch straightaway into the succeeding chapters on the Family, Education, Work and Community which make up Part Two of the book.

These four topics are then discussed in this order because we wish, initially, to relate our unfolding of the discipline of sociology to the reader's own experience of life. The normal experience is to be brought up in families, then to go to school, and later to go out to work and to come under wider community influences.

Each of these areas of social life has given rise to a different specialized sub-division of the general subject-matter of sociology: the sociology of the family, of education, of work, of urban and rural community life, etc.: and so we use these divisions as the subject-matter of the separate chapters in Part Two.

At the same time we introduce basic concepts and raise important theoretical issues which we illustrate with material on the family, education, and so on. Thus concepts like 'the role-set' and functionalist theory are introduced in Chapter 3 and Chapter 5. Subsequently, these concepts and theories are used in quite different contexts: the concept of 'role' is thus used in analysing community life, social class membership and so on. Similarly, the notion of 'function' is introduced in the chapter on the family, but is later also utilized when discussing the educational system. Thus each chapter has a double purpose: it introduces the reader to a particular 'substantive' area of social life as studied by sociologists, and it also familiarizes him progressively with key concepts and theoretical ideas. We thereby hope to avoid giving the reader the mental indigestion which would result if we started off with strings of concepts and pages of abstract discussion on theory. To do so, moreover, would reinforce the evil tendency in British thinking towards dichotomizing 'theory' and 'description', and we want firmly to show that you cannot even manage description well without theory. We wish, then, to raise problems and to assist the reader's own thinking about these problems, not primarily just to convey information to him.

This is why we have not gone on, mechanically, to write further chapters on each major conventional division of social life, commonly recognized in everyday usage and used also as the basis of the divisions in sociology textbooks: sections on 'political sociology', 'the sociology of religion', etc., etc. Instead, we deliberately chose to break away from these conventional divisions in Part Three by raising wider questions of the way societies are held together despite being divided horizontally (e.g., into classes) and vertically (e.g., into town and country, or different ethnic areas), and despite the existence, commonly, of sizeable groupings of people who reject the norms of 'respectable' society.

At the back of the book, the reader will find a list of references containing all the titles of books and articles referred to in brackets in the text; the list contains the authors' names, followed by a year, and then page references if any (thus: Weber, 1952, pp. 100–121). We have tried as far as possible to use only work that we think interesting enough for the reader to follow up, but we have also added, in addition to these references used in the text, a set of suggestions for further reading, chapter by chapter.

Finally, we should explain that each chapter was written by an individual: Chapter 1 was written by Peter Worsley; chapter 2 by J. Clyde Mitchell; chapter 3 by D. H. J. Morgan; chapter 4 by Bryan Roberts; chapter 5 by D. H. J. Morgan and Robin Ward; chapter 6 by Valdo Pons; chapter 7 by Roy Fitzhenry; and chapter 8 by W. W. Sharrock. But the texts have constantly been revised after collective discussions. Further, the first draft was used in teaching students during 1968–9. Their criticisms were then taken into account in rewriting every chapter. The end-product is thus very much a collective product arising out of the authors' academic relationship with their students. Much as we have been able to achieve a great measure of agreement, there remain differences of approach and emphasis. These we have not tried to eliminate, because we believe this to be a much more authentic representation of the diversity of contemporary sociology than to write as if there was one body of thinking common to all sociologists.

Part One

Chapter 1
Sociology as a Discipline

One of the most striking intellectual developments in the 1960s has been the growth in popularity of the social sciences. Sociology has perhaps been the fastest-growing, though it is not the largest, of these disciplines. Yet it is by no means popular in all quarters. Some, indeed, fear the dispassionate examination of society; they think that things might come to light which are better left hidden or unexplained. Sociology is thought to make people (especially students) 'radical' or 'critical'. Radical students, conversely, attack it as being too conservative a discipline. Criticism sometimes goes further: it questions not just the uses of sociology, but even its claim to be a science. Thus a leader in *The Times* (9 July 1968) remarked that sociology 'whatever [its] other merits . . . [is not] a rigorous intellectual discipline'.

Because of attacks like these, sociologists have often reacted to criticism of their new science with a touchiness that sometimes takes the form of 'imperialistic' aggressiveness – claiming that sociology is the queen of all the social sciences – and sometimes that of an over-sensitive defensiveness. Others exhibit a conservatism of their own, asserting that the discipline is so exacting that it cannot properly be taught in schools, but only to more mature students.

So in capitalist countries, many think of sociology as a kind of academic synonym for socialism, whilst in communist countries it was banned for decades as 'bourgeois' ideology. Hence, in 1965, a year in which physicists scarcely felt it incumbent upon them to 'defend' physics as a discipline, a popular symposium still opened with an article 'in defence of sociology' (Gould, 1965, pp. 9–19).

Despite all these tribulations, sociology has continued to grow rapidly. It is this very growth, indeed, which excites some of the attacks from those who fear its social consequences or its academic competition. It has grown because yet others find it useful. Indeed, the more serious problem for sociology today is not so much that people look down on it, but that they expect too much of it. Today, sociology departments exist in dozens of British universities and colleges. In the United States, the American Sociological Association had fewer than 700 members fifty years ago; today it numbers over 12,000. And in the Soviet Union sociology is now a legitimate discipline.

A second paradox concerning the growth of sociology raises even more fundamental issues. While these words were being written, human society and culture entered a new era. For the first time, men stepped beyond the bounds of their own planet. To do so, they had to overcome all kinds of limitations set by Nature, including those upon the human body. They succeeded because they were able to bring technical devices into being which overcame these natural limitations. From one point of view, this achievement is quite new in kind. From another, it is merely the latest in a succession of technological break-throughs which go back in time to the earliest successes of humankind in inventing such crucial tools as the knife and the spear.

Yet even when we remember this, it still seems paradoxical that such an outstanding set of cultural innovations as are implied by space-technology should occur at the very time a succession of very popular books are seeking to remind us that Man is an animal – a 'naked ape' – and for the most part, dwelling on his less endearing characteristics.

This kind of thinking about Man does not come about simply because we have now accumulated lots of facts about Man's habits and history. For the facts always have to be placed within some context which gives them meaning. From this point of view, the moral fables so characteristic of our time which we call 'science-fiction' share a great deal in common with quite non-fictional science. For the latter, in the end, has significance for us to the extent that it helps us answer such questions as 'Where have we come from?', 'How did we get to this point?', 'What are we doing?', and 'Where are we going?'

These questions are not simple 'questions of fact', though facts are certainly needed in order to answer them. Fundamentally, they are questions about our evaluation of the significance of life: *why* should we do one thing rather than another? what is the *best* way of doing things? how are we to decide what *is* best? is there any ultimate purpose to it all? will our patent capacity for viciousness and destruction prove more powerful than that other part of our heritage: our ability to co-operate and to create?

Hence, when we look at the sweep of human history, we ask ourselves ethical and philosophical questions, questions of *value* as well as of fact. For though looking at Man as a natural species might seem a purely 'scientific' operation, to do so raises philosophical and ethical questions in particularly sharp form, for men have always projected their values, beliefs, prejudices, hunches, hopes and fears upon 'Nature'. In the nineteenth century thinkers drew many different conclusions from their studies of biological evolution: for some, their studies showed that Nature was 'red in tooth and claw', that 'the fittest' survived; for others, like the anarchist Prince Peter Kropotkin, they revealed a story of a cosmic progression towards co-operation and autonomy and away from competitive individualism; from being controlled and determined by Nature, to the exercise of collective reason so as to maximize human independence and self-determination. In fact, you can always read into the history of the human species, as into Nature generally, almost anything you like.

In the nineteenth century, though they were aware of mass poverty, mass war and mass disease, upper-class thinkers were usually confident that human history was the history of progress, ever onwards and upwards – 'Whig' history, as it was parochially called in Britain. Both conservatives and revolutionaries were optimists who believed that change, by and large, meant improvement, and that the present was the best because it was the latest. Today, though we all accept the patent evidence of human technological advance, there is much less confidence that such advance is necessarily accompanied by a parallel improvement in morality or in our ability to devise better social arrangements that would enable more people to live richer lives than they do now.

The contrast between lunar triumph and the hunger of the majority of men on earth is too striking to permit unqualified optimism today. For at the back of our minds are two World Wars, Hiroshima, concentration-camps and brainwashing. A mood of pessimism coexists with the jubilation over man's entry into space. People wonder whether the conquest of space will not in the end lead to disaster, whether unintentionally (e.g. through contamination) or because one of the key rationales is, in any case, military. For only those who

C. Wright Mills calls 'cheerful robots' (Mills, 1959a) can forget that equal human ingenuity has been deliberately called into service in order to devise chemical, bacteriological and nuclear weapons which now give us power to kill off the entire human species. Within a single decade, we have found it necessary to coin a new word to replace genocide – biocide.

If we do end in disaster, it will not be because we are animals beneath a cultural veneer. It will be because we were not as good at social innovation as we were at natural-scientific. Men are, as we know, aggressive; they are also animals. But they are not solely aggressive, any more than other animals, and when they are, it is often because this is culturally expected of them and instilled in them. Even in attacking each other, they use their reason and their social skills. It may sound strange to describe warfare as 'culture', for this is a term we normally reserve for string quartets, poetry, or – nowadays – films or jazz. But from the sociologist's point of view, it is vital to distinguish what is 'given' in man's physical heritage as an animal – the ways of behaving that he is *naturally* born with – from those ways of behaving that he learns. And the really striking thing about the human child is its dependence on people around it, normally its parents and kin, for a very lengthy period of time, for much of which it is fairly helpless. Unlike the newborn foal, which gets up and runs about within hours of its birth, humans cannot even walk for a long time. They are, however, from their first moments, subjected to an incredibly complex and intensive process of 'socialization', during which they acquire what social scientists call 'culture'. They learn how to behave, starting with control over their bowel-motions and eating-habits. As well as being so constrained and trained from earliest infancy, they are simultaneously encouraged to internalize norms of conduct, to practice *self*-control, as well as – most important – to develop their own capacity to learn and to innovate (within limits set by their culture) without having somebody having to stand over them the whole time.

Biology and Culture

We often assume that many of the things we learn are not learned: that it is 'natural' to dislike people who look different from ourselves;

that pain in childbirth is entirely natural; that different degrees of success in life reflect the amount of intelligence we are endowed with at birth; that poor countries stay poor because their peoples lack qualities of enterprise, etc. Yet slave-owners were so attracted to Black women that whole 'Coloured' populations emerged; the physical experience of childbirth varies enormously between cultures even though every woman belongs to the same physical species, *homo sapiens*; our society condemns nearly half of the most talented youth in the country to humble stations in life; the passive Indians of the Andes are the lineal descendants of their imperial Inca forebears, and industrialized Wales and Scotland contain descendants of those the Romans regarded as primitive barbarians. Even something as basic as sex does not necessarily carry with it a 'natural' set of masculine and feminine behaviours. Unlike sex, 'gender' is a social product: 'One is not born, but rather becomes, a woman. No biological, psychological or economic fate determines the figure that the human female presents in society; it is civilization as a whole that produces this creature, intermediate between male and eunuch, which is described as feminine' (de Beauvoir, 1953, p. 9).

Plainly, these variations cannot be attributed to physical changes or differences. What does change is society and its stock of culture. For human culture, though it constantly cumulates over-all, taking the world as a whole, can also be lost or decline: whole peoples can be de-cultured or stand still, so that those who now lead may be laggards at some other time. True, in isolated areas, the rate of innovation may be almost imperceptible, as with the Australian aborigines before Captain Cook. But the constant enlargement of human culture as a whole is plain enough, as is the growing-together of the human species. (The very last pockets of peoples still not involved in what is in effect a single world society are today being broken into in the Highlands of New Guinea and the jungles of the Amazon.) But if we can talk in this way about general human advance, we do so primarily with reference to the enlargement of human knowledge, particularly technical devices and skills. Whether these advances carry with them any enrichment of the *quality* of life, or whether the Australian aborigines did not have highly complex religious cultures, constantly changing and enriched despite the fixity and poverty of their technical equipment, are not just matters of debate, but of debate according to philosophical criteria. This we cannot embark on here, just as we leave aside such questions as whether there might be other dimensions of experience altogether (accessible perhaps only via religion, hallucinogenic drugs, etc.) outside what we take to be normal waking life.

All we need to appreciate, at this juncture, is that conventional definitions of human culture, which usually restrict this term to the creative 'fine arts' are, to the sociologist, arbitrary and restricted. He is most unlikely to take the view that all human creations are of the same order of value – that 'pushpin is as good as poetry' – and will recognize as well as the next man that Beethoven or Angkor Wat are cultural products of a very superior kind. But these are philosophical and aesthetic evaluations; for sociological purposes he will regard as 'culture' *everything* acquired by human beings that is not physically inherited. From this point of view, sewers are as much 'culture' as symphonies. 'Culture', as traditionally defined, consists of certain forms of the conventionally approved arts: painting, sculpture, creative literature, music: these are indeed 'culture' in the sociological sense too, but so are hybrid wheat, brake-linings and strontium 90.

Our physical inheritance, indeed, includes very little human culture. Neither machine-guns, breakfast-foods, brassieres, existentialism, or the Goon Show are outcomes of biological dispositions or inborn behaviour. They are 'artefacts' or 'ideofacts', produced, communicated, handed down, stored up (in books, on tape, on film, etc., and in men's brains), internalized and taught, transmitted from man to man, and from group to group.

Nor can we explain the great diversity of human cultures by reference to our common biological equipment. For there are many *different* cultures and many 'human natures' which vary from society to society, not one single, physically-determined 'Human Nature'. Though as individuals we have to learn everything 'from the beginning', as it were – whether in school, the family, or elsewhere – collectively we do not, for culture is both a social product and a social property, passed on through teaching from generation to generation, so that, as individuals, we are able to start where the last and most advanced person left off. Hence culture cumulates, and the most creative, too, are always adding to it: they do not merely inherit and receive. At the same time, our biological equipment scarcely changes.

It is this that marks off human society as a qualitatively distinctive phenomenon from even the most complex insect 'society', for the insects do not learn to behave; they do so instinctively. Their society has no *culture* at all. Even the higher apes are sadly limited in the extent to which they can learn, and when they do learn, do not pass their experience on to new generations: the result is that their culture does not grow. Indeed, scientists have brought up chimpanzees and gorillas with their own children. The rate of advance of the apes has, in some respects, been more rapid than that of the children in early years, but the apes soon get left behind. Their fundamental limitation, of course, is that they can learn, invent, and hand on very few words – socially standardized sounds which convey meanings – and it is this inability to produce language (apart from physical limitations) that keeps the apes as they are. For culture is only transmissible through coding, classifying and concentrating experience through some form of language. A developed language, therefore, is a unique and distinctive human trait, and human society is a higher level of organization of behaviour than merely instinctive or animal behaviour. Hence any attempt to explain human behaviour in terms of lower levels of behaviour is bound to be inadequate.

Man, in fact, is the least biologically-determined species of all, because he possesses features absent in other natural species. Whilst ethologists emphasize our resemblances to animals, the sociologist looking at human conflict, for example, sees that men co-operate even in order to fight: they create complex social organizations that far exceed anything animal packs are capable of. Nothing, indeed, is more organized, tight-knit, less 'personal', spontaneous or 'instinctive' than an army. Moreover, whatever potentials for aggression there are within the individual's psyche, the culture or sub-culture he lives in is a crucial intervening variable between his biological predisposition and the overt acting-out of aggression towards others, for if he is a Quaker his aggressiveness will be discouraged, whereas Nazi and Fascist theory and practice reinforced, indeed evoked, aggressive action. In other words, violence may be learned as culturally-expected behaviour in different kinds of society or sub-society: it is not simply 'instinctive'.

Man, though a producer, is certainly not always a creator – one who produces positive values which are helpful to his fellow men, for he creates also the means of destruction. But *reductionist* theories, which simplify the elaborate complexity and diversity of human cultures by trying to reduce it to 'underlying' innate animal instincts are, of course, hard put to it to explain why, given, say, what is assumed to be a fixed 'sex instinct', human beings have developed so many different ways of 'handling' sex: within marriage, where there are many forms from polyandry and polygyny to monogamy (and, in Hollywood, what has been called 'serial monogamy'), to commercial sex, religious sex, and other forms of extra-marital sex in forms which range from the casual encounter to the long-term liaison, or even the deliberate suppression of sex-drives in the form of required or even self-imposed celibacy. We also know that cultural practices, such as erotic advertising and other public stimuli can create 'appetites' that are often assumed to be entirely 'natural', and that non-erotic environments, such as many prisons, can result in a diminished preoccupation with sex. Again, anthropologists have shown how hunters-and-collectors constantly on the margins of hunger have dreams, fantasies and obsessions about food rather than sex.

Human beings by no means simply produce material objects; indeed, these could not be produced unless thoughts and ideas were produced too. A particularly crucial set of human products are the social arrangements men live under – their social organization. Cultural innovation includes more, indeed, than simply technological innovation, for older social forms and cultural behaviours become outmoded as well as machines. Religions and monarchical institutions have decayed in Western Europe and new kinds of social phenomena have emerged across the globe: the Chinese commune, the Ombudsman, the giant metropolis, new 'youth cultures', and so on.

The relationship between technological innovation and the growth of culture is thus more complex than is often thought; not just because progress in technology does not automatically mean social progress, but also because the same technology is compatible with quite different social arrangements. The same tools can be used within the context of quite different 'relations of production', for the relations themselves are not built into the instruments. Yet we are still sometimes tempted to talk as if 'technology' was some kind of quite independent moving force. Thus Clark Kerr and his colleagues assert that, by and large, modern industrialism has a 'logic' of its own, which will ultimately lead to a convergence between capitalist and Soviet society because both are industrial societies (Kerr *et al.*, 1962). It is true that there are no capitalist lathes and no communist lathes, but only lathes. Yet though both societies may employ common technical systems – capstan lathes and nuclear energy – they use them in different ways and turn them to different ends. The upshot is quite different kinds of society. In fact, there is no serious evidence of over-all 'convergence' at all (Goldthorpe, 1964). For basically, technology does not determine the total pattern of social arrangements; it is groups of men, with certain values they wish to realize, who pursue policies that determine what technology and its products will be used for. The patterns of relationship entailed in industrial organization are only part of the social order; society is much more than its technology. Similarly, neither the cultural variety of humankind nor the general patterns of development it has exhibited can be explained by demographic factors, such as population pressure – another common type of reductionist thinking.

The notions that society is directly shaped by demographic pressures or by technology or by economic arrangements are thus too simple; they are 'reductionist' every bit as much as the ethological theories we have discussed. Besides being reductionist, such theories are *deterministic:* they assume that these forces give rise to the same outcome everywhere in an inevitable fashion. This is not to deny that there are limits set to what is possible, and inherent requirements, too, imposed for example, by the economy and by the technology on which the economy depends. These issues will be discussed more closely in Chapter 5. Equally, though we reject the view that social man can be understood simply in terms of his animal characteristics, this is not to say that there are not very important social implications which derive from the facts of man's physical condition. Chronic hunger will certainly affect both our capacity to work, as well as our attitudes towards work and towards those who are more fortunate. Different distributions of certain physical characteristics in different populations also have profound repercussions for society: in Europe, the growing proportion of the aged in the population is creating new problems of the social isolation of old people, at the personal level and nationally, because of the need to provide new social services and other sources of support for those who are 'old and alone'. In developing countries, where more than half the population is commonly under fifteen, the new difficulties of absorbing this growing population into productive employment, and the availability now of revolutionary alternatives, makes for very explosive social situations.

The variety of physical population-characteristics also has consequences at other levels. Race (or ethnicity, more usually) is one of the 'ready-made' physical attributes which, if reinforced by inequalities in living-standards, political power or in social interaction, gives rise to conflicts which are only too obvious (and only too widespread and full of tension) today, whether at the interpersonal or global level.

Finally, there are immense social problems created by the changes in Nature brought about by Man. We are polluting the atmosphere and the waters, poisoning sources of food, and creating the means of universal destruction far faster than we are inventing means of overcoming these dangers. It is the shortfall in these social skills that is Man's greatest weakness. It is for this reason that the scientific study of society, so late in beginning, becomes an urgent need, not as some specialist activity for a few, but as a central preoccupation of all intelligent human beings.

The Divisions of Social Science

Sociology is only one of several social sciences, some of which have been in existence a good deal longer than has sociology, which only seriously emerged towards the end of the nineteenth century. Perhaps the most sophisticated of the longer-established social sciences is economics, which has developed elaborate techniques and a complex body of theory over two centuries. Psychology, anthropology and political science (including 'public administration') are the other disciplines most closely related to sociology, together with law, history and aspects of other fields of study (social medicine, social administration, etc.). All these disciplines have their own bodies of theory, techniques of inquiry and specialized subject-matter, to one degree or another. They have also become specialized occupations (law, business, medicine, etc.). Because of this, the relationships between the social sciences that logically ought to exist, in fact, are often quite weak due to 'professional' divisions and jealousies that are far from scientific in character.

Despite their differences, these specialized subject-matters are in fact all parts of one general subject-matter: man's social behaviour. Certain of these disciplines can be readily marked off as being focussed primarily on one particular kind or aspect of general human behaviour. Thus the rather mis-named 'social administration' has in practice been concerned with the consequences of various kinds of social disadvantage, ranging from illness to unmarried motherhood, for which some kind of social provision has to be made. Yet those concerned with these social problems find that they have to study the organizational contexts within which welfare or medical work, for example, take place. In order to carry out such studies, the social administrator often finds that he has to draw on the theories and the 'substantive' knowledge developed within other related disciplines, such as political science, public administration or sociology. There are thus no hard-and-fast lines between the social sciences, even in the case of those disciplines like social administration which might appear to have a neatly marked-off subject-matter.

The absence of hard-and-fast lines of division reflects the fact that they deal with something that is, in reality – 'out there' – *not* parcelled up into discrete areas. What social scientists actually observe is human beings walking, talking and performing other kinds of physical acts. They then proceed to abstract out of this welter of activity certain aspects to which they give particular attention and to which they also attach certain labels. Certain kinds of actions become dubbed as 'economic' – such as those relating to production. In the process, the analyst will deliberately and consciously fail to pay attention to other aspects of the behaviour in front of his eyes. If he does his study via the use of statistics or documents, the degree of abstraction, of selection out of the complexity of the real world, is even greater.

We will see later that though, in studying factories, an economist might tend to see the work-force primarily as a 'supply of labour', the sociologist would be interested in other dimensions of the workers' social make-up which indeed make them very different *kinds* of worker. He will note that social relationships on the shop-floor are greatly affected by relationships developed *outside* the firm, and that the attachments and antagonisms within the factory are not necessarily produced by the requirements of work alone. So factories manned by unskilled Irish immigrants, skilled female Lancashire cotton-operatives, or craft-conscious engineers, are very different kinds of factory, not just because the work is different, but because people bring their lives outside the factory into the work-situation. The sociologist then, may study exactly the same scene, may watch the same people doing the same things that the economist or the psychologist observes. But whereas the economist normally restricts himself to looking at this reality through certain theoretical spectacles, and so restricts himself to the analysis of the interaction between the factors of capital and labour, or with the operation of the market in terms of price or demand, the sociologist will be further interested in the interconnexions of all this with other dimensions of social relationships in the work-place or the market-place, and with the way work fits into non-work life.

The sociologist, then, does not question the expertise of the economist in dealing with those special aspects of human behaviour that he chooses to concentrate on. Rather, he attempts to relate 'economic' behaviour to other kinds of behaviour, or, more accurately, to see 'economic' behaviour as simply a partial abstraction from the total social behaviour of the individual.

Though the sociologist needs the economist's expertise, he himself is able to contribute this wider perspective. But a discipline which claims an even wider perspective than this, with much justice, is anthropology. 'Social' or 'cultural' anthropology is concerned with the variety of arrangements which men have created over millennia. Its perspective is highly comparative, or 'cross-cultural'. Anthropologists have been especially interested in studying cultures very remote from their own, sometimes by going back into history, but more normally by going to still-existing tribal, exotic and often (though not always) simple societies in the contemporary world. In arriving at an understanding of how such societies work, anthropologists have inevitably thrown a flood of light on general principles of social organization and have enabled us to see how, on the one hand, apparently exotic customs are simply ways of coping with common human problems that we handle in different ways, and that our ways are not necessarily the best or the only ones possible, or, in other cases, that some societies have quite different preoccupations altogether than those that dominate our thinking, so that by studying them we can see ourselves as only one particular kind of society with its own limited concerns.

In some ways, then, anthropology is much wider-ranging than sociology. On the other hand, precisely because of its search for what is culturally different, anthropology has paid little attention to developed societies which are particularly important to us. The great value of anthropology then lies in its comparative 'cross-cultural' vision. Conversely, though some sociologists talk about sociology as the 'widest' social science that includes all others, in fact sociologists have largely confined themselves to contemporary societies, initially industrialized ones, and latterly in the underdeveloped world.

The enormous field of the study of *past* societies has rarely attracted sociologists, who have left this field to the historian. There are many kinds of historians, some of whom see history as simply as 'meaningless' or even 'patternless', unique sequences of events which can only be described quite separately rather than looked at in terms of common patterns or trends shared with other societies. Such writers are suspicious of 'theory' and claim to stick to the concrete facts of the particular situation. This 'empiricist' approach will be discussed later. Suffice it to say here that such approaches, common enough among historians, represent quite non-sociological ways of approaching the study of past societies, however great the value of such researches may be as industrious compilations bringing order into chaos and knowledge out of ignorance, or as implicit analysis. Nor would we claim that the sociologist who turns to past societies necessarily does better research than his historian-colleague (he is probably likely to be as long on theory and short on fact as the historian is the converse). But the best history is, in fact, sociological: the sociology of the past.

What we may claim for sociology, at its ideal best, is a distinctive *perspective* rather than, say, any specific substantive subject-matter or type of human behaviour: it is a way of looking at Man's behaviour as conditioned by his membership of social groups – a perspective which may seem self-evident to some, but is by no means accepted by those, for example, who see history as determined by the activities of great men, or those who see Man's social behaviour as simply the outcome of his animal nature. To make the contrast, a reductionist is likely to see warfare simply as an outcome of aggressive instincts which people, as individuals, are born with. Thus Anthony Storr remarks: 'We are the cruellest and most ruthless species that has ever walked the earth –

each one of us harbors within himself those same savage impulses which lead to murder, to torture and to war' (Storr, 1968, p. 9). War, here, is the outcome at the social level of pre-social human characteristics inherited by the individual. The social scientist, on the other hand, is sceptical of this appeal to instincts, noting that 'three out of four die from causes other than violence', that 'most forms of human rivalry explicitly preclude the use of violence' and that 'Man is not just a wild animal whose ferocious instincts must be curbed by society or sublimated into other channels, [but] . . . a social animal who is taught by society to exhibit hostility in some situations and friendliness in others. The difference is fundamental' (Leach, 1968, pp. 26, 28).

Sociology is thus concerned with socio-cultural behaviour, a different – and higher – level of behaviour altogether than those kinds of behaviour that are the outcome of innate drives built into the individual. This is not to say that the latter do not exist, simply that they may be overlaid, elaborated, repressed, counteracted, by complex sets of social forces which the individual is subjected to *because he lives in society* and because he is not an isolated entity who simply 'behaves' in response to internal or external physical stimuli or psychological drives. Perhaps the best-known attempt to interpret society in terms of innate instincts is Freud's psycho-analytical theory, which places such great emphasis upon inborn drives, particularly the sex-drive. Yet Freud himself constantly stressed the way such drives could be frustrated by cultural controls, and towards the end of his life placed more and more emphasis on culture as against simple instinct.

Psychology is a sister-science that contains both sub-social and social 'wings'. Physiological psychology is concerned with the physical processes through which thinking, feeling, etc., take place. But most of the rest of psychology is in fact to one degree or another *social*. What is commonly labelled 'social psychology' is in fact only a part of this wider 'social' part of psychology. Social psychology usually deals with a rather arbitrary collection of topics, not necessarily related, such as the study of small groups or of crowd behaviour. But *all* non-physiological psychology is in effect 'social' psychology, since it is concerned with the processes by which human behaviour becomes culturally standardized, expected and obligatory: in other words, the ways in which society enjoins certain patterns of behaviour upon the individual.

Are not both psychology and sociology, then, it might be asked, equally concerned with the way individual behaviour is socially conditioned? The answer is 'Yes', but the psychologist's point of attention is usually the individual, the sociologist's that of the groups and categories to which the individual belongs. But that is to put it too crudely, for psychologists do study groups and categories, too: the attitudes, say, of miners, disc-jockeys, sadists, or women. The real difference is that the unit or frame of reference for the psychologist is the behaviour of the individual, whether his inner 'psyche' or its external manifestations observable in his relationships with others. The sociologist approaches perhaps exactly the same piece of behaviour 'from the other end', as it were, and asks what are the significant regularities and patterns in a person's behaviour that enable us to see him as typical of others who have been similarly socialized, undergone parallel life-experiences, or belonged to similar groups. Social behaviour is thus not simply the putting-together of all the separate 'natural' behaviours of many individuals – what is called 'aggregate psychology' – it is a qualitatively different *level* of behaviour, not 'given' in the *individual* psyche independently of his experience of society, as it were, but produced *in social groups* and internalized within the individual as a result of his exposure to the pressures of these groups. Both psychologist and the sociologist, then, may study the same behaviour and ask similar questions. It is not, crudely, that one studies the group and the other the individual, but that the focus or 'point of entry' will be the individual, for the psychologist, and for the sociologist, the society and culture of which the individual is a part. They will thus frequently converge in their studies, and at the border lines it becomes rather arbitrary whether one labels a study 'psychology' or 'sociology'. Yet the psychologist, basically, is interested in the way the individual's behaviour is organized so as to constitute a 'personality', the sociologist in the way the individual as a person relates to others.

The differences between sociology and psychology, on the one hand then, are differences of *perspective*, in the same way as the differences between a sociologically-minded historian and an 'empiricist' historian are differences of perspective. The differences between law, political science and economics, on the other hand, are differences of what one might term *domain*, in that each has a prime interest in certain substantive areas only within human behaviour in general, that is, the lawyer in the study of the way men resolve 'trouble issues', the economist in the study of production and consumption. Of course, at the widest, the lawyer who looks at the connexion of law-making agencies to the rest of society, or who studies how different kinds of behaviour become defined as 'good' or 'bad' and how these definitions become embodied in law, is studying law in very sociological ways.

Researches within any one specific discipline may be vital to another: thus the sociologist may draw upon the economist's knowledge of the female labour-market as a part of his study of the family; conversely, the economist may use the sociologist's national surveys or local, intensive studies in order to enable him to estimate where and when likely supplies of labour, or demand for commodities, can be expected.

Thus the different divisions of the social sciences are only relative; they cut off what is in reality a 'seamless web' for convenience of analysis and in order to permit specialized study, so that where we see people behaving, we label their different actions variously 'economic' behaviour, 'religious' and so on.

Sociology itself has been subject to the same processes of specialization that characterize industrial production, the arts, or the natural sciences. Within 'sociology' as a general perspective, there are now specialized 'domains' also, of which industrial sociology and the sociology of education, in Britain at least, are the most popular – for obvious reasons, since both deal with key social institutions which employ sociology and sociologists, finance research, etc., on a scale that is not the case, for instance, with the sociology of religion or law. These special areas or domains are, however, held together by a common body of theory and a common body of available methods. Other major divisions are urban sociology, political sociology, social stratification, race relations, the sociology of the family and so on. All these, of course, are only divisions of convenience. There can be, in principle, as many sociological domains, or sub-domains, as there are classes of social activity. Thus we have a 'sociology of jazz', of dying, of war, and even a sociology of sleep, since sleep is, in part, a socially-conditioned activity (Aubert, 1965, pp. 168–200). And the sociology of deviance, that is, the study of those activities stigmatized and designated as 'improper' or 'nonconformist' behaviour – from prostitution to membership of marginal religious sects – is a well-developed field.

Sociology studies all these separate topics only as particular manifestations of its overall subject-matter: men's social relationships to one another. Although each domain does develop its own special body of theory, it always draws upon the *general* theory of sociology. In its turn, it contributes to general theory, so that industrial sociologists may learn a great deal from theoretically-oriented (as against merely descriptive) studies of schools, and a sociologist studying religion may profit greatly from reading studies of child-rearing. Certainly, anyone who sticks too rigidly to his chosen specialism is likely to be both a poor specialist as well as a poor sociologist-in-general.

Sociology in Society

So far, we have defined sociology by discussing those special characteristics that mark it off as a discipline distinct from other, related disciplines. This definition is in fact an ideal statement of what sociology *ought* to be about. We now need to look at sociology, not so much in logical or ideal terms, but in terms of the actual organized forms in which it is found 'on the ground', and in terms, too, of the kinds of things sociologists actually do. For, like any other science, sociology exists not just in people's minds, but in the form of institutions within which sociological work is carried out. And though the field claimed for it is extremely wide – no less than the study of social relationships, of whatever historical period and in whatever culture–nevertheless, sociologists do, in practice, concentrate predominantly on certain kinds of problems within certain kinds of societies.

When sociology emerged as a new science at the end of the eighteenth century, it was very wide-ranging and comparative, covering the whole development of man. It attempted to classify the variety of forms of society throughout human history and throughout the world, and to locate these different species of society within a general theory of the development of society. Under the impact of the Darwinian revolution in biology, most major nineteenth-century sociologists continued this tradition. The great sociological theorists – Marx, Saint-Simon, Comte, Durkheim, Spencer – to name no others, all developed evolutionary schemes that embraced all the main types of social organization then known.

Yet in the later nineteenth and early twentieth centuries, during the period when sociology was becoming an established academic discipline in universities, there was a turning away from such ambitious comparative and developmental study in the direction of an increasing preoccupation with contemporary industrial societies, usually the study of the society in which the sociologist was living. Underlying this shift of attention was the assumption that the industrial countries which dominated the world then were the 'wave of the future' and that the rest were outmoded 'traditional' societies, destined to follow in the wake of the advanced countries. Sociology thus became both less cross-cultural and less historical, concentrating mainly on contemporary society, and witnessed a revolt not only against evolutionist thinking but against large-scale generalization of any variety concerning the over-all direction of man's social development.

This loss of historical and comparative vision has persisted to the present day, though of late there has grown up a revival of interest in the larger problems of 'development' under the stimulus of the arrival on the world stage of the new revolutionary societies of the U.S.S.R. and China, and the transformation of many former colonies into newly-independent states, all bent upon rapid modernization.

In this century, then, sociology has, until recently, primarily concentrated upon the analysis of the social systems of a very limited number of highly developed societies. It has mainly flourished in the United States and in Britain, France and Germany. Within these countries, it has existed in institutionalized form in the shape of a discipline taught in universities and colleges, and in the form of research conducted in these places and in special research institutes. It has also been found in governmental research units; in market-research and consultancy bodies (usually commercial organizations); within pressure-groups and 'cause' organizations; and has reached the reading-public mainly via such books as William Whyte's *Organization Man* (Whyte, 1957) and Vance Packard's *The Hidden Persuaders* (Packard, 1957), which are serious attempts by non-professionals to tackle sociological problems whilst making their analysis comprehensible to the general reader.

Good books like these can be written by non-professionals. Both Whyte and Packard are, however, thoroughly familiar with and use the writings of professional social scientists. But people can write perceptively about society without having read any sociology at all, if they have that special capacity to generalize intelligently from their own experience, to relate this experience to the lives of others, and to trace out the forces shaping the conditions under which people live out their relationships with one another. People who lack these gifts, however, and who are at the same time ignorant of the literature of the social sciences, nevertheless readily pronounce about society. They are likely simply to produce spurious 'conventional wisdom' at best, and positively dangerous nonsense at worst.

Often, however, laymen write books simply because the sociologist has failed to do so, and the gap needs to be filled. When Anthony Sampson wrote *Anatomy of Britain Today* (1965), he had the courage to ask a very big question which few sociologists had dared tackle – who runs Britain? And however critical one might be of his attempt to answer this question, he did make the attempt. John Gunther's books are another instance of a journalist chancing his arm at a task the social scientist had left alone: high-level surveys, not simply of whole societies, but even of continents (Gunther, 1947). The neglect of such key problems by sociologists may be in part, of course, simply a function of the small numbers of professional sociologists: until ten years ago, there were only 450 members of the British Sociological Association, and not all of these were working sociologists. But the causes of such neglect run deeper than this: it is also a failure of intellectual nerve and a narrowness of horizons that has been excoriated by C. Wright Mills in his book *The Sociological Imagination* (Mills, 1959a).

We do lack sound scientific studies of many areas of social life, and sociologists commonly defend themselves for not having produced such studies on the grounds that they cannot produce scientific analyses where the basic research has not been done. Against this one can argue that we will probably never have all, even much, of the data we would ideally like. Yet we do have available data of various kinds, which we can use within a sociological framework of analysis. If we wait for perfect information, we will never be able to say anything.

Mills declares that the shortage of data is not accidental. Academics, he suggests, are usually people of middle class (and nowadays often working class) background. Their upbringing and work rarely involves them in any direct acquaintance with the lives led by the wealthy and the powerful; they mostly occupy lower and middle-level positions in institutions such as universities which are separated off from the worlds of business and politics where the key decisions are taken. The academic, too, often interprets the scientific ideal of objectivity to mean 'non-involvement' in public issues, and refrains from researching such controversial areas as 'Who runs Britain?' and from expressing any views on such matters. He is in danger, Mills suggests, of becoming exactly what the Greeks – who thought men should be engaged in their society – defined the 'idiot' to be: the completely private man. The result is that many of the 'big', the controversial, and therefore the really important problems never get researched into at all. Conversely, the social scientist, all too often, confines himself not just to small-scale studies (which are perfectly justifiable), but to studies of the socially marginal and unimportant.

Since every one of us knows something about society, to many people the study of society does not seem to call for any special expertise. Moreover, journalists, creative writers and others – not social scientists alone – write perceptively about society.

Yet increasingly people are coming to appreciate that to study society scientifically demands special skills, and produces, though it does not displace, a quite different kind of understanding from that provided, say, by the novelist. They hope, too, that this knowledge will be of use, just as sociology emerged in the nineteenth century in response to the needs of various kinds of groups – mainly governments and social reformers – interested in using social science. The contemporary 'customers' for social science are equally varied.

We will now consider the uses made of social science under three broad heads: the demand for information; the need for explanation; and the use of sociology in policy-formulation and execution.

The Assembling of Information

It would be naïve to assume that governments, any more than ordinary people, necessarily only want accurate information. They may want to mislead others with lies; they may be incapable of facing the truth, and may wish to have their favourite prejudices comfortably supported; or they may use 'inquiry' itself as a political device to avoid actually doing anything, whilst making it appear that something is being done. Thus the Morton Royal Commission on Marriage and Divorce in 1951 in Britain, has been described as 'a device for obfuscating a socially urgent but politically inconvenient issue' (McGregor, 1957). Nor does the inclusion of a sprinkling of social scientists on a commission guarantee by any means that the inquiry as a whole will be scientific. Even less does it ensure that any conclusions will be translated into action. The Kerner Commission into the U.S. riots of 1967 concluded its report with these words from Dr Kenneth B. Clark, a distinguished Negro psychologist called as 'expert witness':

I read [the report] . . . of the 1919 riot in Chicago, and it was as if I were reading the report of the investigating committee on the Harlem riot of '35, the report of the investigating committee on the Harlem riots of '45, the report of the McCone Commission on the Watts riot.

I must again in candour say to you members of this Commission – it is a kind of Alice in Wonderland – with the same moving picture – reshown over and over again, the same analysis, the same recommendations, and the same inaction (Report of the National Advisory Commission on Civil Disorders, 1968).

But governments, like firms or individuals, do need a great deal of information, too, and many inquiries are mounted in order to get it. The coming of industrial society made it increasingly imperative for governments to assemble information about populations that were highly mobile and therefore highly unsettled, as hundreds of thousands of people were pushed or pulled off the land into the new, teeming cities. In the era which followed the French Revolution a terror of Jacobinism akin to the McCarthyite fear of Communism in this century gripped the comfortable classes. Simple repression was the main response: early trade unions were banned and more troops faced the Luddites in Britain in 1812 than Wellington had had under his command in Spain in the Peninsular War.

But, increasingly, governments found that the sword brought no solution to problems that were essentially rooted in social distress; they turned, in consequence, to analysis of these sources of popular discontent and began investigation of the lives of the new masses who now lived in cities and worked in factories, and who responded in new ways to these new conditions of life. Before action could be taken, the size and nature of the problem had to be estimated. How many people were there? How many were literate? What did they earn? How did they make a living? Did they make a living at all? The asking of such questions in Britain, the first industrial society, underlay the introduction of the Census (1801), the classic Reports of the Factory Inspectors and the Poor Law Commissioners. This was the beginning of what we now call the 'information explosion'; complex societies, from thence forwards, could no longer be run on the basis of ignorance.

Many of the great series of nineteenth-century governmental inquiries were also concerned with modernizing ancient institutions. The Civil Service, the Army and the Public Schools were all redesigned in this way. Disasters were a singularly important stimulus to such critical examination, as when the cholera epidemic of the 1830s, and the ignominious performance of the British Army in the Boer War, led to agonizing reappraisals of the health of the nation.

Studies of popular responses to these new conditions, however, were less common. The Religious Census of 1851 was an exception, and was not repeated. But public official inquiries are not the only way to assemble information. Popular moods and organizations were in fact watched, and less respectable ones were watched in less respectable ways: by police-informers and *agents-provocateurs*, just as the CIA and FBI do a great deal of un-public research in twentieth-century America and elsewhere. The records of these public private eyes, and the archives of court and prison, only become available to later generations, if at all. They are as valuable to the social historian as they once were to those who paid for them, and have enabled historians like George Rudé to add to the *dramatis personae* of traditional historical studies those who inhabited prisons rather than palaces (Rudé, 1959).

Though governments produced information for their own purposes, they could not prevent their opponents using Government publications for their own, quite different, purposes. Reforming radicals and revolutionaries made great use of official reports. Karl Marx used them to write *Capital*; social reformers used them as ammunition. But the radicals and reformers mounted their own independent inquiries as well. Liberal reformers like Francis Place, Ernest Chadwick and Lord Shaftesbury helped pioneer the modern extensive survey, and Marx's colleague, Frederick Engels, pioneered the sociology of the new industrial cities in his classic study of Manchester in 1844 (Engels, 1953). Later the Fabians, notably Beatrice and Sydney Webb, developed the factual social survey in a monumental series of studies that helped shape the entire cast of thought of the Labour Party.

The long tradition of fact-collecting surveys in Britain, and their use by the Establishment and its opponents alike, in part explains why so many people still see social science as simply the collection of facts, and why so many people make the further assumption that since facts are neutral, the collecting and ordering of the facts must be a neutral operation too. The facts, they believe, speak for themselves.

Now if there is one thing that facts never do it is to speak. What does happen is that *men* select certain facts, interpret them, and then take actions which may or may not be closely dependent upon the analysis they have made.

There is, obviously, some element of truth in this popular assumption that fact-collecting is 'scientific'. The scientific aspect of fact-collecting lies in its being *uninhibited*, in two senses; firstly in the sense that the scientist imposes as few barriers as possible on himself (even if others may do so) in collecting the evidence he needs, and in analysing and publishing it 'without fear or favour'; and uninhibited in a second sense, in that the scientist tries to free himself from fixed preconceptions, prejudices, *a priori* judgements, 'pet theories', etc. Ideally, he questions everything, even his own habits of thought. For him there are no tabooed topics, no areas where inquiry should be avoided for fear of breaking rules imposed by non-scientists – whether they be political rules ('security'), or just social conventions (e.g. taboos on discussing sexual experience) – and thereby offending authority or the general public or some particular interest-group. The slogan 'publish and be damned' reflects the spirit of this aspect of social science well.

In more academic form, the same spirit manifests itself as what is called *empiricism*. The empiricist model assumes an individual researcher who runs across or thinks up some intellectual problem, which stimulates him to collect facts in an open-minded way, which lead him in turn to certain conclusions which he publishes without any consideration for practical implications and without committing himself to any moral judgement or recommending any course of action. Though this model contains elements of truth, *in toto* it is quite inadequate as a sociological model of the way science works. Firstly, it assumes that facts can be collected without the prior existence of a framework within which they can be put into some kind of order. Facts do not order themselves, and even in the simplest inquiry there are theoretical assumptions built into the researcher's mental equipment that suggest to him what sort of facts to look for, what kinds of facts are likely to be irrelevant and may therefore safely be ignored, what likely causes to look for, what connexions might be worth following up, and so on. Moreover, as we shall see in Chapter 2, very little research actually follows the postulated sequence of operations.

Because of this constant endeavour to take nothing for granted, much of the time the scientist appears to be simply documenting the 'obvious'. In fact, much that is held to be 'obvious' is anything but, and 'received ideas', 'conventional wisdom', or popular stereotypes are often quite misleading. Not that popular assumptions are necessarily wrong: the real inadequacy of such ideas, from a scientific point of view, is simply that they are unexamined and untested.

The scientist does more than question particular interpretations of the facts; he questions the very claim that they are the relevant facts, and asks whether other relevant facts might not have been ignored. For all facts are a selection from a complex mass of phenomena which confronts us. Out of this welter of events, we select some for particular attention because we think them to be relevant to some problem we have in mind. Not all facts are relevant: it is the 'frame of reference' which determines which are likely to be. Even where facts seem to be self-evident, then, we are already reading significance into them by even selecting them for attention.

Such problems arise even when we are engaged in such apparently 'factual' matters as estimating the distribution of income. First of all, what do we include under the term 'income'? In peasant economies, food produced for subsistence is often the biggest item in a peasant's total income, but it is not purchased for money: can we impute a value to it in money terms? Next, what is the income-unit: the individual, the family, or the household? Can we lump together the profits of small shopkeepers, the wages of skilled workers, the pensions of the retired, etc., as 'income', merely because they receive the same amount of money? Are they not different *kinds* of income?

When we start asking such questions, the simple notion that obvious facts are lying around waiting to be collected can be seen to be an illusion. The categories we use to select and order facts will depend upon our purposes: to follow our example, a taxation official will only classify as 'income' those kinds of income specified by legislation as liable to tax. A sociologist studying the family might regard as 'income' forms of wealth such as trusts and covenants which are not conventional individual income (Titmuss, 1962).

If the categories we use are affected by our purposes, so are even the things we perceive, for we are conditioned by our cultural training to perceive some facts and not others. We do not inevitably even see the same things when we do look. 'What a man sees', Kuhn points out, 'depends upon what he looks at, and also upon what his previous visual-conceptual experience has taught him to see' (Kuhn, 1962). Thus a landscape artist and a farmer both *look at* the same reality, but *see* (or 'perceive') quite different things: the one a valley good for wheat, the other a pattern of tonal values. We may be trained to see the world differently from the way other people see it, especially if we are training to be a specialist. The police-recruit, for example, must not look at everyday reality as everyone else does, but instead is taught to look for clues which might indicate the existence of crime. Most of us do not see the world as being filled with potential miscreants. The policeman's role demands that he does exactly this: 'As he drives down the street in his patrol car, the significant elements that he attends to are evidence or remembrances of criminality . . . "That shoeshine parlor has gambling in the back; this bar used to have bloody fights every night, but it has quieted down now . . ."' (Buckner, 1967, p. 163).

It is not the case, then, that we 'see' identical things which automatically register themselves on our minds, like light on photographic paper producing identical images on each sheet of paper. Rather, we are all equipped with different pieces of sensitized paper, since we have all had different cultural experiences: our cultural conditioning sensitizes our minds to special kinds of things which we share only with those similarly sensitized.

But it is not only the observer who is socialized into interpreting the scenes he observes. The people he is observing, too, are themselves doing the same thing all the time. They may even be observing him.

This, indeed, is the basic difference between most of the natural sciences and the social sciences: that the former do not have to cope with *consciousness*. For unlike rocks, amoebae or machines, men think, appraise and feel: they have aims, grievances, aspirations, hopes, fears, dreams, utopias, horrors. This consciousness is not simply *cognitive* knowledge, for men also *evaluate* their experiences as 'good' or 'bad' and react to them with feelings, whether of pleasure or fear. Because of these special features of human behaviour, Max Weber, the classical German sociologist (1864–1920), insisted on using the phrase 'social action' to distinguish such behaviour – behaviour characterized by *meaning* – from man's purely animal behaviour or from the behaviour of plants or insects.

Some of our behaviour is of the latter kind. Just as an insect reacts to a source of light by flying towards it, so we, because we are animals, respond to physical stimuli instinctively: a sudden shout makes us jump. But we control our natural tendency to jump out of our skins, because we don't want to seem 'seven-stone weaklings' in the eyes of our girl-friend (we evaluate the social effects of our own actions on others). Behaviour of this kind is not 'natural' at all: it is social. We also immediately interpret such behaviour. We try to find out who has shouted, what he was shouting about, whether he is hostile, or perhaps simply someone we know giving us an over-hearty greeting; whether he is addressing himself to us at all or perhaps to some other person; and we adapt our own response accordingly.

Even when we are physically quite alone, we carry our society around with us in our heads, just as Robinson Crusoe did on his island. So we refrain from stealing a wallet we find in an empty room because we have absorbed ideas about honesty from our society. Conversely, we may be socially quite isolated, though physically surrounded by people: we can be very lonely in the big city. David Riesman, indeed, has characterized our whole urban civilization as the life of *The Lonely Crowd* (Riesman, 1953). Loneliness is a social, not just a physical condition.

Social action, then, is action which takes into account, or is affected by, the existence of others. It involves understanding or interpreting the meaning of their behaviour – estimating what they are thinking, feeling, and trying to do. We project ourselves into other people's minds. And, of course, they are doing exactly the same *vis-à-vis* our behaviour. This two-sided process has been called 'double contingency'. More complex still, we calculate what others are thinking *about us*, and so on. This is no piece of abstract academic complication for its own sake. It is a perfectly normal part of everyday life, certainly familiar to Lucy and Charlie Brown (see next page).

Though social action takes place at one point or period in time, it is affected by events that have happened before – by 'history'. Thus our estimate of a person's likely behaviour will be affected by our past experience of him, or someone like him in similar situations we have lived through or heard about. Any act thus involves the past as well as the present. We carry history around with us, locked up in our heads, and are constantly referring to it all the time, as historians rightly emphasize. But in acting at any time, we are also making estimates about the future. We pre-figure the outcome in our 'mind's eye'. Even so-called traditional or habitual behaviour – where we 'do this because our forefathers always did it that way' – carries with it the implication '. . . and it will therefore work equally well in the future'. Sociologists, who concentrate usually upon the study of contemporary situations, often underemphasize the extent to which contemporary behaviour is thus conditioned both by the past and by orientation towards the future. In order to understand why trade unionists are sensitive to technological innovation, one has to know what the experience of the Depression has built into their consciousness. In order to understand why the sons of comfortable upper class families go off to live in jungles as guerillas, one has to understand their ideas about the coming of a new kind of society. The simplest piece of behaviour thus involves past, present, and future.

Insofar as all behaviour contains an element of intention, all behaviour is 'future-oriented', even if the future turns out to be just a repetition of the present. Marx pointed out that this characteristic is peculiarly human: even the so-called 'social insects' do not possess it. 'A spider conducts operations that resemble those of a weaver, and a bee puts to shame many an architect in the construction of her cells. But what distinguishes the worst architect from the best of bees is . . . that the architect raises his structure in imagination before he erects it in reality' (Marx, 1942, pp. 169–70).

The capacity to imagine involves a further crucial human skill that the insect lacks: our capacity to 'dream up' future states that have

'Double Contingency'

never yet existed in reality, such as 'utopian' societies or 1984s and similar 'anti-utopias'.

It is this capacity to imagine that is the source of innovation and therefore of human development, for men try to bring these utopias into actual existence, and dreams of a heaven upon earth or a classless society have been powerful springs of action in human history. Karl Mannheim called them 'utopian' orientations (Mannheim, 1948), in contrast to those social ideals which merely justified and helped preserve the present social order. These he called 'ideologies'. Our orientation to the future, then, includes not only what we think will happen (our expectations), but also what we want to see happen (our aspirations).

To understand other people's behaviour we have to make complex calculations about such mental states that underlie their actions. We also have to look at our own actions 'from the outside' as it were; to 'see ourselves', as we say, 'as others see us'. One's own behaviour becomes an object of scrutiny to oneself. George Herbert Mead, the American philosopher (1863–1931) therefore tried to persuade us to stop thinking of the individual as a unitary thing called the 'person', a self which exists, as it were, quite independently of others, but to think of the self as a complex with several different dimensions, built up out of our relationships with what he called 'significant others': people whose behaviour has social importance or consequences for us (Strauss, 1964). The individual actor is a different person to different Others, both because he acts differently towards them, and they to him, and because each interprets the Other's behaviour differently. When the individual considers how his behaviour looks to Others, he becomes a Me (the Self as object of scrutiny) to his I (the self as subject, who is doing the scrutinizing).

The skills needed in interpreting the behaviour of others are thus quite different from those needed in analysing non-social, physical behaviour. They are acquired directly by practising them in everyday life, and indirectly from other people and from special stores of cultural experience – books, films and so forth. Since no two of us have been through quite the same set of identical social experiences – we have each had different parents, have been of different seniority in the family, have had different teachers in school, read different books and had different friends, etc. – each of us ends up (apart from being differently endowed by nature) with a distinctive personal store of culture. It is this idiosyncratic culture that constitutes our individual personality. Conversely, millions of us occupy quite similar life-situations, have lived through the same events and have been raised in very similar ways, so we also share social characteristics with millions of others. If we did not, social science would be impossible, for society would be composed of a multitude of unique cases.

This rich variety of social contacts sets us a problem, then, for each role we play connects us with others who have expectations about what we are likely to do, and ideals to which they try to get us to conform. The attempt to pressurize other people to conform to our normative expectations is what we often call 'politics' or 'social control'. There is, indeed, a coercive element in all behaviour, not just the behaviour of governments and political parties.

But different Others have different norms. Each tries to get us to behave in the way he wants. We cannot satisfy everybody. Yet we must, in the end, act. Sometimes we can arrange things so that we meet these competing Others separately; we solve the problem by behaving 'situationally'. In so doing, we are not simply being hypocrites. Total inconsistency we call 'being all things to all men'; yet social life certainly requires what we more generously call 'flexibility'. Words like 'hypocrisy', 'inconsistency' and 'flexibility' are different *moral* evaluations of what, sociologically, is an inevitable consequence of social relationships. For every role we occupy brings us into contact with several different people, each with different expectations of us. And we enact many such roles, as we will see when we discuss roles and role-sets below (pp. 213-14). In some situations we cannot so easily compartmentalize our behaviour, however. We may have to decide to risk hurting A because, in the end, B is more important to us. Or we may try to strike a balance, by behaving in a way that will totally alienate nobody even if it totally satisfies nobody either. Often, then, we have to calculate 'How will people *in general* treat us or respond to our behaviour?' We produce a kind of lowest common multiple or highest common factor of behaviour in adapting it to the differing expectations of all those different Others. Mead called it adapting our behaviour to a *Generalized* Other.

The Construction of Explanations

Given this complexity of social meaning, even in 'simple' social acts, we can see how inadequate the notion of simply 'collecting the facts' is. Strictly, we cannot separate information-gathering from explanation, which involves interpreting the meanings social actors attach to their behaviour. Secondly, the theories we have in our heads will tend to influence not simply the explanation of the facts we assemble, but the very process of assembling them and the categories we use to classify them.

Much of sociological theory consists in the clarification and development of these categories, for without agreement upon them we cannot even speak the same language about society. Terms such as 'role', 'socialization', or 'pluralism' are necessary tools of the trade, just as natural scientists have their terms with agreed meanings. But we need to distinguish two types of terms. Firstly, there are those like 'hydrogen' or the 'matricentral family' which describe some particular arrangement of matter (in the first case), a particular structure of social relationships (in the second). They describe bits of reality which exist 'out there' in Nature and society. Let us call these, following mathematical practice, 'parameters'. Terms like 'role', on the other hand, are not particular kinds of social arrangement in certain societies, but can be applied to the analysis of any piece of human behaviour. The difference is such that people in a given society can recognize a 'clan' or a 'trade union' for themselves, and indeed have a word for such parameters as the 'clan' and names for particular clans, whereas they do not necessarily have any equivalent for such sociological concepts as 'social mobility' or 'interaction', 'deviance' or 'bureaucracy'. A lot of sociological work, especially in cultures less familiar to us, has consisted simply in creating a 'parametric terminology' by labelling the institutions of which the society is made up – what a 'clan' was, or how 'patronage' worked, the structure and functioning of families, trade unions, parties, etc., in a given society or type of society. 'Concepts', however, are tools we need to tackle the study of *any* society. Both kinds of category are needed in order to analyse social arrangements.

Similarly, in constructing explanations, two different kinds of operation are involved. One researcher may be interested primarily in the religious beliefs of the English. Another may only be interested in these beliefs as a particular example of 'ideology' in general, or as an instance of the wider problems of how human beings respond in a variety of ways to the universal situations of 'birth, copulation and death'. He may, that is, be interested in religion rather than the religion of the English.

Most researchers are interested in both, but the two approaches are distinguishable. Just as we have distinguished 'parameters' from 'concepts', so we can distinguish that kind of sociological theory whose prime focus is upon the culture of the specific society or societies under study as 'substantive' theory (because it is concerned with the content, the 'substance' of the society) from that kind of theorizing which concentrates upon establishing general propositions about the properties of human relationships – which we call 'formal' theory. Formal theory thus deals in concepts and propositions applicable to various kinds of behaviour that differ widely in terms of their 'subject-matter'. 'Substantive' theory on the other hand is theorizing about particular kinds of cultural phenomena: the Soviet power-apparatus, or the English medieval family, or more widely, single-party states or family-systems in industrialized societies.

Formal theory often develops from and is applied to real social situations. Conversely, concepts developed in formal theory are useful in research which is quite practical in orientation. Thus 'small group' theory developed in quite artificial situations (by studying American students through one-way glass screens) has then been used to study real-life street-corner gangs.

The most abstract kind of formal theory focusses upon kinds or dimensions of social relationships that are universal. This extreme kind of theorizing is typified by the work of the German sociologist Georg Simmel (1858–1918) who was concerned with such matters as conflict, authority, and interaction, whether they appeared in religious or economic contexts, in ephemeral interpersonal encounters or in permanent organizations (Simmel, 1950). Thus a formal sociologist concerned with the study of 'authority' could equally well study authority in strip-clubs, the Athenaeum, or pets' homes.

Most of the sociology the reader is likely to be familiar with is of a very different kind: sociological research into specific problem-areas such as crime, race relations, housing, or the family. It is usually research into areas where it is believed that things have 'gone wrong'. The concern of such researches is usually with quite substantive matters – documenting and explaining the patterns and causes of delinquency, illegitimacy, or overcrowding. Its primary aim is not the construction of theory or simply to arrive at an intellectual understanding of why things are as they are.

Men whose prime aim *is* simply to theorize in this way are not irresponsible people, unconcerned with human problems. As citizens, they are often quite as concerned about social problems as the next man. Indeed, they may choose to specialize in theorizing precisely because they believe it necessary to understand the workings of society clearly before one can act in ways likely to prove effective. Their main aim as scientists will thus be to help people think more clearly about society, for we cannot solve social problems until we have thought about social problems sociologically.

Social problems are not the same things as sociological problems. Sociology is a scientific mode of analysing social relationships, and a problem, for sociology, is any pattern of relationships that calls for explanation; the challenging problems are those where the relevant factors and causes are not obvious. A 'social problem' is some piece of social behaviour that causes public friction and/or private misery and calls for collective action to solve it.

Now if a sociological problem is constituted by any piece of behaviour of which we want to 'make sense', it will be obvious that it is not only with 'trouble' problems – problems of breakdown, welfare, or so-called 'social pathology' – that the sociologist is concerned. The explanation of why divorce happens, why it happens to some people with certain social characteristics and not others, or its rise and fall, constitute problems of explanation for the sociologist. Divorce thus throws up sociological problems. It is, at the same time, a 'social problem'. But the sociologist confronts equally different problems of explanation when he looks at marriages which persist rather than break down, for any husband or wife knows that marriage is no bed of roses; it is a relationship suffused with tensions, even where – indeed, because – there is a specially close relationship. Again, Finer has argued that whilst the series of recent military take-overs in African states is a social phenomenon requiring explanation, equally interesting is the sociological problem of explaining why it is that the military, who have decisive control over the means of violence, do not take over in *every* society (Finer, 1962, p. 5).

So 'normalcy', persistence, continuity, order, the things we regard as 'natural' and 'normal', are all quite as much sociological problems as are those of breakdown, conflict or deviation from normalcy – homosexuality, marital discord, etc. – the phenomena we conventionally label 'social problems'. From the point of view of the State or the neighbours, that is, 'quiet' families are not 'problem families'. Sociologically speaking, they are.

Since sociology emerged largely in the context of movements of reform or modernization, we tend to retain nineteenth-century conceptions of social science as the study of 'social problems'. More than that, we retain nineteenth-century definitions of only certain *kinds* of issues as social problems; delinquency and crime, unemployment, disease, malnutrition, poverty, drug addiction, alcoholism, prostitution, bad housing, sexual deviance, divorce, etc. The major things that these quite diverse items have in common is that they are all things which the nineteenth century saw as *bad* things, and about which people used sociological inquiry in order to provide them with ammunition in an essentially political and moral debate. This debate centred on the issue of whether these things occurred because the individuals involved were personally inadequate, or whether social arrangements and not simply individual shortcomings led them into such straits.

Even today, 'social problems' are still thought of in a way that reflects a nineteenth-century preoccupation with problems of poverty and with an individualistic approach to its solution. Thus the social services are largely focussed upon a 'case-work' approach to solving the individual client's personal problems. Only very recently have 'community-action' approaches to problems of health, education, poverty and housing begun to break away from the individualistic 'case-work' approach. Moreover, increasing leisure is seen as the source of new kinds of social problem; problems of 'affluence' as well as poverty. Further, researchers like Titmuss (1958) see such individual problems not merely as the product of inadequate interpersonal social relationships within the family or within the firm, but as outcomes of decisions and arrangements at national level and as part of national politics. For 'welfare' problems cannot be fully analysed without relating them to the wider structure of society which produces such problems for the individual as being out of work. Others are trying to transform 'social administration' by applying sociological theory developed in the study of steel-plants or insurance offices to the analysis of welfare organizations, hospitals, and case-work agencies.

Deviations from normal, respectable behaviour create social problems not just for the individuals who suffer, but also for their neighbours, their kin, the State, etc., who have to bear the consequences of their suffering. Such tragedies, that is, are rarely purely private, either in causation or in their consequences. Nor are the individual's problems usually peculiar to him alone. The sociological imagination, C. Wright Mills has argued, consists in the ability to appreciate that the 'troubles' that afflict the individual are the outcome of much wider arrangements within which his life is lived out, and that these arrangements affect the local family and work milieux within which most of this life is acted out. Most people never get beyond seeing their personal troubles as simply personal. Even some social scientists tell people that their problems are mainly caused by personal inadequacy, by inability to adjust, that they are the outward manifestation of innate anti-social drives, etc. The development of a sociological imagination, Mills suggests, enables the individual to see that his 'personal troubles of milieu' are connected with 'public issues of social structure'; that his personal history (biography) is shaped by what is happening to his society (history); that to 'understand what is happening in themselves', men have to see themselves as 'minute points of the intersections of biography and history within society' (Mills, 1959a, p. 7).

The causes of constantly-recurring mass and personal distress, moreover, are to be found in the functioning of what to those more fortunately-placed appears to be a 'normal' and satisfying society. Thus, in an educational system like that in Britain, 'educational opportunity', which represents for some children the achievement of higher education, necessarily entails the 'de-selection' of the rest. Failure for the majority is a condition of the normal functioning of society. We know, too, that large numbers of the most talented children are excluded while many of the less-gifted go on to college and university. This, also, is part of the 'normal' functioning of society.

Those who suffer, therefore, often criticize the structures that produce these results as themselves constituting 'social problems'. Traditional 'social problems' research, they say – the study of what has been variously defined as the study of 'nuts and sluts' (or 'peers' and 'queers') – merely deals with the end-products of this normal society: its 'welfare' problems. But this social machinery itself, as well as war, political corruption, the private ownership of newspapers, the starvation of millions at home and abroad, are every bit as much 'social problems'.

The 'sociological imagination', then, involves acquiring an understanding of how the day-to-day life of the individual is connected to the higher levels of social organization and to wider processes in society.

The sociologist thus sees society as exhibiting order: patterned regularities, not just a collection of random, disconnected events or facts. A society is a *system* insofar as it is made up of parts which mesh together. Changes in one part will have effects on other parts (though the effects may not necessarily be direct or powerful). To relate together these different parts of society and different areas of experience, to draw a coherent 'intellectual' map of the world and to locate ourselves on this map, we need to match together the different pieces of our mental furniture also. Some of it may need consigning to the rubbish-heap because it does not fit the over-all intellectual pattern or style, or is worn-out and needs replacing by more modern and better-fitting furniture.

In order to understand these interconnexions in the world 'out there', then, we need a body of theory which itself is systematic. We cannot, in social science, operate effectively with bits and pieces of ideas unconnected to each other, as we so often tend to do in everyday life. Most people in Britain, for example, use bits of classical liberalism, bits of socialist ideas, and bits of Christianity, without necessarily subscribing to any one of these belief-systems as a whole, and without fitting the bits together very systematically in their minds. True, few people see no interconnexions at all; their life would be very chaotic if this were so. But they are quite capable of refusing to believe, for instance, that Hell exists as well as Heaven (Gorer, 1955, p. 252) – or where they acknowledge the existence of Hell, refuse to admit that anyone they know and love is destined for Hell.

Scientists can be quite as inconsistent and unscientific in their private lives as anyone else. They are obliged, however, in their work to order their thinking more rigorously, if they are to make serious sense, and be able to demonstrate to their colleagues that they have made serious sense. Without some kind of intellectual scheme which is comprehensible and acceptable to their colleagues, they cannot do this.

Once we begin consciously to relate our ideas about society to each other to form a more coherent outlook, we are beginning to think systematically. The most unlikely and apparently remote phenomena may now be seen to be related: thus Max Weber argued that the rise of capitalism in Europe and the rise of Protestantism were by no means unconnected (Weber, 1952). There is, of course, a danger of artificially *over*-connecting things. There are sociologists who seem to think that if there are two football teams in a town, one must be Protestant and the other Catholic (an assumption which holds true probably only in Glasgow).

Systematic thought is essential for comprehending the world that itself is a system. We can, indeed, look at the whole world as one single social system (Worsley, 1967, ch. 1). Within this world system are sub-systems such as the nation-state. There are also sub-systems within the State: county and parish levels of government, for example: as well as other separate and parallel organizational sub-systems within the same society: national organizations of transport workers, national associations of motor-car owners, dahlia-growers, etc., each with its own internal divisions and levels. There are also non-organizational systematic regularities, as when all families – both by legal requirement and long-established custom – are systematically monogamous. There are thus regularities even though there is no formal organization to which all families belong. The concept of system allows for the existence of many kinds of system and sub-system, as well as *levels* of society, from the lowest level of direct face-to-face interactions in 'primary groups' to the level of nation-wide and even international groups and associations.

Though today what goes on in any one country is profoundly conditioned by world-wide developments – so that no nation-state is an island – most of the groups and categories that immediately affect our lives are still contained within the nation-state. Between the level of the nation and the level of the primary group, there are many types and levels of society: Parliament, a housing estate, or a school class in their form-room. Theory can be said to be high-level or lower-level according to the different levels of society it deals with. Thus theories about the functioning of the national party system are often described as 'higher' level theory than studies of local party branches. This implies that the level of a theory is a function of the range of phenomena it deals with, and some go on to argue that the study of national organizations or of such nationwide units as the family (e.g. by carrying out nation-wide surveys) necessarily engenders theory which is 'higher level' than that which arises from studying twenty families intensively.

Now in one sense, a theory which deals with a larger area of reality is, of course, more 'general' than one which handles smaller portions. But very good theory can be generated out of studies which are quite limited in size. Thus Elizabeth Bott studied only twenty families, but produced some of the most stimulating ideas about family life in general that have come out of recent sociology (Bott, 1957). Again, general theory can be applied to, rather than emerge from, small-scale or low-level situations, as when a psychiatrist applies all his knowledge to the cure of a single patient or when industrial sociologists intensively study a single shop in a factory. It is possible, if one is equipped with an adequate sociological vision, to study the Chinese Revolution through the examination of only one village (Hinton, 1966).

We can thus classify theories not only according to the *level* of social organization to which it applies, but also according to the *range* of phenomena the theory covers. The kind of theory we have called 'substantive' is said to be 'high level' when it tackles things which are large in scale or widely distributed. But the degree of generality of *formal* theory is of a quite different kind and is measured by the extent to which concepts and propositions are fitted together to form a coherent body of *ideas*, rather than the degree to which the theory concerns a particular level of *society*.

Formal theory, then, is concerned with theoretical range rather than with social level. Extreme formalists aim at establishing propositions which will hold good for any social situation in any society in any epoch. Naturally such proportions are very abstract and limited in number. Thus, we may see certain resemblances in three-party relationships, whether these be the 'eternal triangle' or nations at war, but the differences between these are much more crucial than any such resemblances.

But in order to comprehend processes of development, and especially the emergence of quite new social forms to displace older ones, a more historically-informed sociology is needed. The great sociological theorists, such as Max Weber and Karl Marx, were thus neither simply 'formal' or 'substantive' theorists. It seems best to label them 'general' theorists, for while they developed complex bodies of theory concerning the basic properties of human society, they used this to delineate the general patterns of human historical development within which studies of particular societies were located.

Many theorists have been attracted to formal theorizing because they have hoped to be able to establish general laws of human behaviour that would hold true irrespective of what particular society was being studied in what particular period. They hoped to emulate the natural sciences by working out the laws governing social behaviour. Once we knew these laws, we could become 'social engineers', able to control the future by taking the appropriate action.

This set of ideas about the role of science in society is known as *positivism*, a term coined by Auguste Comte (1798–1857), the man who also coined the term 'sociology'.

Positivism is based on a number of assumptions. First, it assumed a mistaken conception of the natural sciences, for natural scientists do not simply 'collect' facts any more than social scientists do. Different scientists develop different theoretical frameworks or 'paradigms', as Kuhn calls them, and these are often in rivalry, as when astronomers began to find that Ptolemaean conceptions of the cosmos could not explain certain observed movements of the heavenly bodies. Copernicus then devised an alternative 'paradigm'. Science proceeds by the resolution of such problems, not simply by the amassing of more and more facts.

Secondly, modern natural scientists no longer conceive of the operation of the laws of Nature in the way that their predecessors did in the eighteenth century. The conception of law with which the natural scientist operates today is based upon notions of probability in the statistical sense, rather than upon notions of an absolutely determined universe. In this conception of law, there is still order, but the behaviour of any particular item cannot be exactly foreseen – unless we can acquire exhaustive knowledge of everything that might possibly affect it (which we can never do, though we can get near enough to it for many practical purposes including some extremely sophisticated ones). The positivistic social scientist, then, is really modelling himself upon outmoded, not contemporary, natural science.

But social science cannot, in any case, entirely imitate the natural sciences because of that fundamental central difference in subject-matter we have emphasized: that the sociologist's subject-matter includes conscious, active men. One of the major implications of this consciousness, we have also seen, is that men can retain their experience, storing it up as 'culture'. They also increase it by innovation. Hence social life is characterized not only by the communication of culture from one society to another and from one generation to another, but also by the emergence of new forms. Social development tends to show sharp discontinuities as well as more gradual change, since a society may be converted to Islam, or undergo a revolution: whereas no ant society is ever going to be affected by the ideas of other ants, because they do not have any.

The construction of a body of sociological theory capable of handling the variety of human society and culture over time is plainly enormously difficult. It encourages social scientist to give up the attempt, and to concentrate instead on becoming a specialist in only some limited area. Sociology becomes a series of compartments: there is now industrial sociology, 'small group' sociology, conflict sociology, and so on, rather than, simply, 'sociology'. The results are often disastrous: theorists spin elaborate structures which are ill-connected to researched knowledge, and field-researchers fail to demonstrate what the general theoretical implications of their work might be.

A further lamentable result is a distortion not so much of intellectual as of moral vision. C. Wright Mills has pointed out that some areas are remarkably understudied, considering their social importance. This neglect he saw in part as the expression of a limited 'middle level' imagination which the social backgrounds and social role of most researchers engendered. But it also occurred because academics simply gave in too readily to social pressures not to delve too deeply into areas that the powerful might prefer to keep shielded from scrutiny. What gets studied clearly depends greatly upon whether support for research is forthcoming. What is done with the studies equally depends upon people other than the sociologist. But he does have some say himself, and at this point, science, politics and ethics are all involved, and create problems of choice and of social responsibility for the sociologist.

Sociology and Political Action

For social research to take place at all, research must normally be sponsored and paid for. Moreover, various groups in society are interested in using the results of inquiry, whether simply to clarify their understanding of social processes or in order to develop and carry out specific policies.

But even the act of publishing or reading a quite 'academic' book is a social act which has social consequences. The reader may have his beliefs undermined, his prejudices reinforced or his 'eyes opened' by being exposed to new possible interpretations of the world. The specialized production and consumption of knowledge, indeed, has become a source of unique power in an age where mass communications become ever more influential.

The 'pure' scientist professes to be unconcerned or unaffected by such things. But the distinction between 'pure' and 'applied' science is quite misleading if it is taken to mean that the scientist, even if he is unconcerned about any possible applications of his work, bears no responsibility for its social consequences, or that there *are* no social consequences to 'pure' science. However 'pure' research is intended to be, the distinction between 'pure' and 'applied' science is not absolute. All that we can really say about 'pure' science, is that it is either that knowledge which has not *yet* been used, or which is 'fundamental' – basic to other scientific work. For we cannot know what the applications of even the most abstract theory may be. After the dropping of the atomic bombs on Japan, Einstein, on whose early 'pure' and utterly 'academic' mathematical work the development of nuclear weapons depended, remarked, 'Had I known, I would rather have been a watchmaker'. Conversely, theoretical findings of great importance have resulted from research undertaken for quite practical purposes, as the scientific breakthroughs of two World Wars demonstrate.

In fact, the scientist faces moral dilemmas at every stage of his work. The classical liberal view of science does not prepare him for these problems, for it teaches him that science is neutral. It also contains within it ideals which most of us accept as highly desirable – the ideal of the untrammelled search for the truth, and the ideal of the unrestricted free interchange of knowledge between fellow-scientists and between human beings generally. Yet we know that in reality knowledge may be used for evil purposes: there are people whom each one of us, if we could, would debar from acquiring certain kinds of knowledge because we know they would use it for anti-human ends. Such decisions, in reality, are more often made *for* the scientist than *by* him: control of the flow of information is a matter of institutional rather than individual decision. But the individual still has to decide whether to conform to that decision.

Society, in fact, by no means always allows the pursuit of knowledge as an absolute. Much natural-science information is 'classified' for 'security' reasons; social science, too, is inhibited by refusal of research facilities, restrictions upon publication, or upon communication with foreigners.

Thus the liberal conception of science fails to provide an adequate sociological model of the practice of science. Nor does it even pose satisfactorily the ethical problems of science. It holds that science cannot flourish without the submission of knowledge to the critical inspection of the whole scientific community, because we need to co-operate with other minds. 'Secrets', therefore, are said to be a hindrance to science. Yet clearly, the communication of knowledge is not what the patrons or controllers of science are necessarily interested in at all; they are as much, sometimes more, concerned, notably in the fields of atomic and bacteriological research, with preventing knowledge getting to other scientists, who work for their political rivals and enemies. Knowledge produced by social scientists, if important, is usually labelled 'intelligence'.

Scientists themselves also secrete their findings, perhaps less dramatically. They may do so for reasons quite unconnected with the 'reasons of State' we have so far mentioned. Scientists are no more or less ambitious, avaricious, idealistic or egoistic than other human beings, as Watson's account of his work on DNA vividly shows (Watson, 1968). The institutionalized pressure to 'publish or perish' in the race for personal advancement, or consideration of status, can induce researchers to secrete their findings, so that their rivals do not 'jump the gun'.

Not only is the liberal ideal of the free flow of knowledge a long way removed from the actual practice of science, but its strict necessity becomes dubious in an age when scientific organizations are now so large that they can live largely off their intellectual resources, just as big corporations finance their growth out of retained profits. Being big, these organizations automatically attract recruits, as big nations do via the 'brain drain'. By impoverishing scientific institutions elsewhere, they have less need to pay attention to the work of other, minor institutions. Moreover, such advanced scientific work can be carried out within quite unfree societies, for scientists can work and live in 'encapsulated' privileged worlds or be allowed freedom in their work only. The production of knowledge within massive organizations – however 'socialized' it may thus have become – is clearly by no means dependent on free communication and co-operation. Furthermore, the utilization of this knowledge can be used to the disadvantage of people, or in ways repugnant to the values of the researcher.

It is unscientific, then, simply to assert that science is intrinsically 'liberalizing' or beneficial. It can be used to destroy as well as construct. Social science, likewise, is increasingly being used as part of 'counter-insurgency' programmes, brain-washing and village-concentration campaigns, as well as for the activities with which it has been more commonly associated in the past: town planning, social welfare, etc. Though science has always been put to harmful uses, today it is being used for purposes which its least optimistic and liberal forebears might have found horrifying.

The classical liberal model of science further asserts that the scientist should not refrain from scrutinizing *any* area of human behaviour because he finds it abhorrent or sacred, because of fear of offending the mighty or of offending against social taboos against the frank examination of certain topics or institutions, or from some desire to protect his own pet beliefs from scrutiny or testing.

On the other hand, privacy is a major value, too, and people have the right to freedom from social science inquiry into their lives. And there are scientific studies we would not do. None of us would study the concentration-camps, even though Erving Goffman (1961) has shown how the literature of the camps usefully helps us understand behaviour under much less appalling conditions, in 'total institutions' such as the ship, the mental hospital, or the army unit (see pp. 229–31).

Peter Berger has called this capacity to alter one's perspective 'alternation'. Others call it 'relativism'. It is embodied, in more popular language, in such sayings as 'seeing the other man's point of view'. By looking at very unfamiliar social situations, we are undoubtedly enabled to escape from our conventional ways of thinking about society, even about our own society. This has moral as well as intellectual implications.

Such shifts of perspective may be destructive of dogmatic beliefs or habit. Social science, indeed, often does show that dogmas are unfounded, that 'the facts' can be interpreted differently, or that there are assumptions, acts of faith, beliefs or values lurking behind what people think to be 'self-evident' truths or 'natural' behaviour. If this left us in a position of absolute relativism – believing that nothing is true, or that everything is true, depending on how you look at it – it would be morally unnerving. But insofar as we avoid this and the opposite absolute – that there is one simple and self-evident truth – we are encouraged to think relatively and critically.

Comparative sociology thus leads us to challenge uncritical modes of thought. It is unlikely to eliminate them entirely, since men do not hold their views solely because they have arrived at them as a result of hard thinking. They are least likely to alter their thinking when there is one socially-approved way of thinking, when to think differently would invite social loss, as when to challenge racial stereotypes would be to invite ostracism, or raise fears of social competition for houses, jobs or women.

There are limits, then, upon the power of scientific knowledge alone to effectively change men's thoughts and actions. People are adept at 'compartmentalizing' their thinking, and compartmentalizing their thinking, feeling and acting, so that to accept an idea intellectually does not necessarily mean that this will change one's whole behaviour. People live quite happily with contradictory beliefs. They believe in spermatozoa and ovulation in the biology class, and the 'divine spark of life' in the religious instruction period. We believe in democracy and equality – but often only for 'people like us'. We think, that is, *situationally*.

Most people are, in fact, hardly concerned with systematizing their world-view at all: they are concerned with solving their particular problems: what to do about those coloured people who have come to live next door; how to avoid getting called up for the Army; why it was that my child, and no other, died of the 'flu.

Some intellectuals make such problems their work. Many, as we have seen, are as 'fragmented', even in their work, as the non-intellectual. But if intellectual systemization eludes him too, the scientist in the laboratory situation, on the other hand, does come near to the ideal of criticality. Yet even in the apparently purely technical activity of carrying out experiments, he is driven by a complex of personal and social motivations which have little to do with the pursuit of knowledge, and a lot to do with the pursuit of money, status and power, with religious or political beliefs, or even with sexual insecurity. The white coat is worn as much to emphasize rank, to tell the world that one is a professional, as for reasons of hygiene. And when he goes home and is talking to the children about sex, for example, the scientist may be as bigoted and inept as the next person.

To understand the causes of social problems does not, of course, necessarily enable the scientist, or anyone else, to solve these problems, any more than a knowledge of the causes of an illness necessarily enables us to cure it every time. However convincing analysis may be, however sensible proposals for reform, decisions as to what will be done, or even whether anything will be done at all, lie in other hands.

In one way, most of us will be heartened to realize that the power of the social scientist is limited, for besides having hopes of social science, we are also all haunted by the 'anti-utopian' nightmares of totally-controlled societies master-minded by sinister social scientists who manipulate the people who inhabit these Brave New Worlds and 1984s. The social scientist is in fact never likely to be in this position, both because real power lies elsewhere – with the élites and with the masses he manipulates so easily in the nightmare – and because our scientific knowledge of society is never likely to be as perfect as the positivistic social engineer thinks it can be.

We need not be overly pessimistic or humble about what social science *can* do:

A sociologist worth his salt, if given two basic indices of class such as income and occupation, can make a long list of predictions about the individual in question. .., about the part of the town in which the individual lives, as well as about the size and style of his house . . . , the interior decorating of the house and . . . the types of pictures . . . and books or magazines likely to be found. .., what kind of music the individual . . . likes to listen to . . . which voluntary associations [he] has joined and where he has his church membership. .., [his] political affiliation and his views on a number of public issues. He can predict the number of children sired by his subject, and also whether [he] has sexual relations with his wife with the lights on or off . . . (Berger, 1963, pp. 96–7).

Yet, in the end, we cannot, however carefully we examine the present, accurately predict the future. Rather than predict what *will* happen, in some foredoomed sense, social science enables us to make up our minds in an informed way about what the problem is and how to go about solving it in the way that we would prefer. The social scientist may well provide people with improved information and explanation and with better intellectual tools which they can use for themselves. But decisions, in the end, will be made as the outcome of sets of complex pressures from many kinds of people: idea-mongers, power-wielders, organized citizens, etc., not social scientists alone, and not solely on the basis of knowledge or reason.

Some kinds of prediction can be made, both long-range predictions about large-scale processes, and short-term projections about small-scale matters. We can be fairly confident both about some of the bigger looks into the future – that there will be major famines by the 1980s, for instance – and about lesser extrapolations, such as the projection of divorce-rates for the next decade, or even smaller predictions such as the likelihood of a particular newly-married couple's marriage ending in divorce and when, or their chances of producing a child within a given time. The last example may seem so simple as to be merely commonsense or trivial. Since it is the kind of calculation we make every minute of the day, we do not usually think of it as 'prediction'. But it is, just as we go to a popular film-show early, because we *know*, in advance, that there will be a queue.

To be accurate, most of the explaining we do in social science is not 'forward' prediction at all. It demonstrates the interconnexions between events at a given point of time, rather than explaining how they came to happen or what will happen in the *future*. Strictly, research is 'retrodiction', looking backwards at past events and making sense of them. From this point of view we may attempt to extrapolate forwards, to make what some contemptuously call 'prophecies' because our estimates about the future cannot, in the nature of things, be as definitive as retrospective analysis.

There are special reasons why there are limits upon successful forecasting in the social sciences. The social scientist's data is especially complex not just in volume – in that there are so *many* factors to be taken into account – but in quality, because consciousness is both part of his subject-matter and because he, too, is a conscious human being who can never completely insulate himself from involvement with his subject-matter.

People may be objects of study, but they are also subjects with their own consciousness and interests. People can change their minds, can think and act in one way in one situation, and differently in another, under different sets of pressures. They can even deliberately set out to mislead those who seek to govern, bamboozle, or even just study them.

They resist other people's pressures upon them, and may reject official orthodoxies and develop their own definition of the situation, creating their own group life embodying their own separate culture and independent interests. Even the most all-embracing, repressive, or complex organization can never establish total social control. There is always a degree of latitude, autonomy, conflict, looseness of 'fit', even if in exceptional situations, like that of prison, the room for manoeuvre may be very restricted indeed. The larger and more complex modern organizations become, moreover, the more they depend upon the harmonious working-together of all the parts, and the more vulnerable, in consequence, to the malfunctioning of even one part. Thus the withdrawal of labour by even a few hundred key workers can bring to a halt plants employing tens of thousands.

It would be foolish to underestimate the power of those who control large organizations. But it is also possible to underestimate the degree to which self-assertion and capacity to make changes are possible even in 'organization society'. To take the very different situation of agrarian societies, the passivity, even fatalism, of peasants was assumed to be a 'natural' characteristic of a population bound to the unchanging rhythms of the agricultural year, and, as often, bound by oppressive laws, by landlords and money-lenders. But in the twentieth century, peasants, far from being passive, have been a major revolutionary force. People can, then, respond to a given social situation in new ways, once their consciousness is changed or their capacity to act altered (e.g., when a revolutionary party gives them direction).

The subject-matter of the social sciences – the relationships of people to one another – is thus peculiar, owing to this special capacity of people to think about themselves and to modify their behaviour. It is a capacity which separates Man from the rest of Nature, and therefore the social from the natural sciences. It inevitably makes for special difficulties in making extrapolations about future behaviour on the basis of an examination of the past.

Nevertheless, sociologists often do make such prognostications. They even make recommendations, though here they are acting as citizens rather than scientists. A social scientist, *qua* scientist, cannot tell anyone what to do. He can make reasonable guesses as to what will happen if we choose to do A rather than B, but that does not tell us whether A is *better* than B. Whether it is or not depends on the values you hold. If you are shown that wealth is unequally distributed, you may react with disgust, indifference, or possibly pleasure (if you are wealthy yourself, say, or believe in the inevitability of inequality).

Whether he openly prescribes or not, a sociologist's assumptions, theories, values and attitudes always shine through. Any skilled reader can usually tell what they are, just as any intelligent reader of the daily Press does when he observes the way different newspapers treat the same events. Sociologists, however, sometimes refrain from making explicit recommendations or forecasts (though there are always some possibilities they silently exclude) because they regard it as their job to analyse, not to prophesy. Even less do many of them consider it their duty to prescribe: to say what should be done. For to recommend involves taking up a position, the abandonment of a 'neutral' position. The search for knowledge is held to be an absolute; if the scientist takes sides, his open-mindedness is likely to be impaired. He may close his eyes, consciously or unconsciously, to things which he would prefer not to see because they might offend his deepest beliefs, his party or his religion. We may refuse to subject those beliefs which our values would lead us to like to believe were true to the test of rigorous scientific method. These procedures will be discussed in the next chapter.

There is a real danger that we may close our eyes precisely where they need to be kept open. It is for this reason that the scientist does not so much set out positively to *prove* a particular hypothesis, but deliberately to test its validity by subjecting it to precisely that kind of evidence that he thinks might *dis*prove it.

We should not confuse objectivity with neutrality. The social scientist, indeed, cannot escape from the social implications of his role as scientist or his other social responsibilities either. He has inescapable moral obligations towards the people he studies and thus tries to avoid publishing anything which might damage people who have helped him. The moral choices he faces are not always so easily made. They are not even necessarily perceived as moral issues, nor, if perceived, can a single answer acceptable to everybody be given.

The ethical problems of social science, then, do not reduce themselves to such simple issues as whether direct recommendations are made or not. Even if there are no recommendations, there are social effects, no matter how few people read one's work. The more diffuse consequences are often forgotten, because the more direct consequences are the more obvious – as when people protest publicly about interpretations contained in a research document, or when a social scientist's work is used to somebody's disadvantage, say, to make money out of them or control them. The social scientist bears responsibility for the social implications of his work at every stage. He cannot shrug it off with the all-too-familiar response: 'the social scientist only reports: he does not recommend – that is the politician's choice', or 'the social scientist simply indicates what the likely outcome will be if courses a, b, c are followed'.

There are ethical choices throughout. Who pays for research, who uses it, who ignores it or censors it, are some of the major issues. They involve the social scientist in taking decisions in the light of his values as a citizen, not simply according to some kind of 'purely scientific' criteria devoid of value-implications. For social science, like the social scientist, exists within a social context, which does not disappear however much the scientist wants to be uninvolved, thinks he can be, or tries to be. The position of being 'uninvolved' is, of course, itself a position. It tacitly entails letting things go on as they are. It is for this reason that the notion of total uninvolvement has elicited the sardonic remark that a man can be 'so open-minded that his brains fall out'. The ultimate immorality of total non-involvement has been expressed in the words Tom Lehrer credits to the nuclear technician:

'Once the rockets are up, who cares where they come down?
"That's not my department", says Wernher von Braun.'

Chapter 2
The Logic and Method of Sociological Inquiry

Given that the sociologist is likely to be misled by his own value orientations, it follows that he must exercise particular care when making observations about the character of social relationships and of drawing conclusions from these observations. Problems of 'method' of this sort are an integral part of any scientific discipline, and sociology is no exception. Perhaps because of the difficulties arising out of the unique quality of their data sociologists have possibly paid more attention to these problems than natural scientists.

Basically the question is: among sociologists working with the same set of general theoretical concepts, in what way can an investigator satisfy his colleagues that they can trust that he has accurately described what he has seen, and that the conclusions he has drawn are valid? Clearly, as we have seen, the set of theoretical notions the sociologist works with will determine the way in which he perceives social reality. Yet at the same time his observations will be used to test the adequacy of his theoretical propositions. Theory and observations are thus closely interrelated and support each other.

The specific, though simplified, interrelationship between theory and observation may be represented as the steps in the so-called scientific method, or more technically the hypothetico-deductive method as in the diagram on page 70.

The process is cyclical: we start at any point in the process and then proceed through the steps back to the same point, or more accurately, the process is spiral: we arrive back at a slightly changed position. We may commence, for example, with the formulation of an hypothesis – a tentative explanation. We start out, therefore, armed with the knowledge of existing theory about social relationships or social actions, and anticipate finding certain relationships. From our knowledge of existing theory, for example, we know without any further work on our part that delinquent gangs tend to operate with a set of values which is different from that of their parents and local representatives of authority. We then *deduce* that in a community which is sharply alienated from the larger society – as in a Negro quarter in the United States, for example, where this community's values are likely to be opposed to those of the larger society, young Negroes who revolt against their parents are likely to do so by adopting the cultural

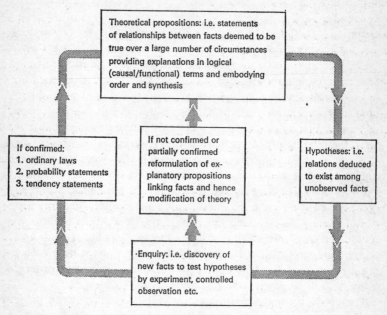

Figure 1 The paradigm of scientific method

characteristics of the Whites to whom their parents are opposed. At this stage, we have merely generated an *hypothesis*. The next step is to see whether what we expect in fact turns out to be true. To do this, we actually look for a set of circumstances that reproduce these conditions; that is, a Negro community which as a whole, rejects the values of the larger society. We then set out to see whether the young people in this community do in fact adopt the values of the wider society.

The outcome of the inquiry may in fact confirm our hypothesis, in which case we begin to have a little more confidence in the general theoretical framework out of which this particular hypothesis was developed. We may then go on to make a generalization about the relationship between dominant values and the values of delinquent youths, either because the relationship always holds true and constitutes a 'law', or – more likely – because it is true more often than not and reflects a 'probability' that the two characteristics will occur together. Though not a certainty, we can still express such a probability quite precisely. At the present stage of inquiry it is more likely that we can only state, much less precisely, that these two characteristics will *tend* to occur together in given circumstances. But we may find that our hypothesis is not confirmed to any degree: that the expectations were *not* borne out and in this case we may conclude that our inquiry did not, in fact, bear out the proposition we started out with. So we have to conclude either that the hypothesis was mistakenly derived from the theory, or that the theory itself was inadequate. At this point we will have to examine our methods of inquiry: in particular we must re-examine the way in which the hypothesis was generated; or we must question the validity of the general theoretical propositions with which we started.

Usually hypotheses are neither completely supported nor completely rejected: they are supported in some respects, and rejected in others. The sociologist then seeks to modify his theoretical statements to take account of this complexity. For example, in the illustration we have used, the investigator may find that not *all* Negro youths adopt the values of the wider society, but only some section of them – as for example the children of *middle-class* Negroes. This then poses a new problem for the investigator and should make him refine and widen his theory.

This is to speak as if scientific inquiry always followed a rigid pattern. But the *logical* procedures by which hypotheses are developed and tested, should not be confused with the way in which scientists, whether natural or social, actually carry out their inquiries. Scientific method, that is to say, is the *logic* of the procedure not the *practice*. The 'perfect' scientific method is more like a systematic set of rules which scientists use in order to organize their analysis in ways acceptable and understandable to their colleagues. But this is usually a very abstract reorganization of what they actually did, arranged so as to bring out the connexion between the various aspects of the scientific procedure in a clear and logical way. If a scientist is to expect his colleagues to accept his arguments, he must be able to cast his procedure in the form of the model or paradigm in Figure 1.

In real-life scientific work, the actual carrying out of research – of theorizing, testing, hypothesizing and reformulating hypotheses so as to arrive at theoretical insights – takes place at one and the same time and in a much more haphazard way. Few scientists in fact actually sit down in cold blood and follow the sequence of working out an hypothesis from an existing theoretical notion, developing an appropriate experiment or inquiry, then systematically testing the hypothesis and finally spelling out the consequences of their finding for theory. Rather they may happen to be reading a research report on some quite specialized topic; see that it suggests certain general theoretical issues; half-remember some inquiry which was relevant (perhaps something *they* have done); develop an hypothesis from what they already know and then pursue inquiries (perhaps using strict experimental procedures) to demonstrate the relationship which they already know very likely exists. Scientists may thus in fact develop the 'theoretical background' only as the inquiry begins to yield preliminary results. In the process they modify their hypotheses or change the direction of the inquiry.

All this may seem very haphazard. In fact it is not: it is simply that sociological research, like any other intellectual pursuit, has to be organized in a systematic way when it comes to making a careful analysis, but the way in which ideas come to scientists does not take place according to neat procedural rules. When scientists come to write up their results they must, however, present their findings within a framework which allows their colleagues, whether friendly or hostile, to check the validity of the steps in their arguments. Here the model of the scientific method as set out in Figure 1 becomes important, for it is only through using an explicit model that their colleagues are able to examine the validity of the procedures they have adopted and to see whether the conclusions they have drawn are in fact justified.

Sources of Data

One of the basic matters on which the sociologist must satisfy his colleagues is to assure them that his generalizations are based on information which has been collected in a way which allows an hypothesis to be disproved as well as proved. We therefore need to consider in more detail how this information is in fact assembled.

The sociologist is primarily interested in seeking out generally-valid explanations of regularly-recurring social phenomena. The framework of ideas and concepts which he uses in this process constitutes sociological theory. These concepts and notions are abstract mental constructions in the same way that 'gravity' is in physics, or 'valency' is in chemistry. The sociologist arrives at these concepts by making a very basic assumption: that there is a regularity in the things he observes. Equally, he may infer the existence of an underlying characteristic from the presence of certain indicators. A sociologist may, for example, notice that the behaviour of workers in a large factory and that of children in slum areas of a large city have certain similarities which may be characterized as a lack of identification with their fellows and a lack of confidence in those who wield authority. He may identify this characteristic as a manifestation of the abstract condition of 'alienation'. He may be able to isolate certain actions or characteristics of people which he regards as indicative of this underlying condition. Later he may wish to relate the 'alienation' of a particular category of people to their class position, or possibly to the way in which they vote.

There is thus a two-way interaction between observation and conceptualization. The sociologist selects from all the social actions going on around him a limited number, which he then interprets in terms of an underlying concept (such as 'alienation'). As we have seen, there is no such thing as completely passive observation: the observer perceives social relationships or social actions, and the act of perception implies that he invests his sense-impression with some meaning. In so far as sociology is concerned, then, a fact is simply some element of perception which is related to the sociologist's conceptual scheme.

It follows that since the essential components in the observations of the sociologist are the abstract concepts they embody, the material best suited for analytical use is that collected by the sociologist with these ideas in mind. Ideally, when the sociologist is collecting information, he ought to be doing so in order to test a specific hypothesis developed from a set of explicit explanatory propositions. Unfortunately this is a counsel of perfection which scientists do not or cannot always follow. Often sociologists have to make do with information which has already been collected (even if *they* have collected it themselves) and must test hypotheses after the event. This is another reason why the model or 'paradigm' of the scientific method outlined earlier is more of an ideal than an actual representation of the way sociologists in fact go about their work. Some of the most imaginative and stimulating sociological thinking has been based on re-interpretations of existing data. Nor does adherence to accepted procedures ensure that one's analysis will produce valuable results – it only makes it easier.

So we may classify the material which sociologists have available either as that which has been collected with specific concepts and hypotheses in mind – and upon which therefore *primary* analyses can be conducted – or material which has been collected for some other purpose, or with quite different hypotheses and concepts in mind, which the sociologist may, however, re-interpret and analyse in terms of his own hypotheses and concepts. In other words he may make a *secondary* analysis of this kind of data.

Existing Material

The amount of material which is potentially available for secondary analysis is enormous, since it includes all the information about social relationships and social actions from any source whatsoever, whether it has been assembled for sociological purposes or otherwise. For convenience let us classify these as (i) statistical records, (ii) historical sources, (iii) contemporary records and personal documents.

Statistical sources

Government statistics – particularly censuses – or statistics produced by large industrial or commercial firms, trade unions or other organizations, provide one important kind of data which sociologists can use in their analyses, and which in fact they commonly do use. An outstanding example of the imaginative use of official statistics is the study of suicide made by the famous French sociologist Emile Durkheim (1858–1917) in the last decade of the nineteenth century

(Durkheim, 1952). Durkheim set out to expose the social basis of this apparently most individual of all acts, and to do so he used official statistics, firstly to identify the sorts of people who were most likely to commit suicide, and secondly to identify the sorts of circumstances under which people were most likely to commit suicide. By carefully searching through the official suicide statistics of the Europe of his day he was able to show that some hypotheses about the causes of suicide did not hold water (e.g. that 'Latins' commit suicide more easily than 'Nordics') and that certain other features of suicide rates were very general and were to be found in country after country and from year to year. Durkheim then concentrated on these regularities, and in order to account for them erected several hypotheses about the way in which the individual is integrated into social groups to which he belongs.

The assiduity and care which Durkheim displayed in the use of these statistics are a model even today. But the difficulties he ran up against illustrate well the difficulties we always encounter in using official statistics and other kinds of data not collected by sociologists themselves. The first is that the statistics are classified into categories drawn up by officials for their own purposes. These categories however may present difficulties to sociologists who try to use them. Suicide statistics are notoriously prone to difficulties of this kind. For example, for 'social' reasons the cause of death for a clear case of suicide may sometimes be entered as some other 'cause' on the death certificate from which the mortality statistics are compiled. Sometimes, indeed, it is very difficult to say whether the person who killed himself had in fact intended to do so. If such distortions of recorded cases of suicide occurred purely at random, they would not lead to much distortion in an analysis based on these figures. But the factors which lead to an under-registration of suicide are frequently social because of the shame that surrounds suicide, as for example in small, intimately-organized social systems, or among Catholics or Moslems, and this distortion may not be apparent from the official statistics. For similar reasons, crime statistics are notoriously unreliable foundations on which to base sociological analysis.

A second difficulty is that characteristics which are important for sociological purposes are frequently simply not recorded. Durkheim found this when he wanted to relate suicide rates to religious persuasion, for the religious persuasion of the victims of suicide was not recorded in official statistics. Yet it was important for his hypothesis that he should be able to measure the effect of religious persuasion upon the propensity to commit suicide. He had therefore to rely upon a questionable statistical procedure, that is, to compare suicide rates in predominantly Roman Catholic parts of Germany with rates in predominantly Protestant parts.

What is relevant for official statistics, which are often collected for fiscal or franchise purposes, may not, then, be important for the sociologist's purposes, and what the sociologist wants to know about may not be of interest to governments. It would be of great value to sociologists if church membership, social class and personal income could be collected in population censuses and in health and mortality statistics. But British sensitivity on these issues precludes this, and sociologists must accordingly make do without these categories of information in official statistics.

A third difficulty arises because statistics are sometimes not presented in a form which is most useful for the sociologist, even when the appropriate categories have been included. Distributions of characteristics, for example, may be presented independently of one another, whereas the sociologist is likely to be interested mainly in the way in which one characteristic varies in relation to other character-istics. Durkheim ran into this difficulty also, for although data on suicide by age, sex, conjugal status, presence or absence of children and province were available, these characteristics were not related to each other in official statistical publications. Accordingly he had to get one of his students, Marcel Mauss, to tabulate by hand the details of 26,000 suicides recorded in documents held by the Ministry of Justice in Paris. The table Mauss prepared enabled Durkheim to separate out the effects of marriage, childlessness, and age respectively on the propensity to commit suicide, a finding he could not otherwise have established. This was of particular importance to Durkheim, but was clearly of no direct interest to the Ministry of Justice.

But the greatest difficulty that sociologists encounter in using official and other statistics is the extent to which the categories in terms of which the statistics are collected can be held to reflect significant sociological variables. Durkheim was particularly interested in the cohesion of social groups, and the extent to which this cohesion influenced the behaviour of its members. He found that members of *élite* regiments of the Army, for example, were more inclined to commit suicide than members of other regiments. This he attributed to the high emphasis on *esprit de corps* in these regiments, with a consequent sinking of the individual's personal identity in that of his regiment and therefore an under-emphasis on individual survival. Durkheim looks at the same issue in several different contexts – long-term soldiers as against short-term; soldiers who have re-enlisted as against those who have joined for the first time; non-commissioned officers as against 'other ranks'. But it would have suited his purposes much better if he could have used a direct measure of the subjugation of the individual's identity to the ethos of the regiment. This he could not do because he was in fact conducting a secondary analysis. Instead, he could only examine a whole series of instances which he took to illustrate indirectly the abstract notions he was trying to demonstrate.

These dangers are made clear in a much more recent study in which the author wishes to show how the growth of towns stimulates and accompanies extensive changes in social systems (Reissman, 1964). He bases his study on material drawn from the recent history of Western Europe and then proceeds to test how four different characteristics of social organization vary according to the level of development of society. These variables are urbanization, industrialization, the growth of the middle classes and the development of nationalism. The only available method of examining the way these variables vary together is to look for such indicators of them as are available in official international statistics. The author does not have much difficulty in finding reasonable indicators of the degree of urbanization and industrialization of various nations, but the other two variables present him with difficulties. As an indicator of the prevalence of middle classes he takes *per capita* income. As an indicator of nationalism, he takes the percentage of people over the age of fifteen who are literate. The use of the latter indicator is based on the argument that: If nationalism is to be an effective determinant of attitudes and behaviour, it is necessary for those responding to it to be able to imagine unity in the face of manifest diversity between the peoples of a nation. Such abstractions do not come easily to illiterate persons who tend to equate reality only with sensed experience. A minimal skill in reading and writing can therefore justifiably be used, he considers, as an index of the ability of populations to understand the concept of 'nationalism'.

Reissman is well aware of the weakness of his position and he warns readers that his approach is tentative. But even so, to try to represent such a complex phenomenon as nationalism by such a simple indicator as the proportion of adults who are literate is scarcely adequate, even if we were to accept the validity of Reissman's justification for it. A combination of *several* suitable indicators might get nearer the mark, if they could be found, but there is in fact no way of measuring nationalism by means of official statistics.

Much of what has been said about difficulties in the use of official statistics would apply to the 'secondary' analysis of social surveys conducted by other sociologists. It is true that such surveys are likely to include more variables which are potentially important to sociologists, and that many of them include such key variables as social class, membership of social groupings, value-orientations, and so on. It is also likely that the results of social surveys conducted by other sociologists will contain more cross-tabulations of findings, so that the association between variables can be estimated. But even here a re-analysis is likely to involve asking questions which the original survey was not designed to answer, and this can easily lead to difficulties in trying to represent abstract notions by inadequate indicators.

Historical documents as sources of data

Records and accounts of a qualitative (i.e. non-statistical) kind – for example, relating to beliefs, values, social relationships or social behaviour – may also provide data for the sociologist. Such records and accounts may be contemporary or may refer to earlier periods. But in using either kind of data, similar problems arise and there are specific advantages and disadvantages whichever kind of data we have available.

Consider first the use of documents and records relating to former times. The sociologist is interested in tracing regularities in social relationships and social action. Data from earlier times are therefore particularly valuable in providing information about the extent to which patterns of social relationships persist as contrasted with the extent to which they change.

But several difficulties immediately present themselves in the use of records from the past. The most important of these is that few chroniclers of the past have been interested in recording observations of social relationships and social actions in the systematic way in which sociologists are. There are often intriguing and sympathetic accounts, of, say, peasant life, but information which is vital to the sociologist is often missing, presumably because the chroniclers of those times did not think these points significant. Thus, from studies of African societies, we know that who accuses whom of witchcraft is a valuable indicator of wider social oppositions and tensions in small face-to-face communities. A systematic study of witchcraft accusations in a seventeenth-century English village, therefore, might equally throw light upon social conflicts within it. But records of witchcraft accusations are limited to those that were brought to court, and these were probably only a small proportion of all accusations made. Where records of accusations do exist, they frequently lack the detailed information which would enable us to see the framework of social relationships within which the witch and her accuser operated.

As with official statistics, a sociologist using historical records has to accept the fact that the records have been created for purposes other than for sociological analysis. He must, therefore, select indicators of the sociological concepts he wishes to handle, and then make inferences about the operation of these explanatory principles from the indicators he has available.

One attempt to do this is J. A. Banks's study of *Prosperity and Parenthood* (Banks, 1954), in which the author sets out to examine the relationship between standards of living and family-limitation in England during the Victorian period. Methods of preventing the conception of children had been known for a long time before the late 1870s when evidence of a clear decline of fertility among middle-class people became apparent. The problem then is: 'why was it that voluntary control of the size of the family became popular when it did, and what was the relationship of the decline in fertility to the economic circumstances of middle-class people at the time?' For although the number of children a couple may have decided to have may appear to be a highly personal matter, as with suicide, there is little doubt that general social circumstances have a distinct influence on these personal decisions, since, for example, middle-class couples began to limit the number of children they had earlier and more generally than working class couples.

This problem arose out of the population controversy at the end of the eighteenth century, when Thomas Malthus pointed out that population numbers inexorably pressed upon the means of subsistence available to that population. By the middle of the nineteenth century, it was becoming common for members of the middle classes to postpone marriage until they could afford both to have children and at the same time to maintain the standard of living to which they had become accustomed. The incomes of middle-class people were assumed to rise in such a way as to allow them to support their children in a middle-class style of life as they grew up. But incomes did not continue to rise. Some twenty-five years after the expansion of standards of living in the 1850s, that is, in the middle 1870s, there was an economic recession which forced middle-class parents to limit the number of children they had, or, alternatively, to suffer a decline in their standards of living.

In order to examine the relationship between standards of living on the one hand and size of families on the other, Banks searched through contemporary records and reports of many different kinds. Some were papers written for learned societies; some were official government reports, others were books, both popular and learned, on a variety of topics. Banks also used pamphlets written for propaganda purposes, letters to the papers, and novels of the time (particularly those by Jane Austen and Anthony Trollope). He was able to show convincingly how the attitudes and opinions of representatives of the middle classes reflected their concern with the public demonstration of their social status, as shown by their standard of living, and how the expense of bringing up children – particularly of educating them and giving them a start in life – conflicted with this desire. Yet, as Banks points out himself, the final steps of his argument are not filled in. The need to keep family-size under control to ensure a middle-class standard of living did not alone provide either necessary or sufficient conditions for voluntary limitation of the size of a man's family. To complete the causal connexion between these two aspects of social life, we would have to document how the couple came to the conclusion that they could not afford another child, what choices they had before them, what factors induced them to make the choice they did, and finally, what action they took to prevent the conception of another child. Information bearing on these vital links in the argument was not available to Banks. If he were studying this problem in contemporary England, he could, of course, endeavour to find out about these matters and so complete the links in the argument. But since he had to use data assembled without these questions in mind, his argument necessarily remains incomplete.

Contemporary records

Similar difficulties arise in connexion with the use of contemporary records when used as a source of information in sociological studies. Contemporary records are seldom used as the sole source of information in a sociological study; they are usually one source of a particular kind of information. We may, for example, use them to study ideologies. Thus in the field of communications-research a great deal of attention has been paid to the way in which ideas or values are presented through various media.

Studies of newspaper readerships, for example, involve the analysis of the way in which different newspapers, directing their custom to different types of audience, present the same item of news in different ways. This method is also applied to the study of political, religious or other doctrines as they are presented in such mass-communication media as newspapers, magazines, radio broadcasts or television programmes. Here the object is to identify and characterize the content of the communication and not to test sociological hypotheses. A sociologist, however, is more likely to use information derived from an examination of contemporary records by using it to test some hypothesis which links, say, people's aspirations with the frustrations the consumers of the mass medium experience.

Contemporary and historical records are often analysed systematically through a procedure known as 'content analysis'. This involves constructing certain categories for classifying information on certain themes in advance. The records are then perused and the incidence and use of the categories and themes noted. Sociologists often examine records less rigorously by creating a 'quantitative index' in which the frequency with which themes are mentioned is counted *without* first establishing a list of themes on the basis of some prior hypothesis or theoretical assumption. (In some questionnaires, again, the questions are laid down in advance in order to elicit a precise answer: other questions are designed to allow the subject to respond freely.) The sociologist is left with the problem of reducing the 'freer' responses to some systematic set of categories he can use for his analysis. It is here that a quantitative index is useful, for by means of such an index he can record the number of times the different themes are mentioned in response to a question. Coding the responses to these questions is usually a tedious task, but recently some steps have been taken towards using computers to recognize patterns of words and to count up the themes mentioned by enumerating the different word-patterns that emerge.

The distinction which is significant there, however, is not that of whether a record is analysed by 'content analysis' or a 'quantitative index', but that of records which come into being by reason of a sociologist's inquiry with a specific hypothesis and conceptual scheme in view on the one hand, and records which have come into being originally for some other purpose, but which the sociologist nevertheless uses as a potential source of information, on the other.

Our emphasis so far has been on records produced for purposes which are not those of the sociologist. We must now turn to information which the sociologist gathers directly for his own specific purposes.

Data Collected with an Hypothesis in View

When a sociologist sets about systematically gathering information about a problem that he wishes to find an answer to, he is faced with certain conflicting demands on his time. On the one hand he needs, ideally, to extend his inquiries over a large number of instances in order to take account of the full range of variation in the phenomenon he is interested in. On the other hand, he needs to become sufficiently well-acquainted with each particular case to enable him to obtain enough understanding about it in order to be able to make trustworthy judgements. Clearly, the more he satisfies the one need, the more he frustrates the other. The techniques of information-gathering available to the sociologist therefore may be ranged along the two dimensions of 'numbers involved' and 'personal involvement'.

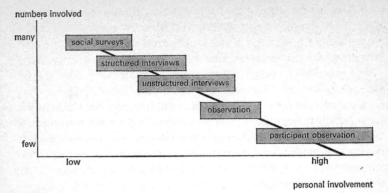

Figure 2 Relationship between number of respondents and degree of personal involvement of sociologist

Social surveys

The man in the street particularly associates the social survey with sociologists, since he often thinks that this is the only available technique that sociologists have for collecting information. The survey is certainly a very important way of assembling data, but it is by no means the only way.

The basic procedure is that people are asked a number of questions focussed on that aspect of behaviour the sociologist is interested in. A number of people, carefully selected so that they are representative of the population being studied, are asked to answer exactly the same questions, so that the replies of different categories of respondent may be examined for differences. Since one of the virtues of the survey lies in the large number of respondents that can be included, it follows that both the method of getting the questionnaires completed, and consequently the formulation of the questions to be asked, must be very carefully worked out.

One type of survey relies on contacting the respondents by letter and asking them to complete the questionnaires themselves before returning it. A variation of the procedure is that an assistant delivers the questionnaire to the respondent, asks him to complete it, and makes an arrangement to pick it up later. Sometimes questionnaires are not completed by individuals separately but by people in a group under the direct supervision of the research worker, as for example a class

The Logic and Method of Sociological Inquiry   83

of students in a university or a group of workers at a trade union meeting. In other surveys a trained interviewer asks the questions and records the responses on a schedule for each respondent. These alternative procedures have different strengths and weaknesses.

Mail-questionnaires are relatively cheap and can be used to contact respondents who are scattered over a wide area. But at the same time the proportion of people who return questionnaires sent through the post is usually rather small. The questions asked in mail-questionnaires have also to be very carefully worked out in order to avoid ambiguity, since the respondent cannot ask to have questions clarified for him. The questionnaire which is picked up by an assistant, similarly, must be very carefully designed. The personal attention of the assistant usually ensures a higher rate of completion, but it obviously costs more than a mail-questionnaire. Using *groups* to complete questionnaires means that the return rate is good and that the information is assembled quickly and fairly cheaply (though difficulties are encountered in selecting appropriate groups and in securing their co-operation in completing the questionnaires). The research-worker is also able to explain the purposes of his study and to clear up misunderstandings, but unless strict control is maintained the respondents may discuss the questions with one another and so impair the accuracy of the results.

Interviewing respondents individually is probably the most reliable method, although it is usually expensive. Several trained interviewers may be employed to contact specified individuals at addresses or locations. These interviews may be short or of several hours duration; they may either stick to a very closely specified wording and question-order, or they may be fairly free interviews in which the interviewer is allowed to pursue the topic in an indirect and oblique way. Different topics may require different methods of interview.

Where 'attitude' questions are included, great care must be exercised to see that the wording, emphasis and intonation are standardized between different interviewers and from respondent to respondent. Respondents may react to slightly different intonations or difference in wording; this can make results obtained by one interviewer systematically different from those another interviewer obtains, and make the results useless for comparative purposes.

As a rule the questions will cover two somewhat different types of information. One part of the questionnaire will be concerned with the main (or 'substantive') part of the inquiry. If the inquiry were concerned with the factors influencing family planning, for example, a number of attitudinal questions might be asked about peoples' aspirations for their children; conceptions of the satisfactions and dissatisfactions which might come from having children; their attitudes to methods of contraception; their value-orientation in respect of marriage and the family; a number of factual questions on the number of children desired; their actual practice of contraception, and so on. The other part of the questionnaire (sometimes called 'face sheet data') would consist of a set of factual questions about the couple's education, social background, religious persuasion, income, ages, date of marriage and so on. Much of the analysis which follows will involve seeing whether respondents with specific social and demographic characteristics answer the questions in the substantive part of the questionnaire in the same way or not.

An important aspect of the survey, as in other procedures of data collecting, is the way in which the units of inquiry are chosen. The kind of unit selected depends on the frame of reference of the inquiry. It may be a group, or organization, or an individual. In an ideal world, the sociologist would be able to examine every unit he wanted to acquire information about. Sometimes this is possible – there are after all, a limited number of trade unions or political parties in any one country. More commonly, however, there are more units than a research worker can possibly contact in any practicable way. He must therefore employ other tactics. One of these is to limit the units to be examined to a number which he can handle given the time and resources he has available. The research-worker, then, must first of all decide how many units of inquiry he can examine, taking into account how long each investigation (or interview) will take, how long it will take him to get there, whether he will be able to analyse all the material he collects and so on. Having decided on the number of units he can handle, he must now choose which actual units he will examine.

Immediately a problem presents itself: how can he ensure that the units he selects really reflect the characteristics of the whole population about which he wishes to make generalizations? Several devices are used to achieve this. One of these, known as 'quota sampling', requires that certain specified characteristics of the units should be present in the sample in the same proportion as they are in the general population. For example, if the sample were of adult males, and we wanted to find out the extent to which they belonged to voluntary associations, the sample may be so designed that the proportions falling into different age-groups, incomes and occupations are the same as those in the general population. The interviewers then have to contact a given number of males in these specified age-groups, income-categories and occupations. This type of sampling is used widely in public opinion polls, and has the great advantage that it is relatively simple and cheap to administer. But there are certain difficulties with it. One of these is that the final selection of units is left to the interviewer, who may unconsciously introduce a bias. Another is that certain mathematical procedures based on probability theory cannot justifiably be applied to the results.

For scientific, as against commercial work, some form of 'random' sampling is usually recommended. Random sampling does not mean *haphazard* selection. It is instead a method of selecting units for study in such a way that the probability of selecting each unit can be exactly specified. This means that formulae based on probability mathematics can be used to calculate within some range of accuracy, what the chances are that the sample so drawn is typical or not typical of the wider population from which it is taken. The commonest way of doing this is to allocate a number to each unit in the whole population (or 'universe'), and then to use a set of 'random numbers' to select the actual units to be included in the sample. The way in which the set of numbers is constructed ensures that no bias is introduced into the selection of the sample and that the probability basis of the sample is maintained. Note that the actual proportion of units drawn out of the total population does not play a very important part in the procedure. Rather the minimum number of cases that will allow adequate cross-tabulations of characteristics, and the maximum number that can be handled with the resources available, is decided upon. The actual size of the sample is determined by these considerations, and this in turn determines the ratio of the size of the sample to the population out of which it is drawn, that is, the 'sampling fraction'. If the sampling fraction turns out to be rather large (say, over 10 per cent) then adjustments will need to be made to some of the calculations. But this is done later – at the stage of *analysis* – by modifying some of the values in the computations, and does not affect the sample.

It is essential that before a sample is drawn, all the elements of the population being studied (it may be a 'population' of industrial concerns or schools) should be identifiable and open to selection by the method of sampling chosen. These requirements may present some difficulties. Let us suppose that we wish to obtain a representative sample of the young people of England and Wales. Let us further suppose that we are able to define those people of ages fifteen to twenty-four who have been in England for one year at the time of the survey as constituting the universe of people we want to make generalizations about. Ideally, our sampling requirement demands that we should have available a record of each person with these qualifications, so that he or she is exposed to the possibility of being selected. But how do we in fact give each person with the requisite characteristics a number which may be used to select a sample from our table of random numbers? There is no easy answer. In fact, the problem is usually solved by choosing first of all a number of geographical areas in a random way. Sub-areas are chosen within these, and sub-sub-areas within these, until we arrive at a unit of identifiable residences. These are then sampled in turn to find out whether there are in fact people with the appropriate qualifications in the households. Some of the elaborate procedures involved are discussed in books on methods of social investigation such as that by Moser (1958).

Before the inquiry can begin it is usually necessary to conduct a 'pilot' study, in which preliminary ideas about the problem, the overall research strategy, the design of the 'research instruments' – the questionnaires, interview schedules, etc. – are tested. It is usual for the preliminary schedules, for example, to be tried out in the field to see whether they present any particular difficulties in use. Only when the schedule has been tested in the field will the stage be set for the full study. A workable set of research procedures should thus emerge from the pilot study.

There is usually a good deal of office organization needed to run a social survey. Schedules must be prepared with sample identifications (for example the addresses of houses or firms). If a mail questionnaire is to be used, the envelopes have to be addressed, stamped and posted. If the inquiry is based on interviews, the interviewers will have to be very carefully briefed. When the schedules are completed and returned, it is usually necessary for someone to read them through to see if all questions have in fact been completed so that omissions may be attended to. Then it is usually necessary for the individual responses to be translated into a code which can be punched on to a card, or on to paper tape or transferred to magnetic tape for computer analysis. The preparation of a code, and the actual coding, often takes longer than the actual interviewing: a fact which has led to the tendency to prepare a code in advance ('pre-coding') so that the way in which the interviewer records the reply (as for example, by putting a ring around a number printed on the schedule) *automatically* codes the response to the question.

There has been a good deal of controversy about the reliability and validity of results obtained from social surveys. Many of the critics of social surveys have little idea of the care that goes into the design of such studies, the wording of the questions, the testing of schedules before they are used, and the precautions taken in training interviewers and in selecting the sample. Commonly, too, uninformed people criticize individual questions without taking into account their relationship to many other questions in the schedule, or without appreciating how the research-worker proposes to use the responses to this question. There are undoubtedly limits to what may be inferred from a particular kind of response to a question in a social survey, in the same way that indicators may only partially represent an underlying phenomenon. But within these limits, the results of social surveys can be useful and meaningful.

There are other objections to the use of the survey method in sociology, however, which are more difficult to counter. One of these concerns the extent to which *individual* characteristics may be assumed to relate to social properties – a point which will be discussed further below. Another concerns the validity of the replies to questions which are obtained in social surveys. This objection is based on the argument that the interview in a social survey is a special kind of social situation and that social interaction under these conditions may influence the way in which respondents react to some types of question. Some factual questions, such as age, occupation, or educational level reached, may be relatively straightforward (though this is not always so: it is difficult to get middle-aged women to say what their real age is, for example). But certain attitudinal and opinion questions may be sharply influenced by the nature of the interview-situation. Information about private aspects of behaviour such as the use of contraceptives or sexual habits may be difficult to collect, mainly because respondents tend to give 'safe', standardized and not necessarily accurate responses to these questions.

Clearly the means used to collect data must be suited to the sort of information that is required. While mail-questionnaires may be perfectly adequate for information on a number of straightforward and unambiguous topics, other topics may require the more subtle approach of a skilled interviewer. Social surveys, therefore, may or may not involve interviewing depending on the topic being studied. Where interviews are involved, however, new problems are raised.

Interviewing

Social surveys, as we have seen, may depend either on questionnaires which are self-administered, or on schedules which are completed by trained interviewers or by the research-worker personally. Interviewing then, is not a method of data collection distinct from social surveying, but rather a technique which may vary from the brief formal contact – as when the interviewer is working for a firm of public opinion consultants or a market-research organization and simply asks a housewife a few highly specific questions on a limited range of topics – to a long and rather rambling interview in which the research-worker allows the respondent to develop points at leisure and take up others as he chooses. The brief formal interviews, in which the wording of the question and the order in which they are asked is fixed, is called a 'structured' interview, while the more free discursive interview is called an 'unstructured' interview.

The object of using structured interviews is to standardize the interview as much as possible, and thus to reduce the effect that the interviewer's personal approach or biases may have upon the results. And even when structured interviews are used, proper training can do a lot to ensure further the reliability and validity of results. Tests made with both untrained and trained interviewers showed that more accurate and fuller results were obtained from trained interviewers, and that there were also fewer 'refusals' and 'non-contacts'. Not only the personality of the interviewers, but also the social characteristics which the respondents attribute to him, may influence the results. His accent, for example, may lead to different reactions from people of different class backgrounds from himself. Little can be done about problems of this kind apart from using, where practicable, what are known as 'interpenetrating samples'. Here each of several interviewers with different personal characteristics are allocated interviews at random in each of the areas to be surveyed. The effect of interviewer bias can then be estimated by comparing one interviewer's results with another's.

The problem of interviewer bias in *un*structured interviews is much greater. Here the interviewer is left largely to his own devices as far as the way he approaches the respondent is concerned. There is no fixed list of questions to work through; instead, the interviewer may work from a guide which will remind him of the topics he wishes to cover. But what topic he raises first, and how he leads on to the next is left entirely to him, as long as he eventually covers all the issues in the guide.

Clearly the training of the interviewer is crucial here: not simply training in the social skills of keeping a conversation going on a topic which the respondent may not be very interested in, but also in acquiring a sensitivity to those things his respondent tells him which are specially relevant to the theoretical topic he is pursuing. This means that unstructured interviews can only be carried out by people trained in sociological theory. They are then able to seize upon stray comments made by respondents which can be developed and lead on to important theoretical insights.

A good example of unstructured interviewing is provided by the study Elizabeth Bott made of twenty London families (Bott, 1957). She was interested in the way in which husbands and wives divided the domestic tasks between themselves, and wanted to relate this division of labour to the structure of friendships the couple had with others. It would have been difficult to use other methods of investigation. A structured interview was hardly appropriate on a topic as delicate as this and was in any case impracticable, since Bott had not yet worked out the details of her hypothesis. This was done only *during* her inquiry. If she had decided to work by observation, she would have had to confine herself solely to those families she was able to live with.

Her best procedure was a series of unstructured interviews, covering the background of the families, the organization of family-activities, the informal relationships of the family with outsiders, the formal relationships of the family with outsiders, and the set of value-orientations the different families worked with. On the average, Bott conducted thirteen interviews with each family. These lasted on the average for about one hour and twenty minutes, about ten minutes being spent in initial conversation, an hour covering the topics she wished to explore, and about ten minutes casual conversation at the end. Bott introduced the topic to the couple and the couple discussed it with her. If they wandered off the topic, she did not bring them back to it immediately, because part of the study was to see how the couple managed their interpersonal relationships. The interviews tended to be a friendly exchange of information rather than a matter of question and answer.

There is little doubt that interviewing of this kind can provide a sociologist with immensely useful insights. But there are difficulties. One of these is that an interviewer, whether conducting a structured or an unstructured interview, is in fact playing a role and the content of the communication between the respondent and the interviewer may be very heavily influenced by their individual conceptions of that role. Interviewing after all is a kind of formal social interaction in which the actors adopt behaviour which they consider appropriate to the situation. The fact that most sociologists would be thought of as members of the middle class, for example, in a working-class area is likely to colour the information sociologists collect by interview in such an area. Interviews on emotionally charged topics such as race relations, religion and political attitudes are particularly prone to biases of this kind.

But it is not simply a matter of a stereotyped role that a respondent may attribute to an interviewer. If the role is recognized the interviewer can make some allowance for it in recording his findings. It is rather that it may be very difficult for a respondent to understand what exactly an interviewer is trying to do. The notion of a scientific inquiry which is concerned with some apparently abstruse theoretical issue may be very difficult for the ordinary man in the street to grasp. He may therefore attribute to the interviewer a role quite different from the interviewer's own conception of what he is doing, and may quite unconsciously structure his comments in accordance with his conception. This may lead him to avoid the very issue in which the sociologist is really interested, and it will be very difficult for the interviewer to appreciate that this has happened.

Bott found that she acquired *three* (partly contradictory) roles in relation to the couples she was studying. First, she was, of course, a *scientific investigator* interested in obtaining certain information, the import of which was not always clear to her respondents. She also tried, initially at least, to present herself as a *friend of the family*, so that in the early interviews she 'submerged' the role of scientific investigator and did not take notes in front of the couple nor raise specific topics. Thirdly she was looked upon, to some extent, as someone who was interested in the 'problems' of the couple which she could 'put right'; that is, as a *therapist*. The contradictions between these different roles led Bott into difficulties, which were considerably reduced when she defined her role clearly as 'scientist' and started making notes in front of the couple and 'directing' the interviews to specific topics.

One major danger, we have suggested, is that when people are asked to report on their own behaviour, or to consider in abstract terms the ideas and values that lie behind their actions – as they might be asked to do in an interview-situation – they may tend merely to state the formal rules of social behaviour, rather than recount accurately how they or other people actually behave. Bott found this in her study. She knew that one woman held strong views about the desirability of easy divorce. Yet in a meeting of a women's association, the same woman spoke out *against* easy divorce. In the formal public meeting, clearly, she felt it necessary to emphasize the 'respectable' norm of the sanctity of marriage even though her private opinions were at variance with this. The same thing can happen in interviews. People may simply reiterate formal norms and values and behave quite differently in practice, or make a general statement about their behaviour, when in fact they behave differently in different situations.

Observation: participant and otherwise

Some of the difficulties arising out of the use of interviewing in sociological data-collection can be overcome by combining observation with interviewing, or perhaps by using observation alone. The rationale behind the use of observations in sociological research is that the sociologist should become party to a set of social actions sufficiently to be able to assess directly the social relationships involved. The degree of involvement may vary considerably from being merely a watcher on the side-lines to being deeply involved and part of what is going on.

Completely non-participant observation is as rare as full participant observation. In social psychology, one-way observation screens have been used to watch groups in action so that they are unaware that they are being watched and the observer cannot affect their actions by his presence. But in sociological studies, which are usually studies of everyday situations, the observer is usually visibly present in a situation. Sometimes he may be relatively unobtrusive, as he might be when studying a football crowd, where he appears merely to be another spectator in the situation and does not influence the situation any more than any other member of the crowd. But more commonly the sociologist is visibly present and part of the situation either as a sociologist or in some other guise. Simply entering into personal relationships with a number of people will involve a sociologist in a set of obligations towards them, so that he will have to explain to them what he is doing. Much will depend upon the sort of relationship the sociologist becomes involved in and the situation he finds himself in. As a member of the football crowd where the interpersonal contact is slight little explanation of his role seems called for but in situations involving deeper personal involvement as in studying a gang for example the sociologist would need to justify his presence in order to be able to have access to the information he needs. In any case, professional ethics demand that the sociologist should not deceive his subjects: they should know he is a sociologist studying *them*.

Where the sociologist is merely an observer it is usually assumed that he knows enough about what the actors are doing to be able to understand their behaviour. It would be pointless, for example, for him to attempt to study the behaviour of some quite foreign people merely by observation, for he would know so little about the culture of the people that he would have difficulty in understanding why the people were doing what they were doing. Even the uninitiated Englishman watching American football is in this position. Any sociological observer has then, to some extent, to be a participant observer – he must at least share sufficient cultural background with the actors to be able to construe their behaviour meaningfully.

But the degree of participation and of sharing of meanings may vary considerably. The fact is that all people who join groups come to play some part in the activities of these groups. This means that, like the interviewer, the observer is allocated a role. The role that he is allocated will at least be defined by such basic characteristics as age, sex and possibly ethnic or racial status. Even if he participates only very little in the activities of the group, like some social anthropologists in the past, at least he will be given some minimal roles, and his ability to gather information will be affected accordingly. A man will find much of the behaviour of women beyond his observation, and vice versa: a young researcher may find it virtually impossible to associate with the old in order to see what they do and what they talk about, and vice versa. Coloured people and Whites may have associations from which people of the other colour-group are virtually excluded. The role that the observer assumes or is allocated, therefore, has a considerable influence on what he may see and hear.

To escape this dilemma, some observers have attempted to hide their observer role completely. They have adopted roles which were familiar in the groups they wanted to study, and carried out their observations clandestinely. Thus a group of American social scientists wanted to study a very exclusive cult which believed that the end of the world was to come on a certain specified day, and took part in its meetings by pretending to be believers (Festinger *et al.*, 1966).

The ethical dubiousness of this sort of subterfuge is obvious. Here, however, we are concerned primarily with the procedural difficulties involved. One of the advantages of an overt as against a covert participant-observer status is that the observer is able to ask for certain obscure aspects of behaviour to be explained to him. The people who have accepted him into their midst acknowledge his observer role, as well as any other role that he may have taken. Though he may never be fully accepted into the group, therefore, he does have certain rights and a certain special degree of freedom at the same time.

The roles that participant observers assume – apart from the basic roles dictated by age, sex, etc. already mentioned – vary considerably. Ideally, it should be a role which will enable an observer to sink himself in the activities of the group but at the same time give him the maximum opportunity to see and hear what is going on, and, if necessary, to take notes about what is going on. Frankenberg, who studied a small Welsh village, found it convenient to take on the role of Secretary to the Football Club. This gave him a *raison d'être* for being at all the meetings, for knowing what was going on, and also for keeping extensive 'minutes' of the meetings which could double as field notes (Frankenberg, 1957). Lupton, who made a study of the social relationships of workers in an engineering workshop, took on the role of a sweeper, which enabled him to circulate freely amongst the workers and to talk to them all (Lupton, 1963).

But to remain an observer when one is becoming more and more involved in the activities of the group may prove difficult. One of the best accounts of the problems of participant observation is by William Foote Whyte, who made a study of an Italian slum 'street corner' gang in Boston just before the Second World War (Whyte, 1954). Whyte was introduced to the leader of the gang, Doc, who became his patron. Whyte learnt Italian and participated in all the activities of the gang – gambling, bowling and even participating in rather shady electioneering for a senator – while at the same time being known to the gang as someone who was 'writing a book' about the slum. But he eventually became aware that he was becoming so absorbed with his life as a gang member that he had stopped being an observer. He commented 'I began as a non-participating observer. As I became accepted into the community I found myself becoming almost a non-observing participator.'

Indeed, the peculiar strength of participant observation demands not complete detachment, but the involvement of the research worker in the lives of the people he is studying. (He has of course to submit this experience to dispassionate analysis.) His general experience and knowledge are extended by his contact with the actors, and his sharing of their activities with them. He is then able to understand the meaning they attribute to the actions of others, and so better to appreciate the logic of their behaviour. This gives him a deeper insight into the behaviour of the people he is studying.

But to do this involves the investment of a good deal of time and energy in achieving this closeness to them, so that he can only become really accepted by a few groups. Clearly the problem of choosing which groups to study is a difficult one, since it does not depend entirely on *his* choice but also on whether a given *group* allows the sociologist to become 'one of them'. Now whether the group is representative of the wider category of groups he is interested in is not always within his power to ensure. Thus intensive studies have their problems as well as 'extensive' (e.g. survey) ones.

In so far as the intensity of personal contact and numbers of persons involved are concerned, participant observation is at one polar extreme, then, and the large scale social survey at the other. There is often much debate about the desirability of one method of collecting sociological data as against another, with the protagonists of survey methods commonly arrayed in hostile ranks against equally belliger-ent supporters of participant observation. The Solomonic judgement, of course, is that the method of data-collection must be related to the sort of problem on hand and to the social situation which presents itself to the sociologist. If we were to undertake a sociological study of a small group – say the operation of a Board of Directors of an industrial concern given that access to it is assured – there would seem to be little point in trying to use social survey techniques. Participant observation can be turned to good account in practically any situation, but the findings which emerge from its use will be of a different kind and quality from those derived from a social survey. A study conducted by participant observation provides detailed examination of the actions of persons occupying specific social positions in particular social situations, together with their appreciation of the meanings which they attribute to the actions. But we would not be able to say how general this behaviour was, that is, whether it occurred in other situations or in other groups. For this, data derived from a *series* of observational studies or from some carefully designed social survey, would seem to be necessary.

There is, then, no one 'best' way of collecting data. The sort of generalization that the sociologist wishes to make, and the nature of the subject-matter he is dealing with, will jointly determine whether he primarily uses existing material, a social survey, interviewing, or observation, participant or otherwise. The danger is that the ease of accessibility of information will determine the sort of data the sociolo-gist collects and therefore indirectly determine the sort of problem he considers. It may be easier to conduct a social survey than involve oneself in participant observation, even though the problem at hand demands participant observation techniques. If the sociologist is swayed by the ease of data collection in these circumstances then the quality of his analysis may be severely impaired.

The Analysis of Data

As our paradigm of scientific procedure shows, the data which the sociologist has collected, by whatever means, must at some stage be subjected to analysis. This means that the sociologist must search systematically through his observations to discern the patterns of relationships which emerge and must try to explain these regularities by means of general sociological principles.

In actual fact the processes of observation and analysis are rarely independent of one another. Problems often become redefined as the research proceeds, and this means changing the kinds of observation made. In the social survey, for example, the pilot stage is vitally important, since the sociologist derives preliminary information from it which he then uses to test existing hypotheses in a crude way. He may then have to modify both the hypotheses and in consequence the techniques, for example, the schedule that he is using. Unstructured interview-techniques and observation are particularly suitable where the questions must be changed as the analysis begins to throw up new problems which demand new information in order to answer them. But once the sociologist becomes immersed more in analysis than anything else, he must obviously stop collecting data – at least for a while. A successful analysis is one which explains much of what has already been observed, and directs the sociologist's attention to new areas of observation. Thus having related youth sub-culture to delinquent behaviour, he immediately has to ask why some kinds of youth behaviour involve sub-cultures and others do not.

The analysis of data, therefore, involves sifting through observations with the object of determining in what circumstances certain relationships manifest themselves and in what circumstances they do not. This is partly a matter of abstraction and definition (that is, of identifying the phenomenon or the relationship) and partly a matter of routine (that is, of examining every possible instance to see whether the phenomenon or relationship is present or not).

By far the more demanding task is that of deciding upon the definitions and criteria of phenomena and relationships which are relevant to the analysis. Once these are decided upon, various routine and mechanical procedures may be adopted to speed up and simplify the tasks of sorting and classification. These may involve a simple perusal of notes and records so as to select descriptions of social actions which may be relevant, or more formal procedures such as 'quantitative indexes' or 'content analysis' mentioned above. In social surveys it is standard procedure to classify responses into categories to which numerical codes are assigned, so that mechanical methods of quantitative analysis may be used. For example, occupations may be classified in a two-digit code – thus, sixty-five, the first digit representing the broad type of occupation, i.e. professional, managerial, white collar, skilled, etc.; the second digit referring to some sub-classification within the broader groups, for example, managers of large firms as against small firms, or invoice clerks against insurance clerks. With mechanical tabulators or computers, it is very easy to count up the number of occupations, either in broad categories, i.e. by the first digit, or in finer categories, i.e. by both digits. When the full set of details are coded for each unit of analysis, it is simple to tabulate one item against another (cross-tabulation) which might be of relevance in an analysis (e.g. occupations against voting preference). The increasing use of computers for data analysis has led to some relaxation of the need for rigorous coding from the beginning. Material in quite detailed form can be stored on magnetic tape in a computer and classified by the computer in several different ways for analysis. Occupations, for example, may be classified into one of 211 different types though for analysis they may be reduced to seven socio-economic 'classes'.

However, coding is, although largely a routine procedure, in effect, a first step in the abstraction of regularities from the observational material. The coding categories themselves must be carefully thought out so as to bring out effectively the relationships between the phenomena which the analyst is interested in. When the appropriate categories have been decided upon, a code-number has to be allocated to each case. This usually means ignoring what are considered to be irrelevant details, and allocating a code-number accordingly. The actual process of classification and preliminary analysis thus starts at this stage. In coding, the vast complexity of details is reduced to a relatively small number of broad categories. Thus the actual ages of individuals are reduced to age-groups which the sociologist may single out as being especially significant, as, for example, those under and over the age of twenty-one, or those over and under the age of eligibility for an old age pension. Again, the plethora of occupations may be reduced to professional, managerial, white collar, skilled and manual categories. The sociologist thus has to decide what sort of categories are likely to be important *before* he starts his coding. Subsequent analyses may use these code figures to relate phenomena to one another in much more complex ways, but the validity of this second stage of abstraction will depend on the validity of the preliminary phase of coding.

The process of analysis basically, then, involves finding out how phenomena affect one another. The classical scientific way of doing this is by conducting controlled experiments. Experimental procedures, however, are seldom feasible in sociological analysis. Experiment involves selecting two sets of cases which, at a given point of time, are considered to be identical in all observable (or measurable) relevant characteristics. An experimental stimulus with observable (or measurable) effect is applied to one of the sets of instances (the 'experimental' group), while the other set (the 'control') is isolated from the effect of the stimulus. The observable characteristics of both experimental and control group are then examined to see whether any changes in them have taken place. Changes in the experimental group which have not taken place in the control group are attributed to the experimental stimulus.

It is not difficult to see why these classical experimental procedures are not common in sociology. To create a situation in which a designated group of people are isolated from some social stimulus, while another identical in relevant characteristics is exposed to it, is hardly feasible. It is true that sometimes something approaching this state of affairs may occur by accident. For example, in several parts of Africa the arbitrary acts of statesmen have divided a single tribe so that one part has fallen under the colonial administration of one nation, while the other has fallen under another régime. It has been possible to study the differences between the two parts of the same people after the elapse of time and so to estimate the effect of differences in political culture upon them. But there are many difficulties in this procedure, the most important being that it is almost impossible to prevent people from moving to and fro across international boundaries, and so intermixing the two experimental populations, or at least communicating with each other, thus violating the rule that the experimental stimulus should apply to one group and not to the other.

Even if it were possible to isolate the experimental from the control group, it is still difficult to ensure that the two populations are as nearly identical as possible before the stimulus is applied. One device which has been attempted is matching, in which each experimental subject is matched exactly by a control subject on as many variables as the research-worker thinks is necessary. The best reported instance is described by Chapin (1947). The research-worker wished to study the effects of education on occupational advancement. The experimental group was composed of students who had a college education; the control group of those who had not. The two groups were matched on six factors (i.e. father's occupation, whether both parents were alive, neighbourhood, age, sex, academic rating) before their occupational histories were examined. The procedure of matching is set out on page 101.

The net outcome was that the research-worker ended with 46 subjects out of an initial set (or 'cohort') of 2127, 23 of whom were experimental subjects and 23 controls matched individually with the experimental subjects on all 6 factors. The exclusion of so many subjects involves a waste of time and money for a small return and does not commend itself to the average research-worker, particularly if the advantages from matching are not very great. If the research worker had been prepared to sacrifice the rather severe requirement that each experimental subject should be matched individually with a control subject, she would have been able to work with 290 subjects (145 experimental and 145 control subjects). But in this case, the research-worker would have balanced out the factors so that the over-all distribution of the characteristics that she wanted to hold constant would have been the same in both the experimental and the control groups. Imposing the condition that the combination of characteristics for each individual subject in the experimental group would match exactly with those for one other individual subject

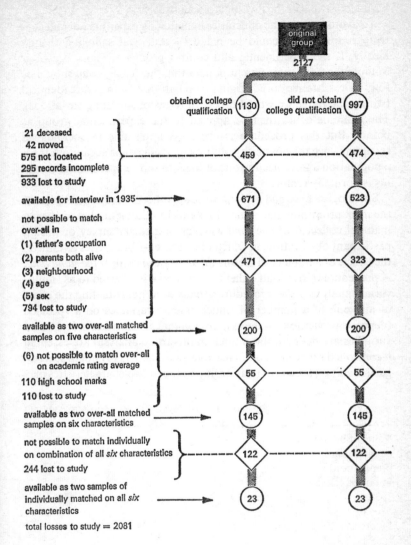

Figure 3

in the control group, in fact, imposes a very severe constraint on the number of subjects the investigator can use.

To avoid some of the difficulties in matching experimental and control groups appeal could be made to statistical sampling theory, ideally. If the experimental and control groups are both drawn at random from the same parent population, then each group should be fully representative of the original population, and therefore identical (within the range we would expect in terms of sampling variations). The stimulus could then be applied to the experimental group as before. But this procedure is even less applicable in sociological research, since the possibility of drawing two groups at random from a population and subjecting one of them to some experimental stimulus is normally remote.

Sociologists have had perforce to adopt other procedures. At present the most promising line of inquiry seems to be a method of analysing material collected *at one time* whether in a social survey or during participant observation, in which the research-worker tries to unravel the effects of a number of factors *all of which operate at the same time*. A procedure of this kind – there are several – is referred to as 'multivariate analysis'. The procedure usually aims at estimating the effect of any one of a number of 'independent' variables on a specified 'dependent' variable on the assumption that all the other independent variables are held constant. Such multivariate analyses are essential if controlled experiment is not feasible – and it is usually not in sociological inquiry – because a relationship between two characteristics may

	'38	'39	'40	'41	'42	'43	'44	'45	'46	'47	'48	'49
Value of perfumery and toilet preparations imported (Base, 1938)	100	100	129	140	128	91	192	233	349	376	314	472
Number of marriages registered in following year (Base, 1939)	100	83	76	75	60	69	70	101	107	122	117	119

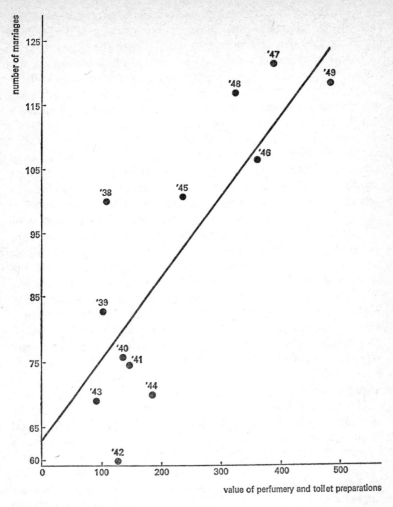

Figure 4 Relationship between value of perfumery and toilet preparations imported into Rhodesia and the number of marriages registered the next year: 1938-49

arise simply because they derive from a common circumstance and have no sociological significance other than the 'spurious' relationship through the common factor.

An example is provided by the association between the imports of

The Logic and Method of Sociological Inquiry   103

toilet requisites into Rhodesia, on the one hand, and the number of marriages contracted in the following year (over the period 1938 to 1949), on the other. The relationship is shown by the graph in Figure 4, in which the points, labelled by the date to which the information refers, are placed at the appropriate value in relation to the vertical axis (number of marriages in succeeding year) and the horizontal axis (value of perfumery and toilet preparations in the stated year). The line is drawn through the points in such a way as to make the deviations from it as small as possible.

It is clear from these figures that as the value of perfumes and toilet waters imported varied, so did the number of marriages that took place in the following year. The degree of association may in fact be measured by a 'correlation coefficient' which takes the value of $+1 \cdot 0$ when two characteristics vary in the same way exactly; $-1 \cdot 0$ when the two characteristics vary together, but in exactly *opposite* directions; and a value of 0 where there is no association at all. In this case, the correlation coefficient is $+0 \cdot 83$, which is high. But commonsense leads us to distrust the implication of this correlation. We can scarcely believe what some advertisers would have us believe – that marriages are brought about primarily because men cannot resist the allure of perfume! Though a correlation can be found, therefore, there is no direct *causal* connexion. Rather, both marriage rates and the volume of imports of perfumes were the consequences of a common set of circumstances – a period of marked over-all change during and following the war.

The example chosen was deliberately simple. In actual practice the position is a good deal more subtle and difficult to disentangle. This is because social phenomena are usually interconnected and affected by *many* determining factors, some of which may not be immediately appreciated by the observer. Let us return to the example of suicide. We know, for instance, that suicide is more common among divorcees than among married people of the same age and sex. But there may be *several* explanations of this: that suicide is caused by the distress and isolation experienced after divorce is one possible explanation. In other words a third factor, such as isolation, distress or perhaps financial strain, has intervened between the divorce and the suicide, explaining the causal connexion between them. Diagrammatically we may represent the situation thus:

But there is also the possibility that it was the very personality characteristics which inclined the person to commit suicide which also put the marriage under strain and led eventually to its break-up, in which case the assumption that suicide was the consequence of divorce is spurious, so that the position is as follows:

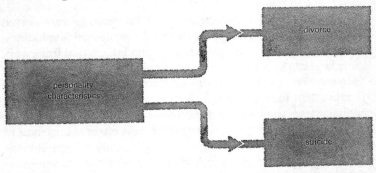

There is also the further possibility that the divorced person will commit suicide only if certain other factors are also present (say, for example, if he has no children – children normally being a 'protective' influence against suicide). Or perhaps there need to be *several* such 'conditions' before a divorcee is likely to kill himself, giving rise to the following situation:

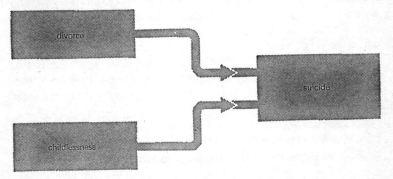

Finally, there is the possibility that a divorced person may only be likely to commit suicide because stresses and strains arise *after* divorce which he might have been able to withstand if he were still married, for example loss of employment. In this case the relationship among the events would be:

There are several ways, therefore, of interpreting an observed association between two phenomena of sociological significance. The research-worker, then, must have a sound theoretical framework before he starts his study so as to be able to identify the sort of factors which are likely to have a bearing on the problem he is interested in. He must then look at the operation of *all* these factors operating simultaneously some of which he can take to be both logically or chronologically *prior* to the phenomenon he is interested in, some of which he can take to be logically or chronologically *subsequent* to the phenomenon he is interested in, and some of which are 'functionally' related to the phenomenon he is interested in – that is, they may be taken as *either* cause *or* effect with equal validity.

Analysis is mainly concerned with stating causal or functional relationships between variables in this way. But before this can begin, the sociologist must make sure that the abstract notions he is chasing are adequately contained in the events he has been able to capture in his observations. The language of sociologists contains very general abstract concepts like 'social status', 'alienation', 'anomie', 'status inconsistency' or 'social cohesion' as well as less abstract notions which refer to relationships like 'kinsmen of', or 'manager' or 'middle class person', all of which, he assumes, manifest themselves in what people do and in how they *interpret* what they and other people do, but which are in fact not open to easy and direct observation.

Sociologists argue that even if they are not open to *direct* observation, they are nevertheless open to *indirect* observation. A label such as 'middle class person', for example, is usually based on the examination of a large number of characteristics related to social class and cannot be determined from any single characteristic of an individual. The argument is that different attributes of individuals may reflect, in different degrees, the middle class status of that individual. For example, each single attribute – where he lives, what school he has been to, his taste in music, the job he does – may not by itself be a trustworthy indicator of the 'class' of the individual, but a consistent response on all of them will be much more reliable. Some summary or adumbration of a number of these 'indicators', therefore, will enable the sociologist to gauge the dimensions of the intangible underlying disposition he wants to reveal.

The underlying disposition is sometimes referred to as a 'genotypic' phenomenon, that is, as the phenomenon which gives rise to the external and observable characteristics. The observable characteristics, on the other hand, sometimes called the 'phenotypic' phenomena, are directly observable and apparent. Many of the problems of devising indexes and scales in sociology arise from the difficulty of inferring underlying characteristics from their observable manifestations. The logic of most of the procedures turns on the notion that if we select a number of characteristics of individuals or groups, which, our theory suggests to us, reflect some underlying disposition we are interested in, they ought, if they are all manifestations of the same underlying disposition, to vary in the same way when the underlying disposition varies. Therefore, if we examine a number of sets of indicators of, say, social class, we would expect them all to move in the same direction as we successively move from looking at the behaviour of upper class people to looking at middle class people and then working class people. We would anticipate, however, that some of the indicators would reflect social class differences more faithfully than others. Different indicators could then be weighted by their relationship to the underlying disposition and be combined into a single index of social class. Something like this was done by the American sociologist Lloyd Warner (Warner *et al.*, 1949). He devised a mathematical expression which allocated a person to a social class on a scale made up out of a combination of indicators: occupation, amount of income, source of income, education, type of house and residential area. The statistical reasoning behind such procedures may be fairly complex and may depend upon certain mathematical assumptions, but with the widespread availability of computers to cope with the arithmetic involved, the use of these techniques should become commonplace before long. Sociologists will therefore have to know how to use these techniques, though they will not necessarily have to know how the answers are in fact worked out, in the same way that a psychologist may use a complex piece of equipment to study the operation of the brain without knowing much about the electronic circuit upon which it is based.

In computing such indexes and constructing such scales however, there is one serious difficulty that the sociologist must take into account. The basic assumption behind these procedures is that the characteristics we observe are the characteristics of *individuals*. Our interest as sociologists, however, lies not in the individuals themselves but in the relationships the individual has with other individuals or the beliefs and values that he shares with others. The underlying sociological relationships must usually be adduced from these personal characteristics: they are usually not immediately observable. Often, when statistical tables are prepared in which the personal attributes of many individuals are cross-classified the sociological phenomena that they are taken to represent are not made explicit. What passes for sociological analysis merely becomes what Coleman (1964) has called 'aggregate psychology', that is, the behaviour of the persons is seen to be the summation of a series of individual reactions, without any reference necessarily to their common beliefs and values, or the social relationships they have to one another.

If we correlate the incidence of suicide amongst men and women, young and old, married and single, town-dwellers and country-dwellers, for example, we are merely dealing with the joint occurrence of characteristics in a collection of atomized individuals. We are saying nothing about the social relationships between these individuals, including the meanings which people give to the actions of others. Much social survey analysis, indeed, does not go much beyond this.

Personal characteristics such as age and sex may be construed in several different ways. They may be related at one level to personality structure, so that the relationship of suicide to the characteristics can be understood in the framework of general personality structure. But age and sex, at a sociological level of analysis, may be taken to signify social relationships, so that being both old and a man may indicate the social isolation that characterizes men in industrial society when at the later phases of the life-cycles they have stopped working and lost their position in the family. In terms of Durkheim's analysis an isolated person of this kind is particularly prone to commit suicide. The personal characteristics in this sort of analysis, therefore, indicate abstract sociological notions: the propositions are about these sociological notions and not directly about the observed personal characteristics at all.

The Return to Reality: Models and Case Studies

The basic ideas with which the sociologist is working therefore are necessarily abstract and not directly observable. Abstraction is one of the essential characteristics of the scientific method. Yet the starting point of sociological analysis is the reality of what people do and what governs that behaviour. The purpose of abstraction is to provide a means of deepening our understanding of social reality.

At present there seems to be two rather different ways in which the general principles that sociologists have developed may be related back to reality. One of these is by way of 'models', in which the sociologist sets out the admittedly simplified connexions between phenomena in terms of his abstract theoretical principles. Such models ought to reproduce what happens in the real world at least to some extent. The other procedure is to examine a specific set of ongoing social actions and to show how the abstract principles manifest themselves in these actions. This is the approach through the 'case-method'. Case studies and model-building, then, are at once opposite and complementary procedures, the one showing how theoretical principles underlie real phenomena, the other how theoretical principles reproduce real phenomena.

In sociology model-building has not yet reached the pitch that it has in economics. It manifests itself mainly in what are known as 'simulation' studies. These are strictly models which set out to show what will happen when some specified changes take place. One field in which simulation studies are widely used is in international relations and in conflict-studies generally. In these studies, ordinary individuals are given roles to play representing people in important positions in the structures whose behaviour is to be simulated, for example –

nations. The decisions they make, and the effects of these decisions upon one another, are correlated and co-ordinated and fed back to the actors. They are then in a position to make new decisions in the light of this information, and these decisions are, in turn, fed back into the situation. The social scientists who make these simulation studies are then able to examine the possible outcome of different decisions, and their effect on the pattern of social relationships in their models. Ideally the extent to which the behaviour of the simulated structure resembles the behaviour of real structures should be assessed but there are several difficulties in estimating this due to the complexities of real social structure as compared with the necessarily simple models we must use.

A simple example of this procedure is provided by a study in which a model of organizational behaviour, much respected by sociologists, was tested by linking the various components of the model in an appropriate way in a computer. By feeding arbitrary values into the model and testing to see how the interconnexion in the model affected the various components it was easy to show that the model as set out by the author simply could not work: in this way the *logical* coherence of the model could actually be tested (Markley, 1967).

A more restricted use of model-building is by starting with some very simple assumptions, and then developing more complex arguments from these. In this technique, the consequences of people's actions are traced out on the basis of some very simple assumptions. These are then compared with an example of what happens in fact and the initial assumptions are then modified. An example is provided by Coleman (1964) who predicts what the movements of persons would be among a set of towns on the assumption that the movements are conditioned partly by the size of the towns and partly by the distance separating them. Next he compares his predictions with actual migration statistics and finds several significant departures. He then seeks to explain these differences in terms of the specific characteristics of the cities involved, for example the amount of travel to the Federal capital, Washington, which is disproportionately large in relation to the size and distance of Washington from other cities.

The attraction in these procedures lies in the fact that the basic assumptions and the logical relationships involved are explicit and clear. Models start from a number of postulates about the relationships linking parts of a structure: the extent to which the model predicts observed phenomena is a measure of the adequacy of its explanatory power. The case-study, however, starts from observation and proceeds to show how general abstract explanatory principles manifest themselves in observed reality. The approach here is similar to that of a medical scientist who has before him a diseased person and a history of the course of the disease up to that point. He also has a number of symptoms and clinical signs, and possibly a number of other diagnostic aids such as blood-counts, microscopic examinations of tissues, serum reactions and so on. The medical scientist weighs up these various indicators and fits them together into a meaningful whole, guided by what he knows about the patterns of disease in general. Given this interpretation, he is able to check his assumption by carrying out further tests.

In the same way, a sociologist making a study of a 'wildcat' strike may have before him a history of events leading up to the strike, an analysis of the structure of the factory, and a knowledge of the relationship of the various actors in the situation to one another. From his general knowledge of industrial sociology, he will be aware of a number of generalizations about the role of informal relationships among workers in industrial organizations, the differing effects of authoritarian and permissive managements, and so on. By examining the course of events he may be able to make a number of propositions about the way in which social relationships operate in industrial situations, and the courses of action workers may adopt in such situations.

The time duration of the case-study may vary from a single isolable instance – a social situation – through to a series of situations which develop one from another in a connected series of events, possibly over several years. Both types of analysis, however, share one basic characteristic: the situation, or set of situations, provide the occasion on which the sociologist is able to point to the operation of certain basic principles of social organization. Turner (1957), who calls his extended case-studies of one African people 'social dramas', uses situations of crisis to examine the latent conflicts in social life. 'Through the social drama,' he says, 'we are able to observe the crucial principles of the social structure in operation and their relative dominance at successive points in time.' The sociologist using this technique, therefore, selects a strategic set of events – a ceremony, a demonstration or a dispute – and uses his general knowledge of the social situation in which these events are taking place, and his detailed knowledge of the actors, to analyse the set of social situations and thereby show how the actions of the *dramatis personae* reflect their position in the social structure.

In arriving at his interpretation, the sociologist makes use of as much knowledge and information about the actors and their social relationships as he can assemble. He draws on historical data, official records, social surveys, interviews with people in strategic positions, and insights and understandings he may have acquired through participating in the activities of the people concerned. He also uses his knowledge of the social system as a whole as a backdrop against which he interprets the behaviour of the individual actors. All this is fitted together so that the whole forms an intellectual synthesis in which the connexions between the actions of people occupying positions in a social structure and the meanings informing those actions are made understandable.

The general validity of the analysis does not depend on whether the case being analysed is representative of other cases of this kind, but rather upon the plausibility of the logic of the analysis. The generality is of the same kind that enabled Sir Ronald Ross to announce the 'cause' of malaria when he found the malaria parasite in the salivary gland of a single female Anopheles mosquito in 1897.

The demonstration of the logical connexion between events gives the scientist the means of asking further questions about the phenomenon he is examining. To answer these questions he must start once more systematically to collect and analyse data. The subject thus grows by the constant interaction of painstaking systematic checking of observations and the inferences that may be made from them, on the one hand, and insightful, imaginative synthesis – as in model-building or case-studies – on the other. Together they allow order to be seen where formerly none was discernible.

Part Two

Chapter 3
The Family

Wives, submit yourselves unto your own husbands, as it is fit in the Lord.

Husbands, love *your* wives, and be not bitter against them.

Children, obey *your* parents in all things: for this is well pleasing unto the Lord.

Fathers, provoke not your children *to anger*, lest they be discouraged.

Servants, obey in all things *your* masters according to the flesh; not with eyeservice, as menpleasers; but in singleness of heart, fearing God.

(The Epistle of Paul the Apostle to the Colossians, iii 18–22)

Abolition of the family! Even the most radical flare up at this infamous proposal of the Communists.

On what foundation is the present family, the bourgeois family, based? On capital, on private gain. In its completely developed form this family exists only among the bourgeoisie. But this state of things finds its complement in the practical absence of the family among the proletarians, and in public prostitution.

(Marx and Engels, *The Manifesto of the Communist Party*)

The juxtaposition of the above two quotations is not done in order to make any political or religious point, but to illustrate, in a dramatic way, some of the widely differing assumptions and values which underlie people's thinking about the family. On the one hand, we have an ideal model of the family stressing stability and reciprocity. On the other hand, we have a picture of the family as part of a class-divided social structure, reflecting consequently, conflict and antagonism as much as love and obedience. On the one hand, we have the apostle announcing the ideal after which all should seek; on the other, the revolutionary seeking to 'demystify' the family, to dig beneath the idealistic words to reach the 'real' structure of human relationships.

Even if most people's views are less decisive than these two sharply-contrasting orientations, their ideas about the family are still closely linked to their ideas and the values they cleave to concerning the relationships of people within society. Thus, for example, central events in the life of the family – birth, marriage and death – are, for the most part still celebrated in church, even by people who never attend church at any other time in their lives. In 1962, out of every 1000 marriages, just over 700 were solemnized in a religious setting; similarly, there were 531 live-birth baptisms per 1000 in the Church of England (Church of England, 1965, pp. 54, 57). Geoffrey Gorer has shown, too, that for most people, these 'life-crises' and the hope of rejoining their loved ones in a future life, are central strands of popular religious thought (Gorer, 1955, pp. 242, 258). Politically, too, the churches still act as important pressure groups, more on matters related to the family, such as birth control, abortion and divorce, than on anything else.

The close relationship between the family and some deeply held and widely diffused values may be illustrated in a variety of ways. Thus because family relationships are so basic, familistic terms are often used in *non*-family circumstances to emphasize certain ideal types of relationships. Thus the term 'brother' is used in the context of the labour movement or in a religious context, since the use of this term stresses the values of equality and solidarity. Similarly, the use of the terms 'father', 'brother', 'sister' and 'mother' towards nuns, priests or monks, again emphasize certain ideals of fatherhood and motherhood. The virtues of the family and home life are, of course, emphasized over and over again in many other ways: in proverbial expressions and popular songs.

This close intermeshing of deeply held values and family life presents certain problems for the sociologist. In the first place, he is part of the society in which these values are stressed. Problems of objectivity, while always present, perhaps exist in a specially acute form in relation to the family. In the second place, research into the family is difficult because it touches upon an intimate and 'central' area of life. It is perhaps for this reason that we lack the richness of detail about family life in developed societies which anthropologists have presented for tribal societies. For more intimate or dramatic pictures of family life at close quarters we usually have to rely upon the creative artist rather than the sociologist, who has tended to paint a broader picture.

Biology and Culture

Two related arguments appear to lie beneath much of the debate about the family which we have already indicated. The first may be stated as the universalist versus the relativist argument, in short: 'Is the family a universal social institution or not?' The second argument is a slightly more sophisticated version of this question: 'Is the family a *dependent* or an *independent* variable?' On the one hand, the family is said to be a *dependent* variable if it can be shown that the family is caused by something *outside* the family, such as, for example, the cultural or economic framework of society. On the other hand, the family is seen as an *in*dependent variable if its form and presence cannot be attributed to something outside itself, and if the family is seen as the cause *of* other elements in society.

We have not yet, however, presented a definition of the family. For the present, let us simply assume that the area of discourse includes such matters as sex, marriage, parenthood and kinship, and that the subject is not exhausted by considering the small, relatively isolated monogamous family with which most readers will normally be most familiar.

The argument about the 'universality' of the family may be examined from three different points of view. In the first place, we can ask whether the family corresponds to some universally defined biological 'need' or 'drive'. In the second place, we can ask whether the family – or at least certain arrangements and practices associated with the concept of the family – are to be found in all existing (or once-existing) societies. Finally, we can ask whether the family fulfils some universally applicable *functions* in society. In practice, of course, the three questions are closely related. It is this first question – whether the family corresponds to some universally defined biological *need* – to which we will now turn.

One argument for the universality of the family often goes as follows. Sexual reproduction is essential for the maintenance of the human species. This automatically creates a triangular relationship between a male, a female and offspring. The family, therefore, is seen by some as a response to the need for the species to reproduce itself, together with individual *drives* for sexual intercourse. Put in these bald terms the argument may appear to be excessively crude although it is not too distant from the theories of Malinowski (1944, ch. 10). Malinowski is concerned with the scientific examination of 'culture' and sees the major cultural institutions as responses to the 'organic needs of Man'. In the present context, for example, kinship is seen as being the cultural response to the basic need for reproduction.

In all fairness, of course, a few other steps need to be added to this argument. Thus we have the first 'basic' need:

1. The need for reproduction. The individual expression of this is in the sexual drives.

To this we need to add the following proposition:

2. That there are basic needs for nutrition, and protection from natural and social dangers.

3. The human infant is not in a position to seek its own food or to protect itself, and needs others to do this on its behalf. Further, it remains in this state of dependence for a much longer period than other animals.

Such an approach, even with these additional clauses, is not so much wrong as unhelpful. It may be a 'scientific theory of *needs*', but it cannot be a 'scientific theory of *culture*'. It does not really answer any questions, but merely takes us to the base from which we may start asking important questions. We may ask, for example, if it is necessary for *all* persons to partake in the process of reproduction? The answer is 'obviously not', for at all periods of history groups of people have practised celibacy. Secondly, it may be asked whether it is necessary for the biological father to *remain* with the biological mother and their joint child? Again, the answer must be 'no'. Finally, we must ask whether it is necessary for the needs for reproduction, on the one hand, and the needs for care and protection on the other, to be carried out *by the same persons*?

In order to expand this point let us consider the relationship between sex differences and parenthood. To take the first point, sex differences, in the simplified Malinowskian approach we would see a direct relationship between the biological fact of sexual differences and cultural institutions, such as marriage. This may be represented diagrammatically:

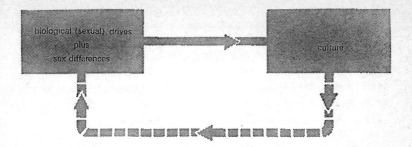

Malinowski recognizes that culture does exercise some 'feedback' influence on biological drives in that sex-drives may either be intensified (eroticism) or reduced (celibacy). (Hence the broken line in the diagram.) It is drawn as a broken line, however, because it is not the primary direction of the relationship, which is from the biological to the cultural.

An alternative approach may be presented in a slightly different form:

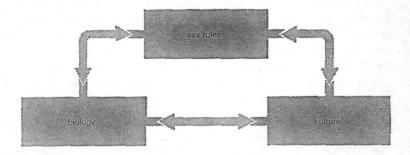

The alternative suggests a *three*-cornered relationship between sex differences, biology and culture, each one influencing the other. In more sociological language we need to distinguish between the biological and cultural dimensions of sex *roles*.

In the first place, it might be observed that even biologically speaking there is not always a clear-cut distinction between male and female, as the problem of defining the sex of certain athletes indicates. In the second place, it needs to be stressed that there are no fixed temperamental patterns associated with the fact of being male and female. References to days 'when men were men and women were women' are not so much inaccurate as meaningless. In a famous case study first published in 1935, Margaret Mead argued that the temperamental differences between the sexes differed radically in three different New Guinea societies (Mead, 1964). Mead's study has not been accepted in its entirety by all scholars, but even so, it may serve as a corrective against viewing the family, and sexual relationships in particular, solely from the viewpoint of one's own society.

Finally, it can be seen that differences in sex-roles may be accentuated or reduced according to culture and circumstance. In the early stages of the development of a kibbutz, for example, the differences between the sexes (in dress, for example) tended to be minimized, as intense romantic attachments were regarded as potentially disruptive in the early revolutionary stages of building a community. In our own society, it can be seen that while it might be desirable, perhaps even required, to stress sexual differences at a party or a dance, the same considerations might be frowned upon at a prayer meeting or a university seminar.

Similar considerations apply to parenthood. Anthropologists distinguish between the *genitor* (biological father) and the *pater* (social father). In our own society, the two roles tend to be played by the same person, although there are exceptions (e.g. adoption). In other societies, however, the distinction between the *pater* and the *genitor* is more highly elaborated and central as for example in the institution of *ghost marriage*. Gluckman describes the system of ghost marriage among the Zulu in these words:

There are two forms of this: (a) if a man was betrothed and died, his fiancée should marry one of his kinsmen and bear children for the dead man, as if she were a widow; and (b) a man may 'waken' a dead kinsman who was never betrothed by marrying a wife to his name and begetting children for him (Gluckman, 1950, pp. 183–4).

We have argued, then, that important distinctions need to be made between the biological facts of sex and parenthood, and the social *roles* attached to sex and parenthood. If anything, culture often accentuates the biological differences between the sexes. If we are to argue that the family is a universal institution, this argument is not universally supported by the 'facts of life'.

Sex, Love and Marriage

Marilyn Monroe was reported as having said 'Sex is part of Nature and I go along with Nature'. Rather differently, a popular song of the 1950s included the lines:

Love and marriage, love and marriage go together like a horse and carriage, . . .
You can't have one without the other.

But as a sex-phenomenon herself, Marilyn Monroe was very much the product of a particular culture, since the image of sex she embodied was a product of Hollywood as well as of her gene-structure. Moreover, she did not link sex up with marriage and the family at all. Sex was part of *Nature*, not yoked, 'like a horse and carriage', to *marriage*. Indeed *sex* is not even mentioned explicitly in the song. Love is. 'Love and marriage', in fact, is a more popular (and also more social) version of the universality of the family theme, based, not on biology, but on the idea of the universality of something called 'love', the ideal and 'normal' expression of which is through the institutions of marriage and the family.

Taking a cross-cultural point of view, it is *not* empirically the case that 'love and marriage go together like a horse and carriage'. There are four possible, and actually existing, combinations of 'love' and marriage which we outline below:

		Love	
		Present	*Absent*
Marriage	*Present*	1 (++)	2 (+−)
	Absent	3 (−+)	4 (−−)

In the present context, we are distinguishing 'love' from physical intercourse and are using the term to refer to an emotional feeling-state existing between an adult male and an adult female. We shall consider the four 'cases' in turn, ignoring, of course, the fourth 'cell' where both love and marriage are absent.

1. This may be said to respect the ideal as expressed in the song. It assumes a complete overlap between sex and marriage and an almost complete overlap between love and marriage. The popular sequence might be expressed as follows:

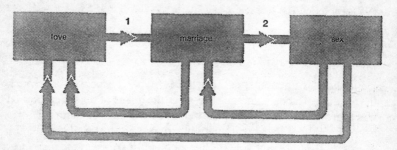

This ideal is emphasized by religion and teaching in schools, reinforced by much popular culture. A process of 'feedback' is assumed to take place, whereby the marriage reinforces the love, and satisfactory sexual intercourse reinforces both the marriage and the love. It can be said that, while the relationship between this ideal and actual practice remains a matter for investigation, practice does conform to the ideal in at least some instances in the Western Christian cultural environment and therefore represents one combination of the factors of love, marriage and sex.

2. This represents the case where one has marriage but not love. In our culture, this is often seen as being a tragic deviation from the Western Christian ideal. Elsewhere, however, it may be said to be the norm in a wide range of cultures and cultural situations, as in that institution so widespread throughout the world and throughout history: the 'arranged marriage'. In this case, while it need not be said that love is absent from such a relationship, it may be argued that if it is present at all, love is a consequence of marriage and not the reverse. This stress upon individual romantic attraction is also clearly inappropriate in societies where the husband–wife relationship has to compete in importance with relationships between the respective spouses and other kin. Gluckman remarks that:

... among the Bechuana it is ... [believed] ... that love potions may be used by the wife and her parents to gain her husband's full attentions, against the conventional requirements that a man should continue after marriage to spend his time with his kinsmen and his wealth in their support. If a man is too devoted to his wife, Barotse and Bembas say that she has bewitched him out of his senses ... (Gluckman, 1956, p. 60).

While these cases are not necessarily examples of marital situations where love is totally absent – for it does often exist – they do show that marriage is not necessarily a consequence of love, not is it the sole focus of loving relationships.

3. The situation where love is present but marriage is absent is not an unfamiliar one. On the basis of a detailed cross-cultural survey Murdock concludes:

Among those of our 250 societies for which information is available, 65 allow unmarried and unrelated persons complete freedom in sexual matters, and 20 others give qualified consent, while only 54 forbid or disapprove premarital liaisons between non-relatives, and many of these allow sex relations between specified relatives such as cross cousins. Where premarital license prevails, sex certainly cannot be alleged as the primary force driving people into matrimony (Murdock, 1949, pp. 5–6).

Even within the Western Christian tradition, for example, in the 'courtly love' of the Middle Ages, there has been a strong and institutionalized (often highly formalized and public, and at least informally and regularly recognized) pattern of love outside marriage. Indeed, to some at least, 'romantic love' is the antithesis of marriage rather than its natural setting. Thus the mistress has often played an important role in history and in literature.

Thus, taking a broad cross-cultural and historical perspective it can be seen that love and marriage are not bound together in some necessary relationship.* There are various combinations, all of them possible (although not all equally prevalent) and all of them, to some extent at least, institutionalized in certain ways. We have also noted that, even in societies where there is a clear, formal ideal that love and marriage should go together, there are usually deviations in practice.

* We have not considered the fourth possibility, namely where there is neither love nor marriage. Possible examples might be prostitution, routinized cohabitation, etc.

A survey of the sexual behaviour of teenagers in Great Britain found that 20 per cent of the boys interviewed and 12 per cent of the girls had experienced sexual intercourse. In many cases, this 'premarital intercourse' *was* 'premarital', however, in the strict sense, since most of those who fall into this category will go on to marry their sexual partners (Schofield, 1965, pp. 29–30, 163–4).

Just as it is difficult to trace the relationships between biological 'drives' and patterns of sexual and family practice, so, even if we accept that there is some universal thing called 'love', it is difficult to explain the variety of marital arrangements that exist. There is wide variation from society to society in the number of spouses a person may have; in the limits placed upon whom a person may marry; limits on the age of marriage, and so on. If love is the basis on which the family rests, it is a basis which supports a rambling edifice with many different rooms.

Furthermore, just as there are several meanings which may be assigned to the word 'marriage', so too there are many meanings which can be applied to the word 'love'. In the present culture, in relation to the sexes, the word love usually conveys the idea of an emotional attachment to another person, a relationship in which the person is valued for his or her own sake rather than being valued for some benefit outside the bounds of the particular relationship. Thus we may distinguish the 'love' relationship between a male and a female from the relationships, say, between a shopkeeper and a customer, or between a manager and a worker.

Expressed in these terms, as we have seen, the relationship between love and marriage is not all that obvious. There are cases where this kind of relationship is not a characteristic of the marriage tie and, more frequently, there are cases where this is not an *exclusive* characteristic of marriage. However, the concept of love, at least as popularly expressed, is a little more specific than this. Thus, while such intrinsic emotional attachments may be a general characteristic of a multiplicity of relationships, including the marriage relationship, the 'romantic love' concept is something which has been specifically applied to sexual love relationships and which appears to be characteristic of only a few cultures.

The romantic ideal of love entails a few features additional to our definition. It implies, for example, that love is *prior* to the formation of a sexual or marital relationship, and not the *consequence* of that relationship. In the extreme statement of this ideal, love would apparently exist even before verbal interaction; 'star-crossed lovers' are 'destined' for each other – and no one else. Secondly, the concept implies that such relationships transcend any other considerations. Such romantic love is so intensely focussed on the individual, so total in its commitment that its authenticity is often measured by the extent to which it cuts across, flouts or defies other, social, considerations, such as barriers of class, nation or race. Since the romantic love concept implies this singleness of devotion on both sides, monogamy is usually seen as the institutional expression of the romantic love ideal (although this may not perhaps be entirely the case: courtly love was essentially extra-marital).

Here, we are not concerned with this view as an *ethic*. But we must observe that it is not even the case in our society, where there is an ideal of romantic love, that one's choice of mate is simply dependent on romantic attraction. In the first place, there are legal limits on whom one is able to marry; notably the rules of incest and laws defining the age of majority, enforcing monogamy, controlling divorce and remarriage, etc. But even outside these formal limits, there are powerful informal rules delimiting, for example, the social area within which one may marry. Ethnicity has been one of the most powerful considerations here: informal disapproval of Negro–White intercourse or marriage, for example, has even been supported in some parts of the world by legal penalties. Religion, too, is a factor likely to limit the choice of mate. In the United States this is a very strong consideration among Jews, less strong among Catholics, and much less strong among Protestants (with the exception of some Protestant sects (Lenski, 1961, pp. 35–9). Finally, the factor of social class also acts as an informal barrier to intermarriage as do certain physical characteristics such as age or height.

The formal rules restricting random mating are what anthropologists describe as rules of exogamy and endogamy: rules delineating those whom one should or should not marry. Many societies go beyond such broad injunctions, and go on to specify categories of 'preferred' partners who are the appropriate people to marry. With many religious denominations also, both the negative and positive rules go hand-in-hand. Thus the negative restriction that a Jew should not marry a Gentile goes hand-in-hand with the positive prescription that a Jew should marry a Jew. In general, it might be said that in Britain norms relating to whom one must or ought to marry are less clearly stated than norms about whom one ought *not* to marry. This contrasts with the situation in other societies where preferred mates are very clearly stated, as in the case of 'cross-cousin' marriage, where it is preferred that marriage should take place with the daughter of a mother's brother or a father's sister. To the extent, therefore, that our society lays greater stress on negative rather than positive roles, and to the extent that these prescriptions are informal rather than formal, it may be said that marriage is *achieved* (that is, the consequence of an individual's decision) rather than *ascribed*. To this extent, also, the romantic ideal in our own society has some basis in fact, even if there is still a gap between ideal and practice.

Finally, although we have spoken as if the 'romantic love' ideal is something which is widely held and believed among those in the Western Christian tradition, there is much evidence that people commonly take a more matter-of-fact approach than is suggested here (e.g. Gorer, 1955, pp. 83–161). If this is the case, then the relationship between ideal and practice is a little more problematic than we have suggested. Obviously whatever their views on love, most people look for a partner who will provide them with economic, social and personal security.

We have considered the relations between love, marriage, sex and the family. It has been suggested that the institutions of marriage and the family cannot be adequately explained either on the basis of certain basic drives, or on the basis of some universal state of feeling called 'love'. We must look beyond these considerations for an explanation of the institution of the family.

Is the Family a Universal Institution?

Empirical evidence for the universality of the family must be sought. As we have seen, an attempt has been made at a broad cross-cultural examination to see if there is, in fact, any empirical evidence of the existence of the family as a universal institution at all. Having conducted an analysis of 250 societies, Murdock concluded that it could be argued that the *nuclear* family was universal. Such cross-cultural studies, however, have been subjected to a good deal of criticism and they must be treated with a certain degree of caution.

Murdock defines the family as:

... a social group characterized by common residence, economic co-operation, and reproduction. It includes adults of both sexes, at least two of whom maintain a socially approved sexual relationship, and one or more children, own or adopted, of the sexually co-habiting adults (Murdock, 1949, p. 1).

Within this broad definition, Murdock defines the 'nuclear family' as:

... a married man and woman with their offspring, although in individual cases one or more additional persons may reside with them (p. 1).

On the basis of his investigations, he considers the nuclear family to be a 'universal human social grouping'. In thus separating out the *nuclear* family (in contra-distinction to his more general definition of the family) Murdock makes no allowance for the fact of polygamy. In fact, he sees the nuclear family as a basic unit from which other types of family (polygamous and extended) are compounded. To some extent, this qualification weakens Murdock's main contention, as it begs the question as to whether a nuclear family within the context of a polygamous or extended family is the same thing as a nuclear family which, as it were, 'stands alone'.

Exceptions to Murdock's main contention about the universality of the nuclear family seem to be very few. The Nayar case has been much debated in the literature (Mencher, 1965; Gough, 1960) and attention has also been directed to the West Indian family as another possible exception (Greenfield, 1961, pp. 312–22). The case of 'Tally's Corner' – examined in some detail towards the end of this chapter – provides a modern urban example. There have also been some deliberately established communities which attempted to abolish, or to weaken the effect of, the nuclear family. The Israeli kibbutz has often been cited in this connexion (Spiro, 1960; Talmon, 1965) and mention may also be made of the 'utopian' communities deliberately established in America in the nineteenth century (see, e.g. Nordhoff, 1961).

Certainly, however, no society practising complete promiscuity has lasted long. In all societies, some principle exists whereby the legitimacy of offspring (that is the person's social identity) is established, and in nearly all societies there is something which might be defined as 'the nuclear family'. But such generality is obtained at the expense of meaning. What is of interest to the sociologist is not so much the fact that some basic form of relationship can be found to exist, but rather the richness of variety of contexts in which it exists and the various functions which it performs.

The Varying Context of the Family

It is this crucial question of the variety of family situations which we must now take up. Let us begin with the fact of common residence, which most people would consider to be a basic characteristic of the family.

Normally, the nuclear family is *included* within residential boundaries, although the residential boundaries may also contain persons other than the spouses and their children. Sometimes the nuclear family sharing a common residence, will be 'incomplete' as when the father (whether *pater* or *genitor*) lives apart from the mother(s) and children. This is the situation encountered among the Nayar and which is also found (in a variety of forms) in the West Indies, or, as we shall see later, among poor Negroes in Washington, D.C. Where the nuclear family is 'incomplete' in this sense it is often 'completed' by a succession of fathers and by the addition of other kin such as the mother's own mother.

The complete nuclear family may share its residence with other, non-related persons: with slaves, with the 'stranger within the gates' of the Old Testament; lodgers may be treated as 'one of the family' and the central position of servants in the organization of the household is well known to readers of P. G. Wodehouse.

The concept of 'common residence', however, is not so self-evident as it might seem. In most western societies, it conjures up a picture of discrete domestic units, each occupying a clearly-demarcated piece of territory. But how do we define the large farm, which also houses the labourers and their families? What is common residence among the Bedouin: the tent or the camp? (Peters, 1965). The answer to the question 'Where do you live?' in our society will probably be almost as precise as a map reference, pointing to a clearly-bounded unit, but in other societies, the answer may be much less clearly-defined.

But the nuclear family, within a common residence, is not only extended by the addition of non-related members such as lodgers or servants. Much more frequently, it is extended by the addition of other related members, in one or more of the following ways:

A. *Horizontally*

1. Where a system of *polygamy* exists, the residential unit may include the children of all the spouses. There are two possibilities here: the *polygynous* family, where one man has two or more wives, and the much less-frequent *polyandrous* family, where one woman has two or more husbands.

2. Where brothers or sisters and *their* families share common residence, perhaps under a common head of the household.

B. *Vertically*

This is the situation of the *extended* family, where members of different generations share a common residence. Nuclear families are thus linked vertically, as where grandparents or grandchildren share a common residence with the nuclear family. The situation under A.2, therefore, is often an extension of the nuclear family in both a horizontal and a vertical direction.

We have, then, a variety of ways in which different persons, related or unrelated, share a common residence. These can be summarized in the form of a diagram (see page 130).

But common residence does not exhaust what is usually meant by the family, for there are ties of kinship (that is relationships through birth) and affinity (relationships through marriage) which extend outside any residential unit. There are potentially a very large number of ties which can be reckoned in these ways: in practice, however, there are limits to the number of ties which are effective in actual existing relationships.

Effective ties may be considered under two headings, indicating various degrees of remoteness. Close to the individual, although not sharing the same residence, there are those with whom he has what might be called '*interactional ties*'. These are related persons with whom a person has exchange-relationships of various kinds and

1. common residence equals nuclear family

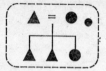

2. common residence does not include complete nuclear family

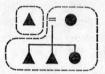

3. common residence includes non-related members

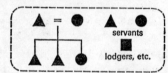

4. horizontal extension
(i) through spouses

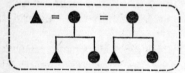

(ii) through siblings

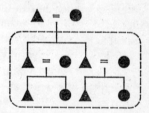

5. vertical extension

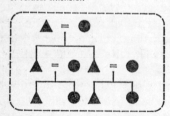

▲ male

● female

= marriage

- - - - - residential boundary

Figure 5 Diagrammatic representation of varieties of common residence

varying degrees of intensity. These may be as minimal as the exchange of greetings in the street, or as important as the regular exchange of goods and services. In working-class districts, for example, it is common for a working mother to leave her child in the care of her own mother, although they may not share the same residence.

Beyond the set of 'interactional' ties, we have the set of recognized ties. 'Recognized' ties exist on the frontier of an individual's set of kinship ties; they exist, and are recognized to exist, but are rarely activated. While exchanges may take place within the set of recognized ties as well as among the interactional ties, these will tend to be much more fleeting, less readily-established and perhaps characterized by a greater degree of formality. Beyond these are all the more remote ties which exist, but which are not, except in extraordinary circumstances, recognized as such. Recognized ties, in our society, may be indicated by the exchange of Christmas cards or mutual attendance at family ceremonies such as funerals and weddings.

There will therefore be considerable variation in the number and character of the kinship ties which exist outside the domestic residential unit. Thus although kinship ties are based on descent, and this is not a matter of individual choice, we do have a choice as to whether we make our kinship relations into relationships involving contact. For example, we may count as our 'uncles', 'aunts', even 'brothers' and 'sisters', people whom we seldom or never see.

Whether or not we activate these kinship ties depends on locality (we may not live near our close kin), on social and geographical mobility (they may have 'risen above' us in the social scale and regard us as 'poor relations' whom they do not wish to know), and on personal likes and dislikes (we may simply find them unpleasant people).

In our society terms like 'uncle', 'aunt', 'grandparent' and 'cousin' do not usually specify whether such a relationship is on the mother's side or the father's side. In many of societies studied by anthropologists, however, such distinctions are of key importance. Descent may be reckoned through males (patrilineal descent) or through females (matrilineal descent), though different combinations of these two modes of descent are used for different purposes. Such distinctions are of importance in economic terms, in political terms and in religious terms, since they determine the particular way in which these kinds of rights and duties together with the social identity provided by the family name are handed on from one generation to another.

When a marriage takes place, the couple live with or near a particular relative, or form a new, separate residence. The various possibilities are listed below:

Virilocal – live at place of husband's people.

Uxorilocal – live at place of wife's people.

Neolocal – set up new residence.

In many cases, although not all, the principles on which a person adopts one or other of these possibilities will be related to the characteristic modes of reckoning descent. These ties, based on locality or on descent, are usually backed by powerful formal or informal sanctions.

In our society, kinship ties involve no such clear-cut principles according to which a person must operate. The individual has more latitude as to whether he makes anything of the relationship or not. This is not, however, to say that he is completely free. The ideal is neolocality, and there is a stress on bilateral descent, but there are considerable variations on these themes, and individuals may choose not to conform to these ideals without fear of serious sanction.

Thus we commonly find that in families which are very large there is close contact with even the most distant kin. Other families are limited to the members of the domestic unit and perhaps only a few close kin outside that unit.

Kinship ties are not the only important ties which the nuclear family has and, indeed, in our society such ties are often much less important than other kinds of relationship which a family's members have with 'outsiders'. Elizabeth Bott has attempted to demonstrate how the 'networks' of family members shape their relationships with one another (Bott, 1957). A 'network' is simply a tracing out of the pattern of an individual's contacts with other persons, and those patterns may be classified as being of different types; thus the network of an individual who sees people who also see each other may be called 'close-knit' in that there are many links (a contact between persons counting as a 'link') between the members of the networks. Such networks, Bott argues, are associated with a sharp and rigid division of labour within the family – for example, a clear separation between the kinds of things that men do in the household and the kinds of things women do; the paradigm of such a situation is, of course, the 'traditional' working-class community in which everyone knows everyone else, sees them often, and has close friendship ties with many of them, and in which the men generally reject any concern with domestic matters. This sort of situation is different from that in which few of the people whom an individual knows have any knowledge of, or relationship with, each other: where there is this situation we may speak of a 'loose-knit' network. Here one finds, Bott argues, a much less rigid separation of the spouses' roles in the household, and much more co-operation between sexes in domestic affairs. The external relation of the conjugal partners – including kinship relations, but also, and often more importantly in our society, friendship, work and other social relations, etc., may therefore be said to exercise an important influence on the internal organization of their domestic life, and should be borne in mind whenever we consider the place of the family in society.

We have looked at the family unit so far as though it did not change over time. But it must be stressed that the family, in all its variety, is a dynamic entity. It constantly changes, in part because the members pass through the life-cycle, in part because it is in a society which changes. Children grow up and leave home, and are now only rarely seen. Others on the fringe of the 'recognized ties' may move closer and enter into the interactional set. The family, like any other social entity, is a process, then, not a thing. Different persons will come to occupy the same role (the role of youngest son, for example): or the same person will take on different roles (as when he takes on the role of husband and the role of father while still retaining the role of son). We see here the difference between change as it affects the *family*: a structure of relationships and roles, the individual occupants of which are constantly changing: and changes as it affects the *individual*, moving through a series of changes in his life-cycle, each stage to some degree recognized by a 'rite of transition', such as christenings, weddings, funerals. Since we normally think of the family as a stable unit, clearly segregated from other such units by the four walls of the home, it is important to stress that it undergoes constant changes in its size, structure and activities as each of its members moves through his personal life-cycle. We must bear this dynamic picture in mind when we come to consider the functions of the family.

The Functions of the Family

Before looking at the empirical evidence concerning the functions of the family, we must look fairly carefully at the conception of 'function', since it is a concept widely used in sociology, but one also surrounded by fierce controversies. In general, it might be said that the 'functionalist' approach arose partly as a reaction against a crude kind of evolutionism which sought to 'explain' the presence of social institutions in terms of their origin in some more 'primitive' form. Functionalism was, at one level, simply an injunction to look at society *as a* system, so that particular customs, beliefs and practices could be understood by looking at them within the context of the society in which they were found, not by looking at their origins, since to do the latter was to ask a quite different question: one of *genesis* rather than function. As we shall have cause to be critical of some of the functionalist formulations in the course of this chapter it is important at the outset to note the important advance that these theorists made in our understanding of human society.

Of the many definitions of 'function' and of 'functionalism', Radcliffe-Brown's has been one of the most influential:

The *function* of any recurrent activity ... is the part it plays in the social life as a whole and therefore the contribution it makes to the maintenance of the structural continuity (Radcliffe-Brown, 1952, p. 180).

The concept of function is thus intimately bound up with the concept of social structure, that is the patterned, non-haphazard ordering of social relationships. The relationship between mother and child is, for example, an element in social structure. To use the language developed in another chapter, social structure is the organized pattern of *roles* within society.* The function of a recurrent (as opposed to the purely idiosyncratic or ephemeral) activity is in terms of its contribution to the maintenence of this structure. The logical flaw in this argument is the assumption that any activity necessarily helps *maintain* society; love for her son may cause a mother to help her son evade the draft, or to quarrel with her neighbours.

Radcliffe-Brown's conception is based on an analogy between the biological organism (e.g., the human body) and the social 'organism'.

*See Chapter 5, pp. 211–19.

Yet though we can see the heart's role in supplying the body with blood, and can think of the transport system similarly, we cannot envisage the heart going on strike, competing with other systems for scarce resources, or as being part of several systems at once. Yet conflict, competition and contradictions are, to varying degrees, built into the social system. Thus what may be seen as being functional for one part of the social system may be less functional for other parts or for that system as a whole. Nepotism, for example, may be functional for the extended family but less functional for the economy.

This problem is partly recognized by Merton in his re-definition of function (1957). He defines functions as: '. . . those observed consequences which make for the adaptation or adjustment of a given system' (p. 51).

In addition Merton presents the concept of *dysfunction:* '. . . those observed consequences which lessen the adaptation or adjustment of the system' (p. 51).

Merton, moreover, stresses that it is important to specify the system for which a given activity is functional or dysfunctional. What may be functional for one system may be dysfunctional for another, and any item of behaviour is part, not only of a single over-all 'system', but of various levels and ranges of patterned relationships wider than the nation-state, tribe or other political unit commonly regarded as 'the society'. Moreover, to say that a given item has *effects* on other social activities, or is *related* to other phenomena, is true enough. But the extent to which they are related, and the intensity or direction of the relationship, may vary considerably, and are matters for empirical investigations. Moreover, to show that two things are *interrelated*, does not help us to tease out whether x *causes* y, or otherwise.

In spite of these criticisms it must be stressed that it is valuable – indeed essential – both theoretically and practically to consider the interrelationships between the parts and the whole of a society even if we do not necessarily view that society as an harmonious or unified whole.

A second virtue of functionalism is that it often enables us to look beneath the surface of social life, to probe beneath official explanations and popular beliefs. The functional approach often helps to free us from certain preconceived notions and encourages us to examine society afresh. Thus Merton introduced the distinction between *manifest* and *latent* functions (Merton, 1957, p. 51). Manifest functions are those which are intended and recognized by the participants in the situation, while latent functions are those which are neither intended nor recognized. Thus, while the manifest functions of a student rag week might be to raise money for charity, the latent functions might be rather different from this; perhaps the function of getting to know and understand each other better through the fun and the collective breaking of social conventions. The major rituals of family life – baptisms, weddings and funerals – can only be fully understood at both of these two levels.

Armed with these concepts and theoretical insights, let us return to the family. What, now, *are* the 'functions of the family'? Murdock argues that these are of four different kinds – the sexual, the economic, the reproductive and the educational – which are central to life, culture and society (1949, p. 3).

It can be seen at once that these functions are not exclusive to the family. We have already seen that sexual functions, even reproduction, take place outside the family. Similarly, economic and educational functions may be carried out in all sorts of institutions outside or beyond the family.

Furthermore, it is evident from observations in many societies, including our own, that the family need not perform all of these functions together, nor need any other single social institution or unit. Nor is it clear in Murdock's formulation for whom or what the family is functional. Of course, strictly speaking, it is individuals who have sexual intercourse; 'society' does not. But there *are* also various kinds of social control over individual sexual activity, from chastity belts to internalized self control. 'Society' does not reproduce itself at all: its organization *controls* and regulates sexuality and that may be said to have functional consequences for society. Thus it might be argued that apart from simply regulating the survival of its numbers, society tends to be organized in such a way as to restrict sexuality in that sexual ties do not come between the individual and his obligations to other individuals and groups: society might be hopelessly divided if sexual relationships and their attendant jealousies and antagonisms were allowed to develop in *any* relationship. For example, doctors are required to maintain complete detachment from the sexual attractions of their patients; if they did not, they might often find their capacity to make medical decisions affected by personal considerations.

This leads us back to the crucial problem: 'functional for whom?' which we raised when discussing functionalism at a more general level. Murdock, as we have seen, is mainly concerned about the functions for society as a whole. But we must also see these functions as applying to the spouses, the children and others. What is functional for the spouses might not be functional for society. Furthermore, the different sections of society – political, economic, religious, etc. – may have opposed interests in the family. Finally our stress upon the family as a dynamic entity, constantly changing in its internal structure as well as being affected by the changes in the wider society will be recalled. It is important to remember that the family, whilst attempting to consider its functions, is continually subject to this process of change.

The Functions of the Family in Industrial Society

We are now in a position to examine the ways in which, and the extent to which, the family has been affected by the associated processes of urbanization and industrialization. Here we examine briefly two widely-held beliefs:

1. That in modern industrialized and urbanized society the family has been 'stripped of its functions'.
2. That the relatively isolated nuclear family is the characteristic unit of industrial society.

For the most part the information presented here will relate to the United States and Great Britain.

In examining the first theme, we will not confine the term 'family' to the nuclear family, and we will take as our point of reference the four functions already mentioned by Murdock, namely, the sexual function, the reproductive function, the economic function, and the socialization function.

The sexual function

As witnesses here we may call the reports in the United States of

Kinsey and his colleagues who showed the importance, and apparently the increasing importance, of sex before and outside marriage (Geddes, 1954, p. 52). We may also call Michael Schofield, whose evidence concerning the sexual behaviour of teenagers was mentioned earlier in this chapter.

If we accept these reports as providing valid evidence that the sexual function is probably less confined to the family than it was in the recent past, to what do we attribute these changes? Explanations in terms of technical innovations in contraception are far too narrow. They do not tell us anything about the values which lie behind the increasing use of 'the pill' or the dissemination of birth-control information. Further, it is not necessarily the case that contraceptives are always used in pre-marital intercourse; a high proportion of sexually experienced teenagers seem prepared to 'take risks' in this respect (Schofield, 1965, p. 107). At the other end of the scale, explanations in terms of the growth of something called 'the permissive society' are much too broad. The sociologist would insist that ideas about 'permissiveness' do not exist in a vacuum but that they are in some way related to the structure of society and to changes within the society wherein these ideas are framed.

Another explanation points to the joint processes of urbanization and industrialization, which weaken the control of the family and the control of the community. Large areas of sexual behaviour are not subject to formal legal sanctions but rather depend upon informal sanctions ranging from gossip to locking up one's daughter. The effectiveness of many of these informal sanctions depends upon agreed meanings and evaluations arising out of a stable community, where work, family and residence to a large extent, overlap. The effectiveness of such sanctions is weakened to the extent that this particular nexus is broken. Religion, also, can no longer be relied upon as a powerful informal force as its relationship to the community becomes more indirect and remote.

However, a few qualifications to the basic premise must be made. We must ask, firstly, to what extent and in what ways is sex outside the family an increasing phenomenon? Kinsey notes that, while there has been an increase in pre-marital and extra-marital sex, the use of the services of prostitutes has declined (Geddes, 1954, p. 161). Furthermore, assessments of an increase or a decline in such a sensitive matter as sexual behaviour must always be subject to a considerable amount of error, that error being the greater the further one goes back in time. Was life in Victorian England necessarily all that chaste? The evidence of social historians and contemporary documents show that it was anything but, certainly for the lowest social classes in slum areas, where family bonds were very weak, and for the younger middle and upper class males who were saving up for a 'good' marriage but who were denied sexual access to their intended spouse, and who provided prostitutes with a large clientele (some of the evidence is summarized in Fletcher, 1962, ch. 3).

Secondly, while it may be possible to see an increase in sex outside the family, it would be wrong to regard sex and marriage as alternatives between which people have to choose. As we have seen, much of the pre-marital intercourse takes place between partners who intend to get married in any case (Schofield, 1965, pp. 163-4). Similarly, of those couples who get divorced, the overwhelming majority re-marry (Fletcher, 1962, p. 143; Nimkoff, 1965, p. 339).

The reproductive function

In considering the reproductive function we are not so much concerned with biological reproduction as with social reproduction, that is, with the way social descent is legitimized. Let us first consider the extent to which this function is fulfilled outside the family-system. At present, one child in every fourteen in this country is illegitimate. In a minority of cases, the mother will keep the child in spite of the great personal hardship. This may be regarded as the establishment of an incomplete nuclear family. In the majority of cases, the child will be adopted, that is brought up in the context of a nuclear family which is different from its procreative 'family' (see, e.g. Wimperis, 1960, p. 243). Inasmuch as institutionalized care is not seen as a major solution to the problem of illegitimacy, these facts cannot necessarily be taken to indicate a decline in the significance of the family as an agency of reproduction.

Furthermore, it is not clear to what extent illegitimacy can be seen as a product of an urban or an industrial society. For example, the illegitimacy rates in Merionethshire have been persistently higher than the British national average, although the two rates have been coming closer together since the Second World War. In one rural parish within Merionethshire, the rates were yet higher (Emmett, 1964, p. 109) and rural illegitimacy is not necessarily a recent development.

While it is difficult, without further evidence, to base an argument on the decline of the reproductive function of the family on illegitimacy rates, there are further pieces of evidence which indicate that this function may have declined in importance. The size of the family has declined from Victorian times, from between five and seven children to just over two children (Fletcher, 1962, pp. 112–15). The factors behind this demographic change are many and complex, but at the very least they can be seen as evidence of a desire on the part of the spouses to limit the family's reproductive function. But this personal decision is itself taken in the light of social conditions affecting the family. Mention need only be made of maternity benefits, child allowances, maternity hospitals and wards in hospitals, and family planning clinics. And, of course, on a global scale, the reproductive function of the family is one that is being increasingly and urgently subjected to close and apprehensive scrutiny.

The economic function

In most, if not in all societies, there has been some division of labour between the sexes within the context of the domestic unit. There is a difference, however, between a situation where husband and wife perform different but complementary tasks within the context of a complete unit, such as a farm, and the situation which obtains in modern industrial society. In this connexion, Viola Klein argues that the process of industrialization has affected the family in three ways (Klein, 1965, p. 2). In the first place, the centre of production is moved from the home to the factory. The family becomes an 'income-unit'. In the second place, the unit of production (i.e. the factory) employs the individual worker rather than the whole family. And finally, the process of industrialization ensures a supply of goods and services produced outside the home but consumed within it. The family is still an 'economic unit' but its economic activities have greatly changed. Now, it is the basic unit of consumption, but not of production or distribution.

As we shall see in Chapter 4 the family is not such a central agency of socialization in our society as it has been at other times and in other societies. Most importantly, specialized *educational* institutions have arisen outside the context of the domestic unit and these institutions are not, and never have been, solely concerned with providing the technical skills necessary for making a living or fulfilling various economic roles in society. Even in the pre-school years, the family has been affected by factors outside itself. Leaving aside the development of pre-school nurseries and play groups, we have the growth of what amounts to an industry in parental guidance and advice, including mothers' and women's magazines, extra-mural classes and Dr Spock's best-selling *Baby and Child Care*. Further, we should not forget the effects of television which may provide models of life and society at variance with those presented in the immediate family.

While the socialization functions of the family have, in many cases, been replaced by other more formal institutions, it would be wrong to suggest that the family and education exist as independent institutions in our society. On the contrary, much of the research into educational sociology has demonstrated the complex inter-relationships between the two: as when, to take two examples, education may serve to segregate the working-class boy from his family (Hoggart, 1958, pp. 241–52; Jackson and Marsden, 1962), or when the domestic environment and parental attitudes influence educational achievement at school (Douglas, 1966). Both the family and the school exist in the context of a stratified society (see Chapter 7).

This leads us to one final point under this heading. If we are to talk about the socialization functions of the family we must ask, 'socialization into what?' This question is dealt with in more detail in the next chapter. We exist neither in a completely unified, coherent society in which there is one model equally available to all members, nor do we live in a society (such as a caste or feudal society) where there are distinct and discrete social groups into which one is born and in which one remains for the rest of one's life. In a mobile, pluralistic society such as ours, alternative models to those one was brought up with do exist, but we do not all have an equal chance of achieving these alternatives.

It is difficult, then, to provide an unequivocal answer to the question whether the modern family has been 'stripped of its functions'. In the case of the sexual function, we see that this is not the exclusive preserve of the family, although the two are certainly usually closely connected. Furthermore, it is by no means clear to what extent there has been a decline here. In the case of the reproductive function, it is possible to see, in British society at least, some decline in the extent to which the family fulfils this particular function. This apparently straightforward statement is full of difficulties which reflect the problems of the functional approach. If by 'reproduction' we mean *biological* reproduction this implies that there is some clear-cut functional relationship between the needs of a society and the numbers of individuals that society possesses. If we mean *social* reproduction (the passing down of a name, various rights and duties, etc., from generation to generation) it is difficult to see a decline here except in so far as industrial societies stress achieved, as opposed to ascribed, statuses. In the case of the educational/socialization function, we see an increase of alternative agencies, and a variety of patterns of conflict and accommodation between the family and these other forces. If the emphasis is to be laid upon any one set of changes, it is on the economic function, as this has entailed a shift from the family as a unit of production and consumption to its becoming a unit of consumption only. This change, however, has taken place over a longer period of time than the others we have mentioned, and it is not clear whether this is a *necessary* consequence of industrialization and urbanization.

It can be argued, however, that this discussion about the family being stripped of its functions is too negative. Thus Parsons argues, for example, that it is not so much that the family has lost functions as that it has taken on new and more specialized ones (Parsons and Bales, 1956, pp. 3–34). Just as society as a whole has become more complex, and its institutions more specialized, so too have the functions of the family. The stress within the family is now upon the socialization of the child and the provision of emotional support and stability for the adult members. The family in modern society forms a sub-system linked to the wider social system through the occupational role of the father. Through this sub-system the children are socialized into taking on the roles of adult members of society and the parents are able to manage the tensions that arise elsewhere especially, for the male, in the occupational sphere. (The popular stereotype of the husband who comes home to a meal on the table and a fire in the hearth fits this model exactly.) It is important, in this connexion, that the choice of marriage partners is ideally made on the basis of mutual attractiveness with the stress on 'compatibility'. Thus there is a functional link between the notion of romantic love which we have discussed earlier and the nature of the family in modern society.

It will be clear that this model of the modern family is 'ideal' in at least two senses. In the first place it must be stressed that it is rare to get the closeness of fit between the family, the individual and the society which is implied in this account. The family, while it may be an area for emotional release may also be the source of further tensions which may not be readily handled elsewhere in society. Moreover, this close solidarity, and the role of the family as a source of emotional support for its members, may conflict with the requirements of other social roles, such as that of 'citizen'. The family may encourage 'privatization' or even 'anti-social' attitudes. In short, there may also be dysfunctions of the family as well as functions. The model is also ideal in a second sense in that it tends to smooth over the varieties of forms and structures of family which exist even within modern industrial society. In the case which follows, for example, we see the possibility of a conflict between the ideal model of family life in modern society (corresponding roughly to Parsons and Bales' model) and the actual, everyday experiences of some members of that society.

An Example: Tally's Corner

Some of the preceding points may be illustrated by a case study (Liebow, 1967). The material is taken from a study of a group of Negroes who hung around a street corner in Washington, D.C. Much of the interaction takes place with Tally's Carry-Out store as a focal point. The men in the study are often unemployed, or intermittently employed in jobs of low pay and skill.

The author, Elliot Liebow, makes the following points about the family life of these men:

1. The father–child bond is often weak or even non-existent. While there are a variety of arrangements, ranging from the situation where

the father denies the paternity of his child to that where mother, father and children live together under one roof, most situations are characterized by this particular weak bond. Liebow shows that the more physically remote the father (in the sense that he does not live with the mother and child), the stronger appear to be the emotional ties between father and child.

2. While a distinction is made between marriage and 'shacking up', the boundaries between the two situations are often fluid and indistinct. Many of the formal marriages end in divorce or separation.

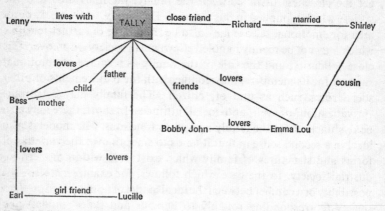

Figure 6 Tally's personal network

3. For the men, considerable importance is given to ties of friendship underlined by the fact that friends are often spoken of in kinship terms. Two men are spoken of as 'going for brothers' although they are not physically related. A man and a woman may call each other 'cousin' although, again, they may not be related; furthermore, this serves to emphasize that theirs is a relationship of friendship and not a sexual relationship. These friendship ties are very much of the present, for little is known of a friend's past or his future. So much weight is put upon friendship relations that they are often not strong enough to survive the strains engendered.

Some of the points are emphasized in Figure 6 which presents Tally's personal network. In presenting this in a diagrammatic form (this is not done in the original work), we have inevitably simplified the material. One point that needs stressing is that this is not

Tally's network at one point of time, but rather his network over the author's period of fieldwork. Relations are established and broken. Some members of Tally's network, such as Emma Lou, depart altogether.

Liebow argues that Tally's corner does not represent a 'subculture' in the sense of a social area encapsulated and demarcated off from the 'wider society'. Rather, the wider society impinges upon the street corner in many ways, through the police, through the social workers, through anthropologists, but most of all through work or the absence of work. The author sees the members of the street corner and their system of marriage and family life as 'the cultural model of the larger society as seen through the prism of repeated failure' (op. cit., p. 221). The men want to get married, for to get married and to be head of a household is part of what it means to be a 'man' in American society. But the head of a household is at the intersection of two social areas: the world of the family, and the world of work; and it is in this latter area that the man, a Negro with few skills or opportunities in the labour market, falls down. He is unable to fulfil the high expectations he has of his position in the family and those that his wife has of him. Failure leads him to the street corner, where he is able to establish some kind of identity. There, his 'failure' in his marriage is rationalized; it is attributed to 'manly flaws', to the fact that he 'has too much dog in him'. Such values, and the ties established therewith supplement and perhaps replace domestic ties and values and so the family is weakened yet further.

Two points emerge clearly from this brief account of a family situation in contemporary society. Firstly, it illustrates the distinction and the overlaps between biological and social ties. In some cases, a man may deny the paternity of his child; in others, he may become 'as a father' to children who are not, biologically, his. People may talk of each other as 'brothers' or 'cousins' – and the relationships will conform to what is ideally expected of these blood ties, though they are in fact unrelated. Secondly, we see that many of the 'functions of the family' are separated from it here and shared with other social agencies. Nor is its membership always complete; male heads are often absent, and the economic function is supplemented or replaced by patterns of exchange among 'brothers' on the street corner. Yet, at the same time, the family still appears as an ideal.

The 'Decline' of the Nuclear Family

In conclusion we shall consider the extent to which the relatively isolated nuclear family has become the typical domestic unit of industrial society. Several lines of argument seem to be implied here:

1. The domestic unit comes to be equivalent to the nuclear family.

2. This nuclear family is relatively isolated from other kin, in both vertical and horizontal directions. There is also a decline in the strength of interactional ties.

3. There is a decline in the proportion of *interactional* ties to *recognized* ties. The number of recognized ties may decline as well. Clearly, this argument is linked with our previous discussion of the changing functions of the family, especially the change in the economic function. The family as a unit of production *and* consumption is likely to be a larger unit (that is, is likely to involve more than just the nuclear family-members) than a family which is just a unit of consumption.

One preliminary question concerns the *direction* of the relationship between industrialization and the changes in the family system. That is to say, was the isolation of the nuclear family a necessary *precondition* for industrialization or was it a *consequence* of industrialization? The first line of argument suggests that changes in family structure were a necessary but not a sufficient condition for the development of an industrial society.

Briefly, the argument is that an industrial society is based upon criteria of profit and efficiency; in Max Weber's sense of the word, it requires 'rationality'. One of the components of this rationality was that personnel be recruited on the basis of their skills, aptitudes and objective achievements rather than on the basis of kinship. Furthermore, such persons are expected to be mobile, and hence to loosen themselves from familistic ties in the process. The rational economy requires that workers should be devoted in a single-minded fashion to their task; their energies and time should not be dissipated in leaving work to look after kin, to plough a relative's field, or to support a family business. From the point of view of the enterprise, there is a need to accumulate wealth, to plough back profits rather than to support a multiplicity of relatives. A strict separation is to be made between the domestic accounts and the accounts of the firm. Weber saw as being a key factor in this process what he called 'the Protestant Ethic'. He saw Protestantism as appealing to a universalistic concept of brotherhood rather than to the narrow ties of blood, as seeking to minimize the special emotional ties of kin and even of the world in general in the greater cause of devotion to Christ (Weber, 1952). One of the *unintended* consequences of this, and other aspects of the Protestant Ethic, was to pave the way for a rational capitalistic society.

The alternative approach sees the changes in the nuclear family as a consequence of industrialization. Thus before an industrial revolution could get under way, an agricultural revolution was required whereby many small single family farms were combined (enclosed) into one large estate using hired labour and rational methods of cultivation and accounting. This process served to release labour for industry, and also had the effect of weakening family ties. The family was further weakened, as we have seen, by the shift of many tasks away from the home to the market and to the industrial enterprise. The growth of industry created a spirit of individual competitiveness which worked against the traditions of family ties. Women were able to undertake paid employment outside the home and developed a new independence. Labour moved where the work was, and new family units were established. Later the State came to take a hand in many areas traditionally dealt with by the family such as care of the sick and aged, assistance to families with small children, and the education of the young. The extended family therefore became less of a necessity.

Proof of one or other of these theories would seem to be fairly simple. If we find everywhere that industry and the family appear to change *together*, then it is likely – although not inevitable – that the two are causally related. If the isolated family is found to come into existence prior to industrialization, then the first theory is confirmed. If the isolated nuclear family is found to come into existence after industrialization, then the latter would appear to be the case.

Unfortunately, in sociology, matters are rarely as simple as this. One of the major difficulties here is the absence of systematic cross-cultural and historical data on the basis of which one could attempt to prove or disprove such theories. The terms themselves are, of course, highly imprecise. Just when, for example, did 'the Industrial Revolution' begin in this country? And, given the fact that some countries became industrialized before others, is it necessary for each country to follow exactly the same course of events? It is unfortunate that many of the attempts to 'prove' or 'disprove' these theories rest upon the citing of one case which is in contradiction to the main theory under examination. Normally, however, sociological theories are not usually presented in strictly 'deterministic' terms (that is of the order, if A happens, then B *must* follow) but rather in 'probabilistic terms' (that is, if A happens *it is probable* that B will follow). This means that a single contradictory case does not necessarily disprove a theory, but rather suggests that the theory should be modified to take account of some other, hitherto unconsidered, factors. This makes our task much more difficult, and it is only possible to indicate some of the kinds of evidence that has been brought forward on one side or another.

The evidence relating to this debate will be presented under three headings. We will first examine the English family before the Industrial Revolution. Secondly, we will look at societies which are at present undergoing the processes of urbanization and industrialization. Finally, we shall examine the structure of the family in contemporary Britain.

1. In recent years our understanding of the history of the English family has been enhanced by the growth of detailed demographic research at the University of Cambridge. Laslett describes one of the early conclusions of this research in these terms:

> In fact the English peasantry and the English townsfolk in the seventeenth or eighteenth century lived in nuclear families, independent families, of man, wife and children, sometimes with additions . . . the family in England ten or fifteen generations ago was not so very different from the family in England as it is today (Laslett, 1965, Ch. 4).

The average size of family was between four or five. The noblemen had much larger domestic units, but the number was increased not as a result of the inclusion of other related adults, but rather the inclusion of domestic servants. A similar family structure was in existence in New England prior to the industrialization of America (Greenfield, 1961, pp. 312–22).

This evidence would seem to lend support to – though it does not prove – the first argument: namely that the isolated nuclear family was a pre-condition for industrialization. Furthermore, it might be argued, on the basis of further comparative investigation, that where this kind of family was absent, the development of industrialization was retarded. However, it needs to be stressed that this research is in its early stages; we need, for example, to know more about regional variations.

2. If the evidence on a historical basis tends, as yet, to be a little scarce and difficult to assess, the evidence on industry and the family in countries at present undergoing industrialization is very rich and diverse. Consider the following quotation:

... labour migration to the urban industrial areas is positively emancipating the individual from his obligations to his kinship group. Again, if a man wishes to accumulate capital to set up as a petty trader or tailor, or to acquire a higher standard of living for himself, and his elementary family, he must break away from his circle of village kin towards whom he has traditional obligations. Everywhere, we see the spectacle of corporate groups of kin disintegrating and the emergence of smaller residential units based on the elementary family (Turner, 1957, p. 43).

Other sociologists and anthropologists have come to similar conclusions. Nimkoff assessed a wide variety of comparative material and concludes that the general course of change, if not the pace, is in the same direction (Nimkoff, 1965, pp. 343–56).

However, it is likely that a detailed examination of actual situations would be profitable here. Some studies indicate that while certain kin ties may be severed, others may become strengthened or renewed. Kinship ties may be mobilized in order to obtain jobs in new factories, and people may go to stay with relatives on arriving at a new town. Loans and exchanges may take place between kin, and there will be frequent return trips to the rural areas. Some factories may even take the likelihood of those return trips into account when planning the use of its labour force (Sheth, 1968). In our terms, while there may be a shift towards the nuclear family becoming coterminous with the domestic unit, this need not be an *isolated* nuclear family, and need not imply a reduction in interactional and recognized ties even if these are now spread over a wider area. What seems to be likely is that kinship ties become one of a whole set of different ties, which may or may not be used according to circumstances. They are augmented and modified, rather than absolutely changed, by the growth of ties based on occupation, class and residence.

3. The evidence reported for British society is equally varied. The studies of Bethnal Green have perhaps been the most prominent studies indicating that in long-established slums and working-class communities, the nuclear family, whilst most likely to be coterminous with the domestic unit, was not isolated and its members lived in a network of interactional ties of kinship (Young and Willmott, 1957a). Other studies of working-class and other communities tended to confirm this picture. What we perhaps lack in some of these accounts is a discussion of the *meaning*, in personal terms, of these ties. Is it the case that ties are maintained simply 'because they are there', or out of a definite preference for these ties over ties of friendship or neighbourliness? What *is* important to note is that these ties are nearly always much more important to the women, who remain at home, rather than for the men, who go to work. In other words, the general thesis concerning the isolation of the nuclear family, suggested at the beginning of this section may be true for men and not for women.

Kinship ties may still be important, in some cases, for men in their work relationships. In some working-class occupations, notably in the docks, men commonly obtain their jobs through kinship ties (Young and Willmott, pp. 73–80). Again this may be a case where kinship ties are one of a whole set of ties which are used in various circumstances but which do not necessarily have an *over-all* precedence over the others. At the other end of the social scale, it is still true that kinship ties are an important part of what has been called the 'old boy net', where relationships of family and education interact to produce a closely-knit *élite*, spread throughout certain top business and political positions (see, for example, Lupton and Wilson, 1959, pp. 30–52). It may simply be that *power* is the crucial resource at stake, and kinship merely *one* convenient way of handling it.

The family exists, then, in a variety of relationships to society. At one extreme, we may just say that the family as an extended network of kin and affines *is* the society: that all that is important in economic, political or religious life takes place within this context, and that each sphere reinforces the other. At the other extreme, we have the secularized, privatized family, relatively isolated in an urban setting, seen

by its members as the only meaningful unit in an increasingly bureau-
craticized and industrialized society. Between these extremes, we have
a variety of relationships and possibilities. In our own society, we
should probably not talk of *the* family at all, but only of the working-
class family, the middle-class family, the privatized family, the extended family, and so on. Similarly, it is probably not very helpful to
talk of *the* functions of the family, for to do this presupposes a
degree of independence on the part of the family that it does not
perhaps possess. Rather, we need to look at the particular patterns of
exchange and influence; the relative weight to be assigned to familistic
and kinship, as against other, non-familial, ties; the relative meanings
which the individual assigns to the concepts of the family; and the
various kinds of kin and affinal relationship subsumed under the
single label 'family'.

Chapter 4
Education

A large part of our social and technical skills are acquired through deliberate instruction which we call education. It is the main waking activity of children from the ages of five to fifteen and often beyond, and is also a major economic activity. It consumes the largest single part of the budget of many developed and developing countries, frequently employing more people than any single industrial activity. For example, in the United States almost two million people are employed in teaching in primary and secondary schools and a further quarter of a million teach in institutions of higher education, which in some states now cater for 50 per cent of the relevant age group (U.S. Bureau of Census, 1967). The days in which someone with no more than secondary education could learn the trade of architect, lawyer or other professions are rapidly receding into the past and in some modern industries not only do executives have to have university education, but foremen as well.

We have come to accept the growth of education as a natural process. Yet the current respect paid to education and the educational system is a recent phenomenon. A hundred years ago, less than one per cent of an age-group would go on to university education in the United States, and as recently as 1916 a now-prominent industrial executive felt he had to conceal his advanced degree in economics (Drucker, 1962, pp. 15–21): 'I told the man who hired me that I had been a railroad clerk since I was fourteen,' he remarked, 'otherwise I would have been turned down as too educated for a job in business.'

As sociologists, we need to ask:

1. Why education has increased so greatly in extent.

2. What education does in modern society to justify its position.

3. And what education contributes to planned and unplanned change in society.

If we begin to answer these questions we have some hope of understanding and controlling what promises to be an increasingly dominant manner of organizing human society.

Education is, however, only one part of the way human beings learn. We have already noted the considerable contribution that the family makes to a child's learning of skills and social behaviour, and in daily life through friends, jobs or recreation, people are constantly learning new skills and information. Even deliberate instruction occurs outside the framework of a formal education system. In some countries political parties, such as the Communist Party, may take a large share in formally instructing children and adults in history, philosophy and social conduct. Industrial firms, trade unions and churches have at different times and different places taken on the formal instruction of their members. To understand the significance and potential of formal education we thus need to consider the relation of education to other parts of learning.

Socialization

Little of man's behaviour is instinctive. Rather, man's behaviour is *learned* behaviour. The kinds of skills and knowledge that man requires to survive and to develop are acquired both through interaction and communication with other men in society, and by the transmission of culture, material and immaterial, from the previous to the present generation. Man *is* man because he shares with others a common culture, a culture which includes not only its living members but also members of past generations and those as yet unborn.

It is because man is a cultural being that sociologists have attached great importance to the notion of *socialization*. By this is meant, simply, the transmission of culture, the process whereby men learn the rules and practices of social groups. Socialization is an aspect of all activity within all human societies. Just as we learn a game by playing it, so we learn life by engaging in it; we are socialized in the course of the activities themselves. For example, if we are untutored in manners, we learn 'correct' manners through the mistakes that we make and the disapprobation that others display. Education – deliberate instruction – is thus only a *part* of the socialization process; it is not, and can never be, the whole of that process.

The process of socialization is something that continues throughout life – we must not think that there is a point in formal education at which a man has learnt everything about his group and that, there-after, he ceases to learn. Man belongs to different groups at different stages of his life. As these groups change, so we must learn new rules, new patterns of behaviour. Furthermore we do not always remain within the same role: although we are members of a family all our life, we are constantly changing our roles within it, acquiring new ones, dropping or modifying old ones: we begin as children, pass through adolescence into adulthood, marry, become parents, enter middle age, retire and grow old. With each role, comes new patterns of behaviour that we must learn and, thus, throughout life, we are in-volved in the socialization process. Even at death's door we are being socialized. The staff of hospitals, for example, have a conception of what is a 'good' way to die and they try to socialize their dying patients into abiding by their expectations, dying in a 'proper' manner (Sudnow, 1967).

Not only do persons change roles within groups, but they also change membership-groups. In some cases, re-socialization – the stripping away of learned patterns and substitution of new ones for them – must occur. Such re-socialization occurs most often when a social role is radically changed, as in sudden downwards or upwards social mobility, or when a person is transferred from a legitimate social role to one that is 'outside' the moral order of the society. A good example of the latter kind of transition is that involved in moving from the status of 'citizen' to that of 'lunatic', the transition of role involved on entry as a patient into a mental hospital (Goffman, 1961).

Men not only learn the culture of the group of which they are immediate members. They may also learn the culture of groups to which they do not belong. Sociologists have, for example, written of *anticipatory* socialization, the process whereby men socialize them-selves into the culture of a group with the anticipation of joining that group (Merton, 1957 pp. 265–8). A person who aspires to join the upper class of his society may take on the style of life, speech pattern and attitudes of the upper class in anticipation of being recognized as a member.

We see, therefore, that socialization is a concept which has many, wide-ranging implications. People may be socialized into groups of which they are already members or into groups to which they wish to become attached. Socialization is not a process which takes place merely in early childhood but takes place at different times and places throughout life. In short, it is a term that refers to the social learning process in all its complexity.

The contrast between industrial and pre-industrial societies serves to bring out the changing place of education within the socialization process. In pre-industrial societies there is *some* education – deliberate instruction, for instance is given to those who would join the ranks of witch-doctors, but the vast bulk of learning is done through socialization, not education. The individual learns largely by participation in work, the family, religion and so on – although spasmodic instruction may be given during the course of such activity. In some cases, in the case of the specialists that such societies support, education is given in the form of an 'apprenticeship' the individual learns at the side of the practitioner.

Compare the situation in a highly industrialized society; here the situation is significantly different. Not only do individuals receive deliberate instruction for a long period of time continuously and consistently, not only do they receive specialized instruction in a particular task or occupation, but they receive also a broad and general education in a number of basic skills (reading, writing and counting) and are taught about matters not directly relevant to any occupation. Such instruction is not given by a practitioner, but by a person whose occupation is a specialized one; a person whose occupation it is to educate.

We can say that education is *differentiated* from other aspects of socialization to a greater extent in industrial society than in non-industrial society. The term 'differentiation' when used sociologically, refers to the extent to which one activity, role, institution, or organization is separated from others.

The differentiation of education is linked to the special position it occupies within socialization in industrial society. Education fits people for increasingly specialized roles. The more education a person receives, the more specialized that education becomes. A child's education begins quite broadly and includes a general introduction to literate skills. With each year in school, the focus of education narrows on to particular subjects and subject areas. In secondary school, a child will often be specializing in two or three subjects, and in only certain areas within these subjects. At university, specialization increases to the point where the fully educated individual will receive his doctorate for knowing more about a smaller field than anyone before him.

Contrast informal aspects of socialization. The social skills and values learned through interaction with family, peers and other social groups are broadly useful in social life. They enable an individual to deal with the range of people and situations which he is likely to encounter in his life. Thus, informal socialization is most successful when it gives us skills and values that are not so specialized that they prevent us understanding the different people and situations we encounter.

Formal education and other aspects of socialization are thus complementary. Formal training produces recruits for the specialized roles that are being increasingly created in industrial society. Formal education was thus less emphasized in pre-industrial society where such specialized roles were less common. Informal aspects of socialization provide people with the skills and values that facilitate interaction and communication between people, irrespective of the specialized role they hold in society.

As we shall see later, values and social skills are also communicated through the system of formal education. This is often done deliberately as when, for example, a school seeks to impress upon its pupils values of achievement or loyalty to the flag. Skills and values will also be communicated to pupils informally by their masters and fellow-pupils. Not only are civic ideals communicated in the school, but also basic ethical notions of honesty, solidarity, and social norms defining, say, ideals of individual competitiveness or group loyalty. The communication is often not overt: it occurs via the playing of games, in the life of school societies, in rituals of school prayers and assemblies. Thus, though we have spoken of formal education as being differentiated from other forms of socialization there is considerable overlap in the influence of the various aspects of socialization. Since learning in all its forms is primarily a social phenomenon – where interaction with others is the main means of transmitting information – it is not surprising that the learning of technical skills also involves learning values and social skills.

The fact that children learn values and social skills at school as well as through family and friends mean that these various agents of socialization are potentially competing with each other for influence over the child. If family and friends emphasize values that are different from those a child is learning at school, then this child may face especial problems in adapting to both school and home. This is illustrated by one account given by Jackson and Marsden of a working-class father who reported the difficulties he had in understanding his son's career in grammar school:

Many a time you'd be out and the neighbours would say, 'Eeh, is your lad still at school? What's he going to be then?'
And I'd have to say, 'I don't know what he's going to be yet.'
And they'd say, 'Doesn't he know yet?' And then I'd come home and I'd sit opposite our lad in the chair, and I'd say 'What do you think you'll be when you leave school?' 'I don't know, I don't know at all, don't bother me,' he'd say and that was it. When the neighbours bothered me, I hadn't got an answer and I felt soft. They'd look at you as much as to say, 'Staying on at school all that time and don't know what he's going to be, well!' (Jackson and Marsden, 1962, p. 116).

For this father and his neighbours the value of education was understood in terms of the job it would bring. The grammar school the son attended stressed more 'ivory tower' values in which learning was seen as good for its own sake. The son was caught between these conflicting emphases and felt uneasy with both.

We spend time later examining the consequence of conflict between home and school for a child's education. Throughout our lives we are socialized by conflicting as well as complementary influences. This is one reason why we must put education within the broader perspective of socialization in order to understand the problems that emerge in schooling. Education cannot be isolated from its social setting since education is only one among many influences that determine what a child learns – even within the school.

We remarked earlier that in an industrial society education is differentiated from other aspects of socialization. This brings us to another important distinguishing feature of education. In most contemporary societies, education is carried out through a large and highly complex organization. We can call this organization a formal organization since it has clearly established goals, and a defined structure and procedures for reaching these goals. Education is thus not only deliberate instruction; it is also organized instruction.

Organizations have both a formal and informal structure. The formal structure of a school, for example, includes the number of classes into which the school is divided. It also includes the procedures by which pupils move every year from a lower to a higher class. The legally established authority of headmaster and staff – and the authority they delegate to prefects – is also part of the formal structure.

Pupils develop relationships among themselves and with staff; the staff acquire likes and dislikes for each other and certain pupils. This informal interaction generates norms of behaviour that are often distinct from the official norms of the school. In higher forms, for example, it is often accepted practice to wear the official school clothing as little as possible; whereas the school still emphasizes the pride a pupil should take in wearing school uniform on every occasion. The informal expectations of pupils and staff can limit the operation of the formal structure of a school.

A student does not merely respond to the formal knowledge presented by teacher, lecturer and textbook. He also responds to the informal patterns of relations and expectations that develop within the student body and between student and teacher. A complete sociological account of the educational process must take into account both the gangs in the playground and the 'streams' in the classrooms, both the student debate or staff-student sherry party and the final examinations.

It is this interaction between formal and informal aspects of education that distinguishes education – which is organized – from other aspects of socialization. Educational organizations require the socialization of their members into the practices that are found within them. Education thus socializes both for the world *beyond* its boundaries and for the world *within* its boundaries.

The specific organizational framework of education merits study. Some forms of educational organizations may be more efficient than others in developing the talents of students. Also, because of their size, complexity, and the informal relations they generate, it is often difficult to change educational organizations to make them more efficient or more responsive to new findings in educational research.

We have thus seen that education is only one part of a more general process which we call socialization. Socialization begins at birth and ends only with death. Education is primarily deliberate learning, which fits the individual for a highly specialized job in society. It contrasts with informal learning which occurs through interaction with others and observations of their behaviour, and which ensures that an individual learns to understand and conform to the behaviour of others with whom he comes into contact during his life.

Values and social skills are also inculcated during education. In part this is deliberately intended. In part it occurs as an unintended consequence of the way education is organized. Since we are educated with others in a large-scale organization, we develop relations with fellow students and teachers and come to terms with the rules of the organization. These relations are expressed in norms and encourage certain social skills. This informal process of socialization is an important part of the educational process, affecting the ways students and teachers relate to the specialized goals of education.

The Growth of Education

In the previous section we linked the contemporary importance of education to industrial society. The recent growth of the English educational system is very closely tied to the rapid industrialization of the nineteenth and twentieth centuries. Before industrialization, formal education was a rudimentary affair reaching a small proportion of children. In many villages school would be given in one class for all ages. The instructor might be an old soldier who was himself scarcely literate but could at least be expected to keep order. The local priest provided instruction in the catechism and religious orders passed on higher learning to those who would follow in the priesthood and to some favoured laymen. Most children of school age would be helping their parents in their jobs, be apprenticed out to learn a trade or be serving in a household. More prosperous members of society ensured that their children received some education by hiring private tutors and governesses for their children. The aristocracy would supplement this education by the grand tour in which the scion of the family would be taken around Europe to places of culture and good breeding to see for himself the products of Western civilization. However, the middling groups of English society who could not afford the expense of the aristocratic education were more interested in having schools for their children. Many of our contemporary grammar schools are ancient foundations attesting both the beneficence of a long-dead notable and the eagerness of the sixteenth, seventeenth and eighteenth century small merchants, prosperous farmers and skilled craftsmen to have somewhere to educate their children.

One of the first major expansions in English education came with the desire of the increasingly prosperous mercantile and landed middle classes of the eighteenth and nineteenth centuries to provide a more adequate public education for their children. This is the period of the establishment and expansion of most of our contemporary public schools. Originally they were conceived as being public in the sense of catering for a wider clientele than was catered for by private tutors, and to the aristocracy the prospering middle classes were the relevant 'public' of the day. The success of these schools became assured with increasing industrialization that created supervisory and managerial jobs for which the children of the middle and upper middle classes had to be educated both socially and intellectually. It was in the late nineteenth century that ancient foundations were re-designed and many new ones created.

In the last half of the nineteenth century, and especially with the Education Act of 1870, education began to reach the majority of the population. The early expansion was mainly concerned with extending literacy and numeracy. The provision of broader and more varied curricula was to come later. The educational reformers sold their reforms to aristocracy and middle classes by emphasizing the extent to which an industrial nation needed literate and numerate workers to man the new machines that became more complex every year. The first provisions of secondary education beyond that of the public school came with the attempt to establish Mechanics' Institutes throughout the country to promote industrial innovation and understanding (Ensor, 1960, pp. 146–51).

This link between industrialization and education is an understandable one. Industrialization basically means an increasing division of labour in which the workman finds himself carrying out a highly specialized task. He carries out this task in the company of a large number of others. Machines do the job and skill is evaluated in terms of being able to carry out instructions and understand what the machine is doing. These are skills highly linked to literacy and numeracy. The old craftsman and farmworker had less need of formal education since his job was learned through years of watching others do the job before him, and the master of his trade was someone who was self-sufficient.

Also, industrialization creates a far wider range of occupations; it gives rise to occupations requiring a great amount of technical knowledge for their mastery. Deliberate and full-time instruction is needed to master these jobs. As society becomes more industrial and more technologically based so there is a demand for ever higher general levels of education. A job that once required a worker to have only literacy, now demands that he finish primary education and then secondary education. For machines become more complex and their manufacturers depend more and more on the increasing technical proficiency of their operator. A modern automated factory requires fewer workers than its predecessor; but these workers must each be more technically skilled and proficient.

These are the 'demands' that industrialization makes on education. Rising levels of education do themselves help to accelerate the 'demands' for more education. As soon as a labour force is literate, then employers are likely to ask for primary education as a means of selecting among applicants for a job – even where the job does not strictly need any training beyond literacy. Even jobs whose nature and complexity have not changed over time now demand much higher educational qualifications.

Formal education has become a vital component of our highly technological society. It is only in full-time educational organizations that there are people with the range of knowledge needed to instruct individuals in the different technical skills that society requires. Technical innovation is so rapid and the accumulation of scientific and humanistic knowledge so great that ever-greater periods of time are needed to instruct a pupil adequately. Thus, to instruct even a moderately skilled person now requires from eleven to sixteen years of full-time instruction. Of course, wise men of past centuries could dedicate their lives to learning and only exhaust a fraction of human knowledge. The difference is that we now expect, and find it necessary, for an infinitely greater proportion of a population to dedicate much of their lives to full-time formal learning.

So far, we have considered the link between education and industrialization as if it was simply a question of the response to the needs of an evolving industrial society. This relationship is not, however, a simple one of stimulus and response. It is also true that education develops in directions that do not serve an industrial economy. Indeed education may develop in directions that harm existing industrial organization; although, as we shall see, such developments may benefit both the individual child and long-term economic and social development – which is to say that serving economic growth is not the only possible or proper function of education.

The growth of English education provides many examples of the lack of fit between education and the 'demands' of the economy. When we speak of education responding to the needs of the industrial revolution, it is as well to remember that this included the increasing influence of the traditional, classically oriented universities of Oxford and Cambridge. It also entailed the emergence of an academic secondary education heavily based on Latin and Greek. Until a short while ago, able students could be rejected for a science course at Oxford and Cambridge for lack of Latin. These historical anomalies are not confined to Britain. Many underdeveloped countries show the same contrast between a traditional, humanistic educational system and an economy attempting desperately to compete in the industrial world. In Guatemala, in Latin America, for example, the national university produced in the fourteen years up to 1964 only twenty-seven graduates in agronomy (UNESCO, 1965). In contrast, the largest university faculties were those of Law and Humanities whose graduates had little special training for the needs of a predominantly agricultural economy.

These historical anomalies between the growth of the economy and the growth of education can be understood in terms of the conservatism inherent in organizations. An educational system is organized in terms of people holding certain positions, and of schools and colleges having a place and importance within this system. Those that benefit from their existing position are likely to be resistant to change and to use their place within the organization to counter change. Since the growth of English education began with schools and colleges oriented to classical subjects, it is not surprising that these subjects persisted. Likewise Oxford and Cambridge were the dominant universities when the contemporary growth of education in England began. New universities founded later were staffed by people from Oxford and Cambridge who continued the traditions of their home universities in the subjects they taught and the degrees they offered. Once a degree is offered, then syllabuses are established, lectures are oriented to the degrees and a whole mesh of bureaucratic procedures is created that constitutes a powerful resistance to rapid change.

We should, however, distinguish between the unintended consequences of educational organization and the intended goals of education. One important reason why the growth of education does not closely relate to the growth of the economy is that the conscious goals of educators have included other than economic considerations. The growth of British education has been directly affected by the work and ideas of philosophers and social reformers such as Matthew Arnold and John Stuart Mill who conceived of education as contributing to the social rather than the economic development of society (Williams, 1958). Included amongst their ideas was an emphasis on the need to educate an individual broadly, to encourage social responsibility and critical thought. They rejected any form of education too narrowly tied to vocational objectives on the grounds that the learning of technical information did not train men to face either personal or intellectual uncertainty. This tradition of thought has persisted in many educational systems throughout the world, providing the rationale by which education in the humanities is seen as a necessary complement to scientific training. Indeed some observers argue that training for such fields as engineering also requires education in the traditional humanities or social sciences. They argue that since technical information is enlarging and changing so rapidly, it is important to train students to cope with and evaluate a mass of information – a capacity that is the central discipline of the humanities.

It is, of course, difficult to assess which particular academic specialism best encourages people to think for themselves. The point to be remembered is that since there is uncertainty over what is the best form of education – even to prepare people for jobs in a technologically-based society – it is unlikely that the growth of an educational system will neatly follow economic change. It is thus likely that education independently contributes to social change by the particular way in which technical information, ideas and values are communicated. Despite all the attempts to quantify the relation of education to the economy we just do not know what kind of education best achieves either economic or social development. Educational controversy and educational philosophy is thus a fertile source of conscious change in education.

The growth of education must also be analysed in terms of the goals of groups unconnected either with education or the economy. The pressures of these groups are further reasons for the lack of fit between the growth of education and the economy. Some of the groups were motivated by religious considerations, such as the British and Foreign School society founded in 1807. The educational aims of such groups emphasized scriptural literacy and moral virtues more than economic considerations. Other pressure groups had political considerations in mind. These ranged from the desire to educate our masters, following the extension of the suffrage, to the provision of élite public schools for training the sons of the aristocracy, and rising middle classes, to take over government positions opened to competition by the Civil Service reforms. The activities of these and other pressure groups were responsible for moulding the curricula and structure of English education in ways that are remote from any needs of the economy. Religious instruction in schools and the élite/non-élite distinction in secondary and higher education are the contemporary legacy of the work of pressure groups on the growth of education.

The work of pressure groups illustrates a more general point to be noted about the relation of the growth of education to society: that education is always conditioned by the existing social structure. The growth of education is linked not only to economic rationality but also to the way power is distributed in society. We can expect this, since education gives access to various forms of power. We have seen that with the growth of education, education becomes increasingly important for determining entrance into occupations. Entrance into the Civil Service becomes dependent on education. Industrial management requires education and can less easily be allocated mainly in terms of friendship or family. Education is thus one means of social stratification and of social mobility. This being the case, those that enjoy a favourable position in society are likely to try to maintain it for their children through securing them privileged education. Note, for example, Asa Briggs's discussion of the reactions to Civil Service reform in the middle of the last century.

The Queen in turn expressed grave doubts about open competition, as did an influential section of the Whigs, and it was left to Gladstone, a few heads of colleges, and a cluster of professors to suggest that the new method would not entail a lowering of social standards in the service – a substitution of *parvenus* for 'gentlemen' – but would rather 'strengthen and multiply the ties between the higher classes and the possession of administrative power'. The civil service was to be thrown open not to the 'raw' middle classes but to the new educational *élite* of the public schools and the universities. Whitehall was to be surrendered not to Manchester but to Oxford. Jobbery was to go, and education was to become the test, but social stratification was to remain (Briggs, 1962, p. 443).

In his study of a Northern grammar school, Hightown Grammar, Colin Lacey showed how the social classes in the town reacted differently to the growth of education (Lacey, 1970). Before the Second World War, the grammar school was mainly used by children of the professional middle class and children of the working class. For both these social groups a grammar school education was a means of mobility for their children. For the professional class, education led to the university and a professional job for their children, usually outside Hightown. For the working class, the grammar school gave children an opportunity to get into a white-collar occupation and enjoy better working conditions than their parents. Under-represented in the grammar school at this time was the child whose parents were merchants or owned small businesses or workshops. The children of this social group did not need the help of a grammar school education since they could follow in their father's business. Lacey shows the changes that occurred after the war with the decline of many small businesses. This meant that it was much more difficult for sons to follow in their father's footsteps. The jobs available, in larger and more impersonal industrial and commercial firms, depended more on education. So after the war, the middle classes moved in bulk into Hightown Grammar, 'displacing' children from working-class homes. In Hightown the share of the working class in grammar school education thus declined over time. This illustrates how education is 'used' by social groups as a means for social mobility. The pressure that social groups place on the growth of education depends on how they assess its importance to their own, and their childrens,' social position.

We can proceed to examine the extent to which the growth of contemporary English education reflects the historical stratification of our society. The origins of the 'tripartite system' of secondary education are particularly interesting from this viewpoint. We have already seen how the public schools commenced as a cheap means of education for the middle classes and became in the late nineteenth century the means whereby the upper and upper-middle classes retained their hold on occupations of power thrown open to competition by examination and qualification. At the end of the nineteenth century, there was a large expansion in the grammar school system. The growth of these schools was a 'response' to the increase in the number of white-collar jobs produced by England's growing commercial and administrative concerns at home and abroad. The grammar schools were intended to train these middle level white-collar workers. They modelled themselves as far as possible after the public schools. Most grammar schools developed a 'house system', a prefect system, obligatory games and a curriculum similar to public schools. Grammar school pupils were not encouraged to aspire to the preserves of the upper classes. A few pupils were allowed to sit the Oxford/Cambridge entrance examinations and might be admitted on a scholarship. Most were expected to leave school at fifteen and take a job in a local business or bank. Some might go to a local university. For the rest of the population, education centred on the primary school and on the extension of the primary school to the age of fourteen. Pupils of these schools took up jobs as blue-collar workers. These schools did not provide the opportunity to sit the examinations that were becoming the normal prerequisite for a white-collar job or university entrance.

The system was drastically modified with the Education Act of 1944 which effectively established the tripartite system in the state sector of education. This system was composed of a primary school sector – up to the age of ten – followed by an examination determining entry into either grammar, technical or secondary modern school. The intention of the Act was to provide a system of separate but equal types of schooling geared to the particular talents of a child. The private sector of education was however excluded from its scope and left undisturbed. The Act thus created four distinct types of secondary schooling, each with a different relation to the occupational world. The private sector retained its privileged connexion with the traditional universities and the higher ranks of business and administration. The grammar schools prepared pupils for university entrance and for the Ordinary and Advanced level examinations that determined entry to most white-collar jobs. The technical high schools emphasized technical subjects to a greater extent than the grammar schools and were intended to channel children to the technical professions. The secondary modern school offered a broad but not heavily academic curriculum that effectively prevented most children from sitting the 'O' and 'A' level examinations.

The Education Act was partly a response to the more egalitarian atmosphere after the Second World War and the advent to power of the Labour Party. It thus aimed to offer better opportunities for educational advancement to children of all social backgrounds. Compared with education before the war, the new school system did provide a broader curriculum, and more opportunity for working and middle-class children to obtain higher levels of education. The university system, too, was opened up to more students by providing government maintenance for successful students and by increasing the number of universities.

Yet, when we look back on this system it still seems heavily anchored to the English class system. Why, for example, should there be four types of schools and not just one? Why should children be examined at the age of eleven to determine their occupations for the rest of their lives? The separation of children into different types of schools from an early age seems a close reflection of English stratification, where each class maintains its own habits and styles of life and rarely interacts with the others. It is striking to compare the English example with that of other countries attempting to make their education more suited to the needs of economic development. It is only in those countries where very strong traditional class divisions have existed that we find a similar partition of education into different types of schools catering for different types of children. Guatemala provides a useful point of comparison. It is a very poor country beginning to expand its educational system as a means to economic and social development. In Guatemala, where almost caste-like social differences are maintained between those of Indian and Spanish descent, where even among the Spanish-descent population there are important cleavages of wealth and status, the secondary school system is also fragmented into a series of state and private schools. Curricula train children from an early age for distinct occupations, allowing little common education between children destined for different occupational positions.

In England, similarly, whatever the intention of the 1944 Education Act, the effect was certainly to stratify education by social class. This is apparent in the statistics in the Robbins Report showing the influence of parental background on a child's chance of entering higher education *even* where the intelligence of the child is taken into account (Table 1):

Table 1

Percentage of Children from Maintained Grammar Schools Entering Higher Education by I.Q. at 11+ and Father's Occupation (Children Born in 1940/41)

I.Q.	Father's occupation	Enter full-time higher education %	Do not enter full-time higher education %	Percentage
130 and over	Non-manual	41	58	99
	Manual	30	70	100
115–129	Non-manual	34	66	100
	Manual	15	85	100
100–114	Non-manual	17	83	100
	Manual	6	94	100

Source: Adapted from Appendix One, *Report of the Committee on Higher Education*, 1963, Table 4, p. 42.

The public schools have remained the preserve of the upper and upper-middle classes, while the proportion of working-class children increases as one moves from grammar to technical to secondary modern school. The universities are heavily attended by students of middle and upper-middle class background. This is strongest at Oxford and Cambridge. In turn, the higher reaches of industry and Civil Service are dominated by ex-students of these two universities. Some 90 per cent of the higher Civil Service attended either Oxford or Cambridge. The social stratification of English education is also apparent in the attitudes of its members. Jackson and Marsden provide a quotation neatly illustrating this sense of social as well as educational difference:

That's right, I saw the headmaster, and I said: 'We've got this form with these schools down, and we don't know anything about any of them.'
'Well,' said the headmaster, 'What's his father's job?'
'He's a lorry driver.'
'Well, then you'd better be sending him to Mill Cross.'
'Mill Cross? Why, is that the best school?'
'No, it's not, but it's the best school for you.'
'How do you mean, it's the best school for me? Where would you send your lad?'
'Oh, I'd send *my* lad to Marburton College. . . .'
So what do you think of that story? Fair cheek, isn't it? (Jackson and Marsden, 1962, pp. 90–91).

It is against this climate that comprehensive schools were introduced, as part of the official policy of a second post-war Labour Government, to eliminate social inequalities in the tripartite system. The effectiveness of the comprehensive school as a force of social as well as educational change we discuss, in the next section, when we consider the general relation between social stratification and the educational process.

The 1944 Education Act was, however, one of the more important steps in increasing the size of the educational establishment. Education may still be as divided by social class as before the war, but numbers taking secondary and university education have substantially increased for all social classes. In Table 2, we see the contrast between the proportions of an age group who stay on in secondary education just after the war and in 1966. For further contrast, we can take the example of Guatemala again. We have already noted that both Britain and Guatemala have some similarities in the stratification of their educational systems. They contrast sharply, however, in the proportions of students at different educational levels. In Guatemala in 1964 less than 1 per cent of an age group reaches university, 5 per cent reach secondary school and 48 per cent are in primary school (UNESCO, 1965, pp. 17–19).

Table 2
Percentage of Children of Different Age Groups Attending Primary and Secondary School in England and Wales, 1950 and 1967

| Age | Proportion of age group attending school | |
	1950 %	1967 %
5–10	99	99
11–14	99	100
15	30	66
16	14	30
17	7	16
18	2	5

Source: Adapted from *Statistics of Education*, vol. 1, 1967, and vol. 1, 1961.

The difference between Guatemala and Britain is a difference between an underdeveloped country just beginning its industrialization and a developed industrial country. The contrast thus allows us to see the changes attendant upon industrialization even where a class system remains relatively powerful. More people are taking formal schooling at *all* levels of education in Britain as compared with Guatemala, and the difference is a considerable one.

The growth of education during industrialization is likely to influence social stratification and social mobility. We have so far stressed the reverse – that education is conditioned by stratification. Yet the sheer growth in numbers of those receiving education makes it more likely that sons will improve upon their father's social position. In Guatemala it is very unlikely that sons of labourers will attain white-collar jobs – there are so few that receive even the minimum of education required for such jobs. In Britain, sons of labourers are at least likely to have minimum educational qualifications required to improve upon their father's position and some are likely to use this education to obtain a white-collar job. Later, we extend this discussion to examine the role that education plays in promoting social change. It is enough to remark at this stage that the growth of education, though conditioned by the economy and social structure, is likely to be a stimulus to change.

The growth of education is thus linked to industrialization. Industrialization introduces a range of specialized jobs, many of which require formal training before entry into the job. As industrialization proceeds, society is increasingly organized on a technological basis, requiring increasing levels of education from all members. Before industrialization, education is mainly confined to the élite. The growth of education is also responsive to changes in educational philosophy and to the activities of pressure groups and the form in which education develops is conditioned by these activities. More generally, the way society is stratified strongly influences the direction and structure of educational growth. The British educational system is thus partly a product of the changing economic situation of the country, and partly a result of the historical impact of social reform and social stratification.

The Functions of Education

Now it is time to look at what education actually does in our society, keeping in mind the distinction between the conscious aims of education and the unintended consequences of educational organization. The perspective in this section is on the *contemporary* relationship between education and society as distinct from our earlier discussion of its historical growth.

We can begin by examining the significance of the values and skills that are imparted by education. We have already seen that there is a definite link between education, the economy and society, and that each influences the development of the other, but we need to understand more clearly what the nature of this relationship is.

Skills can be dealt with first. We have noted several times that education trains in skills that are required by the economy. The full significance of this is often forgotten: the relation between the economy and education can be an exact one. For example, the number and productive capacity of engineering firms are limited by the number of engineers produced by education. This applies to most fields of the economy. It is a common practice for international banks, when estimating what industrial investment they should make in a country, to determine the numbers of people being produced at the different levels of education. One bank when surveying the Guatemalan economy for possible industrial and commercial investment, pointed to the low percentage of children finishing primary school and stressed the difficulty this means in ensuring the future supply of skilled and supervisory labour needed in certain types of modern factory.

This exact relation between education and the economy means that in a modern planned economy the output of skilled people must be consciously geared to the economic and social priorities of the society. The output of doctors, scientists, teachers and so forth must be, and often is, planned years in advance to meet projected economic and social requirements. This means that conscious action must be taken to shape education to these ends. Building programmes, scholarships, teachers' salaries can all be geared to what a government or industry regards as educational priorities. In Britain, the government is constantly emphasizing the shortage of scientific and technical manpower. To remedy this there have been changes in syllabus and incentives for students specializing in these subjects as far back as the primary school. We shall consider below some of the objections that may already be springing to mind concerning such exact planning of the relation between education and society.

The skills learnt in education have wider significance than the narrowly economic significance we have discussed so far. Consider a developing country. One important goal in these countries is the fostering of participant democracy. Participant democracy in any large and complex society depends on literacy. Literacy allows full participation in the mass media and effective voting. Literacy is a product of education. The state of an educational system thus has political as well as economic significance. The literacy and numeracy skills learnt in education are directly necessary to social as well as economic development.

Education is also important for the values that it imparts. The curriculum of a school, its 'extra-curricular' activities and the informal relationships amongst pupils and teachers communicate a variety of social skills and values. This may be done deliberately as when the various activities of a school are geared to impart values and social skills such as co-operation or 'team-spirit', obedience, 'fair play'. History courses may emphasize the virtues and achievement of the national society in comparison with those of other societies, stressing the exemplary lives of national heroes. In most developing countries a large part of the school curriculum is organized around courses and rituals designed to impart the values of national integration. The history and customs of the ethnic groups composing a nation will, for example, receive close attention, and in most nations which face problems of trying to weld together distinct groups of people or distinct geographical areas the educational system is under close state supervision and is required to deliberately communicate common national values. Teachers are moved from one part of the country to another to ensure that they do not develop local attachments, and curriculum is uniform from school to school. Can we explain this concern with values as a product of over-zealous school authorities, or is it related in some systematic way to the structure of society? To answer this we need to look more closely at the relation of values communicated in education to the organization of society.

We have already seen that education can be an *integrative* force in society by communicating values that unite different sections of that society. Contrast the values learnt in the family. The family provides its children with values and social skills appropriate to the present social position of that family. They do not equip a child to take an effective part in a society that is rapidly changing and becoming more interdependent. In such a society an individual must learn new skills and learn to interact with people of different social backgrounds. Educational institutions can provide such learning because *ideally* they are not tied to the values and interests of particular groups in society. The more complex and specialized society becomes the more important is education as the communicator of general social values. According to this viewpoint education has a direct *functional* relation with other parts of society. By functional we mean simply that there is some systematic connexion between what happens in education and what happens elsewhere in society. Education provides the technical skills needed in the economic organization of society. Education also instils the values and social skills that integrate people into the broader society.

Values and orientations which are specific to certain occupations may also be provided. A study of a medical school, *The Student Physician*, shows how medical students are socialized and educated into an orientation which the authors call 'detached concern': the medical practitioner must be concerned about his patients, but must not become involved emotionally with them as this interferes with his judgement and objectivity (Merton *et al.*, 1957). Other values and orientations relevant to the functioning of industrial society are also provided by education. In his essay 'The school class as a social system', Talcott Parsons describes the American school class where emphasis is on performance and where the child is judged by how he performs and not by social status and other criteria external to the classroom (Parsons, 1962, pp. 434–55). Parsons sees this value emphasis of the school class as an essential preparation for an industrial economy, where successful operation depends on people being evaluated by performance and not by status.

To look at education in terms of what it does for other parts of society can be helpful in understanding what goes on within education itself. The presence and endurance of certain types of school or curricula are more fully understood when they are related to education's function for other parts of society. Likewise, change in education can often be explained by changes elsewhere in society. In 1967, when the major problems of British society were seen by government and many citizens to be those of economic survival, the emphasis in education became that of fitting education to the skills then needed by British society. Technical and scientific training were encouraged by the government and local authorities and less apparently useful fields of knowledge discouraged. As a result of other social forces, this encouragement did little to halt the swing from science among students; but it did result in substantial changes in university organization.

To look only at what education does for other parts of society is, however, to miss half the picture. Often what education does *not* do, or the conflicts between education and other parts of society, are more relevant for understanding the process of change in education and society.

Consider this excerpt from a text-book and the comments upon it given by Jonathan Kozol in his book about Negro education in the Boston school system, called *Death at an Early Age*:

'Jumbo and Minko are a black boy and a black girl who live in this jungle village. Their skins are of so dark a brown colour that they look almost black. Their noses are large and flat. Their lips are thick. Their eyes are black and shining, and their hair is so curly that it seems like wool. THEY ARE NEGROES AND THEY BELONG TO THE BLACK RACE.'

Turning the pages to a section about Europe, I read by contrast the following description of a very different and presumably more attractive kind of child: 'Two Swiss children live in a farmhouse on the edge of town. . . . These children are handsome. Their eyes are blue. Their hair is golden yellow. Their skins are clear, and their cheeks are red as ripe, red apples.'

What I felt about the words that I have capitalized above was not that they were wrong, or that there could conceivably ever be anything wrong about saying of a group of people that they are members of a particular race, but simply that the context and the near-belligerence of the assertion make it *sound* degrading. It is not in the facts. It is only in the style. . . . It is from reading a book like this over the course of twenty years that the Reading Teacher and thousands of other teachers like her might well come to believe that you would do a child nothing but a disservice to let him know that he was Negro. The books are not issued any more – but the teachers still are . . . (Kozol, 1968, pp. 76–7).

In this case education is quite poignantly imposing values and attitudes that are quite distinct from those that pupils might have learned in their home background. We can see the same happening in Allan Sillitoe's *Loneliness of a Long-Distance Runner*, a sensitive account of the way in which a correctional educational institution – a Borstal – attempts to use sport to impart values that the authorities desire the boys to accept. The long-distance runner of the story sees his running as a means to escape the pressures imposed upon him by society. Sport is thus the locus of a conflict of values in which the purely technical aspects of the recreation are secondary. To the Borstal authorities the whole purpose of the running was to defeat a team from a neighbouring public school and thus uphold the 'honour' of the Borstal. The runner resolves the value conflict to his own satisfaction by 'winning' the race, but refusing to step across the finishing-line.

It is thus apparent that the communication of values through education often results in conflict with values that the students hold themselves, or with values present in home and community. In the case of the text-book excerpt above, these values even denigrate the racial and social position of pupils reading it.

Education is not only a locus of value conflict, but can also instil values that conflict with those held by the dominant groups in society. Since education cannot be precisely controlled or tailored to achieve some and not other changes in orientations and skills, the fit between education and society is at best a loose one. An important part of research and teaching in education is dedicated to the critical examination of society, and it is not surprising that students freshly exposed to such perspectives should be critical both about their society and about the inadequacies of their education. Students who are most active in demonstrations and other forms of protest study those subjects which are especially concerned with the critical evaluation of society. In Britain, and in other countries, students of sociology and political science and the humanities have been most active in student protest. In Guatemala, for example, such students have been active critics of their society for many years, to a greater extent than students of natural science and technology.

Although student movements reflect unintended consequences of the nature and expansion of higher education – something we deal with in the next section – student protest is chiefly a reflection of conflicts of values, generated intentionally or unintentionally by their education. Students have the time and the intellectual inclination to attend to the politics of their country. They are one of the few social groups available for political action. Characteristically, students have few family or financial responsibilities. They risk less than other social groups in espousing causes hostile to the established interests of their society. It is thus not surprising that in most countries of the world students regard themselves as the vanguard of political action, with a special responsibility for advocating the interests of social groups who are themselves unable to protest. The growth of student protest movements is thus closely related to the emergence of political problems and cleavages within the existing political and economic order of society (Cockburn and Blackburn, 1969).

We have seen that sociologists often speak of *dysfunctions* when the consequences of action hinder rather than promote the attainment of objectives. When education promotes disintegration and not integration, we speak of education being dysfunctional for the integration of society. This is not an evaluative term, and on many occasions we might assess a dysfunction as being 'good' or 'healthy'. Thus, student unrest is dysfunctional for the present integration of society, but may contribute to establishing an improved social order and better education. The use of the term dysfunction is always relative to the problem being studied – action that is dysfunctional in one frame of reference may be functional in another.

The point of emphasizing dysfunctions is that they remind us that we are dealing with a very imprecise area of social planning. We know little about the effects of education and little about how education may relate to planned social and economic change. Also, the effects of education are normally felt a generation after the planning decision is made. An educational decision taken to meet an economic priority of 1969 will produce its fullest effects when economic priorities may have radically changed. Even planning the need for more doctors, for example, is a hazardous business. Not only does a projection of future population at different ages have to be made, but an estimate of changing uses of medical services is required. Add to this the need to find increased staff for teaching hospitals, increased medical teaching plant and to estimate possible changes in medical curricula and training. The analysis of dysfunctions is one way of alerting ourselves to the unintended consequences of planned and unplanned educational change.

To look at what education does or does not do for other parts of society still does not tell us *how* this takes place. Whatever the relation between education and society, the content of education is controlled by people who hold power and make decisions. The positions that these people hold in society determine the kinds of pressure to which education will be subjected. In the United States, control of education is located in a school board drawn from a local area with the general supervision of a state board of education. The national government exercises indirect supervision mainly through a judicious use of funds at its disposal. In general, however, much of the content of primary and secondary education in the United States reflects the values and necessities of the local community. This has its advantages, but it also means that the range of education may be restricted by the interests of the existing power structure of a community. In conservative communities, for example, it is difficult for students to be taught about non-capitalist economic systems.

The possible conflict between community control and the general functions of education was brought out sharply in the controversy between Governor Reagan of California and the State University. Reagan, acting through the Board of Regents of the University, required certain changes in the general content and policy of university education. Specifically, the governor was alarmed at the radical political activities of many students. The President of the University ultimately resigned, claiming that it was an essential part of a university's role in society to allow its students to explore intellectual issues and become thinking and acting members of society. The President was thus claiming a more autonomous role for education than that allowed by the Governor.

It is important to note that the issue was decided not at the level of these different concepts of education but in terms of who held the power in the situation. The Governor was never completely successful in obtaining his demands. For the University was always protected to some extent by the fear of local business and local residents that harming the University would be detrimental to the state's economy. Californian industry had benefited from the presence of distinguished science faculties at the University. Other parts of the Californian economy drew directly on university staff and graduates. Education, though responsive to the social structure, maintains a certain autonomy through the importance of its contribution to society.

In contrast to the American system, the British educational system has been more centralized and more resistant to local community pressures. The effective holders of power in education have been the national government and its Ministry of Education. Schools have thus been able to preserve a greater measure of autonomy with respect to their community. This has meant that the content of education has been relatively free of local pressures. It has also meant that education has not been responsive to local community needs. It is difficult for working-class parents to exercise effective pressure on school-teachers who often come from middle-class backgrounds and are supported by a nationally-linked educational bureaucracy. The power of such bureaucracies is often overwhelming: consider for example the Napoleonic centralization in French education, where, as legend has it, every schoolboy turned the same page in the same text-book at the same time.

No matter whether it is local community, national government, or private interests that control education, this control is exercised by people who are not likely to be representative of all the social groups present in society. The control exercised over education is thus likely to be socially biased control. The form and content of education will be socially biased also. We saw examples of such a social bias in the growth of the British educational system. We saw specific illustrations of social bias in the content of a text in the Boston school system.

Various safeguards may exist to attenuate the pressure of special interests. An example of this is the way in which direct British governmental pressure on the universities is mediated through a University Grants Committee controlled by members of the universities. Yet, to a greater or lesser extent, socially biased control is still prevalent in education. Education systems are sensitive to financial pressure, and education is too important a component in the distribution of social and economic rewards, for those who hold power to be content to leave it alone. Furthermore, education is staffed by people who themselves come from an unrepresentative segment of society – the intellectual middle classes – allowing manifold opportunities for social bias to enter into the educational process. Consider this account by one of Jackson's and Marsden's respondents of his contacts with his son's principal educator:

'Well, we can't tell you much about bloody schooling because they didn't tell *us* so bloody much about the job! Once a year you went to that bloody college, a great big bloody queue, two or three minutes each. . . . You'd see this bloody Glen-Smith fellow and he'd look at you and hum and bloody haw and he'd give you no encouragement at all, none whatever, not a bloody bit of encouragement. . . . We never thought the lad had a chance, and there in the end he gets a scholarship to university. There it is! . . . aye, don't come talking to me about Marburton bloody education, it's time that the bloody ratepayers went and shook them buggers up. We're good citizens, aren't we? We might be poor folks around this way, but we've as much bloody right as any other buggers in this bloody town to get the job done properly' (Jackson and Marsden, 1962, pp. 118–19).

We have now examined the way in which education contributes both skills and values which help in integrating complex and heterogeneous societies. Skills and values learnt in education are directly related to the way in which the economy and the occupational structure operate. The fit between education and society is not an exact one, and education can be dysfunctional for the existing economic and social structure. Education is not, however, independent of society, but is controlled by members of society. This control is likely to be a socially biased control and to produce social biases in the form and content of education. These biases mean that education is likely to be productive of conflict as well as integration in society.

It is now time to look at what goes on *within* education. We by now have good reason to suspect that social background is an important component of the educational process. We also want to look at the ways in which the organization of education is an additional and important factor in the way children learn.

Education as a Social System

One part of our argument so far has been concerned to show that education does something for society that is distinct from other agents of socialization. If this is the case, education must to some extent be independent of the influence of these other agents. We saw how Parsons, for example, stressed the degree to which the school class emphasized values and orientations different to those a child might be used to in home and community. The degree to which a school class succeeds in doing this depends on the extent to which it can exclude external influences from impinging on its internal processes. The independent effect of education on skills and values depends on its being something of a world of its own. The study of this aspect of education is the study of education as a social system. We mean by 'social system' the internal organization and processes of education analysed as a coherent unit distinguishable from other parts of society.

We have emphasized that education can never be divorced from its social setting since the 'actors' in education are social actors who carry with them the symbols and orientations marking them as belonging to distinct sectors of society. A child does not drop his accent or his style of dress upon entering a school. In the discussion that follows the focus is thus on seeing how the social system of education is an additional factor in the way in which social background affects the educational process.

One way of assessing education's degree of autonomy from other parts of society is to look at the boundaries of education and society. The sharper the boundaries, the more likely is education to avoid being permeated by the values and pressures of other parts of society. For example, it is important that when children are in school they should be aware that they are participating in an activity with norms and purposes distinct from other sectors of social life in which they participate.

If we conceive of the school as a *sub*-system, whose staff are concerned to preserve a degree of autonomy, we can better understand many of the rituals associated with school life. The rituals of morning prayer or assembly, associated with the beginning of a school day, derive some of their significance from their contribution to maintaining the boundaries between home and school. School uniform and discipline contribute further to the maintenance of these boundaries. Parent-teachers associations and the channelling of parental contacts with schools, through the headmaster or school secretary, are in part ways in which a school seeks to preserve a degree of autonomy in socializing the child. The quotation we have just looked at from Jackson and Marsden is an illustration of the way a headmaster maintains the 'boundary' between home and school. Other parts of school life also relate to the values and concerns of the external society. Religious instruction and prayers, the cadet corps in British and American schools are important 'boundary' points at which the school relates to the pressures to society while preserving a certain degree of independence.

The boundaries where education is controlled by external forces are also apparent. The University Grants Committee, already cited, is a body that marks the boundary between the university system and financial control by the Exchequer. School Boards of Governors are another example of the way in which an educational system is buffered from direct public control. In Britain, though the boundaries are hazy, education has to a large extent succeeded in maintaining its boundaries. Education is controlled differently from other public services and is less responsive than other public agencies to public and governmental pressure.

We can ask whether this relative autonomy serves any useful purpose. Does it, for example, ensure that the educational potential of children is developed equally irrespective of their social background? Does it permit education to pursue learning unfettered by the narrowing constraints of social prejudice? This does not seem to be the case. To understand why we must take a closer look at the way education's boundaries are permeated by the social structure.

Children who enter school bring with them a certain culture. From their family and neighbourhood they have learnt certain patterns of speech, certain habits and certain orientations to life. These are often subtle and deeply ingrained. Basil Bernstein attempts, through a distinction between what he calls *public* and *formal* language, to show how the structure of speech itself is able to shape the experience and thought of individuals (Bernstein, 1961, pp. 288–314). In his later writings he has called this distinction that between a *restricted* and an *elaborated* code (Bernstein, 1965, pp. 144–68). His distinction can be used to point to the quite considerable differences in the vocabulary and syntax of the language typically spoken by members of the middle classes and by members of the lower working classes. Lower working-class people typically speak a public language, that is one that is grammatically simple, often contains unfinished sentences, poor syntactical form and little use of impersonal forms such as 'one'. This is quite different from the dominant speech mode of the middle classes, the formal language (although middle-class people do use public language in some contexts such as, for example, in relationship with intimates). Formal language has a much more elaborate grammatical and syntactical form, employs a more extensive vocabulary, etc. The import of these two speech forms is this: the working-class person is less able to express his own particular response to situations (because he draws upon the standardized sayings of his community, e.g., proverbs, quite heavily) and to express fine and nuanced discriminations between things, feelings, relationships and so on (because he has a restricted vocabulary), than is the middle-class person who is able to make explicit the details and variations of his own personal experience.

Teachers are usually from middle-class homes and consequently communicate with their pupils through formal language using elaborate speech-forms. The working-class child is usually unfamiliar with such language, bringing patterns of speech to school that are unsuited to the educational process. Irrespective of his alertness or creativity, he starts school with the handicap of having to learn new speech patterns. His own speech patterns are likely to cause problems with his teachers, for the public language does not allow of subtle verbal discriminations that convey a sense of social nicety or distinction. Its use to a teacher, though implying no disrespect, may appear disrespectful to ears used to the discriminations of the formal language. 'Give us this' for example, is the public language equivalent of 'Please may I have that because . . .', yet it falls quite differently on ears attuned to the formal language.

In these last examples, it is apparent that the *interaction* of social background and the educational system is likely to produce social biases in the educational process. Education is staffed and controlled by people who through background or training are socialized into middle-class values and speech patterns. This is itself an implicit bias in the system. The organization of education can increase this bias. Consider: an aim of British education is to train children as highly as their potential allows; this is achieved by competitive examinations that sort children into different schools and into different streams within those schools; to stimulate achievement, rewards are given for successful performance and sanctions for unsuccessful performance. British education has thus tended to be organized in a way that stresses individual competition and the stratification of children by degrees of success and failure. The values implicit in this structure are in closer accord with the values stressed in middle-class homes than they are in working-class homes. Individuality and competition, for example, are values that smack strongly of the dominant entrepreneurial middle classes of the nineteenth and twentieth centuries.

The general point to be remembered here is that the organization of education is never value or culture free. Any system of organization has a system of implicit values and priorities, and we must discover these if we are to judge the social biases present in education. A good example is the statement of a distinguished historian as he surveys the evolution of university education in Britain in the late nineteenth century:

Then in 1884 was born the first of the more modern English provincial universities, the Victoria University. . . . Hitherto they had utilized the examinations of London University; now they had an examining and degree-giving authority of their own. Fortunately the new body did not yield to the temptation to make its degrees too easy, but set a courageous example, which benefited the whole subsequent development of the provincial universities (Ensor, 1960, p. 148).

There is a whole world of value judgements and biases implicit in this quotation. The provincial universities chose to model their degree and standards on Oxbridge. In so doing they forewent other possible forms of educational organization, other possible relations with their community. It is an open question, for example, whether more working-class students would have been educated, and to a higher standard, had the provincial universities been more attuned to the courses and degrees suited to their local communities.

We can now conceive of the educational process as more than the gradual and cumulative learning of skills and values. It is also an organized confrontation between children holding a certain set of expectations and teachers and school administrators who hold another set of expectations. The performance of a child is likely to be affected by the congruence between his expectations and that of the school, and by his relative success in learning the values implicit in the school organization. The relations that a child develops with fellow students or teachers give him a position within the over-all school organization that becomes a further determinant of how he learns.

Social background is relevant to this analysis because it is an initial and continuing source of orientation that disposes a child to enter into certain patterns of association, or to have certain reactions to the school. Social background is not the only factor, however. The relationships a child enters into in a school can be an additional factor in his behaviour. Consider Colin Lacey's description of the effect of school class organization on the learning of two boys in a Northern grammar school:

On another occasion, Priestley was asked to read and the whole class groaned and laughed. He grinned apprehensively, wiped his face with a huge white handkerchief and started to read very nervously. For a few moments, the class was absolutely quiet, then one boy tittered. Priestley made a silly mistake, partly because he was looking up to smile at the boy who was giggling, and the whole class burst into laughter. . . . Finally, the master with obvious annoyance snapped 'All right, Priestley, that's enough!'

This short incident, one of several during the day, served to remind Priestley of his structural position within the class and to confirm the opinions and expectations of the class and teacher towards him. . . .

During this period of observation, I also noticed the significance of the behaviour of another boy, Cready. Cready . . . although his form position was similar to Priestley's (twenty-sixth) habitually associated with a strikingly different group. . . . Cready was a member of the school choir . . . members of the school choir sat in the row next to the piano and [the English master's desk]. . . .

During the first three lessons I observed, Cready answered four of the questions put to the class. If Cready got an answer wrong he was never laughed at. . . .

[Priestley] compensated for his failure in class and lack of academic success by learning the stocks and shares table of the *Financial Times* every week. This enabled him to develop a reputation in a field outside the sphere in which the school was competent to judge. . . . Even this did not improve his standing in the school, especially with the staff. . . .

Cready and Priestley do not . . . conform with the established correlation between academic achievement and social class. Cready, a working-class boy from a large family on a council estate, is making good, while Priestley, an upper-middle class boy from a smaller family, is failing academically. However, this negative case highlights the point I want to make; there was a measure of autonomy in the system of social relations of the classroom. The positions of Cready and Priestley are only explicable in the light of an analysis of the system of social relations *inside* the classroom . . . Cready who had all the major external factors stacked against him, was able to use the system of social relations to sustain and buoy himself up, while Priestley, despite all the advantages that he brought to the situation, had fallen foul of the system and was not only failing but also speedily losing any motivation to succeed in the sphere in which the school was competent to judge him (Lacey, 1966, pp. 245–62).

This excerpt allows us to grasp, more adequately, the implications of the social system of education for the process of learning. Children develop a set of relations among themselves and with teachers within the context of the organization of the school. Contributing factors to the way these relations develop are: the division of the school into classes, extracurricular activities in the school, the grading of pupils between classes and within classes, the attitudes of teachers, the values emphasized by headmaster and teachers, and the social background of pupils. These factors interact and place every pupil in a set of social relations that give him a particular position in the school. This position may encourage a child to succeed according to the goals of the school. This position may also contribute to a child's failure.

Lacey describes the formation of an 'anti-school culture' in his Northern grammar school. This culture develops among a group of boys and becomes stronger with longer stay at the school. The anti-school culture develops among those boys who have fallen foul of the official system. Some came from working-class backgrounds and were always uneasy at the grammar school. Others found it difficult to achieve academically or show required skills and drifted into relations with other 'outcasts'. The process had the characteristics of a self-fulfilling prophecy. Teachers reacted against boys whom they regarded as deviating from the academic or social norms of the school. These boys formed strong relations among themselves and their group became a visible body of deviants that incurred the further wrath of teachers and 'good' pupils. The boys in the anti-school culture were so often identified as the 'bad actors' that they came to believe it and live up to their role, confirming teachers and other pupils in their attitude to them. Lacey shows that in this process academic and social criteria of behaviour become confused. The child that is seen as behaving badly is also assumed to be stupid, and masters quite unconsciously prejudice any examination or written work done by 'bad' pupils.

Any educational organization that ranks and differentiates students is likely to produce the phenomenon of the 'self-fulfilling prophecy'. In a class, for example, there will be a top, middle and bottom. Irrespective of their intelligence relative to children in other classes or other schools, children at the bottom are likely to be treated by other pupils and teachers as 'slow' or 'stupid' and over time these pupils come to believe this. The bottom form of one grammar school may have performed better at the eleven plus than the top form of a less prestigeful grammar school. Yet, this bottom form is likely to be regarded within the social system of its own school as not performing to the norms of the school. Soon the form is regarded as full of deviants, discipline problems, unmotivated children. At the end of their school career, these pupils will probably have come to accept the position they are assigned. They are likely to drop out of school early and certainly will do less well in the Ordinary Level examination than pupils from the top stream of the less prestigious school.

These effects are not confined to primary and secondary schools, but also influence performance in higher education. Universities and colleges are organizations that confront students with administrative requirements and a patterned sequence of learning. As Merton demonstrates in *The Student Physician* the ordering of how a student learns can have an impact on what he learns that is independent of the content of his curriculum: the particular sequence of courses a student takes, the stage at which he is exposed to practical experience, the prestige that institutions give to different features of the field, are all factors that are systematically related to the professional attitudes and skills that a trained physician develops. Other sociologists have emphasized the role that residence versus non-residence, examination uncertainty and college goals pay in developing distinctive orientations among students (Becker, 1963). Educating higher percentages of an age-group in colleges and universities has involved large increases in the size of colleges and universities – universities of 30,000 students are common throughout the world. The task of co-ordinating such numbers through a choice of subjects for the attainment of a specialized qualification requires a large bureaucratic apparatus making extensive use of anonymous means of recording, handling and teaching students. Problems of size and impersonality thus add to the difficulties of a student's career in higher education and become an important component in the analysis of the intended and unintended consequences of higher education. In this situation, since teaching is an activity that is not visible to those outside the classroom, and brings little general prestige, the teacher in higher education often finds that he obtains more material and intellectual rewards from research. Research and the publications that follow from it are visible nationally and internationally and provide an available index by which to judge performance and allocate rewards. The consequences of these factors in the expansion of higher education is a growing distance between students, staff and administration.

The social system effects of education are broader than those we have so far considered. Education is a linked system of primary, secondary and higher educational institutions. Each stage bears a definite relation to the next and a child's progress is highly determined by the point at which he starts on this ladder. We have already seen that the path to university is disproportionately through grammar and public schools. Not to enter these around the age of eleven is to forgo the opportunity of higher education. It is not so often realized that primary school is also important. In any city it is often remarked that certain primary schools are more successful in sending their children to grammar schools than others. Parents talk about sending a child to one primary school rather than another. 'Don't send Johnny there, that school never does well. Mill Lane always gets good eleven plus results.' Even in the United States where there is no eleven plus examination, parents often show an equal concern that their child should go to a certain primary school.

We can call the difference among primary schools an 'ecological effect'. This means that the characteristics of a neighbourhood are reflected in a school, and in a way that exaggerates the effect of a child's social background. A primary school in a middle-class neighbourhood draws middle-class children who, as we have seen, have speech and behaviour patterns readily adaptable to the educational process. Teachers are likely to find such a school relatively pleasant to teach in and teachers stay several years in such a school. The equipment and buildings of the school are well looked after. An environment is created in which everything conduces to children learning rapidly and easily. Contrast a school in a working-class area. The children who come to the school are not used to the values and speech patterns of a formal learning environment. They are also unused to the discipline requirements of formal learning. An environment is created in which difficulties are accumulated. Teachers do not find the school rewarding to teach in and leave quickly, so that there is a constant turnover in the teaching staff. Instead of children reinforcing each other's desire to learn as in an academically orientated middle-class school, they reinforce each other's desire not to learn. This is what is meant when we talk of a school exaggerating the effect of a child's social background. A middle-class child performs worse than the 'average' middle-class child when he is in a working-class school and a working-class child performs better than the 'average' working-class child when he is in a middle-class school.

This 'ecological effect' is a serious factor in the educational process because the spatial patterns of towns and cities emphasize the spatial segregation of social groups. Urban areas are relatively socially homogeneous. There are working-class areas, middle-class areas and so on. A neighbourhood school is thus likely to be a school drawing from one social class.

These ecological factors are also more serious for working-class children than they are for middle-class children, because the two social groups show very different awareness of how to manipulate the system. A middle-class parent is usually aware of the relative advantages and disadvantages of various schools. This is not the case for working-class parents. The inequalities that can accrue from the different levels of information about education is illustrated by the comparison Jackson and Marsden make between a middle-class parent and a working-class parent choosing their child's school.

Middle-class parent

When they chose a primary school they chose with care. They chose one which not only promised well for a grammar school place, but pointed firmly in the direction of college or university.

This turned out to be quite a feasible forecast. . . . Of these ten sons and daughters [of middle-class parents], nine were placed in what our calculations show to be Marburton's leading primary schools for long term results.

Working-class parent

. . . Their reasons for preferring one [school] rather than the other were warm and child-centered, but extraordinarily short-term. Mrs Black chose in this way for her little girl: 'Yes, there *were* two schools in Broadbank but we didn't know much about them. Well, there were some children passing on the road and I said, "Which school do you go to?" and they told me the Church School. So I told our Doreen, "Those children go to the Church School. Would you like to go to that school?"' (Jackson and Marsden, 1962, pp. 28, 84).

Parental lack of information can be a handicap to a child's educational progress throughout his educational career. The different capacities that different social groups show in manipulating the educational process is thus a further source for social bias in that process.

We are now in a better position to estimate the differences that comprehensive schools will make to education in Britain. The comprehensive school breaks from the tripartite system of secondary education by recruiting all children from its neighbourhood. Within a comprehensive school the range of curricula are provided – vocational, technical and academic. Ideally, each child can choose the curriculum that best suits his interests and development. The choice is not forced at the age of eleven. Also, children of different academic interests and capacities mix throughout the school which *ideally* promotes social integration. Comprehensive schools are usually larger units than the separate schools of the tripartite system. They can thus make *economies of scale*. This means that they can afford to provide more specialized teachers and equipment. The potential advantages of comprehensive schools are thus economic, social and academic. It is claimed that more children can be educated to a higher standard than was possible in the tripartite system.

In assessing the reality of these claims, it is useful to remember that comprehensive education is not a novel British invention. It is, for example, the prevalent form of education in the United States. Consequently there is comparative experience to help our assessment.

One major problem that a comprehensive school faces is that it is a neighbourhood school and is subject to the advantages and disadvantages of the ecological effect we discussed earlier. In the United States, secondary schools are often socially segregated. Schools in Black ghetto areas are not likely to send any child on to higher education.

In contrast, a school in a rich suburb may send as much as 90 per cent of its students to higher education. Indeed there is little evidence that comprehensive education in the United States encouraged more upward social mobility than did the tripartite system in Britain. Manipulation of boundaries, free bus travel for children and the special provision of extra funds are ways that can reduce the impact of ecology on the educational process.

A comprehensive school is a large organization and is liable to those problems discussed with regard to the social system of the school. A comprehensive school may differentially reward and stratify pupils and stimulate the formation of anti-school cultures. Children may be as isolated or as prone to join the 'wrong' groups as in a grammar school. Some comprehensive schools, for example, have introduced as many as twenty streams in a year – a very fruitful field for the emergence of cliques and cultures.

Also comprehensive education does nothing to alter the inequalities arising from the different speech patterns and orientations that pupils bring from their homes. It does not alter the difference in access to information possessed by different social groups.

The chief advantage of the comprehensive school is that it is *potentially* a more flexible instrument of education. It does not fore-close the possibilities of education at an early age. Late-developers can have their chance late in their school career. Children do not feel that they belong to an institution that already marks them out as failures or points them in one fixed direction. It can promote social integration by mixing talents and backgrounds – even where this is limited by ecology. Clubs and sport, for example, are areas where children of different backgrounds and futures meet. There is some evidence that comprehensive education is successful in encouraging children to go on to higher education. The percentage of children successfully taking 'O' Level certificates is higher for comprehensive schools than for the schools in the tripartite system that they have replaced. This finding partly reflects improved standards over time. In the United States a very much higher percentage of children go on to higher education than is the case here. This remains true even when we compare *equivalent* higher educational institutions.

We should remember that this discussion must ultimately be referred to the priorities we and our society have for education. It is a value, for example, to want more children to go on to higher educa-tion. Other people may reject this value in favour of educating a few to a high degree of intellectual and social sophistication. The view taken here is that both mass education and 'high standards' are possible and best achieved when the social biases in education are understood and remedied.

To conclude, education has a certain autonomy from other parts of society. This allows educators to instil skills and values different from those emphasized by family or government. Education is, however, permeated by influences from family and community. It is highly susceptible to pressures from the dominant social groups in society. Education thus preserves, and often increases, social biases present in society. The organization of education, particularly by schools, classes and streams, presents further opportunities for non-educational factors to enter the educational process. The social relations a student enters into at school or university affect his success or failure. The tendency of educational organizations to stratify their pupils acts as a 'self-fulfilling prophecy' encouraging pupils to conform to the role into which they are cast by teachers and fellow-pupils. The location of education in schools in socially homogeneous neighbourhoods produces an ecological effect which is an additional factor strengthening the effect of social background. The differential ability of social groups to manipulate the advantages and disadvantages of educational organizations reinforces the other sources of social bias in education. Innovations in education such as the comprehensive school are limited in their effect by these social biases, despite the greater flexibility they offer for educating students of different backgrounds and abilities.

Education and Social Development

The role of education as an agent of social development is limited by the fact that education is an organization permeated by the social biases of society. The subjects of education are social actors who retain the orientations of their particular position in society. Education is an important channel to the social and economic rewards of society. It is essential to the economy, and it is a large-scale and highly visible organization. For these reasons education is controlled by the dominant groups of society so as to meet their definition of society's priorities. Education is an independent factor in society to the extent that its organizational forms provide some buffer from direct outside control and to the extent that the effect of education cannot be planned or anticipated – the unanticipated consequences of educational organization.

The possible ways of conceiving of the relation of education and development are these: that education *reflects* society, and educational change follows social change; that education *conditions* development, but is itself a product of prior social and economic changes in society; that education is an independent factor in social and economic development producing intended and unintended consequences and conflicts of values and goals. Naturally these 'models' of the relation between education and development are not mutually exclusive. It is possible for education to partake of some characteristics of each at different historical periods or in different parts of the educational system. In previous sections we have noted examples of education conforming to each of the models. It was argued that the tripartite secondary school system was a reflection of the evolution of British social stratification. The tripartite system did educate more people to higher levels of education than before, and this conditioned further social and economic changes – greater social mobility, more skilled manpower for technologically based industry. The comprehensive school system is a planned educational innovation intended to produce social and economic development by encouraging social integration and a more highly educated labour force and electorate.

From our discussion we can draw some conclusions about the role of education in development. Education can be planned to produce social change. We know, for example, that literacy does stimulate economic and social development and large-scale literacy programmes are important tools in the development of many countries. Yet, education is permeated by the existing social structure which limits the extent of planned change and often produces consequences unintended by the educational planners. We have seen many examples of how the British social class system intrudes in all the attempts at educational innovation of the last hundred years.

The point to draw from this is that educational innovation is more likely to produce a desired change if innovation in education is co-ordinated with changing other parts of the social structure. This is to say that effective planning cannot be piecemeal. An illustration of what this implies is given by current attempts to improve elementary education in many developing countries. Often improvements in elementary education are carried out by increasing facilities, the numbers of teachers and offering financial incentives to families. The intention is to effect a planned change in educational standards which has positive consequences for social and economic development. The planned educational change is not usually co-ordinated with changing the social context that has depressed educational standards. In most developing countries, there is an enormous, unsatisfied demand for education because it is perceived as the gateway to an improved social position. The outcome is, sometimes, the over-production of people with skills – usually only simple literacy – for whom there are too few jobs available. In its turn, the fact that there are few opportunities in many of these societies for occupational and social mobility through education becomes a depressant on the desire of poor people to obtain education. Because the poor have for so long been outside the decision-making process in their countries they do not feel part of their society. They are not likely to value goals of development that have never brought them any benefits. Consequently, parents are not motivated to stimulate their children to continue with education. The children do not see any real material benefits that education brings. Irrespective of the educational facilities provided, these are likely, in this context, to be underused and be highly inefficient in educating people. Educational change in these countries thus cannot effectively proceed without changing other aspects of their social structure.

Where education is a *condition* of social and economic change it is more likely to produce intended consequences. This happens because educational change is following other changes in society; the social context is thus favourable to particular change. For example, we can expect educational reforms designed to raise educational standards among low-income people to be more successful in Cuba than in Guatemala. In the one country, educational change follows social and economic changes favourable to the increased participation of low-income people in the national society. In the other country, educational change proceeds without social or economic change and within a society whose structure is not favourable to low-income group participation.

We must remember that even when the above warnings are taken into account the best laid educational plans of men are likely to go astray. Unintended consequences are always present because we cannot precisely estimate the relation between each component of change. The study of unintended consequences is thus an important and continuing part of a sociologist's contribution to understanding and planning social change. This is not to say that unintended consequences are necessarily 'bad' things for social and economic development. It depends on your values. Consider this example: literacy in Guatemala is primarily intended to increase economic productivity by providing workers able to handle sophisticated machinery; literacy has the consequence unintended by the planners of allowing more and more people to read the mass media and political literature. Thus literacy increases political awareness among poor people and makes forms of organization, hitherto impossible among them, possible. Consumer and producer's co-operatives are examples of organizations that depend on the literacy of their membership. These changes introduce wider political changes with the increasingly organized participation of poor people in national politics. The ultimate sequence may be a change in the economic structure of the country in directions totally unintended by the original planners, and perhaps totally unacceptable to them.

The contribution of education to development is thus dynamic and multi-faceted. Educational systems, partly because they are organized, are able to secure some of their intended aims – even when these conflict with the aims of those who control society. Given the length and the complexity of the educational process, it is impossible for outside authorities to exercise a sufficiently detailed control to prevent completely the diffusion of 'undesirable' ideas or information. Further, the length of an individual's exposure to education and the centrality of educational qualifications for jobs in modern society makes education a crucial sector for bringing about planned social change. Also, the unintended consequences and conflicts that arise in the educational process are important and unplanned sources of change in all societies. At the most basic level, allowing large numbers of people the time to think and to read with relative freedom from the constraints of job, family or government, ensures a constant critical re-examination of society.

Chapter 5
Work, Industry and Organizations

In our own society, the term 'work' would seem to have a perfectly unambiguous meaning. It refers to a specialized undertaking, clearly marked off from other activities in time and space. Work is an activity which takes place in an office, a marketplace or a factory – somewhere separate from the home. Secondly, it occurs during periods of time – 'nine to five,' the 'evening shift' and so on – which are likewise segregated from other periods of time.

Yet, while the meaning of this word would appear at first glance to be perfectly clear, there are, in fact, certain problems and contradictions in the way we use it. Thus a person expending considerable physical energy in his garden, or in re-decorating the front room, is not normally considered to be 'working'. In official statistics, housework is not normally regarded as 'work' although the activities of the housewife may be more exhausting that those of her husband. In our society, too, an artist or an athlete may think of themselves as 'working', while carrying out activities which others think of as 'leisure-time' activities. (The problem of defining an 'amateur' or a 'professional' in sport is an indication of this kind of ambiguity.) Though it is possible to make money from 'hobbies' pursued at home, in this chapter we are concerned with work which takes place at particular times in particular places for the purpose of gaining income.

Clearly, work is not the same thing as physical effort or the expenditure of energy. What is and what is not work is *socially* defined; it is not a quality inherent in any particular act. It is true that without the achievement of a certain level of production, society could not survive. But society *can* survive without everybody necessarily working – there are the 'leisure classes'. Yet more often than not, even the leisure classes do some kind of work. Though there are international playboys who live off unearned income, the average denizen of playboy haunts is more likely to be an executive – a manager or a director. Thus even those who are able to live without work commonly do work, because work gives them a valued status in society in other people's eyes, and therefore in their own eyes.

To say that work is a fundamental necessity in human life, then, means much more than saying that society depends upon the production of food, machines, newsprint, etc. As individuals, too, most men need to work in order to satisfy their material needs – in order to eat – but, they also normally need to work in order to satisfy their social and psychological needs – to meet certain obligations, to be seen as significant people, and to feel significant to themselves. Much work, however, is far removed from food-production, or even from direct production of commodities at all. With the growth of service industries in the modern economy, fewer and fewer people work at producing material objects and more and more work at manipulating paper and people.

The difficulty in defining 'work' is further complicated by the fact that the concept of work is invested with varying degrees and kinds of *moral* evaluation. Thus the attitude to work emphasized by Calvinism sees work as a moral as well as an economic necessity. 'Idleness', and its many synonyms, are not merely neutral terms describing the state of non-working, but are in fact also redolent with moral disapproval. Marxists, who, at one level, stress that work is the basis of social life, a co-operative and creative activity that lifts man above the animals, at the same time point out that, in class societies, men work not only *with*, but also *for* other human beings. As a result, work comes to imply exploitation. Secondly, the social division of labour involves most workers in performing only highly-specialized operations. Their work-life thus appears to be controlled by impersonal forces – by money or by machines, by 'technological changes' – because they rarely encounter the people who make the crucial decisions that structure their lives. Thus they feel themselves to be cogs in a complicated machine, performing unsatisfying tasks – like Charlie Chaplin's assembly-belt worker in *Modern Times* – which satisfy their need for income, but not the 'whole man'. The idealized case of the artist who lives for his painting, but starves in a garret, is the opposite situation. He derives his widest satisfactions *from* his work;

whereas for the 'worker' work is merely instrumental, a means of acquiring the resources with which he can satisfy his 'real' needs *outside* work, in his leisure-time or with his family. Yet the worker may define the artist as a parasite, because what he produces is not the basic commodities – food, clothes, etc. – which *all* need some minimum of in order to survive. What constitutes a minimum, however, is always culturally-defined: degrading poverty in Britain would be abundant riches to the poor of Calcutta.

Certain *kinds* of work are thus valued differently by different people. Within a single society there is no general agreement as to what constitutes 'real' work and who are the 'real' workers. Some kinds of work are regarded as more 'fulfilling' or more dignified. Thus the terms 'vocation', 'career' or 'profession', all carry slightly more elevated connotations than the monosyllabic 'job', and a certain distaste for 'mere physical toil' is implied when such distinctions are made. This particular distinction partly reflects a long-established, largely upper-class bias. But it probably derives, equally, from a plebian resentment of obligatory back-breaking labour. Such a low regard for physical labour is not found universally throughout society, even amongst those who have to perform it: what have been called the 'upside-downers' regard *manual* labour as 'real' or 'true' work (Young and Willmott, 1957b). Something of this sentiment is conveyed in the popular image of clerical workers: 'Those chaps who sit on their you-know-whats in offices and push pens' (Lockwood, 1958, p. 12).

But whether we look at work in the materially 'necessary' sense or in the moral-evaluative sense – work is a central focus in society.

Social Consumption

The fundamental necessity of producing enough for sustenance and protection cannot explain how there has arisen an extraordinary variety of patterns of production, distribution and consumption found throughout history and throughout the contemporary world. In other words, society is not merely the *result* of economic or biological 'needs'; it is also, in a sense, the *cause* of these 'needs'. In fact, apart from the minimum level of calories needed to sustain life at all, the rest of what we strive to produce and consume is not required to meet biological 'needs' at all; they are culturally determined 'wants'. Economists go further and distinguish both wants and needs from 'demands', which are wants backed up by the ability to pay in cash or in kind for the things we desire. Thus I need food, I want salmon, and I demand kippers. Salmon here, is not simply wanted because of its nutritional content, but also because it symbolizes a particular status and style of life.

Even in the simplest societies, men prize material goods because of these wider social connotations. The Bushmen or the Australian aborigines, always on the edge of hunger, nevertheless produce and consume in order to satisfy their religious wants as well as their stomachs, and exchange food – even go hungry – in order to meet religious or kinship obligations. Richer societies work hard over-producing food they do not eat at all, but destroy or simply display it so as to enhance their social reputations. An example of this is the 'potlatch', a system of competitive feasting which took place among the Indians of British Columbia. These feasts involved the destruction of food, canoes and other forms of valuable property as rival tried to outdo rival in competitive display so as to enhance his prestige. Malinowski, in his study of the Trobriand Islanders provides another example:

In gardening, for instance, the natives produce much more than they actually require, and in any average year they harvest perhaps twice as much as they can eat. ... Again, they produce this surplus in a manner which entails much more work than is strictly necessary for obtaining the crops. Much time and labour is given up to aesthetic purposes, to making the gardens tidy, clean, cleared of all debris ... [this is] clearly perceptible in the various tasks which they carry out entirely for the sake of ornament-ation, in connexion with magical ceremonies and in obedience to tribal usage. Thus, after the ground has been scrupulously cleared and is ready for planting, the natives divide each garden plot into small squares, each a few yards in length and width, and this is done only in obedience to usage, in order to make the gardens look neat (Malinowski, 1922, pp. 58–9).

We see in this illustration that the Trobrianders produce more than they need in a strictly biological sense; that the work they put into this process of production is more than would seem to be technically necessary; and that work has a meaning in terms of criteria other than the satisfaction of material needs. Many of these kinds of consideration also apply in our own society. The display of wealth, rather than its consumption, is not an unfamiliar notion in a society where 'status symbols', 'conspicuous consumption' and 'keeping up with the Joneses' are household phrases. To attend a dinner may serve to satisfy a person's hunger, but it may also have implications for his business or professional interests. Furthermore, to be invited to a meal places the guests under certain obligations in terms of values of reciprocity and exchange. In short, we must see the economist's conception of 'utility' as something which involves social, psychological, religious and political as well as material or economic dimensions.

Social Production

The process of producing materially-necessary and culturally-valued items is a collective undertaking, involving patterns of co-operation between men, and of interaction between men and nature. Relations of co-operation, involving specialization of complementary tasks, are familiar to us from the discussions by classical economists of the 'division of labour'. This approach is vividly illustrated in a celebrated passage by Adam Smith, in 1776, where he is describing the process of pin manufacture:

But in the way in which this business is now carried on, not only the whole work is a peculiar trade, but it is divided into a number of branches, of which the greater part are likewise peculiar trades. One man draws out the wire; another straights it; a third cuts it; a fourth points it; a fifth grinds it at the top for receiving the head; to make the head requires two or three distinct operations; to put it on is a peculiar business; to whiten the pins is another; it is even a trade by itself to put them into the paper; and the important business of making a pin is, in this manner, divided into about eighteen distinct operations, which in some manufactories, are all performed by distinct hands, though in others the same man will sometimes perform two or three of them (Smith, 1950, p. 3).

Smith describes the way in which this division of labour enhances efficiency. He omits, however, some other divisions which are of great interest to the sociologist. For example, there is the division between the owner of the pin-making enterprise and those who work for him: in short, *class* divisions. Also we have the fact that the worker (and indeed the owner) in the pin factory will often be working to support a family at home; there is also a domestic division of labour.

While such production relationships may be formally separate from other kinds of relationships, in practice it is often very difficult to draw the line between the two. In a farming community, for example, the same people may sit around the dinner table and work in the fields together. Or consider another situation, one far removed from Adam Smith's pin manufacturers. Among the Ndembu of Zambia there are clear divisions of labour between the sexes. Planting is regarded as women's work, while tree felling and clearing are regarded as men's work. Hunting is again seen as being essentially a masculine activity, and there is a clear association between hunting and concepts of social status and masculinity (Turner, 1957, pp. 21–3, 25–8).

There are clearly many differences between the Ndembu situation and the one described by Adam Smith. In the first place, Adam Smith is just describing a segment of his workers' lives. We know nothing about their relationships with their kin, with their neighbours or with their wives. This is not the case in the Ndembu situation. Here, in describing the division of labour, one is describing much of the structure of society as a whole. The people one associates with in the process of production are not just fellow workers; they are also kin. Secondly, in the pin-making situation, it would appear to be irrelevant who actually performs the tasks. Male or female, Black or White, old or young: these distinctions are *formally* unimportant in this situation. What does matter is whether the individual is good at the task. Such distinctions are, however, important in the Ndembu case. While a female might prove to be just as skilled at hunting as her husband, this fact will not permit her to take part in the hunt. Sociologists have elaborated this distinction by distinguishing between *ascribed* and *achieved* statuses. In the case of the Ndembu we are emphasizing ascribed status, that is the positions one is born into, or which one occupies by the fact of the possession of certain inescapable characteristics such as being of a certain age, sex or colour, so that people expect and often require a woman, an elder, a teenager, to behave in certain ways. In the case of Smith's pin workers, however, we are stressing achieved statuses, which one acquires through one's own efforts, for example, through one's technical skill, ability or cunning. This is not, of course, to argue that ascribed characteristics are unimportant in the occupational structure of modern society; the kind of work a person may do is often influenced by considerations such as sex or ethnicity.

What needs to be stressed at this stage is, firstly, that the necessity to work, that is, to apply human labour to physical resources in the production of goods, involves a variety of social relationships. Moreover, these relationships are not merely determined by what is technically more efficient or appropriate for the particular task at hand, but they also involve relationships of control and power. To argue that men must co-operate in order to produce does not necessarily mean that such co-operation will be harmonious or conflict-free. As will be argued in the second half of this chapter, men go to work for utilitarian purposes. Within the industrial enterprise, however, employers exercise control over their employees in a variety of ways: sometimes through direct disciplinary procedures, sometimes through the system of payment and the use of machinery. There is considerable scope for conflict over the use of these controls and over what has been called 'the effort bargain', the diverging opinions as to what is the right relationship between rewards and effort (Baldamus, 1967, esp. pp. 34–7).

These relationships of conflict within the productive process have been sharpened in modern society with the growth of capitalism, the development of urban, industrial society and the growth of bureaucracy. As a result of all these processes, work relationships tend to become segregated from other relationships and tend also to be characterized by impersonality. This is also often the case in the sphere of consumption as well. Here, too, we see relationships mediated through the cash nexus, the use of the monetary medium of exchange. Our interaction with shop assistants, waitresses or bus conductors is often fleeting and impersonal. The price is determined in advance; there is no bargaining in terms of personal criteria, or such notions as 'fairness' or 'need'. It is, of course, possible to overstate this impersonality of modern life. Workers, particularly those in small workshops, still find scope to bargain on an individual basis with their manager, and the shop or pub on the corner still plays an important part in our social life. And even the largest factories may be less impersonal than is sometimes supposed.

Work in Industrial Society

We asserted above that work is 'central' in society and, by implication, that it remains of 'central' importance even in advanced industrial societies. Thus it may be held that work is central in that wage-labour is a central source of income and hence physical survival. Even this statement should, however, be subjected to closer examination. Less than half the population of the United Kingdom is classified as being 'gainfully employed'. Thus for every person at work there is slightly more than one further person dependent upon him. If we regard work as central in terms of the amount of time we spend at it, we find that, in 1962, the actual number of hours worked per week (including over-time) was on average 47·1 (Parker *et al.*, 1967, pp. 138–40). If we allow an average of eight hours sleep, less than half of the average worker's waking hours are actually spent at work. So that while we talk about work as a basic activity, in fact it involves less than half the popu-lation for less than half of their waking hours. The worker spends much of his time not in working but in eating, resting and sleeping at home, and a further amount of time at the pub, in church, at the cinema, or in a countless number of other leisure or domestic activities. Work is only a limited part of his waking life and workers are increasingly spending more of their waking lives in *non-work*.

Yet it is important to see work not merely in terms of time spent but also in terms of its meaning for the workers and the effect that this work has on other areas of life. While work may be activity that is physically and perhaps socially segregated from home and leisure activities it is not necessarily a separate undertaking in the individual worker's mind. In the first place, as we have seen, he will most likely go to work to support his family. Work may also affect his leisure activities, either directly in that he spends most of his leisure time with his fellow workers or, indirectly and negatively, in that he seeks to escape from his work in his leisure.

Work is crucial in that it is a source of income. But the work a person does is also important in other ways, notably in that it gives him identity and status within society as a whole. Thus, when we ask the question 'what is he?' the kind of answer we normally expect is a statement about the *work* that person does – 'he's an engineer' or 'he's a dentist'. Such words are not merely labels which inform us about the kind of technical function a person fulfils in society but they are also a major key to social placement and evaluation. That is why most studies of social stratification use occupation as their criterion of social class or status. People do in fact use occupation as a means of classifying or ranking people in the wider society although they use other criteria as well. Lockwood, for example, argues that the differences between 'white-collared' (or 'black-coated') workers and manual workers can be particularly attributed to the fact that these two different kinds of workers are treated differently *at work*. Clerical workers come in to work at different times, usually eat in separate canteens and use separate toilets and are often physically closer to management (Lockwood, 1958, ch. 3). Again Gouldner has shown how status differences between mine-workers and surface-workers in an American gypsum mine carried over into the community in which both groups lived (Gouldner, 1955, ch. 7). Thus a man's work may affect his social standing.

Yet, here again, the situation is not without its ambiguities. Many of the differentials of skill and occupation which are understood by one's fellow workers often have little meaning in the wider society. Indeed when we try to answer accurately the question 'what do you do?' our answer often gives rise to a polite but uncomprehending, 'how interesting!' In a mining community, by contrast, where everybody understands what the miner's work involves in terms of skill and danger, miners derive prestige and satisfaction from talking about their work with their mates and neighbours in the pub or working-men's club (Dennis *et al.*, 1956, p. 144). Such a close overlap of work and community does not often obtain however and a 'big man' at work may be somewhat smaller in his suburban house and garden.

We come now to the final way in which work might be said to be 'central': the way in which it gives the worker a sense of identity, not just in the eyes of others but in his own eyes. Work may be a source of satisfaction *to the individual* even where it is not necessarily recognized by others as 'important', 'valuable' or 'desirable'. Much of the discussion about 'alienation' concerns the extent to which modern industrial society reduces work to an unsatisfying chore, and thus destroys both the 'self-image' of the worker and his image in other people's eyes. That society may indeed even deny him work itself. The unemployed man loses not only income but self-respect and the respect of others. But even if a man has work it may be just a means to an end. In a sample of industrial workers in the United States, for example, Dubin found that three out of four workers did *not* regard their work and workplace as a 'central life interest'. Only 10 per cent of them thought of their work as the source of their most important relationships. Their friends were not normally fellow-workers (Dubin, 1956).

Clearly, the extent to which work is a source of satisfaction will vary according to the kind of occupation. Berger, for example, has suggested a threefold classification of work. Firstly, there are those jobs which still provide some kind of self-identification and satisfaction, for example, professional, craft or artistic occupations. Secondly, there are tasks which are almost the exact opposite – they are seen as a direct threat to a person's identity, reducing him to the status of 'an appendage to a machine'. Berger argues that these two extremes have declined in modern society, the first because working for large bureaucratic organizations results in a loss of personal freedom; conversely, many unpleasant and routine tasks have been eliminated in modern industry. Instead, a third kind of work, perceived as a 'grey neutral' region has grown up which is neither a direct threat to one's personal identity nor a major source of identity. Such jobs are neither very hateful nor very pleasurable (Berger, 1964, pp. 218–19).

The nature of the task being performed thus affects the attitude which the worker has to his work. But some jobs which, to the outside observer, look like boring routine tasks may be a source of satisfaction to the person performing them. Baldamus has developed the notion of 'traction' which may be roughly defined as the opposite of 'tedium'. He describes traction as: '. . . a feeling of being pulled along by the inertia inherent in a particular activity. The experience is pleasant and may therefore function as a relief from tedium' (Baldamus, 1967, p. 59). Traction, he argues, is akin to a sense of 'rhythm' which a person develops even in performing routine tasks.

Now workers may not necessarily expect to derive any intrinsic satisfaction from their work. It may be felt, for example, that continuous assembly-line production in automobile manufacturing is unsatisfying. Thus several American studies found that work which was 'machine-paced' – that is, dictated by the speed of the assembly-belt – was especially disliked. The fact that it is very often difficult for the workers to interact with each other during this may also be felt as a deprivation. But a more recent English study of car workers in Luton has questioned some of these studies, arguing that they paid too much attention to the influence of technology in shaping workers' attitudes and not enough attention to the attitudes and expectations which the workers brought into the factory in the first place (Goldthorpe *et al.*, 1967, pp. 178–86). The workers, it might be said, implicitly strike a bargain with the firm and say, in effect: 'we are prepared to accept these deprivations *in* and *at* work in exchange for high rewards *for* work.' This may help to explain 'labour unrest' in the highly paid motor industry, especially during periods of redundancy or uncertainty when these high rewards are being threatened. It is to be noted that many of the Luton workers *chose* to work in this car firm, often giving up more skilled, but lower-paid, jobs to this end. One of the conclusions of the Luton study is that, because these prior expectations are so important, the industrial sociologist cannot allow his investigations to stop at the factory gates, but he must also consider the influences that the family and the wider society bring to bear on the individual worker.

Pre-Industrial and Industrial Societies

We may perhaps understand the nature of work in industrial society a little more clearly if we contrast work in industrial society with work in pre-industrial society, a contrast we have already considered in examining social production. One main feature which is said to distinguish work in the two kinds of society is the degree of separation of work and non-work, particularly the separation of work and home. Thus, as we have seen, in industrial society work usually refers to 'gainful employment', thereby excluding the retired man tending his roses or the housewife removing stains from the kitchen sink. A man *goes* to work and *returns* home. For his work he receives a wage or a salary which supports himself and his family. Work and home represent two 'separate worlds'.

This is quite a different state of affairs from that in which people work with members of their family or their kin as in 'cottage industry'. Here, status within the family is closely related to the kinds of tasks performed; co-operation is typically carried out between members of the same kinship group and, consequently, there does not exist a sharp dividing-line between what is work and what is not work, between work and family, between work and leisure. There is also the intermediate situation of 'out-work' where there is a separation between work and non-work, but not a separation between home and work.

Yet there is not quite such a clear-cut line of demarcation between industrial and pre-industrial society. Even in contemporary Britain a worker may be influenced, and perhaps even assisted by his kin in selecting a particular place of employment. Ties of kinship are still important at some of the highest levels of business, finance and government, too, and the term 'family firm' still has some meaning in contemporary society (see Lupton and Wilson, 1959).

We have found therefore that non-economic relationships are important even in analysing people at work. It is often claimed that pre-industrial societies differ sharply, however, in another respect. It is held that a further distinguishing feature of industrial society is the presence of 'rationality'. We do not use this word in its popular sense as meaning 'sensible' behaviour. Rather rationality involves the calculated use of resources for the achievement of a particular goal or set of goals in the most economical way possible. In the light of this definition of rationality, we may speak of individuals behaving rationally when they pursue their goals with maximum efficiency and minimum cost. We can think of the performance of organizations in exactly the same way. Thus business firms carry out 'cost-benefit' analyses or 'O and M' studies. Not only business firms, however, but other kinds of institution in developed societies are said to operate according to 'rational' principles, and the type of institution which is based upon such principles is called, in modern sociology, the *organization*.

In pre-industrial societies, on the other hand, it is claimed that there is little rationality in this sense. These societies are characterized by the converse of *rational* action, *traditional* action, which lays the emphasis on what is handed down from the past, on what, it is believed, 'has always been'. The appropriate kind of institution here is not so much the organization as the *community* or the *primary group*. The concepts 'rational' and 'traditional' represent two extreme analytical categories: in any real situation there will always be a mixture of both elements. Thus highly rationally-organized bodies such as trade unions or co-operatives may appeal to the traditions of the working class and seemingly traditional institutions such as the Church of England will in fact contain strong elements of rationality. The Church is also a 'business' organization.

There is thus no one single pattern of rationality. Moreover, rationality is by no means confined to industrial societies or tradition to pre-industrial ones. Even in developed societies, there is little consensus about what constitutes rationality. Some economists may speak of the capitalist entrepreneur working out his best responses to the swings of the market as behaving rationally; others regard the question of the rationality of the individual or firm as subsidiary. They regard an unplanned market system as irrational, whatever the behaviour of the firms in that market. Thus communists regard capitalism as 'anarchy' and capitalists denounce Soviet-type planning as leading to bureaucratic rigidity and therefore 'non-rational' inefficiency.

Having considered the way in which and the extent to which work has become more of an isolated and specialized activity, and the growth of complex organizations within which work takes place, we must now look at a third aspect of work in modern society which is in part a consequence of these developments. This is the *alienation* of labour which we have already touched upon. The theme of alienation has had a long and controversial history in social science since it was introduced by Marx, although the ideas behind the concept can be traced back much earlier. The term 'alienation' literally means 'separated from' and refers, in the first place, to the position of the worker in his work-place and his relationship to his work. He is alienated from the means of production; typically the worker does not own the tools with which he works, or the capital which is employed in the production process. He is also separated from the product of his work. He produces not for himself but for a market. Furthermore, in many cases, he produces not a complete item but a small part of a finished product or perhaps he carries out a simple routine operation. These may be described as the objective features of alienation. Much discussion, however, extends to considering how far the objective features result in subjective feelings of deprivation or estrangement, a sense of a lack of wholeness, a sense of frustration or of a loss of humanity. It seems that men's lives and work are controlled by *things* – by money, by 'market forces', by technology. Alienation, therefore, is more than just a sense of boredom at work; it also refers to a lack of *power* on the part of the worker. It is held by many that the combination of these objective situations, together with the subjective feelings associated with these conditions, leads to certain reactions on the part of workers such as strikes, absenteeism, accidents, lateness and labour turnover.

It can be seen that this theme of alienation is linked to the two previously discussed features of industrial society, namely rationality and the separation of work and non-work. Rationality entails, among other things, the clear definition of the task to be performed, and the linking of that task to other tasks in the context of an organization so as to produce maximum predictability; in short, the clear specialization of tasks as described by Adam Smith. Rationality also demands that, within the context of the work organization, there be a single-minded attention to the task in hand, undiverted by any interests outside the work situation. The classical example here is the model of the government official, his task clearly defined by many paragraphs of printed regulations, and his position in an official hierarchy clearly determined, so that his attention is directed to his task irrespective of whether his clients are kin or friends, enemies or strangers, attractive or powerful: in short, he reacts towards all equally, without 'fear or favour'. That such a model rarely obtains even in contemporary industrial society does not detract from its very real and special power as a model of conduct.

This leads us to consider the connexion between alienation and the separation of home and work. Not only is it held to be non-rational for the two spheres to overlap but it is also felt that the two spheres represent two radically different kinds of relationship. Modern wage-labour is based upon the notion of a 'contract', in which one party – the employer – undertakes to reward the worker in the form of wages for the work he does. In strict theory, the worker and the employer have no other obligations towards one another. Management is not responsible, for example, for the worker's housing or other such matters that are not part of the work-situation. By contrast, the marriage 'contract', so-called, is in fact a very different kind of relationship. The mutual obligations of marriage are not strongly defined or simply economic. The partners undertake to 'love, honour and obey' and this involves sexual, economic, domestic and many other kinds of rights and obligations. In contrast to the bargain struck with the employer, the marriage contract does not specify the proportion of weekly earnings that a man should hand over to his wife on a Friday night. As Mark Antony remarks: 'There's beggary in the love that can be reckon'd.'

Thus we have the increase of rationality in industrial society together with the increasing separation of home and work; both these serve to sharpen the sense of alienation, which we argue is a third characteristic of industrial society. In the light of this kind of analysis, social critics looking at modern industry, whether they be traditionalists looking back to a past rural society or revolutionaries looking forward to an 'era of freedom', both see work in industrial society as lacking in 'wholeness', in that it is divorced from the totality of human life. 'Non-alienated' work, it is argued, should be seen as a reward in itself and not something which is performed just for the income it provides. Work ought also to satisfy a sense of craftsmanship or of achievement and give the individual a sense of contributing usefully to society. In short, it is argued that work ought to be, to a much larger extent, 'expressive' as well as 'instrumental'. It would be overstating the case to argue that the alienated/non-alienated distinction corresponds exactly with the industrial/pre-industrial distinction. Indeed it has been argued that the technology of advanced industrial society provides one of the preconditions for the reduction or elimination of alienation in that it can reduce the number of purely routine tasks that have to be performed.

It might be noted that there are two senses in which work can be expressive. The first stresses the rewards *in* work, the rewards to be gained from doing a job well or with some sense of individual fulfilment. The other refers to the rewards *at* work. This includes the sociable relationships which are formed at the workplace, and the social ties established in such different settings as the trade union branch or the canteen. It is clear that both these elements – the rewards in and at work – have their place in nearly all jobs, together with the instrumental aspect, the rewards *for* work. It has been argued, however, that we have an increasing emphasis on the last reward and a decreasing emphasis on the first two kinds.

We have now examined and qualified some of the contrasts commonly made between work in pre-industrial and industrial society. These contrasts have far-reaching implications. One, which we do not often think about because it is so much of our everyday life, is the very concept of 'time' itself, a concept which E. P. Thompson has argued has two very different implications (Thompson, 1967). One concept of time depends upon what Thompson calls 'task-orientation'. Time is reckoned by the regularity with which certain tasks are performed (milking, sowing, etc.) or by the expected *length* of time taken to carry out a particular task. He argues that this way of thinking about time reflects a social order in which people's lives are not sharply divided between work and the rest of their life, and also a way of life which was and is condemned by others as non-rational, wasteful and lacking in any sense of urgency. This sense of time is held to be characteristic of 'pre-industrial' society, although Thompson is reluctant to use the term. The other concept of time is 'clock time', symbolized in the work-situation by the clock-card and the time-keeper, and arising out of the problems of organizing large numbers of people under one roof whose labour has to be synchronized: 'Time is now currency; it is not *passed* but spent.' (ibid., p. 61).

Roles

We have seen that, even in industrial society, work is not a completely 'walled-off' activity segregated from other areas of life. Work is affected by many aspects outside the workplace, and non-work – leisure for example – is often affected by aspects of the work situation. Sociologists often express the fact that the worker is not only a worker, but that he also possesses certain other characteristics and is involved in many other sets of relationships by using the concept of *role*. As this is a key concept in much sociological writing it is worth paying some attention to it. Obviously a theatrical metaphor is being used here; many sociologists not only use the term 'role' but related theatrical terms as well: 'actors', 'playing their roles' to 'an audience'. As with most metaphors the point may be over-stretched; even so, let us remain in the theatre a little while longer. An actor plays a part which is usually written for him. The part exists independently of any particular actor and independently, too, of 'significant others':

people such as the author, the audience, other actors, the critics who have certain expectations as to how that part should be played, and all of whose expectations affect the actor playing the part.

At the same time, the actor is not totally constrained by these expectations. Firstly, as is well known, different actors interpret the same part in different ways; there is a certain latitude left to the individual actor. Secondly, the part may be played in a slightly different way to different audiences. Matinées of Christmas pantomimes may be less ribald than their evening performances, and some audiences may be faster at picking up jokes than others: the player will modify his behaviour in terms of the particular audiences. The player may also select some sub-set of his audiences for particular attention as the expression 'playing to the gallery' indicates. One final point about this theatrical metaphor is that one actor, if he is lucky, will play many parts. Thus he may play for the Royal Shakespeare Company, appear as a guest performer in a television series and have a lead in a horror film all in the same few weeks. (Actually, players in a game of football are in some ways more like social actors than players in the theatre, because theatrical actors are tied down by lines, whereas footballers are only controlled by very general 'rules of the game' and the moves of others.)

We can see that this extended theatrical metaphor does have wider sociological applications. A role exists in a particular social setting in relation to other roles. What the role entails is normatively defined either by some official statement such as an organization chart or a book of rules, or less formally in terms of tradition or custom. Various expectations surround the performance of a particular role, expectations which are held by others. It is important to note that we are dealing with relationships here; a role exists only in relation to other roles. Thus the role of father implies the role of child, the role of worker implies the role of employer, and the role of doctor implies the role of patient.

A person will play many such roles. Thus a machine-operator in a factory will be playing one role in relation to his foreman and his workmates but may also be a member of his union, of the Labour Party and of the Methodist Church. He will also be a husband, a father, a brother, a cousin and an uncle, a ratepayer, a taxpayer, a neighbour and a voter. At certain times of his life he will be a patient, a guest, a customer and a passenger. All his life he will be a male. Throughout the course of his life he will, as Shakespeare reminds us, play many parts which are entailed in the processes of maturation and ageing (these phases of life and the behaviour expected of people of different ages are culturally-defined: it is a *socio*-biological cycle). Some roles, again, are played together; some are clearly separated. Some are played in a sequence; some played once and for all; some fleetingly, and some over a period of years. Clearly, there is scope for conflict in this multiplicity of roles which any one individual is expected to play. In the strike situation, for example, the role of the family man may conflict with the role of the unionist. In being asked to go drinking in the working-men's clubs, his role as a Methodist may conflict with his role as a fellow-worker.

The various roles we have mentioned in this one example are not all of the same order, then. They differ, for example, in their degree of importance and pervasiveness, in the extent to which they enter all or a wide variety of situations. The role of woman, for example, is much more pervasive than the role of shop-steward. Various attempts have been made to classify these differences. Thus Linton has distinguished 'ascribed' from 'achieved' roles, a distinction we have already commented upon (1963, pp. 113–31). Banton has suggested that roles may be arranged on a kind of continuum from the most basic roles at one end (sex roles, for example) to the most specific at the other (occupational roles), through general roles in between these two extremes (1965, pp. 33–6).

A further distinction however, must be made. In the example we have given, we have seen that a man plays a multiplicity of roles. This situation of multiple roles must be distinguished from the situation which Merton describes as the 'role-set' (1957, pp. 368–84). In playing any one particular role, the actor is related to several different 'role-others'. These role-others may be individuals or they may be collections of individuals. Thus our machine-operator will enact that particular role in relation to specific role-others such as the machine-fitters, the foreman, the rate-fixer, his fellow machine-operators, and the shop-steward. There is thus potential conflict *within the role-set* just as there is potential conflict *between the different roles*. Thus the foreman may make demands upon a man which are incompatible with the demands made on him by his fellow-workers.

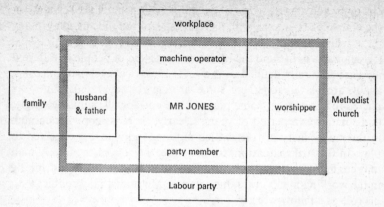

Figure 7a Multiple roles

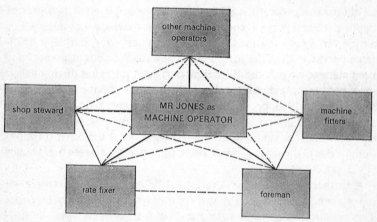

Figure 7b The role-set

This very brief account of some of the concepts used in role-analysis shows that here we have a useful set of tools which can be applied in the study of work-situations no less than in the study of any other social relations. Thus when a worker enters a particular work-situation he is confronted by several constraining expectations. Some of these constraints are built into the work-situation in that they are part of the formal expectations of management. Thus it is laid down, in the form of definite rules, that the worker is expected to work in a particular place and to do a particular job for a particular period of time. Now in much of the literature of industrial sociology, the term 'formal' tends to be used to refer to management's expectations only. The expectations of the workers and the ways in which these expectations are embodied in work-practices are, in contrast, termed 'informal'. Yet the workers' expectations can be equally 'formal' in that they are clearly defined and regularly institutionalized, seen to exist, and sometimes approved of even by management. 'Informal' norms – which we often call 'conventions' – are to be found at all levels of industry, not just amongst workers (e.g. executives use company cars and telephones for private purposes, even where this is not approved of by the company, and cover up for each other). Similarly, workers do have their own 'informal' conventions controlling how much is to be produced or how long tea-breaks should be, as well as 'formal' rules (e.g. trade union practices).

This analysis, so far, has been limited to the confines of the work-situation. These roles and the role-others connected to the roles are contained within the factory or work-situation. But other roles will overlap with this work-situation, thereby linking the work with other areas of life. Thus, for example, the work-situation will overlap with the domestic situation. One way in which this overlap can be examined is to look at these processes over a period of time, rather than at a single point in time. At first, the worker may be a single man with few outside responsibilities. He may be less tied to a particular job or locality. Later he will get married, so that his attitudes to the job will be affected not only by the kind of work that he does, but also by the fact that he now has a wife. (This kind of problem is particularly acute, for example, for working mothers or for professional couples.) Later, the man will become a father, and will acquire a house with concomitant mortgage or rent, and hire-purchase commitments. He may, as a result of these commitments, be further constrained to stay with a particular job and to accept the constraints of that situation, however irksome they might be, or he may try harder for promotion. Thus his particular life-situation is not merely a reflection of the work which he does but also the various commitments and responsibilities outside work. There is, in short, a dynamic interrelationship between the work situation and the home situation.

We may briefly illustrate the application of role-theory by taking a case-study. Our incident is imaginary but it is based upon the real-life situation analysed in a study of the American restaurant industry (Whyte, 1948).

We can take the apparently quite simple and personal situation in which a waitress burst into tears and, using the insight provided by this study, look at it in terms of the conflicts in which she finds herself at work. Firstly, work in a large restaurant entails a high degree of interdependence and co-ordination. There are many stages in the preparation of food, its cooking, the passing of orders to the kitchen, the sending of food to the dining room, the checking and running and waiting. Each person is under pressure, or is constrained by something or someone else. Equally he or she is in turn often able to put pressure on someone else. The customer demands food; the order is passed down to the kitchen. The chef is under two counter-pressures: the one demanding that he does not waste food by cooking too much in advance, the other demanding that the food be brought speedily to the customer's table. These kinds of pressures exist all along the line, and the waitress is caught between the demands of the customer and the pressures of the kitchen staff. In terms of role-theory different members of the role-set are making incompatible demands: the waitress is 'pulled both ways'.

Secondly, the changing rhythm and intensity of work at different times of the day are crucial characteristics of the work-process. These changes of pace clearly heighten the tensions we have described. The reader will find a vivid account of the hectic mealtime rush in Paris and London restaurants in Orwell's *Down and Out in Paris and London* or in Arnold Wesker's play *The Kitchen*.

Thirdly, Whyte devotes a lot of his book to the examination of the complicated system of status within the restaurant industry. Prestige accrues to the type of task (the role of chef as opposed to the dishwasher), the type of food attended to (asparagus as against potatoes), to sex, age, length of service, and many other factors. Yet one normally-recognized mark of status is the fact that one person is able to give orders to another. This can sometimes conflict with other dimensions of status in that a person who is of relatively low status (say a 'runner, who carries the orders from the dining room to the kitchen) is able to give orders to, or at least put pressure on, someone of higher status, namely the chef.

Status-considerations enter into the waitress' situation in several ways, and affect her relations with different sets of others deeply. Firstly, she is able – indeed required – to put pressure on the person at the service-counter, usually a man. In terms of the wider culture, it is not usual for a woman to give orders to a man and this fact alone may give rise to patterns of antagonism.

Consideration of status, built into the two associated roles, also affect the waitress in her relations with the customer. Here, too, there may be contradictory expectations. The master/servant type of relationship is said to be incompatible with the values of democracy, yet here is a situation which resembles the master/servant type relationship. There may be, especially for inexperienced waitresses, a certain amount of ambiguity here as to who is to take the initiative. Further, it is possible that, in a 'superior' restaurant (although these are more likely in fact to be staffed by male waiters), the waitress might feel that she herself is of a status which is higher than that of the customer, for even though the customer 'calls the tunc', the waitress 'borrows prestige' from her place of work and may 'patronize' a patron who is poorly-dressed.

Finally, one of the factors which often attracts girls towards becoming waitresses in the first place is a desire to 'work with people'. This is usually one of the characteristics of work of this kind which gives it higher status in some people's eyes, than, say, factory work. Yet the waitress – like the airline hostess – is likely to find that the 'working with people' aspect of her job is illusory, that the contacts are usually fleeting and sometimes heated, that the customers are highly demanding and just 'faces in a crowd'. There is a conflict, therefore, between the waitress's original expectations of her role and the actualities of role performance.

Thus all these pressures and cross-pressures, these conflicts and contradictions may build up to a 'flash-point' where the waitress bursts into tears. Of course, such an account cannot tell us precisely why one waitress bursts into tears (or one waiter snaps at a customer) rather than another, why it is Jane rather than Mary. But it does show the complicated cross-pressures exercised by different members of the role-set, and just how complete the interrelationships between role and status, and between the work situation and the world outside are.

Of course, we are not claiming that the American restaurant industry provides a model for all kinds of industrial situations. But this type of analysis can make us more sensitive to the kinds of patterned conflicts that are built into almost any work situation. Thus, there are complex patterns of interdependence between the machiners and the 'makers' (who work by hand) in the waterproof garment industry (Cunnison, 1966, pp. 121–63), and clerical workers in an employment agency may find a conflict between their desire to serve the public, on the one hand, and their interest in securing an adequate number of 'placements' on the other (Blau, 1963, pp. 36–81). These points of tension and contradiction, to be found in any work-situation, need analysing, however, not merely in terms of the immediate demands of the workplace but also in terms of the processes and expectations which exist in the wider society.

This chapter has, so far, indicated certain paradoxes, perhaps even contradictions. In modern industrial society work is central; but it is also marginal. Work is undertaken as an isolated activity; yet it is closely related to other areas of life. How can these seeming contradictions be resolved?

In the first place we may note that there are various kinds of attachment to the workplace. Thus, to say that work is central in that it provides the worker with a wage to support himself and his family is not necessarily to say that the work is expressively central for that worker or that his occupation is necessarily a source of status and identity for him in the wider society. Indeed, it is precisely this contrast between the material necessity for work on the one hand and the low degree of personal involvement on the other which has led to the concern about alienation in modern industrial society.

We may similarly examine the second contradiction. On the one hand modern economic organization demands that work be an undertaking separated from the home, carried out without interference from domestic or outside considerations, involving a given number of hours in exchange for a given rate of remuneration. At the same time the workplace does not embrace the totality of the workers' lives. Role-theory reminds us that the worker is also a father, a man, an Irishman and many other things and that there are inevitably links, and sometimes conflicts, between the expectations at work and the expectations arising out of non-work situations.

Within industrial society there are many ways in which work is related to non-work. In the mining village we may see a close overlap between home and work and leisure. In the newer estates of Luton, on the other hand, we may find the workers arguing that 'mates are not friends' and that the major link – perhaps the only link – between work and non-work is the pay-packet (Goldthorpe *et al.*, 1968, pp. 30–39). The fact that these differences exist *within* industrial society should at least persuade us to treat with caution contrasts between industrial and pre-industrial societies made in terms of characteristics such as rationality or separation of home and work. There are many similarities as well as many differences between both types of society.

We have examined work largely in terms of its position in society as a whole, its relationship to the fundamental economic problems that face any society, to the values relating to kinds and degrees of labour, to the patterns of co-operation and conflict arising out of the social division of labour. In the analysis of the role of the waitress in the restaurant, we have attempted to show how face-to-face encounters can be analysed in such a way as to bring in these aspects of the wider culture and society. We have not, however, specifically dealt with the fact that many work encounters take place in the context of organizations and that, indeed, much of our life is lived out in relation to organizations.

Organizations

We have seen that work in small-scale, tribal societies is performed by groups of people who are not usually brought together solely for that purpose. Frequently, the family acts as a unit in the productive process; at other times, wider social groups, even a whole village, may co-operate to bring in the harvest or to move cattle from winter to summer pastures.

In industrial societies, however, work tends to be based on social units specially organized for that purpose. This process has been accelerated by the growth of modern technology, which has led to a rapid increase in the variety and content of work-roles and consequently has brought increasing problems of co-ordination. Work in industrial societies thus takes place in organizations: in factories, mines, offices, warehouses and similar units.

These changes are not entirely new, however. Factory production is at least four thousand years old. Other, non-economic kinds of organization are equally ancient. For centuries, as well as being employed in mines and factories, men have fought in armies, languished in prisons, sent their children to schools, prayed in churches, and played in gymnasia. Organizations have thus existed not only to facilitate production, but also, for example, to make and enforce legal decisions and to decide upon and administer government policy.

But such organizations were rudimentary in comparison with their modern counterparts. Let us first look at three quite different spheres of life in which organizations have come to the fore in modern industrial society: warfare, the law and mental health. Though wars have been fought for as long as history has been recorded, the warriors were not normally professional soldiers. They were usually peasants, who had to bring in their harvests before they could turn themselves into soldiers and fight battles. And when battle was joined, combat was largely an individual affair. Men brought their own weapons and used them as best they could. In industrial societies, by contrast, the military machine is much more sophisticated. Work-roles are more complex and diverse; recruits must be professionally trained; and the command structure is more intricately co-ordinated. It may still be 'a man's life in the Army', but what is demanded of the modern soldier is more often a technical skill, rather than an exhibition of a 'noble art'. The means of advanced warfare (tanks, guns, etc.), too, are owned by the organization – the Army. War is a social activity requiring complex and centralized organization and lengthy specialized training.

Again, legal systems, according to which certain behaviour is defined as wrong and the offender punished, have become increasingly organized. Only in fairly 'developed' societies is the definition of crime and the punishment of the criminal the duty of specially-constituted organizations – courts, police forces, prisons. Tribal societies often operate without judges, sheriffs and gaols, and rely more on the controls exercised over the wrongdoer by his kin or his fellow-villagers. So societies have only gradually developed specialized organizations of social control, with legislative, judicial and penal functions. The blood-feud, for example, based on customary law, requires no official adjudication, and organized punishment is not carried out by specialist officials. Moreover, the solidarity on which the stability of society is based today no longer necessarily rests on a deeply-held agreement about moral values. Such agreement can be extremely powerful, and render prisons and policemen unnecessary. Malinowski quotes the case of a South Sea islander who was known to have had sexual relations with a woman with whom this was not permitted, and felt his shame so keenly that he climbed a coconut palm and threw himself off in full public view. And because such societies have not until recently been subject to rapid social change, ideas about what constitutes 'punishable behaviour' have not had to be regularly reviewed by any formal body. In *The Division of Labour in Society* Durkheim suggested that this kind of consensus has been replaced by what he called 'organic' integration, where a society holds together not because of fundamental common agreement about ideas of right and wrong, but because its constituent parts depend on each other. Thus, though they have different functions and interests workers and management have to co-operate if production is to continue. Rapid change in society generally produces continual organizational change in specific institutions. Thus the pace of social change has involved constant alterations in the criminal law, and new ideas about the treatment of offenders have led to the development of a complex system in which prisoners are not simply kept in custody, but fed, clothed, educated, trained, employed and given access to specialized religious, educational, medical and other welfare services.

Finally, to take a quite different sphere of social life, the revolution in medicine has meant that the treatment of mental illness has also become highly organized. Mental hospitals, in fact, are a modern development. In the past, mental disturbances have often been put down to possession by demons, and offenders were put to death. The Mosaic law required that 'a man also or a woman that hath a familiar spirit or that is a wizard shall surely be put to death ' (Leviticus, xx, 27). Similarly, the seventeenth-century treatise *Malleus Maleficarum* went into great detail in prescribing appropriate torture and burning for the medieval insane. As recently as the 1850s trippers went on outings to Bedlam to poke and prod at the chained lunatics. Modern concepts of the diagnosis and treatment of mentally sick persons, on the other hand, have led to the development of complex organizations through which these new ideas can be put into practice (Stafford-Clark, 1952, chs. 1 and 2).

These and other kinds of specialized organizations have not grown up by chance. Before they could develop at all, there had to be a sufficient level of scientific and economic development to produce a surplus of resources great enough to release personnel to perform specialized technical roles.

In industrial society these organizations have come to be widely accepted as the most rational way of solving the varied problems confronting such societies. Thus, increasing specialization of work roles and complexity of the division of economic activities in production is paralleled by an even greater growth of complex organizational machinery of distribution, which channels the product to the market and, ultimately, to the consumer – market research, advertising, consultancy, and other specialized organizations. The ratio of administrative to productive employees constantly increases, and while this is partly due to the mechanization of production, it also reflects the increase in scale of corporations and the need for machinery to co-ordinate their diverse activities.

Hence our society has come to be called an 'organization society', peopled by 'organization men'. Indeed, some sociologists have emphasized the extent to which organizations have come to control man, rather than the reverse (Presthus, 1962). In the rest of this chapter we shall examine two principal aspects of this process:

1. We shall look at the basic structural resemblances between organizations which, at first glance, are of quite different kinds, noting the main 'types' of organizations, and observing how such structures mould the behaviour of the members.

2. The way in which people come to participate in organizations is not random. They may choose appropriate organizations for themselves – factories, churches, clubs, etc. – or *they* may be chosen because of their 'suitability', and placed under varying degrees of pressure to become members, as in prisons and hospitals. In either case, they are selected according to their social characteristics, on the basis of which they are grouped into such categories as Negro, professional, Catholic, pensioner, etc. They also come to find their way into organizations through the social networks in which they are embedded, that is,

those with whom they have dealings. We need to look, then, at the way in which membership of such categories and networks affects the organizations in which people are involved.

The Structure of Organizations

Let us now tackle a question we have so far avoided: 'What do we mean by an organization?' Sociologists have often given examples rather than satisfactory definitions of what constitutes an organization. But usually they emphasize that organizations are bodies, persisting over time, which are specially set up to achieve specific aims (cf. Blau and Scott, 1963, ch. 1; Etzioni, 1964, ch. 3; Presthus, 1962, ch. 4).

Of course, those who control organizations may not be very effective in achieving their stated aims. In the first place, there may be varying degrees of *internal opposition* to these aims. For example, the interests of prisoners are largely in *conflict* with those of the staff. In industry, on the other hand, despite conflicts of interest, workers and management do, nevertheless, also have *complementary* interests in keeping the factory going. Finally, in churches, pastor and flock share *common* beliefs and have a common interest in the success of the church, though they will not totally agree, of course, about everything.

Secondly, there is likely to be *external opposition* which may inhibit the success of organizations. A religious sect, for example, such as the Jehovah's Witnesses or the Doukhobors, may be proscribed by Government; a business may be hit by new tax laws or by technological advance in other companies sharing the same market; a prison may find its task of rehabilitating inmates made more difficult by a public outcry for maximum security at all costs.

Thirdly, in all organizations members will have *personal interests* which conflict with official aims, and social relations will develop among members which have the effect of reducing organizational efficiency. This does not mean that they are trying to sabotage the organization. The fact is that most of the personnel in an organization may not be held or feel responsible for its success. But the way they express their sectional interests, and the social relations which develop, are limited by their attachment to the organization, the way they are controlled by it, and the need for it to remain a viable unit. Employees are aware that if a strike persists for too long, the factory may close down. If sufficient members of a religious sect develop heretical ideas, they may split the church in two. Even in prisons, inmates realize the advantages of acquiescing in the smooth running of the organization.

Thus there is some value in talking of organizations having goals, even though many of the members do not personally share them. (Prisons, factories and churches continue to function without their personnel regarding themselves as model prisoners or parishioners, or having a zeal for productivity.) Furthermore, organizations differ from communities and societies not only in having explicit goals, but in the means used to achieve them. Etzioni states that organizations are characterized by:

1. Divisions of labour, of power, and of communication responsibilities, such divisions being deliberately planned to achieve certain goals.

2. The presence of power-centres which control the concerted efforts of the organization and continuously review its performance, and re-pattern its structure, where necessary, so as to increase its efficiency.

3. The substitution of personnel, i.e., unsatisfactory persons can be removed and others assigned their tasks, and people can be transferred and promoted (Etzioni, 1964, ch. 3).

This definition is based upon the classic model of bureaucracy developed by Max Weber. We must appreciate that Weber looked at bureaucracy only as part of a much broader subject: the whole basis of authority in society. To him, one of the most striking features of industrial society was that when organizations were administered in a strictly 'bureaucratic' way, they were capable of achieving the highest degree of efficiency. Bureaucratic administration, he wrote, was 'superior to any other form in precision, in stability, in the stringency of its discipline, and in its reliability. It thus makes possible a particularly high degree of calculability of results . . . and is formally capable of application to all kinds of administrative tasks' (Weber, 1964, p. 337). Thus, bureaucratic administration was in principle equally applicable to businesses, charitable organizations, hospitals, churches and political parties. Let us turn, then, to a summary of Weber's conception of bureaucracy:

There is a series of officials, each of whose roles is circumscribed by a written definition of his power. These offices are arranged in a hierarchy, each successive step embracing all those beneath it. There is a set of rules and procedures within which every possible contingency is theoretically provided for. There is a 'bureau' for the safe keeping of all written records and files, it being an important part of the rationality of the system that information is written down. A clear separation is made between personal and business affairs, bolstered by a contractual method of appointment in terms of technical qualifications for office. In such an organization authority is based on the office. Commands are obeyed because the rules state that it is within the competence of a particular office to issue such commands (Pugh *et al.*, 1964, pp. 6–7).

Under these conditions, far from being synonymous with irrelevant form-filling, red tape and inefficiency in general, bureaucracy, Weber says, can be the most efficient and rational means known of organizing human resources to obtain desired ends. Yet the term has not come to have pejorative overtones without reason, and Weber's view needs some qualification.

It is precisely because men in bureaucratic structures perform specialized, 'segmental' roles, over which they have no control, and in which they have no opportunity of using their rational judgement – the very features Weber praises – that they so often feel a sense of 'alienation' in industrial society. Instead of a man being responsible for his own behaviour at work, he feels that he is controlled by it and separated from the product of his labour. Bureaucratic relations are not conducive solely to efficiency: they may have unfortunate, even if unintended, consequences.

Merton, in his article 'Bureaucratic structure and personality' (Merton *et al.*, 1952, pp. 361–71), examines further possible 'dysfunctions' of bureaucracy. He shows how, to be effective, bureaucrats must behave consistently, and follow regulations strictly. This limits the capacity of bureaucrats to adapt to changing circumstances which were not envisaged by those who drew up the rules. The officials still think in terms of rules which are not to be questioned, and overlook the fact that absolute rules which make for efficiency in general produce inefficiency – even injustice – in specific cases. A different view is taken by Blau, who argues that such 'ritualistic' behaviour arises not from over-identification with rules so much as insecurity in established social relationships within the organization (Blau, 1963, p. 236). We shall look briefly at two examples.

Bureaucracy, as conceived by Weber, stresses that the official should be detached and not become closely involved in personal relations with his colleagues. But Merton stresses that this pressure for formal, impersonal treatment may be harmful when *clients* come to the bureaucracy, as in a maternity clinic or employment exchange, because they desire and need more individual attention (Merton *et al.*, 1952, p. 366).

Again, Blau, in the study of a state employment agency mentioned above, shows that the bureaucrats themselves who had to deal with clients, disliked such an emphasis on formality, and that in a department in which impersonal treatment was stressed relations with clients were unsatisfactory. Impersonality produced a loss of efficiency. In another department, officials tended to ignore the recommendation to treat all clients in a 'clinical' fashion, but instead dealt with them all as individual cases. This made the officials more satisfied with their work, and was also to the advantage of those clients that they enjoyed helping. But clients who were less 'rewarding' received worse treatment, so supervisors had to go back to bureaucratic regulations. Blau shows that in this and other ways bureaucratic practices instituted to increase efficiency have corresponding limitations. The task of management consists in continually adjusting bureaucratic and non-bureaucratic elements to secure the most effective combination at any time.

A key limitation upon the efficiency of bureaucratic administration lies in its difficulty in coping with uncertainty and change. Bureaucracy relies on tasks being convertible into routine. The more unforeseen contingencies arise, the less comprehensive and effective are the rules and regulations. Blau argues that in the agencies he observed bureaucratic conditions did generate favourable attitudes towards change. Officials welcomed innovations, for example, which would remove irritations in their present work-roles. They were identified with policies that required the expansion of the organization, etc. But it was not the bureaucratic elements in the administration which brought this pressure for change. Further, the fact that some of the officials favoured changes of a specific kind does not mean that the agency was organized in a way which would allow change in general to be easily instituted (Blau, 1963, pp. 246–7).

Again, Gouldner, in a study of a gypsum mine and plant, shows how work-processes in the plant on the surface were largely predictable, and could be organized in a bureaucratic fashion. But the miners had to cope with much more uncertainty, and when a new manager tried to raise production by increasing bureaucratic control over the organization, this was successful in the plant, but the miners underground were able to resist it. The uncertainties of the physical environment made bureaucratic organization of the work-processes unsuitable, and the greater solidarity of the miners, partly a consequence of the uncertain conditions, enabled them to resist the imposition of bureaucratic controls.

Another major contribution to the study of bureaucracy uses a similar line of argument. In the course of their study of a number of firms in the electronics industry, Burns and Stalker (1961) found it necessary to use two models of work-organization. One, which they called 'mechanistic', was suitable where conditions were stable; the other they labelled 'organic', and used to describe situations where changing conditions constantly gave rise to unforeseen problems which could not be suitably resolved with a 'mechanistic' type of organization. The interest of this 'mechanistic' type is that it corresponds very closely to Weber's notion of bureaucracy, while the 'organic' system is notably different. Some of the bureaucratic principles of the 'mechanistic' model and their counterparts in the 'organic' system are contrasted below:

Mechanistic management system	*Organic management system*
Specialized differentiation of functional tasks into which the problems facing the concern as a whole are broken down.	Organization on the basis of contributions from various specialists to common tasks, across the boundaries of clearly-demarcated jobs.
The specification of what shall be done by whom, and the co-ordination of the separate tasks by those who are formally the immediate superiors for each level in the hierarchy.	Adjustment and continual redefinition of individual tasks through interaction with others.

Mechanistic management system	Organic management system
Precise definition of 'responsibility' as a set of rights and obligations and of technical methods of work which are attached to each functional role.	The shedding of 'responsibility' as a limited field of rights, obligations and methods. (Problems may not be 'posted' upwards, downwards or sideways as being someone else's responsibility.)
Emphasis upon the rights, obligations and work-methods attached to a particular position at work.	The spread of commitment beyond the limits of immediate work-roles to wider levels of the organization.
Hierarchical structure of control, authority and communication.	A 'network' structure of control, authority and communication.
Insistence on loyalty to the concern and obedience to superiors as a condition of membership.	Commitment to the concern's tasks, and to the 'technological' ethos of material progress and expansion, is valued more highly than loyalty and obedience.

(Burns and Stalker, 1961, pp. 120–21.)

Burns and Stalker and Gouldner both point out a crucial ambiguity in Weber's original discussion of the bureaucratic model. Weber spoke of a man's authority as being based upon his tenure of an office to which he had been elected on the basis of his technical qualifications. But Burns and Stalker show that, with the rapid growth in technical knowledge, not only does the hierarchy of offices become less distinct, but it is less obviously based on 'grades' of technical qualifications. That is, there comes to be a conflict between authority based on position and authority based on skill. In modern industry authority simply based on official position is no longer adequate. Rather, people contribute their special knowledge to whatever task is before them, and their standing is affected by the value of the contribution they make. Nor is this process confined to business organizations: similar changes have occurred in other types of organization, for example in the technical wing of modern military forces (Janowitz, 1964).

A further point which Burns and Stalker emphasize is the increased 'commitment to the organization' in the organic system. If a man's participation is not simply confined to a clearly-specified set of activities, involving only a limited part of his personality, then a great deal more of his human capacities can be harnessed by the organization. In the extreme, W. H. Whyte has suggested, not only must the modern technocrat be a 'company man', but his wife, too, must be sociable and adaptable to the requirements of the company (1957).

There are bureaucratic elements, then, in most formal organizaations. Wherever routine administration is necessary, it is likely that it will be bureaucratic in character. So far, we have dealt mainly with economic organizations, in which much of the work performed can readily be converted into routine. The work of a Civil Service is even easier to reduce to routine. But we find bureaucratic elements even in organizations which work under much more difficult conditions: in prisons and hospitals, for example, where much of the work is performed not only *with* other people, but *on* these people and there is a continuous change of prisoners and patients.

Yet sociologists too readily assume that the bureaucratic model can be used to study any kind of organization. From what we have already seen we should expect to find much less bureaucracy in organizations in which people participate as 'whole persons'. We shall examine next an extreme type of organization of this kind – that in which the members sleep, work and take their recreation on the same premises.

Total Institutions

Prisons, hospitals, monasteries, military camps, whaling ships, holiday camps and boarding schools all look vastly different – and are – but all do share one important common feature also: they are all institutions in which participants *live* in the organization. They are, as Goffman calls them, 'total' institutions, in part formal organizations, in part residential communities (Goffman, 1961). All these organizations, he claims, have a basically similar social structure, regardless of the personal characteristics of the members. The basic arrangement of 'normal' society is that home, work and leisure are separate areas of life. People play, sleep and work in different places, in the company of different people, and under different controls. This is not so in 'total institutions'; here the members –

whether they be patients, inmates, prisoners, monks or residents in a holiday camp – lead an enclosed, formally-administered round of life, and undergo similar experiences.

In each of these 'total' organizations, there is a prescribed 'career' for members (or 'inmates', as Goffman generally calls them), and a privilege system which is devised so as to reward them for conforming to this career and for their co-operation in causing as little inconvenience as possible to those who run the organization. Though inmates tend to react to this kind of régime in quite individualistic ways, they nevertheless see themselves as united in one respect: in their common opposition to the staff, who form a quite separate, superior category. They long for release, Goffman claims (thinking presumably of prisons and mental hospitals, which provide much of the illustration for his essay); but soon after graduation they are talking of the happy times they had.

Goffman shows that when people are living in 'batches', similar institutional arrangements are devised to administer them efficiently despite the different purposes the institutions serve (monasteries as against prisons, for example). Of course, there are also important differences *between* these various sub-varieties of total institution. In some, such as the holiday camp, entry is voluntary, in others, such as the armed forces, it is not necessarily so. There are also basic differences between those total organizations which exist to perform a work-task, such as ships and military camps, and those which exist to 'treat' people, especially without their ready consent, as in the case of some prisons and mental hospitals.

Treatment organizations, for example, often exist so that specialist staff can change the way the patients see themselves. A good deal of coercion is often necessary, and a natural rift develops between staff and patients. Patients (or inmates) in treatment organizations tend to be stigmatized, and frequently react by dissociating themselves from other patients, regarding themselves as different (i.e., 'normal'). Because they feel a need to preserve a set image of themselves, they are reluctant to form intimate primary groups with those from whom they wish to dissociate themselves.

In contrast, some work organizations have to be located in places which by definition make them 'total'. Thus, seamen live in a total community while at sea. The fact that a ship is a total organization does not imply that the crew need 'treatment' of any kind. This is simply a condition of their work. In such organizations the same division of labour is found as in factories on land, authority is not normally based on coercion, and close friendship groups are characteristic of such total communities. Thus, not only are there different types of total organizations; in some respects these different species are just as much like other non-total organizations as they are like each other. Schools, after all, have some similar features, whether they are day schools or for boarders.

| | | Organizational scope | |
		total	non-total
	work	merchant ship	factory
		military camp	department store
Organizational aims	treatment	mental hospital	clinic
		boarding school	day school

Goffman's essay on total institutions is important not because all total organizations are alike in every way – this is manifestly untrue – but because when people spend periods of their life within an enclosed space with the same companions, certain patterns of social relations tend to develop, whether it happens to be a prison, a monastery or a military camp.

The Classification of Organizations

We can divide organizations, as above, into work organizations and those which exist to act on people in a specified way. We now add a third type, those which provide a setting for people to share common interests, frequently referred to as 'voluntary associations'. These include religious, political and leisure associations. This rough classification thus divides organizations into three types on the basis of the kind of aims or goals they have.

A similar division of organizations is achieved by Blau and Scott (1963, pp. 42 ff.), who classify organizations according to the four different kinds of 'prime beneficiary' that organizations may serve. The main group to benefit may be the rank-and-file participants, in others, the owners or managers, in yet others, it is the clients, or 'public-in-contact' (people outside the organization who yet have contact with it), and in the last group it is the 'public-at-large', that is, members of society in general. These four types are correspondingly labelled 'mutual benefit', 'business', 'service' and 'commonweal' organizations.

Finally, let us consider one other useful classification which is based upon a different criterion for distinguishing types of organizations. Etzioni (1961) divides organizations according to the kind of power relations that exist between those administering the organization and its lower-level participants. Members may comply with the demands placed upon them by their superiors because they are coerced (they are made to conform), because of utilitarian considerations (they get material rewards, e.g. money or goods), or because they accept or share the assumptions, norms, ideas, values and so on, of those who take the decisions. Many of the significant differences to be found, as between one organization and another, derive from the different kinds of power that are most commonly used and the corresponding variations in the way the members are involved.

Though this typology is based on a different criterion, in fact it produces much the same clusters of organizations. This correspondence does not occur by chance. For the utility of each scheme is not that it enables tidy-minded sociologists neatly to pigeon-hole organizations; rather each mode of classification concentrates upon one aspect of a whole set of interrelated structural features: power, compliance, aims, beneficiaries. Each scheme isolates one significant variable and systematically shows how it will have different values in different social contexts.

Though these typologies take quite different dimensions of organizations as their starting-point, then, there is an underlying pattern which links together their aims, their prime beneficiaries, the types of power used by the leaders and the involvement of the lower participants.

Etzioni's classification is based on the element of 'compliance', itself the product of these two elements: the kind of power wielded by those who take the decisions, and the kind of involvement in the organization of the lower participants. There are three types of power – coercive, remunerative and normative – and three types of

Aims	Treatment	Work	Voluntary activity
Interests of leaders and led	Conflicting	Complementary	Common
Prime beneficiaries (Blau and Scott)	Public	Management	Members
Power exercised by leaders (Etzioni)	Coercive	Remunerative	Normative
Involvement of lower participants (Etzioni)	Alienative	Calculative	Moral
Examples	Prisons	Factories Commercial enterprises	Clubs Churches Political parties

involvement – alienative, calculative and moral. Etzioni argues that there is a tendency for certain types of power and certain types of involvement to occur together. Thus, in organizations where the staff have coercive power, the involvement of the members is alienative; where they have remunerative power, the involvement is calculative; and where they have normative power, it is moral. Etzioni admits that more than one type of power and involvement may be present in an organization at any one time. But these 'congruent' types of compliance patterns are particularly effective because they enable organizations with special kinds of goals to achieve them most easily.

Thus, in organizations which have what Etzioni calls 'order' goals, such as prisons, we can expect to find that the staff use coercive power and the inmates are alienated from the organization. We should expect friendships between staff and inmates to be rather brittle; and the problems of making prison industries efficient are partly due to the inadequacy of economic incentives for people whose involvement in the organization is alienative.

Secondly, we should expect organizations with 'economic' goals to have a utilitarian compliance structure. For example, a recent study of car assembly workers at Luton showed that they had a strongly marked instrumental orientation to their work (Goldthorpe *et al.*, 1968). On the other hand, one school of industrial sociologists has emphasized the advantages of the 'human relations' approach in industry, and the benefits of permissive management. But these can only operate within the framework of a contract in which management and men agree on a suitable balance of labour and earnings. A utilitarian compliance structure is thus more appropriate in an economic organization than, say, coercion. Indeed, the collapse of slavery in some places has been put down to the sheer inefficiency of continually having to coerce workers to perform their tasks.

Thirdly, organizations with 'culture' goals are generally run on a basis of agreement. Churchgoers are not expected to get any economic benefits from their presence in the pews, nor do they expect to be pressured into church attendance; they attend because they hold certain beliefs, or respect social pressure to be seen at church – both are kinds of normative compliance.

Etzioni's 'congruent' types clearly apply to many organizations, such as prisons, factories and churches; his *incongruent* types also help us to understand, for example, military organizations. He describes the peacetime military camp as an organization which is predominantly utilitarian, but has a secondary coercive pattern. The combat unit, however, is a dual normative-coercive organization. This contrast is reflected in the different recruitment methods used in peace and war. During peacetime, advertisements emphasize what recruits will get out of a period in the army, for example, a degree, technical training, a chance to see the world. In wartime however, 'your country needs you': the appeal is to one's duty, to sentiments which are shared with those in the fighting forces. But at any time recruits can be conscripted – coercion can also be used. In fact, many modern armies consist of both a core of economically-motivated regulars and a large body of conscripts. Strains may be set up within the organization where these two compliance-patterns occur together. Social background, career prospects, payment levels, indeed basic orientations to the military in general will tend to differ between these two groups.

External Influences on Organizational Behaviour

We noted earlier that people do not usually pick the organizations they want to join at random. They may follow their friends into a club, see an advertisement for a job which suits them, cultivate their minds by attending evening classes. On the other hand, they were probably sent to school whether they liked it or not, and they may also have been obliged to go to hospital or to do military service. Whatever the circumstances, it is certain that either *they* thought they were suitable for the organizations they joined, or *someone else* – the State, the doctor, parents – thought they were suitable and had the power to get them to enter the organization.

The fact that people who belong to organizations are normally in some way 'suitable' for them is vital to the success of the organization. Schools admit children who are at a particular stage of physical and mental development; monasteries must select their recruits with the greatest possible care. People joining associations are often found to share similar political and religious backgrounds (cf. Stacey, 1960). And although prisons have to take all-comers, even here there are special prisons, or wings of prisons, in which men are separated from women, long-termers from short-termers, the younger from the mature prisoners, etc. Thus, the character of an organization may depend to a great extent on the people who happen to belong to it, and these characteristics, part of the world outside prison, will affect its internal organization.

We shall look at three aspects of this interplay between the organization and the world outside:

1. How does the *orientation* of members to the organization affect its functioning?

2. How is organizational life affected by the *categories* which the members represent?

3. How do the *personal networks* in which members are involved affect life inside the organization?

Orientation to the organization

Let us take a few key examples of the quite different ways in which the orientations of members towards the organization affect the pattern of organization:

(a) Prisons are organizations in which the authorities almost always are obliged to administer people against their will. They therefore have to make arrangements to ensure that work continues despite opposition from the inmates. Thus, there are walls to keep them in, and constant checks to ensure they have not escaped or acquired the means by which they might escape. Such arrangements are not an inevitable consequence of organization. They are 'built in' to a particular *kind* of organization only – those in which the inmates have an 'alienative' involvement in, or orientation to the prison. (It is a negative 'involvement', for they are alienated *from* the organization.) In one unusual prison in Scandinavia, however, which contains members of the Jehovah's Witnesses who refuse to be conscripted for military service, no such 'alienation' exists, since the prisoners accept their sentence because of their religious beliefs. The internal organization of the prison therefore differs markedly because of these different attitudes: the only guards on the perimeter are there to keep sightseers out, rather than the prisoners in.

(b) A very different kind of organization is the monastery, where attitudes to the institution not only affect the monks' experience inside, but are crucial in determining even whether they are accepted as members at all, for applicants are only admitted after rigorous selection procedures. Yet though membership is voluntary, unlike the Jehovah's Witnesses prison, the attitudes of the members are so positive that their *will* to play their part in the efficient running of the system makes utilitarian and coercive modes of control quite insignificant.

(c) Indeed, we can generalize further from monasteries to all 'voluntary' or 'mutual benefit' associations, in Blau and Scott's terminology, for, in this kind of organization, the prime beneficiaries are the members; hence we should expect their orientation to be of the greatest significance in determining the character of the organization.

Attitudes towards the organization will obviously vary according to the degree to which a club or church or political party branch is controlled from outside. If it is part of a centralized body, members may have less scope in moulding the organization according to their inclinations. This is, in fact, a frequent source of tension in voluntary associations: the headquarters staff are engaged in bureaucratic administration, and are relatively free from the pressures and attitudes that influence behaviour in local groups. Union leaders will have different attitudes towards employers from branch members. A headquarters official of a religious sect will speak in a church meeting of 'our friends, the Roman Catholics' while local members are uttering veiled threats about 'popish devilry'.

But attitudes towards the organization are affected by what goes on within the local organization, as well as between the branch and the district or national centre, for instance over decisions about what kinds of activities a voluntary association is to undertake and how they shall be organized. Should the R.S.P.C.A. campaign against blood sports? Should a village football (or county cricket) team be representative of the village (or county), whatever the results, or strengthen its side by bringing in outsiders? Personal relations as well as club organization in a 'social' tennis club will differ from one in which all the members are dedicated to becoming star players.

(d) One striking sociological account of the effect of members' attitudes towards an industrial organization is the study of car assembly workers already mentioned (Goldthorpe *et al.*, 1968). Previous research in a variety of industries tended to emphasize the importance of 'internal' factors, such as management styles (cf. Roethlisberger and Dickson, 1964), or the technological environment (cf. Woodward, 1965), in determining how men reacted to their working conditions. But Goldthorpe and his colleagues showed that these car assemblers had a prior orientation to their work, which was not an 'internal' product of life on the job, but something they brought with them from outside, and which crucially affected the way the workers saw their situation. Their past experience of social and geographical mobility, their position in the life-cycle, their present patterns of family and community living, all helped to give them a distinctively 'instrumental' approach to their work. They were not unduly worried by the pressures of assembly-line jobs and the relative lack of 'social' satisfaction at work – 'belongingness'. The lack of such satisfactions *in* and *at* work was less important to them than a good, long-term 'money-for-effort' bargain (though, clearly, they did not enjoy repetitive, 'un-social' assembly-line work).

Categorical relationships

Having looked at the way in which the attitudes (or the 'orientation') of members affect the kind of organizational pattern adopted, let us now look at the way the running of the organization is affected by the categories that they belong to, that they put themselves in, or that other people put them in. People who enter organizations, whether they are schools, prisons, factories, clubs or other types, acquire a 'formal' role upon entry. They are expected to behave in a way that will enable the organization to function smoothly; they are given specific tasks, and are expected to conform to yet other rules and regulations which guide their behaviour more generally. Interpersonal relations between members, as we have seen, will naturally reflect their particular formal roles within the organization: their position gives them a certain amount of authority; it makes them dependent on others in order to carry out their work, etc. But every organization also has its 'under-life', its set of 'informal' relations, which is to varying degrees independent of the institution and is not 'laid down' by any formal rules.

Naturally, people do not enter organizations as blanks, waiting to be impressed with the organizational stamp. They have attitudes, feelings, beliefs. As we saw above, they have orientations to the organizations they join. Such orientations help to determine not only the formal life of the organization, but also the kind of underlife that develops. That is, their status within the organization and the way people behave towards them will depend not only on their formal work-role, but also on their *latent* status characteristics: age, sex, skin-colour, social background, religion, etc.

Some categories may be of minimal social significance. For example, the fact that some of the members may have red hair will probably not affect their social relationships within the organization. The fact that all of them have addresses, again, will often not *mean* anything to their fellow members. Occasionally, however a particular address, in a high or low status area, will be of social significance to other people in an organization – a shop assistant applying for a job at a fashionable store will be accepted on condition that she changes her address; a junior manager who is already living in the stockbroker belt may find that this makes him more acceptable to his colleagues.

Other categories may be far more important. For example, members who have coloured skins may find this is very significant in determining their life-chances. They may be equally qualified for and competent at a job, but because they represent a particular category of people, who are considered by racially-prejudiced people to be incompetent, they may be denied promotion. There are circumstances in which colour could affect one's capacity to do a job. If an Englishman applied for a job as a waiter at a Chinese restaurant, for example, he would be turned down because of a category he represented – in this case a relevant one. But in most situations in which colour is taken into account, it is quite irrelevant as far as the performance of formal roles within the organization is concerned. Instead colour categories are used to 'pigeon-hole' or 'stereotype' people, and provide a guide to others as to how to relate to them, by treating them in a standardized way irrespective of their other characteristics – their religion, their ability, their age, etc. These racial categories are a way of simplifying or codifying behaviour in situations where there is some ambiguity about what is appropriate, though, in fact, they *over*simplify (Mitchell, 1966, p. 53).

In principle, skin-colour could be ignored in social relations in the same way that hair-colour is. But in reality, it is rarely ignored and so takes on a social meaning. This affects the lives of coloured members in two principal ways:

(a) People are treated in categorical terms on occasions when there is an element of doubt or ambiguity as to how they should be treated. That is, the more 'structured' the situation is (the more the relationship is clearly defined for the actors), the less scope there is for categorical relationships. Thus observers have been struck by the fact that when men are jointly engaged in combat, Black-White differences cease to be relevant. But under more normal conditions and especially in leisure activities racial status is likely to be important in military organizations. Again, there is some evidence that 'coloured' children in England feel more at home in organizations where uniforms are worn, and in which many of the activities are organized for them, than in those youth clubs where it is left to them to guide their own behaviour and establish their own activities according to their personal feelings and preferences.

(b) Such categories may still be built up as an organizational requirement, no matter how irrelevant they may be in terms of a person's ability to do a job or to co-operate with others in doing it. In fact, other employees may simply not accept him. An employer may thus get into serious difficulty if he sticks to a purely 'technical' policy of recruiting men with the requisite skills, for he may thereby violate expectations that certain jobs should only be given to men of a particular ethnic group – a consideration that has nothing to do with individual skill at all, since it is only concerned with people as categories.

Personal networks

We have shown the importance of the orientations of members towards the organizations in which they are involved, and of the categories they represent. These two factors are not of course entirely independent: orientations are partly a product of being Negro, or old or coming from a particular social background. All of these will influence the social networks of members. First, then, let us define what we mean by 'networks', and then suggest why they are important.

Although the term network is a comparatively recent addition to the language of sociology, it has already acquired numerous meanings. For our present purposes, however, we shall take a network to refer to the cluster of personal links which a person has around him, together with the links between these other persons. The importance of having the right 'connexions' was appreciated long before sociology became a discipline. We use terms such as 'contacts', 'cliques' and 'nepotism' to refer to aspects of a man's network which are used for furthering his interests, often in a way that is not entirely approved of. In the same way, when sociologists and social anthropologists use the term, they stress that networks do not just 'exist': people are selected and incorporated into a network who can be relied on for support; they are a means of mobilizing resources.

Even before a man becomes a member of an organization, his network may be important in gaining entry for him. This has frequently been true of traditional industries such as the docks. It also occurs when applicants for membership carry some characteristic which is likely to impede their entry, such as nationality or skin-colour.

This leads to the rise of intermediaries whose networks include both management and men seeking entry, and who are rewarded by management for providing them with reliable recruits and by the men for securing them entry.

Once a man becomes a member of an organization, his network will gradually be built up, on the basis of all three of the factors we have already described. Thus, in the first place his structural position within the organization (the way his official role is defined) will largely determine those with whom he will have contacts: at one extreme is the prisoner who is specifically cut off from many social contacts and as a result acquires an intimate knowledge of a very small number of people who can be manipulated for various purposes; at the other extreme is the shop assistant who spends most of her time within the organization interacting with a large number of people in such a superficial way that it is difficult to 'use' any of these contacts.

However, whether in prisons or shops, a man's relations do not remain confined to those with whom he has formal dealings. Here his status characteristics, or categories, become relevant: he will prefer to spend his off-duty time (tea-breaks, meal-times) with people whom he finds acceptable, possibly those from the same suburb, others with small children, fellow-Pakistanis. These have their uses: confidential information may be entrusted to them; he enjoys a game of cards with them; conversation with them helps the time to pass quickly.

Finally, he is likely to go out and look for other contacts, not because they are people of the same sort, but because, having a certain orientation towards the organization, he is hoping to achieve some specific end, or at least build up contacts which will be useful in the future when occasion arises. Burns shows well two of the many ways in which networks are built up with such aims in view in his discussion of 'cliques' and 'cabals' in occupational settings (1955). These are both types of primary groups that are entered for the sake of building up support in specific social situations: 'cliques', in this usage, are groups of people in a precarious position whose mutual support reassures them that they have not in fact 'failed'; 'cabals' consist of aspiring people who use their influence to obtain illegitimate control and thereby success. In each case, groups are formed with a particular aim in view and cease to exist when that aim disappears.

An excellent study which shows the way in which networks can be used to explain social behaviour in an organization is Kapferer's analysis of a dispute between two operatives in an electrozinc plant in Broken Hill, Zambia (Kapferer, 1969). One of the older workers, Abraham, complained to Donald, a young man, about his fast working pace. Donald retorted angrily suggesting that Abraham was using witchcraft on him. Abraham admitted this, saying that those who did not respect their elders deserved to be bewitched. Each of them appealed to others for support, and in the end Donald had to back down and signalled his defeat by applying for a transfer to another department.

Kapferer analyses the networks of the two protagonists to show why Abraham was able to mobilize more support, although in some ways he was in a weaker position; why it was Abraham who made the accusation and not one of the other older workers; why Donald was accused and not his partner, who was working at the same pace; why in the course of the dispute more stress was laid on subordinate issues, such as whether Donald was showing disrespect to an older man, than the basic question of rate-busting and the accusation of witchcraft. All these questions are answered by identifying each man's sources of support in the department, and the support which the supporters themselves could call upon.

Sociology thrives on the resolution of contradictions, not simply on the cumulation of uncontroversial findings. The scientific method is based on continuously refining hypotheses as a result of comparing conflicting findings which have to be explained. Such conflicting interpretations are prominent in the sociological study of organizations.

Some studies, for example, have shown racial status to be a key factor in social relations at work. But other studies have described work-situations where skin-colour is entirely irrelevant, where White and Coloured perform the same jobs, belong to the same trade unions, eat at the same tables in the canteen and have the same friends, even though the same White people do their utmost to ensure that no Negro is able to buy a house in the attractive all-White quarter of town (Reitzes, 1960). Some English churches find it impossible to attract West Indians; in others, integration has reached an advanced state.

Again, one study will emphasize the significance of internal factors in understanding organizational behaviour, whilst another stresses factors influencing members from the outside. Thus some studies have explained why it is that mental hospital patients do not easily form friendship groups by examining their social position and their place in the communications network inside the hospital; they may be desperately keen to present themselves as 'normal' people, in contrast to all the other unfortunates, with whom they prefer not to associate (Salisbury, 1962). They find it difficult to maintain friendships because, in the hospital communications-system, things spoken 'in confidence' are, in fact, often taken into account in evaluating patients' medical progress and used as evidence against them. On the other hand, the reason for patients being in the hospital at all may be that they have found it difficult communicating in the outside world.

However, these apparent contradictions can usually be resolved if we examine the factors underlying each case and are prepared to refine the explanations we have given. This does not mean treating every case as different – that would spell the end of sociology – but it does mean that the infinite complexity of social behaviour cannot be adequately explained by a few gross principles.

Sociologists have not yet developed a satisfactory framework for analysing the whole range of internal and external influences on organizational behaviour we have discussed. But we should stress that the social experiences that members undergo within organizations feed back into their life outside, into primary groups such as the family, and into their general relationships in the community and elsewhere. In fact, whatever their official philosophies, organizations despite their structural constraints, never operate without paying regard to what their members bring to the organization. Equally, social behaviour in the 'outside' world is affected by people's experience within organizations. As we go on to look at community and class, we shall do well to remember that 'No organization is an island': that while we all belong to families, most people in developed societies spend most of their time within the framework of one organization or another. Unlike the simpler societies, kinship by no means constitutes the dominant mechanism in social life.

Chapter 6
The Community
in Modern Society

In preceding chapters we have discussed a number of specialized institutions, groups and organizations which are relatively discrete units, and can therefore be analysed to some degree as if they were independent systems of social relations. At the same time, we endeavoured constantly to relate those particular units to the wider social context within which they were lodged. We now shift the focus of our attention from institutions, groups and organizations as units operating within larger wholes to the wholes themselves. A simple progression has thus been unfolded in our presentation: we began by examining social relations in the family and the school and then in the factory or office, because these are basic units within which so much day-to-day life takes place. We now need to widen out to examine the nature of *communities*, and the perplexing variety of settings for social life which the villages, towns, cities and metropolitan regions of the modern world provide for man. Our progression from the specialized social units already discussed to the community may at first seem simple and unproblematic. In fact, the study of the community involves us in problems which are by no means simple. They have generated a great deal of debate in the past and continue to do so.

There is, indeed, great diversity in the range of images evoked by the term 'community'. We often still think of a 'village community' in much the same way as Mary Russell Mitford did, writing in the 1820s, as 'our village' – 'a little world of our own . . . where we know everyone and are known to everyone, interested in everyone, and authorized to hope that everyone feels an interest in us' (Mitford, 1951, p. 3). The term community, however, can carry quite different connotations. We often use it, for example, to refer to the large sprawling metropolis of industrial society, and our image of community may in this case involve thoughts of the loneliness and discomfort of commuting to work, or of the dullness and uniformity of supermarkets, or of the bewildering effects of advertising and television, or of the tedious routines of mass-production. In short, the *metropolitan* community is often seen not as a setting for friendly mutual relationships but as a place of 'anomie', of 'alienation' and of 'mass culture', of individual impotence in the face of industrialism and capitalism, of personal struggles against impersonal bureaucrats, technocrats and the like.

The 'village community' and the 'metropolitan community' so conceived are but two extreme kinds of community encountered in the modern world. Others that readily come to mind are the 'local town' which may be the service centre for a surrounding rural area, or the 'urban village' which, unlike the physically isolated rural village, may be embedded within the framework of a modern metropolis yet be inhabited by a distinctive category of people who share certain ways of living.

If the term community is liable to evoke images as markedly varied as the above we may well ask ourselves whether it has any value for the analysis of modern society. One response might simply be to suggest that we need to define the term closely before using it. This would be reasonable enough, were it not for the fact that sociologists and others have already expended a great deal of effort in trying to define community without reaching any appreciable degree of consensus. Thus, after reviewing ninety-four existing definitions, Hillery (1955) claims that 'beyond the recognition that "people are involved in community" there is little agreement on the use of the term'.

This wide range of images evoked by the term community is not the only obstacle to clear thinking on the subject. A second closely related difficulty is that the term is commonly used to perform very different functions in the description and analysis of society. Thus it is often used as above to refer to particular units (e.g., this village or that city) or to denote *sets of units* (e.g., villages and small towns, as against, perhaps, cities and metropolitan centres), but at other times is used in an evaluative way, as when we say that this village is a community but that one is not. These difficulties all stem from the fact that the term has long been used in a variety of ways in everyday life. So we need to distinguish between the layman's uses ('folk models') and the sociologist's uses ('sociological models') of the term.

We are not, however, setting out to provide a new definition of community or to endorse one or more existing definitions. Our object is not to continue the undoubtedly vain search for a definition of community that would be satisfactory for all purposes and for all time. It is, rather, to discuss various concepts of community in the current sociology of the modern world, and to assess their value and limitations. In order to do this, we must inevitably refer to certain important existing definitions, but our main purpose is to examine community as a recurrent *theme* in sociology and to consider the ways in which this theme usefully contributes to the description and analysis of society. At the end of the chapter we shall then be in a position to assess whether the concept of community retains any value.

Since sociological uses of community derive so largely from everyday life, let us begin by presenting a dictionary definition of the term. The *Concise Oxford Dictionary* contains the following entry:

Community, n. Joint ownership, as community *of goods*; identity of character; fellowship (community *of interest* etc.; also attrib., as community *singing*, in which all present join); organized political, municipal, or social body; body of men living in same locality (*community centre*, place providing social and other facilities for a neighbourhood); body of men having religion, profession, etc., in common, as *the mercantile* community, *the Jewish* community; *the community*, the public; monastic, socialistic, or other, body practising *community* of goods.

One working notion of community might thus have a multiplicity of criteria: a community might be a body of men inhabiting the same locality and having identity of character; some joint ownership of property; some degree of political organization; a sense of fellowship, and a uniform set of religious beliefs, while also being ethnically homogeneous and perhaps performing a particular professional or other occupational function. Such 'bodies of men' do indeed exist and have often been studied by social anthropologists and occasionally by sociologists. Many small-scale preliterate societies display all or most of these features, as do many groupings in Western society. One example from Western society is the French-Canadian parish of St Denis studied by Miner in the 1930s. In his introduction to Miner's account, Redfield sums up the salient features of the community of St Denis as follows:

The *habitants* [small farmers] live in terms of common understandings which are rooted in tradition and which have come to form an organization. The fundamental views of life are shared by almost everyone; and these views find consistent expression in the beliefs, the institutions, the rituals and the manners of the people. In a word, they have a culture. Furthermore, the sanctions which support conduct are strongly sacred: the faith which all share provides endorsement of certain behaviour and condemnation for other behaviour. The priest tells them this is right and that is wrong; but the point here is that the people feel the right and the wrong and act from such a feeling, not from mere expediency. Furthermore, this society, like many others more primitive and outside of the European world, is strongly familial. The fabric of society is woven of threads of consanguineous and connubial connexion; the family system is strong, pervasive, and certain in its effects. . . . The familial organization . . . has the definition of outline, the importance or role in the total society, and the intimacy of connexion with other parts of the total structure which we are accustomed to find in the study of aboriginal simple societies. There is little disorganization and little crime (Miner, 1963, pp. 13–14).

St Denis clearly constitutes a community according to the conception which we formulated by putting together certain criteria listed in the *Concise Oxford Dictionary*, and some sociologists use the term primarily to denote 'bodies of men' of this kind. But we are bound to ask ourselves which, if any, of the criteria used are *essential* to the conception. In the case of St Denis, is the fact that 'the fundamental views of life are shared by almost everyone' essential for it to qualify as a community? Is the fact that 'the fabric of society is woven of threads of consanguineous and connubial connexion' crucial? And so on. When we pose such questions we soon find that it is difficult to argue that some features of St Denis are necessarily more central to its existence as a community than are others. The sense in which the term community is readily applied to St Denis is very different to that in which it can be applied to a 'metropolitan community' or an 'urban village' or even to a 'local town'. In the study of St Denis we have an example of a community in which certain kinds of 'order' and 'stability' may strike even a casual observer as salient features of the social scene. There is a clear over-all organization which is relatively easy to grasp. But this is not the only kind of community organization which can produce 'order' and 'stability'.

When we move into the urban field we often encounter quite different mechanisms of social control. Indeed, as Norton Long (1961) stresses, in many local communities there often appears to be little or no inclusive over-all organization. In a middle-class suburb, for example, we may find a plethora of seemingly disparate 'private' voluntary organizations all contributing to the maintenance of a social order which is, however, also to a large extent maintained by the controls and constraints of various 'public' bodies and official municipal, county and national bureaucracies. Such a combination of 'private' organizations, 'public' bodies and statutory bureaucracies may at first sight not appear to be integral parts of any one identifiable community. Yet closer observation may soon reveal a multiplicity of interconnexions. In one way or another, various agencies produce and maintain an intermeshing and co-ordination of activities and patterns of daily life in a manner which is unplanned and often unwilled or unintended by any individual or any one agency.

Or again, in sharp contrast to the middle-class suburb, we find a slum community, like that analysed by Whyte in *Street Corner Society* (Whyte, 1954, first published in 1943), in which gangs and rackets are important agencies of social control. Yet these gangs and rackets are of a kind which many middle-class people might regard as symptoms of 'disorganization' rather than of 'organization'. If this is so, we are obliged to conclude that St Denis is certainly *a* community, but that it is *only one kind of community*.

The features listed in the description of St Denis, however complex, still by no means constitute an exhaustive set of attributes of community. We can readily think of various 'bodies of men' with a territorial basis (such as military camps) which could just as logically be claimed as communities but which nevertheless have other features of social organization which mark them off very sharply indeed from St Denis.

While 'bodies of men' with territorial bases correspond to one popular view of community inherent in the dictionary entry, they do not necessarily correspond to other parts of that lengthy entry. Thus, if primary emphasis is laid on the community as 'the public' rather than as a body of men living in the same *locality*, St Denis is not in itself a community but only a segment of the wider community of *habitants* in French Canada. Certain elements of community as outlined in the dictionary, indeed, can be found in dispersed groupings whose members may share a wide range of attitudes and interests without necessarily being resident in the same village, town, or city, or even in the same nation or state. (A good example, included in the *Concise Oxford Dictionary*, is 'the Jewish community'.)

In general, then, we see that the everyday meanings of community can be extremely various and that the term is far from specific. In this connexion, it is interesting to note an important difference between the English and German languages. English is somewhat less specific than German, in which *Gemeinschaft* is commonly used to refer to the community in general, while *Gemeinde* refers more specifically to the local community. The absence in English of separate words that would allow us to draw a distinction between the local community and the community in the sense of 'the public' or 'people in general' means that we have to make do with a single term that inevitably contains many ambiguities.

The ensuing problems cannot be fully clarified either by a listing of large numbers of characteristics, or by attempts to frame a single abstract overall definition. For to list all the possible features of entities that have been called communities is to combine things that in fact are radically different, whilst any general definitions will be so abstract as to be of little use in analysis. This becomes all the more apparent if we go on to consider the community as an entity or basic unit of society more closely.

The Community as a Unit

Many sociologists conceive of the community as a unit and consider that, despite the many different forms it may take and the different contexts in which it may occur, it always remains an entity in its own right. Thus, for example, König (1968) argues that the community is 'a basic form', and that it does not disappear or dissolve in the wake of industrial and urban revolutions as has often been argued or implied. Similarly, Schnore (1967) launches a discussion on the community with the categorical statement that the 'community is a basic unit of social structure', and then proceeds to discuss its main aspects such as the demographic aspect, the ecological aspect and the structural aspect. One difficulty about such approaches is that it is sometimes unclear whether their proponents are using terms like 'unit', 'entity' and 'basic form' to imply that the community is something that exists as an entity in the real world, 'out there', or whether it is simply a category of analysis. We will return to the point later in our discussion of the urban community. At this juncture, we will confine ourselves to a discussion of the small village-type community as some initial points are more easily made in this way.

The view of the small community as a basic entity in society is usually associated with the name of Redfield, who, in his book *The Little Community*, makes the unambiguous claim that 'humanity presents itself to the view of common sense in just a few kinds of integral entities' – the units of which society is made up. The 'little community' is one of these; others are a person, a people (*ein Volk*), the national state and a civilization. These are all 'conspicuous forms in which humanity obviously comes to our notice', and by implication, they are each capable of being studied as separate units (Redfield, 1955, p. 1). But although persons, peoples, nations, civilizations and 'little communities' may be entities from a commonsense point of view they are extremely disparate entities and, in our view, one could not go very far towards constructing general models of society by using simple 'folk models' of this kind.

Here we do not wish to discuss Redfield's general ideas, however, simply his particular conception of the 'little community', since it is representative of a way of conceptualizing community that has often recurred in the history of sociology and which remains central to a great deal of work in this field. Redfield saw the 'little community' as having four defining qualities: distinctiveness, small size, self-sufficiency and homogeneity of inhabitants. This conception, like many others similar to it, has been criticized on a variety of grounds.

Firstly, it has been pointed out that the features put forward by Redfield as defining qualities are not distinguishing criteria of the 'little community' in any strict sense of the word 'little'. For example, numerous studies of small communities have illustrated that it is seldom, if ever, possible to find units whose boundaries are as clear-cut as Redfield suggests. Similarly, homogeneity and self-sufficiency are very relative and arbitrary characteristics. Every village contains people of varying occupation or social class; their religious and political affiliations may vary, and so on. Again, as we will see, villages are usually tied into a market system that may even be international in range. Redfield was, of course, well aware of these points and himself stressed that, since the course of human history has on the whole run in such a way as to reduce the distinctiveness of the 'little community', we are not in the present historical era likely to find communities that are plainly distinct and self-sufficient. This led him to the recognition that 'to describe a village completely we must reckon with parts that have their centres and their principal being elsewhere than in the village' (Redfield, 1955, p. 114).

Redfield, then, did not intend his four defining qualities of the 'little community' to be taken as a description of empirical reality. His statement on the 'little community' is, rather, an 'ideal-typical' construction, and we cannot engage in any meaningful comment on the statement without first explaining the nature of an 'ideal type'. When we say that the 'little community' is an 'ideal type', we do not mean that it is 'ideal' in the sense of being considered desirable, but in the sense that it is an imaginary perfect representation of the essence of the phenomenon of 'little community'. To take a quite different example, we may think of an author constructing an 'ideal type' of, say, totalitarianism. Such a construction would have to include the features of totalitarianism which its author considers to be *essential* aspects of the phenomenon of 'totalitarianism' in its 'pure' or 'ideal' form – which might hardly ever occur in reality since it will always be mixed up with the other kinds of political arrangements which constitute departures from the pure 'ideal type'. Thus a given society may be predominantly totalitarian, but allow, say, a degree of self-expression to trade unions as long as they confine themselves to matters concerning work. Similarly, an 'ideal type' of democracy might well include, say, popular participation in government and representation on the basis of universal suffrage, even though the author of the 'ideal type' is well aware that free decision-making 'by the people' is always subject to the constraints imposed by political party machines, by a powerful Press, and the like. The construction of such an 'ideal type' may provide a convenient basis for analysing democracy, however, even though we may agree that no *pure* democracy exists in the real world and, indeed, that social reality confronts us with many different kinds of democracy *none* of which approximates at all closely to the 'ideal'.

If we now look at Redfield's characterization of the 'little community' as an 'ideal-typical' construction, it follows (as Redfield recognized) that we cannot expect to find pure or perfect examples of it in the real world. Our assessment of its value must therefore be not in terms of whether it adequately *represents* reality but in terms of its uses in *understanding* reality. This inevitably leads us to ask, as Redfield did, whether it is possible and useful to 'describe as a whole a community whose life is modified by bits of other communities' (p. 114).

At this point in the argument, therefore, we are naturally led to consider two types of community that differ from the self-contained village model: communities within communities, and over-lapping and interpenetrating communities.

Instead of thinking of a discrete unit such as the village, we can conceive of the village as akin to a magnet exercising its pull over a magnetic field. Social relationships take place within fields of force at the centre of which there may lie, not a magnet, but, say a village, a farm-settlement, a town, etc., each exercising attractive power over a certain area. Strong 'magnets' (such as towns) exercise their attraction over larger areas within which weaker magnets (say, villages) also exercise some more limited pull. There are thus a whole range of overlapping social fields for every unit (person, village, etc.) and one may be subjected to the contrary and unique pulls of a number of such magnets. Thus the town exercises a wider attractive pull because it provides specialized or better quality services unavailable in the village even though the latter may be nearer. But for everyday shopping, the latter is good enough.

These 'fields' differ from geographical areas since they are relative, not fixed – the relevant field activated depends on what the social activity is, and they overlap. In social life, of course, the metaphor breaks down because there are different kinds of 'pulls' – economic, familial, religious, etc. – not just one undifferentiated magnetic force. To illustrate this let us now consider extracts from two rural studies which, while compatible with much of Redfield's thinking, go beyond it in important respects. Both studies give us penetrating examples of 'community life' which is not restricted simply to the physical boundaries of a village and in which, far from living in unitary communities, the population is differentiated so that different sets of people are involved with different others at varying ranges in various situations.

Our first example comes from a well-known study, *Family and Community in Ireland*, based on field work conducted by Arensberg and Kimball in the 1930s:

In rural Ireland what we have called the 'rural community' is no simply defined geographical area. Any one of the recognized divisions of the countryside in Ireland, a townland, a group of townlands, a parish, an old barony, a mountain upland, a portion of a valley floor or plain, except perhaps the newer administrative divisions, is in a sense a community. The lines of relationship among the smaller farmers are continuous from one of these to any other across the land. Geographic barriers serve only to deflect the lines of this continuum, not to divide it.

We observe of a farmer of Luogh, for example, that he *coors* [co-operates with neighbouring farmers] largely in Luogh townland. But he has kinsmen scattered around about as far as Mount Elva, four miles to the north and Liscannor, three miles to the south. He attends the parish church of Killilagh, a two-mile walk from his house, but he sends his children to school at Bally-cotton, only a mile off. He does most of his shopping in Roadford, a crossroad settlement two miles away. Yet he takes his larger produce for sale and his larger needs of purchase to the market town of Ennistymon, some eight miles off, or the smaller one of Lisdoonvaran, some five miles off. He votes and pays his taxes as a member of a certain electoral district which overlaps exactly with none of these regions. He associates himself in tradition with Clare and Munster as a North Clare man, rather than with Galway and Connaught, though he may have seen very little of either beyond his market towns. The smaller farmer of Luogh has allegiances to all these communities. He is quite ready to find his emotion stirred in any one of them. He is ready to back the men of Luogh against the men of the neigh-bourhood townland; to back those of the mountain regions against those of the valley lands; those of the parish against the rest; those of the country-side against the towns of Lisdoonvaran and Ennistymon; those of North Clare against other sections of the country; of his class against all others; of his religion against all others; of his nation against all others (Arensberg and Kimball, 1940, pp. 282–3).

The notion of community is thus central to the analysis but the authors make it clear that any conception of a unitary community would be grossly misleading and quite contrary to social reality. Farmers in rural Ireland have various interests or sets of interests and they are liable to pursue these within a series of 'communities' which do not necessarily between them add up to a neat clearly-demarcated whole.

In our second example, drawn from Frankenberg's *Village on the Border*, the emphasis is somewhat different: upon the social connexions of members of each of two broad categories of inhabitants. A key division in the community life of the Welsh village to which Frankenberg gave the name of Pentrediwaith, is that into 'Pentre people' on the one hand and 'outsiders' on the other. But Frankenberg shows that one can only speak of the characteristics and social connexions of 'Pentre people' who 'belong' to the community in a relative way. There is no absolute set of criteria in defining who 'belongs', and varying criteria are invoked in different situations:

In Pentrediwaith social classification of each individual is . . . carried on in various social contexts. Its ostensible purpose is to find out if a person, X, under discussion 'belongs'; that is, to answer the question: 'Is he one of us?' 'He's a stranger really', or 'He's not really a Pentre person', are commonly heard expressions in Pentre. . . . When I was surveying from door to door on the housing estate, after I had introduced myself and said I was studying Pentre, I often got the response: 'Of course, I am not a Pentre person myself.' Sometimes as an objective observer I could accept this, but more than once I found subsequently that the speaker had lived in the village for twenty or thirty years, or had even been born there . . . the criteria that distinguish 'Pentre people' . . . are not absolute. A *'stranger' in one context is 'one of us' in another.* [our italics] To list the characteristics of the 'perfect' villager is only the first stage in understanding the role of social groups within the village.

In some cases it is enough to live in Wales to be 'one of us'. In different contexts this narrows down to North Wales and to the village itself. When there was a broadcast about the village it was argued that only those born in the village were really entitled to speak. [But] to be 'one of us' in some [other] circumstances, membership of a particular family or Chapel is crucial (Frankenberg, 1957, p. 46).

Frankenberg is clearly concerned to show us that awareness of community is not just something in the sociologist's mind but is important to the people whom he studied too. Yet the use of the notion in his analysis by no means requires them or us to view Pentrediwaith as constituting a single community with any particular set of administrative or geographical boundaries.

In both the 'communities' analysed in the above studies, the inhabitants lived their daily lives within a variety of contexts, inter-acting with differing sets of people for different purposes. These vari-ous sets of social relations had different geographical and social bases and were often enclosed within differing administrative and institu-tional boundaries. The important question explored in the two studies was thus not so much the nature of the two 'communities' as basic units, but the way in which these multiple sets of social relations were related to each other as well as to the variously-defined geographical localities in which they existed.

Our broad conclusion is, then, that the notion of 'communities within communities', and its natural extension to cover overlapping and interpenetrating ranges or areas of social relationships, are necessary analytical devices. But the very use of these devices involves more than the abandonment of any simple view of the community as a unitary whole; it also encourages us not to dwell exclusively on unity and harmony but to look also at division, specialization, conflict and competition.

Indeed, one of the major criticisms that has been levelled at Red-field's 'ideal type' is that the whole construction appears to be based on the assumption that the 'little community' is an integrated homogeneous whole, free of tensions, and somehow more harmonious and unified than a large community. This assumption is highly suspect. Indeed, it may well be that internal conflicts, under certain circum-stances, are much greater in a small community precisely because the members are closer to each other. And it is a striking fact that in using the concept of community numerous authors, like Arensberg and Kimball writing on rural Ireland and Frankenberg on rural Wales, have invariably been led away from the model of a self-sufficient unit to the analysis of divided and ill-defined communities in which the 'parts' do not necessarily make up complete and consistent wholes.

'Contrast' Conceptions and Theories of Social Change

We have so far largely refrained from dwelling on any of the several 'contrast' conceptions that are to be found in the large volume of sociological writings on the community in many discussions from the nineteenth century to the present day. The main pairs of contrasted concepts are those between rural and urban communities and, in a sense, those between 'community' and 'non-community'. In broadening our discussion to cover these contrasts we will, at the same time, introduce the subject of social change and attempt to show how sociologists' interests in community as an aspect of social structure have themselves changed over time. Our discussion here, then, is now not about the local community, but about community understood as referring to a certain *quality of social relationships* or to the variety of ways in which individuals and groups of individuals can be bound together and dependent on each other.

We previously stressed the diversity of images of community in the modern world held by different users of the term 'community'. We should now add to this view the suggestion that the ambiguities and complexities taken over into sociology from these diverse 'folk models' of community are to a large extent a reflection of the fact that sociology as a discipline has emerged during a period of far-reaching change. From the nineteenth century to the present day, sociologists have focussed on the community not as some isolated academic exercise, but as an integral part of an extended public discussion on the changes which have continuously engulfed the world of their observations. Living in a changing world, they have naturally focussed on contrast and on change. The history of sociology is, from one point of view, a history of theories of change. Thus we have in the literature a variety of far-reaching theories which see change as a movement from the 'pre-industrial' to the 'industrial' order, as a movement from the 'traditional' to the 'rational', from the 'rural' to the 'urban' way of life, from small-scale 'personal' society to large-scale supposedly 'impersonal' society, from the supposedly simple structure of the 'primitive' to the observed complexity of the 'modern', and so on. These theories contain various conceptions of the community and of its place in the changing social order. Though they may sometimes be implicit rather than explicit, such conceptions are invariably quite central to the theories concerned.

We now proceed to examine some of the main categories of thought contained in theories of change which we have for the most part inherited from the nineteenth century, but which continue in varying degrees to influence our thinking in the twentieth century. We may note right away that change from the 'old' to the 'new' in society has often been conceived as a process of social disorganization involving the erosion and sometimes even the very *disappearance* of community life.

We begin by presenting the major concepts in the work of Tönnies and Durkheim writing in the nineteenth century. We shall then consider connected developments in the later writings of Cooley and MacIver before returning to Redfield to show that his conception of the 'little community' – as well as his broader theory of the folk-urban continuum which takes its departure from the 'little community' – are by no means new, and that the difficulties inherent in them are also present in earlier studies.

Tönnies' book, *Gemeinschaft und Gesellschaft*, first published in 1877, embodies two of the concepts we wish to consider in its very title. Like many nineteenth-century treatises it was an ambitious work which has been described as an attempt to answer the fundamental questions: 'What are we? Where are we? Whence did we come? Where are we going?' (Loomis, 1955, p. 9). The central categories of thought in Tönnies' answer to these broad questions concerning the nature of human society were the twin concepts of *Gemeinschaft* and *Gesellschaft*, usually roughly translated as 'community' and 'association'.

In Tönnies' view, the society of his time in Europe was in the throes of a relentless progression from *Gemeinschaft* to *Gesellschaft*. Urbanization was only one aspect of a whole set of interrelated social changes which affected the whole of society as it became ever less dependent on agriculture and ever more commercial and industrial. He conceived of *Gemeinschaft* as characterized by a unity based on intimate personal living together. Such contacts satisfied fundamental wants and sentiments, and were built into deep-rooted and rich personal relationships. *Gesellschaft*, on the other hand, was characterized by impersonal and limited contractual relations established as a result of calculation and reflection. To illustrate the way in which Tönnies developed and used these twin concepts, we quote the following brief statements from his treatise:

All intimate, private and exclusive living together . . . is . . . life in *Gemeinschaft*. *Gesellschaft* is public life – it is the world itself. In *Gemeinschaft* with one's family, one lives from birth on, bound to it in weal and woe. One goes into *Gesellschaft* as one goes into a strange country. . . .

Gemeinschaft is old; *Gesellschaft* is new . . . all praise of rural life has pointed out that the *Gemeinschaft* among people is stronger there and more alive; it is the lasting and genuine form of living together. In contrast to *Gemeinschaft*, *Gesellschaft* is transitory and superficial. Accordingly, *Gemeinschaft* should be understood as a living organism, *Gesellschaft* as a mechanical aggregate and artefact (Tönnies, 1955, pp. 37–9).

It is important to note that while Tönnies saw *Gemeinschaft* and *Gesellschaft* as two quite opposed ways in which men can be bound together, he considered that there were elements of both *Gemeinschaft* and *Gesellschaft* in all social relationships and all societies. *Gemeinschaft* and *Gesellschaft* were not to be thought of as rigid exclusive categories but as tendencies or influences which pervaded different societies in varying degrees. The second point to note is that he considered the trend of change in the over-all course of human history to be clear: it was towards an increase in the influence of *Gesellschaft* and a corresponding decrease in the influence of *Gemeinschaft*.

A similarly influential study is Durkheim's essay, *The Division of Labor in Society*, first published in 1893. Durkheim sought to show that societies in which the social division of labour was not very marked – in which there were few specialized roles – exhibited a particular kind of social solidarity which he referred to as 'mechanical', whereas societies with a marked division of labour and a high degree of occupational specialization were characterized by another type of solidarity which he referred to as 'organic'. The major features of 'mechanical' solidarity were the relative homogeneity of the population, the uniformity of beliefs, opinions, and conduct, and the dominance of repressive criminal law. In contrast, 'organic' solidarity obtained when a population was 'mentally and morally' heterogeneous, when there was diversity of beliefs, opinions and conduct, and when the principles of law become restitutive rather than repressive. Durkheim suggested that in societies with 'mechanical' solidarity social cohesion derives from a certain conformity of the behaviour of individuals to a common standard. He thus saw 'mechanical' solidarity as based on the *similarity* of individuals, whereas he considered 'organic' solidarity to be based on *interdependence*, arising out of diversity and complementarity.

Like Tönnies, Durkheim saw change as consisting of a progressive one-way movement, and he considered this movement to be irreversible: '. . . it is an historical law that mechanical solidarity, which first stands alone, or nearly so, progressively loses ground, and organic solidarity becomes, little by little, preponderant' (Durkheim, 1964, p. 174).

There are important differences between the formulations of Tönnies and Durkheim. Thus, for example, Tönnies considered that the contrast he described could be attributed to the will of individuals whereas Durkheim was particularly concerned to avoid any type of psychologistic explanation. Our present concern, however, is to point to similarities in their thinking. From one point of view, indeed, their writings are variations on an eternal theme. Theories of this kind did not originate in the nineteenth century but can, as Sorokin and others have frequently stressed, be traced back to the very beginnings of systematic social thought (Sorokin, 1955, p. 6). Nor, as we shall proceed to show, did the appeal of such theories disappear with the passing of the nineteenth century. On the contrary, they have provided the general framework within which systematic field studies in rural and urban sociology have been conducted by many twentieth-century sociologists, and they were clearly very influential in the formulation of conceptions such as those of Cooley and MacIver to which we now turn.

In 1909 Cooley coined the phrase 'primary group' in a statement which was to be repeatedly quoted and discussed for several decades:

By primary groups I mean those characterized by intimate face-to-face association and co-operation. They are primary in several senses, but chiefly in that they are fundamental in forming the social nature and ideals of the individual. The result of intimate association, psychologically, is a certain fusion of individualities in a common whole, so that one's very self, for many purposes at least, is the common life and purpose of the group. Perhaps the simplest way of describing this wholeness is by saying that it is a 'we', it involves the sort of sympathy and mutual identification for which 'we' is the natural expression. One lives in the feeling of the whole, and finds the chief aims of his will in that feeling (Cooley, 1964, p. 311).

In the discussions which followed Cooley's original enunciation of 'primary groups', various authors came to write of 'secondary groups' as, simply, all those which are not primary. Thus another pair of concepts was added to the discussion.

A further influential pair of 'contrast' concepts was MacIver's twentieth-century variation on the theme of 'community' and 'association'. MacIver suggested that we define a community as any group of individuals living together in such a way that they shared 'not this or that particular interest' but 'the basic institutions of a common life'. 'The mark of community,' he wrote, 'is that one's life may be lived wholly within it, that all one's social relationships may be found within it' (MacIver, 1937, pp. 8–9). On the other hand, in contrast to a community, he conceived of an *association* as a group specifically organized for the pursuit of an interest or group of interests. 'The difference is obvious,' he wrote: 'we contrast the business or the church or the club with the village or city or nation' (p. 11).

All these formulations – and others expressing the same broad lines of thought – have passed into the intellectual equipment of present-day sociologists, both as particular concepts and as general characterizations of the processes of change involved in moving from a rural to an urban way of life. Just as Tönnies and Durkheim expressed these changes in the general formulae 'from *Gemeinschaft* to *Gesellschaft*' and 'from mechanical to organic', so Cooley's followers used the conception of the gradual displacement of 'primary groups' by 'secondary groups', and MacIver's followers saw 'associational life' growing at the cost of 'community life'.

The pairs of contrasts we have selected are just some from a wide range of similar pairs of concepts. In the writings of Tönnies and Durkheim they are parts of wider theories of historical change, characteristic of the nineteenth century. The contrasts associated with the work of Cooley and MacIver, however, are examples of more limited pairs of concepts which are not used so much in the analysis of changes in the entire structure of the society as in analysing more specific and limited aspects of particular societies. This difference reflects an important change from the 'old' to the 'new' in sociology itself. Tönnies and Durkheim were writing in the nineteenth-century tradition of the creation of general theories of historical development; Cooley and MacIver were contributing to the formation of the twentieth-century tradition with its great emphasis on field studies and with its consequent need for more specific operational concepts.

Tönnies' and Durkheim's concepts are essentially 'ideal-types' whereas Cooley's and MacIver's come closer to operational definitions which have a ready use in field studies.

This observation brings us back to the kind of problems which we began to consider earlier in discussing Redfield's notion of the 'little community'. We are now able to return to the 'ideal type' of the 'little community'; we can see that it was by no means a completely original notion, but simply another contribution to a rapidly-developing literature on social change based on the notion of the rural-urban contrast. Like Cooley, MacIver and many other sociologists of more recent times, Redfield elaborated his views on the community under the influence of a great deal of earlier theory and speculation, and saw folk society and urban society as polar opposites in much the same style of contrast as *Gemeinschaft* and *Gesellschaft* or as mechanical and organic solidarity. For Redfield, urban society constitutes a disorganized social milieu, whereas folk society is, like the little community, more orderly and harmonious. According to this view the little community is clearly an aspect of folk society and, because Redfield tended to see the essential qualities of community as those expressed in his notion of 'little community', he naturally inclined to the view that urban community is virtually a contradiction in terms. In our view this is an erroneous conclusion which stems directly from the major conceptual confusions in past writings on the community. In saying this, we do not mean to imply that such difficulties are present in the same degree in *all* the past formulations on the theme of change. Durkheim's thesis, for example, is far less open to interpretation as a contrast between either rural and urban or community and non-community than that of Tönnies. But the theme of change from community to non-community, and the rural-urban contrast conception, did, to a greater or lesser extent, converge in the mainstream of the prolonged discussion which came to furnish the principal conceptual inspirations for community research in recent decades. The consequences of this for studies of the urban community are among the topics to which we now turn.

The Community in Urban Studies

The growth of cities and the urbanization of the modern world are impressive facts which clearly constitute a major challenge to the sociologist. The authors whose views are examined above were very much aware both of the facts and of the challenge, but their points of departure were invariably the rural rather than the urban world. Their observations and experience of the rural world were compared to, and contrasted with, notions of the urban world which were often much less solidly based, being impressionistic rather than built out of systematic research. From the early decades of the present century, however, American sociologists in particular have increasingly focussed on the urban community as a field of systematic empirical study. It is mainly to their work that we now turn in order to see how some of the major developments in the concept of community have been used in urban studies.

We shall first devote a section to the formulation of Louis Wirth, who was closely associated with the wide programme of urban research initiated by Robert Park in Chicago in the 1920s and 1930s. We then turn to the 'community study', which also dates as a relatively distinctive type of study from the 1920s, and then to the work of Maurice Stein who, writing much more recently, makes an imaginative attempt to review seemingly disconnected strands of development in the field of 'community studies'. In contrast to this general overview of community studies, we then turn to the study of a community within a modern city – a suburb of Toronto. Finally, we pass on to the more general problem of conceptualizing social space and social boundaries *within* a modern metropolis, and for this purpose make use of a study of Paris by Chombart de Lauwe and his associates.

Our selection of these particular studies for discussion in the sections to follow is partly arbitrary. The field of studies is too vast to allow us to attempt to cover it in any but an illustrative way. Yet our selection has a definite guiding purpose. We attempt, as we move from Louis Wirth's formulation to Chombart de Lauwe's delineation of social areas in Paris, to present a series of approaches which have progressively freed themselves from the model of the small rural community and increasingly include other themes of wider and more general sociological relevance.

Despite the fact that Wirth was associated with a wide programme of research in the modern city of Chicago, his approach to the problem of community remained in many respects very similar to that of

Redfield. This is frankly stated in his well-known essay, 'Urbanism as a way of life', written in 1938, in which he suggests that our starting point for the analysis of the urban community should be the contrast between the 'ideal-types' of rural-folk and urban-industrial society. These, he claims, are our 'basic models of human association in contemporary civilization' (Wirth, 1963, p. 47), and he posits them as the opposite ends of a continuum of human organization. But, being interested primarily in the urban pole, Wirth was less inclined to look for a comprehensive theory of community, and in any case was more concerned to illuminate the nature of city life than was Redfield, who concentrated primarily on the 'little community' and the 'folk society'. Wirth stressed that his conception of the city, which we present in some detail below, was only a very tentative statement intended to guide empirical research and to be constantly subjected to elaboration and revision in the light of field studies. Nevertheless, he also thought that some principal features of urban life were already well-established as enduring and invariable.

The distinctive features of the urban mode of life have often been described sociologically as consisting of the substitution of secondary for primary contacts, the weakening of bonds of kinship, and the declining social significance of the family, the *disappearance* of the neighbourhood, and the undermining of the traditional basis of social solidarity. *All these phenomena can be substantially verified through objective indices* [our italics]. Thus, for instance, the low and declining urban-reproduction rates suggest that the city is not conducive to the traditional type of family life, including the rearing of children and the maintenance of the home as the focus of a whole round of vital activities. The transfer of industrial, educational and recreational activities to specialized institutions outside the home has deprived the family of some of its most characteristic historical functions. In cities mothers are more likely to be employed, lodgers are more frequently part of the household, marriage tends to be postponed and the proportion of single and unattached people is greater. Families are smaller and more frequently without children than in the country. . . .

Being reduced to a stage of virtual impotence as an individual, the urbanite is bound to exert himself by joining with others of similar interest into organized groups to obtain his ends. This results in the enormous multiplication of voluntary organizations directed toward as great a variety of objectives as there are human needs and interests (Wirth, 1963, pp. 60–61).

Before commenting on the above extract as part of Wirth's general conception of the city, let us examine some particular items contained in it in the light of change in society as well as in the light of developments in empirical studies since the essay was written. Looking at the essay thirty years later, we see that history itself has proved Wirth wrong in certain particulars, while better and more comprehensive analyses than were available in 1938 have proved him wrong on others. To illustrate the former, we may take his contention that low and declining reproduction rates were essential features of city life. He thought that the failure of the urban population to reproduce itself was 'a biological consequence of a combination of factors in the complex of urban life', and that the decline in the birthrate generally could be regarded as one of the most significant signs of the urbanization of the Western world. Thus he was led to see cities as 'consumers rather than producers of men'. And he was equally led to assume that large-scale rural-urban migration was, and would remain, universal and permanent.

The facts are, of course, that by and large the above propositions are no longer true of the cities of the Western world. Equally, it is no longer essentially true that 'marriage tends to be postponed' in the cities as compared to villages of the Western world. Wirth based himself on the available empirical evidence of the times mainly from Chicago, from which he drew inferences about city life in general which are very misleading.

Other findings from more recent investigations have proved Wirth wrong on a matter quite central to his general formulation. These concern the supposed *substitution* of secondary for primary contacts in the city, and the supposed *disappearance* of the neighbourhood. Since the 1930s, various studies have shown that both primary contacts and neighbourhoods remain crucially important in the daily life of many city people. The joining of voluntary associations is by no means a general feature of town life. Wirth was certainly correct in pointing to the multiplication of voluntary organizations in urban communities, but investigations such as Stacey's (1960) study of Banbury and Bottomore's (1954) study of Squirebridge show that membership of formally organized groups is only widespread in certain specific sections of the urban population, namely in the middle class and then principally among the middle-aged.

That history and an increasing number of empirical studies have proved Wirth plainly wrong does not necessarily mean that his approach should be dismissed as of no value. It remains one of the most comprehensive statements on the assumptions and concepts which informed a great deal of research into the urban community in the 1920s and 1930s and which have continued to do so up to the present. But it is important to realize that as long as we work *only* with this range of assumptions and concepts we are allowing our imagination to be unduly constrained. The basic shortcoming with Wirth's formulation is that it shows one central – and defective – assumption in common with Redfield's thinking. For if we retain the models of rural society and the rural community as our reference points, we are likely to see city life as 'disorganized', since it *appears* so much more fluid, less integrated and so on. And, as long as we are influenced by this view, we are less likely to develop better perceptions of just how it *is* organized.

The Eclipse of Community?

Wirth was acutely aware of the relative newness of the modern city and of the fact that, as a social phenomenon, large-scale and widespread urbanization was still unfolding itself before the eyes of even the Western world. From one point of view it may thus seem strange that he was so deeply affected by the rural-urban contrast conception. There were other sociologists who had by the 1920s and 1930s already begun to look at the urban scene without *necessarily* referring back to the rural background of the townsman. Yet because many of them devoted themselves mainly to 'community studies' – in the general sense of descriptive and exploratory case studies of towns or sections of a town – and because their researches were often only loosely related either to each other or to any particular 'school' of sociology, their findings are difficult to summarize and do not easily lend themselves to any single system of classification. More importantly, their findings did not influence urban theory as much as they might have done: Wirth did not himself make great use of them, and wrote somewhat disparagingly of 'the miscellaneous assortment of disconnected information which has hitherto found its way into sociological treatises on the city' (Wirth, 1963, p. 62). Hence the rural-urban contrast and mistaken theories about urban life continued to inform urban sociology.

A miscellaneous assortment of disconnected information, it is true, does contribute nothing to systematic sociological theory. But from another point of view, we cannot agree that general 'community studies' are without value. In our view 'community studies' are often extremely valuable precisely to the extent that their main themes and concepts are not based on hard-and-fast preconceptions such as Wirth's, but on suggestive leads or ideas partly current in sociological theory and research, but always, too, grounded in and emerging from the research itself. 'Community studies' are essentially accounts in which the researcher develops his own knowledge and analysis of the community under study. Stein puts it well in his book, *The Eclipse of Community*:

On first reading . . . any good community study, the ordinary reader is likely to be overwhelmed by the mass of detailed facts included. Observations pile upon observations so that the guiding themes are not introduced until the final chapters, if they are made explicit at all. . . . Community studies cannot be read like geometry text-books in which the argument proceeds from postulates to inferences in exact sequence. Instead, the reader has to allow his impressions of the social structure to grow gradually – *quite as does the field worker in the original situation*. Details have to be mulled over as their meaning changes with shifts in context, and general comparisons must be treated by renewed inspection of the reported data (Stein, 1960, p. 8).

Though we regard the title of Stein's book as unfortunate and misleading, many of his views are of considerable importance for the study of the urban community, and to our mind they go a long way towards redressing the balance of the classical view that local communities are somehow less prominent in towns and cities. Stein formally states the purpose of his study as being to develop 'a framework for relating disparate community studies to each other' and 'to devise an approach to community studies in which each investigation becomes a case study illustrating the workings of generalized processes in specific settings.' He carefully examines a series of well-known American community studies including some from the 'Chicago school' inspired by Robert Park, the Lynds' two studies of *Middletown* and *Middletown in Transition* and the Yankee City studies by Lloyd Warner and his associates. In the course of this review he comments on the seemingly disparate materials before him in the following terms:

The range of variation found among the many community studies in the literature is great, making the task of reconciling them difficult. Each research report is a synthesis by the author of several orders of data about a particular community, arranged according to his sense of significant social structures and processes. This synthesis rarely takes into account the relation of the material to other related studies nor do most research reports contain chapters which satisfactorily present generalized conclusions. The community sociologist has been a better ethnographer than a theorist and this is probably as it should be. Weaving the scattered strands of a single community into a coherent picture is in itself a difficult task (p. 4).

Despite the lack of any direct prior connexion between most of the studies, Stein is able to show some continuity and comparability in the community patterns they reveal. Starting with the Chicago studies of the 1920s and 1930s, he draws our attention to the relation between the character of Chicago and the nature of the problems which Robert Park and his followers chose to investigate there. He shows how the Chicago studies were essentially about *a particular kind of urbanization*. He dwells on the fact that the growth of Chicago was very rapid and that it involved the immigration of an ethnically very heterogeneous people, many of them from other countries. The growth-pattern of this particular city is put into perspective and the findings of the Chicago school are presented to us anew as depicting a crucially important, but by no means universal, type of urbanization.

Turning to the Lynds' studies of *Middletown* (a study conducted in 1924; published in 1929) and *Middletown in Transition* (a re-study in 1935; published in 1937), Stein draws attention to important differences in the problems which these volumes present to the theorist as compared to the Chicago studies. He reminds us of the salient characteristics of Middletown: a town of 35,000 inhabitants in 1924; an almost all-White population made up largely of persons born locally or in the immediate rural hinterland; a community which had received its initial stimulus from a 'gas boom' in 1890 when, with a population of 11,000, it was little more than a large village. His emphasis, in assessing the two studies, is that whilst *Middletown* is essentially *a study of industrialization*, in that it recorded in detail the way in which an urban population had adjusted to the recent change-over from a craft economy to factory work, *Middletown in Transition* focusses on *the effects of economic depression* on the changes earlier set in motion by the industrialization reported in the first study. Taking both studies into account Stein interprets the Lynds' work as a case-study of changes in community patterns which display resemblances to those found in cities undergoing rapid growth through absorbing immigrants, but in fact stemming in Middletown from rather different processes – the growth of industrialization and, later, an economic depression over which the inhabitants of the community had no control whatsoever. Urbanization and indus-trialization, that is, do not *necessarily* go hand-in-hand (though they commonly do), nor are immigration of ethnic minorities and depres-sion inevitable parts of urban life *per se*.

From the Lynds' studies, Stein turns to the Yankee City studies conducted between 1930 and 1935 and in particular to *The Social System of the Modern Factory*, in which Warner and Low analyse an industrial strike as a community-wide occurrence. Stein stresses how the authors had to look at the *national* scene before being able to understand and interpret a *local* strike, and also how their attention to the strike led them to focus on certain changing features of the community that might otherwise not have emerged so centrally in their over-all analysis of Yankee City. He recalls the reasons for which Warner and his associates had chosen Yankee City for their studies, namely that they wanted a city where the ordinary daily relations of the inhabitants were not in a state of confusion or rapid change. They wanted a stable community, and they set out in the hopes of studying 'order' and 'organization' rather than 'disorder' and 'disorganization'.

As it turned out, however, Warner and Low found themselves in Yankee City at a time of severe industrial unrest in the local shoe industry, and they were scarcely able to fulfil their hopes of studying 'stability' as against 'instability'. Instead, they were led to turn their investigation into an attempt to explain why a community which had a previous record of weak union organization, and of 'good' indus-trial relations, seemed to rapidly transform itself into a community with strong union organization and 'bad' industrial relations. An important part of the answer to which they came is, in brief, that Yankee City was at that particular juncture being increasingly drawn into a web of social and economic relations that spread far beyond the boundaries of the town.

Following the line of analysis developed by Warner and Low, we come to see Yankee City in terms of the interplay between the growth of bureaucracy in industry and the decreasing isolation of a local community. This process had important implications for both the industrial organization and the community structure of the town, and Stein uses the study to highlight the importance of a third basic process, namely *bureaucratization*, over and above the processes of *urbanization* and *industrialization*, in the transformation of the social structure of American communities.

There are several features of the studies referred to by Stein which deserve close examination by readers who are interested in research procedures and in the methods of investigation used in 'community studies'. The Lynds' re-study of a community after a lapse of ten years is one such feature, the excellent use made by Warner and Low of a fortuitous historical event another, and the strategy employed in the Yankee City series of conducting several studies in one town, so that both expected and unexpected interconnexions could be fully explored, is a third. But it falls beyond our present purpose to discuss these points. Our present interest lies primarily in Stein's clear demonstration that the modern urban community warrants analysis in terms *other than those of the rural–urban contrast model*.

In drawing on the studies of Chicago, Middletown and Yankee City, Stein shows an insistent concern with *social change in and of the city*, and with the construction of a model that would allow us to compare various urban communities at various phases and stages of development. In our view this is Stein's achievement: he began to sketch a model of social process *in* and *of* the urban community which is more general, has more dimensions, and is also more flexible than the rural–urban contrast model. Basing himself on a wide variety of community studies, he nowhere found it crucial to accord overriding importance to the rural–urban contrast model handed down to us from the nineteenth century. For him, the processes of urbanization – of the growth of towns and of the urban incorporation of rural immigrants – constitutes only *one* of three basic processes, the other two being industrialization and bureaucratization.

When we examine the urban community as presented in the kind of 'community studies' which Stein reviews, we become aware that many researchers have, indeed, wittingly or unwittingly, abandoned the rural–urban contrast conception as their model in urban community research. It is, however, often more difficult to see what particular model or models they have used in its place. The value of Stein's contribution lies in his attempt to extract a model from a variety of disparate studies, and this model – in so far as he succeeds in establishing one – lays emphasis not on the urban community as a unit or structure, nor on the rural–urban contrast, but on the three interconnected processes at work in the communities he studied: urbanization, industrialization and bureaucratization.

Having dwelt on the constructive aspect of Stein's work, we must now be somewhat more critical about the basic assumption implied in the title of his book. Why, we may ask, should the processes of urbanization, industrialization and bureaucratization be seen as necessarily spelling the *eclipse* of community?

The considerations which brought Stein to this view are quite explicitly stated. For example, writing of *Middletown in Transition*, he comments that the study reports 'the final breakdown of any sense of character or workings of the whole community among its residents' (Stein, 1960, p. 65). Somewhat similarly, in writing of Yankee City, he remarks that 'relations between (workers and managers). . . were henceforth to be mediated by impersonal contacts arrived at through negotiation between representatives of the top echelons of the two bureaucracies – management and labour . . . [and that] their sense of belonging to a common enterprise, whether it be the shoe factory or the city itself, seriously declined' (p. 90).

Such passages are the clue to Stein's contention that the studies he reviews reveal the passing of community. But his stand on this point does not seem to us to be well-founded. As we see the problem, Stein is in his study as a whole drawing attention to two different aspects of community. On the one hand, he points to certain specific interlocking consequences for the community of urbanization, industrialization and bureaucratization. Among these consequences there are, for example, the increased interdependence and decreased local autonomy of previously well-defined territorial communities, and the increasing determination of the life-chances of local inhabitants by national and international forces outside the local community.

On the other hand, he also points to criteria which are of *a different kind*, such as the sense of belonging, the feeling of change experienced by the inhabitants, and the feeling of *some* that they were becoming strangers in their own towns. ('What of the newcomers?' we may ask in passing.) Our contention is that such criteria cannot by themselves be taken as indications of the eclipse of community. If we use them as such, we are in effect once again using the model of the rural community, a step fraught with difficulties and possible misconceptions. In this connexion, we may usefully recall Arensberg and Kimball's study of rural Ireland and Frankenberg's of a Welsh village. We saw there that the facts of division, of being classified as a stranger, and the like, do not require us to abandon the notion of community. Why should they do so in Middletown or in Yankee City?

Stein's dilemma here is that, in the studies he reviews, he is confronted with two sets of criteria. Some of these criteria are structural and objective, but others are of an altogether different – subjective – order. Both sets of characteristics are of cardinal interest for the sociological analysis of the local community. But they are different, and in handling them we need to be very careful not to return to a nostalgic view of the community. This, we suggest, is what Stein does at the end of his study when he complains that all the communities in mass society look like so many minor variations on a single major theme. We suggest that this vein in his work derives less from his invaluable review of a series of 'community studies' than from a nervous popular view of mass society. In fact, community life persists strongly in cities, whether we have in mind localized communities or 'communities of interest' spread across the city and beyond. Again, the absence of a strong sense of identification with the immediate neighbourhood – the absence of distinctive 'urban villages' within the city boundaries – does not mean that we do not identify ourselves as Mancunians, Parisians or Chicagoans. 'Village'-type community is not the only type. We suggest, therefore, that before convincing ourselves that the forces of mass society will inevitably reduce the rich diversity of urban community life to some irrevocably standardized common pattern, we should recall the fate that history has meted out to some of Wirth's assertions of only thirty years ago. Our criticism, however, does not in itself provide any indication of how the concept of the local community can be usefully modified and applied in the study of modern cities and metropolitan centres; we therefore turn to a study which attempts precisely this.

Community in the Metropolis

As our example of an urban study which demonstrates the value of retaining the concept of local community structure, we take the study by Seeley, Sim and Loosley of a suburb of Toronto which they call 'Crestwood Heights'. In this prosperous, modern upper middle-class area, the adult male population consists mainly of independent businessmen, professionals and senior executives who leave their suburban homes daily for their offices in nearby Big City. Thus at least one major life activity – work – scarcely enters into the analysis. Yet the authors still refer, quite usefully in our view, to the suburb they studied as a community, and they take care to tell us precisely what they mean by it:

Since the word 'community' will be used throughout this study in reference to Crestwood Heights, it is important that the sense in which the term is apt be established in the very beginning. Although Crestwood Heights is officially a separate municipality within a greater metropolitan area, it is also something else. *It exists as a community because of the relationships that exist between people – relationships revealed in the functioning of the institutions which they have created: family, school, church, community center, club, association, summer camp, and other more peripheral institutions and services.* [our italics] ... These relationships develop within a material setting of brick, stone, wood, concrete, and steel – and of flowering gardens, shaded in several sections by trees which once arched over an earlier and a very different enterprise, the clearing of the forest by a more simple type of pioneer (Seeley *et al.*, 1963, pp. 3–4).

The authors then proceed to explain how there is one central feature of social life in Crestwood Heights which gives it coherence as a community. Unlike many communities, work is not a factor making for strong local identification. Instead they write, 'the major institutional focus is upon child-rearing' (p. 4). Participation in the community is largely related to this concern – a concern with a set of ideals about manhood and womanhood and about the way in which these ideals can be passed on to their children.

Crestwood Heights is not merely a dormitory of Toronto. It is, the authors stress, the locus of a common life. Though most Crestwood Heights fathers carry on their occupations outside the limits of the suburb, their removal from the day-time activities of their families and friends is far from complete, for both telephone conversations and lunch-time rendezvous are frequent.

In brief, then, Crestwood Heights is a largely residential community in which adults are in one way or another primarily engaged in producing and rearing children. Directly and indirectly, the institutions of Crestwood Heights are geared to turning out young people to certain specifications that are well accepted in the community. Crestwood Heights is clearly not a community according to the concepts of, say, Redfield or MacIver, if only for the reason that the adult male residents could not conceivably live their lives wholly in Crestwood Heights. And although women and children could conceivably live almost entirely within the suburb, they do not in fact normally do so. But Crestwood Heights is still a complex network of social relations based in a given area and taking place within a limited set of converging institutional structures. In some ways, then, Crestwood Heights is comparable to one or more of the overlapping and interpenetrating 'communities' located around Arensberg and Kimball's Irish townland of Luogh or Frankenberg's Welsh village of Pentrediwaith. Crestwood Heights, that is, is obviously not a complete or self-sufficient community, but it is patently an 'interest community'.

That many residents of Crestwood Heights have no children and therefore do not share with fellow-residents the major local interest of child-rearing does not mean that they do not participate in local institutions. Nor does the fact that numerous residents – especially the men – participate in important activities outside the suburb necessarily imply that they do not also participate locally. The complex networks of social relations centred on local institutions, and particularly those related to child-rearing, give rise to interwoven patterns of differentiated participation, to divisions and alignments. The inhabitants of Crestwood Heights share, admittedly within a limited range, a diversity of interests and activities. They pursue their total daily lives within a variety of multiple contexts, of which a sufficient number are centred in the suburb to give it *an important element of 'community life'* and to make the concept of local community relevant to them, and therefore useful also to the sociologist seeking to analyse their common life.

We have argued that the processes of modern urban life by no means render the concept of community meaningless, and have used the study of Crestwood Heights in support of this view. However, we cannot claim that the concept is always *by itself* of central importance for an understanding of urban social relations. Indeed, the extent to which the life and structure of a large city or metropolis would lend itself to analysis in terms of overlapping and interpenetrating 'interest communities' remains to be tested, for sociologists have thus far usually approached large cities not from this point of view, but with the quite different aims of merely identifying and delineating types of populations and types of social areas within them (usually called 'human ecology'). Such studies are concerned to classify the different areas of a city in terms of their dominant pattern of use – whether they are industrial, residential, commercial or recreational zones – or in terms of the social composition of the population in each zone, whether (usually) by class (upper-, middle- or working-class areas), by type of housing (owner-occupied, public rented, privately rented, rooming area, slum and so on), or possibly into ethnic zones (by colour, tribe, ethnic origin, etc.), and in showing the relationships between these areas. We now briefly examine one such study precisely in order to draw a contrast between the study of ecological patterns in a large city and the very different division of the city population into 'interest communities'.

In *Paris et l'agglomération Parisienne*, Chombart de Lauwe and his colleagues specifically set out to delineate the populations and social areas of Paris rather than to describe it in terms either of its administrative boundaries or of communities. They explain that for them the population of Paris consists of all the people for whom Paris is a centre of attraction, and they thus include as members of the city not only those who live there but all those who commute there daily or who ever visit it for whatever reason. Thinking of any city in this way inevitably means that transportation routes play a large part in determining its 'boundaries', and the authors are led to liken Paris to a roughly circular area with tentacles which protrude along railway lines and main roads. (And, we could add, which extend round the globe.) They equally point out that, socially, Paris does not have one centre, but several. There is a business centre, a university centre, an industrial centre, an arts centre and so on. And this has its counterpart in the fact that Paris plays a number of roles in

France as well as in the modern world as a whole. Paris is, the authors point out, the result of an extraordinary series of centralizations that have developed over hundreds of years.

Against the background of this first broad thumbnail sketch of Paris, the authors then depict the city as a series of roughly concentric zones. In establishing the zones, of which they distinguish seven, the authors (Chombart de Lauwe *et al.*, 1952) take into account several types of criteria, in conjunction with the density of population, the time taken to travel to work, and the relation between areas in which people live and in which they work:

Zone 1. Elliptical in shape – covers the 'noyau' [the heart] – the business core of the city – an area tending to spread westwards over time. (Limits about 1 to $2\frac{1}{2}$ kms from the centre.)

Zone 2. A zone corresponding to what is called 'the zone of transition' in many American studies, but which the authors prefer to call 'the zone of acculturation'. To some extent a zone of foreigners, though not *only* of economically depressed minority groups, e.g. to the west of the centre there are many wealthy Americans. 'Acculturation' in middle-class areas of Zone 2 is very different from 'acculturation' in the poverty-stricken and 'proletarian' areas. (Limits about 3 kms from centre.)

Zone 3. An inner residential zone lying between the 'acculturation' zone and the 'suburbs'. On the East side, the zone contains a fair amount of industry though virtually no *large* firms. In the West, there are few factories, but numbers of large blocks of flats interspersed among areas of private dwelling-houses. (Irregular shape; limits from 3 to 7 kms from centre.)

Zone 4. The zone of large and very large factories with a largely working-class population – residential areas between the factories consist mainly of small dwellings. A number of formerly self-sufficient towns that have now been engulfed by the growth of Paris are found in this zone, as in the remaining zones to be considered. (Irregular shape; limits 5 to 12 kms from centre.)

Zone 5. A mixed residential zone with a high proportion of commuters to the centre and a low proportion of residents *working* in the areas they inhabit. (Shape still more irregular; limits from 10 to 15 kms from centre.)

Zone 6. Somewhat similar to Zone 5 but less densely populated and with a higher rate of population increase at the present point of history. (Limits 12 to 27 kms from centre.)

Zone 7. A peripheral zone which sends markedly fewer commuters to the centre daily than does Zone 6. A zone 'influenced by the proximity of Paris but not yet really integrated into it'.

Having delineated these zones, the authors then proceed to distinguish between other social areas *of* and *in* Paris which, they suggest, have to be seen as cutting *across* the zones or, alternatively, in other cases, as being embedded *within* one or more zones. Thus, for example, they draw numerous contrasts between the *bourgeois* West and the proletarian East. They point out that even aerial photographs show up marked differences between East and West. The *bourgeois* West has relatively sharp lines of demarcation; its streets are broad and also more regular and more symmetrical. In contrast, the East, viewed from the air, forms a more diversified and less regular pattern with narrower streets and fewer open spaces. The general contrast is equally one which many novelists have depicted, and the authors cite in particular the contrasts depicted in Jules Romain's novels between the poles of wealth in the West and of poverty in the East.

From these contrasts between the West and the East, the authors pass on to comment on irregularities in the dominant concentric patterns caused either by the absorption of formerly 'independent' towns or by the 'spontaneous' growth within them of *quartiers* (neighbourhoods) with distinctive populations or distinctive physical features. Thus they refer to *quartiers* that are *bourgeois* as against those of the *ouvriers*, to numerous ethnic *quartiers*, as well as to *quartiers* which derive their distinctive characteristics from the fact that they are centred on a factory, or a park, or a square.

This study of Paris, like many ecological studies in various parts of the world, tells us a great deal about the life of the city. It is, however, not a study of community in any of the senses previously discussed in this chapter. That there are numerous overlapping and interpenetrating 'interest communities' in Paris can be inferred from the information we are given, but the ecological analysis of populations and social areas is basically a preliminary 'mapping' exercise: it does not by itself explain the pattern of social relations within such communities as exist in Paris, why they are distributed as we find them, or how they are interrelated. The charting and the study of communities within Paris, indeed, more widely, the study of the interrelations between the various types and levels of community in the great cities of the world, are tasks which have so far scarcely been tackled, despite the vast output of empirical urban research over recent decades.

At the beginning of this chapter we set out to examine community as a *theme* in modern sociology and to consider the ways in which various concepts developed in pursuing this theme can contribute to the analysis of society. We began by examining the everyday meanings of the word 'community'. Firstly, we drew attention to the ambiguities and complexities inherent in the layman's notion of community and to the way in which these have affected the sociologist's interpretation of it. We suggested and tried to demonstrate that the multiplicity of meanings and the general confusion over the term are not simply due to muddled formulations, but in part to the complexity of modern history and to the constant unfolding of new sociological perspectives. We then discussed the community as a unit and examined the difficulties involved in attempting to use any concept of community which carries with it the connotation of a unitary whole. On the other hand, we illustrated the fruitful use in field studies of the notions of over-lapping and inter-penetrating communities. We then broadened the focus of our attention to include not only the local community, but also the community understood as referring to particular kinds of shared social relationships, and to a variety of ways in which in-dividuals can be bound together and dependent on each other apart from living in the same neighbourhood. We stressed the importance of some nineteenth-century formulations of the concept, and noted how these were developed in the context of theories of change. We equally examined the carry-over of such concepts to the twentieth century, especially in studies of the rural-urban contrast.

Turning specifically to urban studies, we dwelt on the way in which concepts deriving from theories of change and the rural-urban contrast have exercised an enduring – and often a limiting and con-stricting – influence on the imagination of many research workers. But we also noted the concurrent development of a body of 'com-munity studies' which have progressively freed themselves from these constraints. We then used the example of Crestwood Heights to suggest that, once freed from the more negative and restricting connotations associated with notions of rural society, a general concept of community retains considerable value in exploring modern urban life. The use of the concept involves accepting that there may be as many 'interest communities' in the urban or metropolitan world as there are sets of interests and activities. And these interests and activities are likely to be pursued in settings which are only very partially determined by particular geographical and administrative boundaries.

Indeed, once we extend Chombart de Lauwe's notion that we must include all those who *use* Paris in our analysis, we realize that there are innumerable interest groups who pursue enormously diverse interests within a modern city. Some of these groups are concentrated in particular ecological areas and niches – localities or spots specialized as 'residential', 'recreational', and so forth. Other interest communities bring together people from all over the city, and beyond: supporters of football teams, members of political parties, enthusiasts for old-time dancing, or whatever. A community thus refers to those people who are linked together in any particular activity or institution. There are as many communities as there are interests and activities binding sets of people together (Webber, 1964, pp. 108–20). Their geographical extent will vary considerably from the children's playgroup to the community of astronauts.

If a community of interest is not necessarily a locally co-resident community, it need not even involve its members in direct social contacts at all. One can be a member of a national or even international community though one only has indirect relationships with other members. Our behaviour may be profoundly affected by our seeing ourselves as part of an international community of Christians, Muslims, Communists, speleologists or hockey-players. All of these are, to one degree or another, *organized* groups. Yet one can also feel oneself to be part of much less structured and organized groupings – the international community of scholars, the Underground or the Establishment – in ways that will quite importantly affect one's behaviour, though these are not formal associations.

The idea of community, then, or more specifically, of interest-community, is of continuing relevance in studying urban life. Community studies, in the past, have aimed at and have sometimes claimed to have achieved a complete account of all social activities occurring within a relatively small geographically-defined unit. But it becomes increasingly difficult to assert that modern social life can in fact be adequately approached this way. We can give descriptions of what goes on in a particular area, but a great deal of the activities of the people who live there or spend some part of their time there will be carried on outside the chosen locality altogether. Under such conditions, a 'community study' is likely, at best, to include only a *part* of the lives of the people it discusses. Interest communities today extend beyond the neighbourhood, small town or village, so long the favourite units for community studies. And even the 'urban village' study has its limitations, for not all residential areas have distinctive boundaries, centres or styles of life, and in any case the urbanite is likely to associate with those with whom he has interests in common even if they do not live nearby.

The modern conception of community is thus very far removed from older conceptions based on the model of the village. It suggests that in some ways, though the city does contain the 'unattached' and 'lonely crowds', not only do primary groups – families, neighbourhood groups, church congregations, pub clienteles, etc. – retain their importance, but new kinds of secondary associations are also generated, since in large populations any minority interest, however small, may well bring together scattered individuals who would be completely isolated in a village, but who become part of a community in a big city.

Finally, we should remember that there are communities based on many interests that we may not ethically approve of, and that there may also be a great deal of structured community life in situations we look upon as 'chaotic'. Yet neither criminal communities nor slum communities are 'disorganized'; they *are* communities. Slum areas are often closely-integrated into various structures – churches, criminal 'empires', political machines and so on. The most extreme cases today are probably the shanty-towns of the Third World, where people live in what often looks like disorder physically, but develop elaborate sets of interpersonal ties as well as voluntary associations which range from burial and insurance societies to tribal associations or sports clubs. As in the developed world, however, it tends to be the more fortunate who create, lead and join these associations – it is the middle strata who predominate in local associational life, whether in English country towns or African shanty-towns. It is to this ever-intrusive phenomenon of social class that we now wish to turn.

Part Three

Chapter 7
Social Stratification: Class, Status and Power

In using the term 'stratification' to refer to society, we are using an analogy. In geology, stratification refers to the way in which layers of rock are arranged one on top of another. Social stratification, similarly, refers to the division of a population into strata, one on top of another. But there are several most important differences between social stratification and stratification in nature:

1. Between *social* strata, there are relationships, whereas there is no kind of ongoing interconnexion between successive layers of rock. Each class, that is, is part of a *system* of stratification.

2. This interconnexion involves the different strata in relationships of inferiority and superiority, usually of many kinds: political, economic, 'social', even religious. They therefore have conflicts of interest. And their class-position also affects their behaviour even though they may not realize it.

3. Social strata are collectivities of people who themselves perceive these inequalities, and have their own conceptions of the stratification system which affect their behaviour.

4. Social strata are not therefore inert: they tend to give rise to groups which recruit from the given stratum and which claim to express the interests of the stratum as a whole, and thus affect the rest of the system.

5. Stratification systems change over time; they may do so suddenly or gradually (whereas rock strata have remained set, throughout human history at least).

Complex arrangements for classifying and stratifying people do not arise simply as an intellectual pastime. Stratification is in fact a means of regulating access to what the economist calls 'scarce goods', by which he means not just material objects of consumption like groceries or even material instruments of production like blast-furnaces, but rather all things *valued* (seen as 'good') in society and consequently sought after. So among 'goods' we include 'psychic' and 'immaterial' satisfactions, such as the distribution and receipt of prestige, as well as the distribution and receipt of material objects. As we saw in Chapter 5, men will commonly work hard and spend hard, in order to acquire not just the biological 'necessities of life', but also 'social' necessities (more accurately 'wants') which include using wealth to get power over others and respect from them. This often involves using one's resources not just for straightforward individual consumption, but using them to build up a political following or to maximize one's status.

We have used a very wide term, 'stratification', so far, because, although *class* stratification is the dominant kind of stratification found in the modern world – in capitalist societies deriving from differential access to private property, and in communist societies primarily from differential access to political power – there have been many other kinds of stratification in past history. 'Age-set' societies, feudal 'estate' societies and caste societies, for example, are quite different systems of stratification from those more familiar to people living in class societies.

Estate and caste societies, for example, distribute their members at birth into different strata according to one principal criterion – age, descent, rank, etc., and there is little or no possibility of moving out of that stratum. They also develop explicit theories explaining and justifying why such arrangements exist. In industrial societies on the other hand – whether capitalist or communist – however class-ridden or elitist they may be, there are no formal criteria of this kind which condemn a person to one particular class for his whole life. Class is thus much more informally institutionalized than, say, caste, but is nonetheless important. It will therefore help us to see the distinctive features of social class in advanced capitalist and in communist societies more clearly if we look first at two types of stratified 'pre-industrial' society more closely.

Let us look first at those tribal societies of the 'stateless' type described by Fortes and Evans-Pritchard (1940). These societies lack centralized administration and judicial institutions. The office of chief may not exist at all, or if it does, often carries more ritual than secular power. Nor is succession to office necessarily hereditary. Yet a society may be 'stateless', it may lack chiefs (and thus be called an 'acephalous' (headless) society), and yet still be stratified. Australian aboriginal tribes, for example, are stratified on the basis of age (and sex). Men move from one age-grade to another as they grow older, making the transition from boy to young man, from unmarried young man to married adult, and eventually to 'elderhood'. Membership of the successive age grades is so important that it is socially marked by successive rituals, physically marked also on a man's body in the form of cicatrices successively cut into his chest. In other societies, a whole age group is initiated so as to form an 'age-set' together; it often takes a name derived from some contemporary event (*Panyako*: 'Pioneer Corps' was chosen in one African society because many young men were conscripted in 1940), or takes over a traditional name. These age-sets are the major basis of social organization – thus the age-set of warrior age was responsible for defence, and the older age-sets for various other tasks in the running of the society. Membership of these groups thus controls all aspects of life: it affects whom a man may marry, his right to own land, his ability to participate in certain rituals and so forth; hence membership of such a stratum thus has an extra dimension of religious significance that secular ideologies of class lack.

All aborigines, too, move through the age-grade system: a man becomes successively a hunter, warrior and eventually reaches the heights of elderhood. His social development is identical with that of his age-mates, and is determined by the physical fact of ageing. So although a society like this is highly stratified and constitutes a 'gerontocracy', in which the older men hold the decisive authority, every man in his time becomes an elder. He is not fixed for life in a lowly position. Secondly, he performs exactly the same production-roles as his fellows: all are hunter-producers. Consumption-standards hardly differ either. Finally, there is room for any enterprising person of reasonably appropriate age to win himself a leading part in the economy, in settling disputes, or in ritual, if he wants to. To this degree, this kind of society is an 'opportunity' or 'open' society where ours is not, contrary to much popular assumption and even to much sophisticated social theory about the 'open society'. Yet though there is change of personnel within the system, the pattern of stratification itself does not change: the basic determinants remain fixed: those of age and sex.

This kind of fixity is even more evident where a man is allocated to his place in the stratification-system by birth. In the caste-system of India, relationships in all dimensions of life were affected by a man's caste-membership. The caste-system exists at two distinct levels. One is an India-wide classification into priests, warriors (land-holders), merchants and the broad mass of people on the land. The whole Hindu population, and a number of other groups, are fitted into these four *varna*. But these are not the basic units of caste at village level. Here, instead of the *varna*, we find a division of the local community called the *jati* (also translated as 'caste'). The *jati* is a group of individuals who live in a group of villages, who often (but not always) have the same occupation and who maintain their group-identity by marrying exclusively within the caste. It is this *jati* which constitutes the social reality of caste for individuals in rural Indian society and there are many thousands of such groups; all of them, however, can fit themselves into the four *varna*. A complex structure of norms and taboos derived from religious ideas concerning pollution also prevent members of one caste from eating with members of another or even touching them. The effect is to maintain social distance between the various *jatis* and to preserve the hierarchical system of ritual superiority and inferiority intact as a whole. On the margin of society altogether are the 'outcaste' Untouchables (now called 'scheduled castes') with whom caste-members could have only the most minimal contact for fear of pollution. Formally, the caste system is absolutely closed, both to individual and group mobility. Nevertheless, whole groups have successfully improved their caste-position through the process known as 'Sanskritization' in which a group imitates the customs of a superior *jati*, via exaggerated observance of the ritual practices of that group, by taking up 'purer' occupations, by treating *jatis* of previously equal or superior status as ritually polluting, and by making demands for precedence over them in ceremony.

A caste is thus much more than an occupational group. It is an extreme example of what is usually called a status-group, because the term 'status' involves not just a position in a division of labour, but membership of a group marked off from other inferior and superior groups and accorded different amounts of prestige. Since all occupations are themselves evaluated as higher or lower in status, status is an intrinsic dimension even of a person's economic role. A caste is a very *closed* status-group, but status-groups can be much more open.

It is not only prestige that is differentially distributed in this way. So is power. Any occupation or other social role carries more or less power with it. So we propose to take the three major dimensions of stratification: economic inequalities (usually called 'class' on its own), status inequalities, and power inequalities: and discuss each in turn. They may fit together, but, as we shall see, it is possible to be higher on one dimension than another, and in rapidly-changing societies this is particularly so. Thus an unskilled worker may hold high political office; an aristocrat can be obliged to turn to humble work.

These concepts are not used by social scientists alone. People in society have their own understanding of the class system, of the graduations of prestige, and of the way power is distributed. These 'folk-models' are not merely cognitive – making *intellectual* sense of the stratification-system – they also have a moral or normative element: people evaluate the system as good or bad. Even where individuals or groups operate with the same intellectual model, they may differ in their moral evaluation of the system according to their position in it: the poor may regard their own poverty as divinely-ordained; they may regard it as unjust. Any adequate sociological account of social class in all its dimensions must include and explain the conceptions of the social actors themselves. We will see later how inadequate many well-known models of social class are, because they do not take account of people's ideas; the subjective meaning of social class is as much a reality as any objective measure of a man's income though it is harder to get at.

This is why many researchers, more particularly administrators, use very simple indicators of social class. All they want is something that will work – for research or administrative purposes. They do not necessarily seek a rounded understanding of all the complexities of social life. Indeed, they are not necessarily interested in the group life of a class at all; they are concerned usually with only a limited problem – say, educational failure rates. Of course, to understand that problem fully they would need eventually to go quite deeply into the way social class affects people's lives. But for immediate purposes (like constructing simple tables) a single index of class such as occupation will do quite well. Many quite complex models of the class system as a whole are of this kind: they are analytical constructions of limited sociological depth. And they often fail to grasp adequately class 'out there' in society. The society is classified and divided up in these schemes, but in ways that do not grasp the real groups and 'class distinctions' that are the stuff of everyday life, and in ways, often, that few in society would accept as valid ways of conceptualizing the class-system.

Class

Most people who live in class societies are aware that they do, and their ideas about class may not coincide with the sociologist's model of the class-ststem nor with his evaluation of their particular class position. A person's class position may also be differently evaluated by others besides sociologists: by neighbours, workmates, relatives, etc. There are, however, criteria such as a person's occupation or the amount of money he earns, which *all* can agree about, irrespective of their ideas about class in general or this person's position in particular. It might seem possible, then, to find a way of defining class quite *objectively*. But we all know that it is very often the case that whilst X's neighbours insist that X is working class, X obstinately considers himself to be *middle* class. X's ideas (and his neighbours') cannot be ignored because they affect their behaviour. He is more likely, for instance, to associate with people he regards as middle class, follow middle-class patterns of recreation, try to use a middle-class accent, have middle-class ambitions for his children, etc. His *subjective* perception of his class position cannot, therefore, be simply written off as 'wrong' or – more sophisticatedly – as 'false consciousness', to use the Marxist term, if we are to understand why people behave as they do, for although in other people's eyes a man may be 'wrong' in his opinion of himself, his belief, as W. I. Thomas, the American sociologist, put it is '*real* in its consequences', that is, it affects the way he behaves.

A second major difficulty is that we are dealing with rapidly changing societies, in which social class changes rapidly also, and in which people realize that such changes are taking place. So it becomes difficult to draw hard-and-fast border-lines between classes when hundreds of thousands of people move into occupations different from those of their parents, or marry people of different class backgrounds, or feel perhaps that class is not as important or as rigid as it was in Dickens' day.

There certainly have been significant changes in the way people are distributed *within* the class system. (It is much more debatable whether the system as a whole has changed to any significant extent.) But some kinds of change are obvious, notably the expansion of the 'tertiary' sector of the economy, which has meant a decrease in the number of low-paid manual jobs and an increase in the proportion of jobs in the service occupations, the clerical sector, etc. Though such jobs nowadays are not necessarily paid any better than manual occupations (especially when overtime is so generally worked), they still retain an aura of 'middleclassness' and some real differences in treatment at work and in society generally, too. And with so many of the new jobs going to women, even though the women are less well-paid, their income makes the *family* appreciably better off. Many other kinds of change are equally apparent. We all know that the growth of educational opportunities and expanding industrial production have both led to an increased volume of upward social mobility as well as to new avenues for achieving such mobility, and that the very worst extremes of physical poverty have been eliminated. On the other hand, not only do the poor obstinately remain with us, but their numbers are legion, and welfare provision by the State has lessened in significance in recent years (in some respects, the provision is less effective than it was half a century ago) (Titmuss, 1958, p. 24). Nor has 'progressive' taxation made any serious impact upon the wealthy (Titmuss, 1962). And by and large, enhanced social and political equality – notably the extension of rights formerly restricted to the upper classes to the whole population (Marshall, 1950) – has made little difference as far as the elimination of economic inequality is concerned.

These complex changes have led naturally to varying interpretations. Some argue that one result has been the adoption of middle-class styles of life by the new non-manual workers; others argue that not only has the gap between non-manual workers and the middle class diminished, but that the gap between non-manual workers and manual workers has also narrowed (whether in terms of income or in the uses to which they put their incomes). Yet others accept one or both of these propositions, but go on to argue that class differences of a new kind have emerged: that as gross inequalities diminish, more refined distinctions spring up in their place, usually in the form of visible items of consumption – cars, clothing and so on. (This argument assumes that a sense of deprivation and actual discrimination does not simply arise at a given level of poverty, but depends on the comparisons people make between their own life-situations and those of others. Poverty is a relative socially-defined matter; what is poverty in one society is comfort in another, and the same applies *within* a society. The people we compare ourselves with may be those we live amongst rather than those we only know about at second-hand) (Runciman, 1966).

These fairly common views, which we will examine in more detail below, obviously reflect real recent changes, for people also make comparisons over time: between their contemporary life-experience and the era of the Second World War, the depression which preceded it, or their 'folk-memories' of nineteenth-century conditions. For many of us, the history of massive over-crowding, endemic and industrial disease and alcoholism is a part of family, not simply school-book history. Charles Booth's *Life and Labour of the People of London* and other works showed that around 1890 a third of the families lived in poverty. Only slowly did successive Factory Acts lead to improvement of conditions in the work-place. Trade Unions also gradually recruited more and more workers into organizations which brought collective pressure to bear on employers to raise wages, limit hours and improve working-conditions for those at work, and on the State to provide minimal relief for those without work.

These limited advances, however significant, by no means generated a completely new and autonomous working-class culture, opposed intransigently to the culture of capitalism. Indeed, the very concessions won, both in the field of politics and in industrial relations, made it possible for the power-wielders to generate a new kind of social support. Working-class habits and values of deference, partly derived from the pre-industrial past, were strongly ingrained: in 1868, the Birmingham branch of the Conservative Working Men's Association had nearly 3000 members. This 'great constitutional army' (as

Disraeli called it) grew to 700 local associations and branches in 1875; it was the political expression of working-class deference to established society. But a countervailing strain of rebellious, even revolutionary sentiment, also partly inherited from a rural tradition, affected Victorian political and industrial relations; deference was regularly punctuated by political and industrial resistance. Indeed, the very fear of such resistance was an important stimulus to the deliberate political organization of the masses. 'Tory Democracy' was a response to an era during which the common people had thrown up their own quite untraditional and often radical mass organizations from Chartism through to the wave of trade unionization in the 1880s and the formation of the Labour Party in 1900.

In other industrialized countries, working-class politics and trade unionism were often much more radical, as in the anarcho-syndicalism of France at the turn of the century. Yet, in the longer run, the political parties founded upon the basis of large-scale working-class support, though sometimes Communist (as in France and Italy), were not revolutionary in practice, and mainly oriented themselves to 're-formist' political struggles. We can use the experience of England, then, as an example of this wider pattern of development in advanced capitalist countries, despite the fact that there are also other significant differences which we do not discuss here (e.g. the existence of a revolutionary tradition in countries like France).

Social class, indeed, is pre-eminently visible in England, so that this country constitutes a strategic case to study. It is literally visible in differences of dress and audible in differences of accent. It even continues, if not beyond the grave, at least into the graveyard, where the major differences in mortuary furniture are determined by wealth, not denomination. In the nineteenth century, when the lower classes could be referred to as the 'great unwashed', class was no doubt registered by the nose also. The growing prominence of social class as the major feature shaping the general structure and culture of society was reflected in changes in linguistic usage as well as in new organizations and laws. When we look back at the nineteenth century, it often seems to us a very clear and simple picture, patently a 'class society'. Yet it by no means appeared so simple and self-evident to people at the time, nor did they necessarily perceive it as a highly-visible *system*. They did not even use the term *class* with economic connotations until well into the century. Asa Briggs has pointed out that citizens and writers alike continued to use terms like 'ranks', 'orders' and 'degrees' (Briggs, 1960, p. 43).

Today, class-divisions are plainly of crucial importance in all areas of life. They are much more than just analytical or administrative categories. As we shall see, though classes are, in one sense, certainly abstractions (since they only partially have any institutional form), classes nevertheless produce numerous organizations and other kinds of grouping which tend to behave in the same way (in 'parallel') or to act together. They think of themselves as having like interests, and share similar cultural patterns.

Many researchers are only interested in using some indicator of class for limited purposes, as we noted. They are not in fact trying to carry out a many-sided analysis of social class in general. They are not interested necessarily in *explaining* class, or in explaining how it arises or what consequences it has for the social order, but simply in collecting and using information about it. So they may, for their specific purposes, use a single indicator of class, and this may be quite accurate and usable enough in order to tell you, say, where you would be best advised to put your advertisements. For more complex analyses, however, we need to use several different indicators, as indeed people commonly do in their everyday social intercourse. Thus we classify and rank people by income, by their housing (a recent study speaks of 'housing classes' (Rex and Moore, 1967)), by their educational level, by occupation or by wealth. These are the main aspects of class, and each can be used for different purposes, or they can be combined.

If we do want to economize and use as few indicators as possible, one alone is likely to be satisfactory – occupation. Hence it is widely used by researchers and administrators. It is economical, since other characteristics need not be added; many of these other characteristics, if we do record them, are usually found to be sufficiently closely dependent upon or associated with occupation that to use several of them tells us little extra, so that for most purposes occupation is enough. Given a person's occupation, we can estimate fairly well the probability of the kind of income, educational level, housing, politics, etc., he will have, for these things tend to hang together.

Many operations of classifying the population are not concerned at all with the all-round behaviour of people in different classes, or with the nature of the relationships *between* the classes. They are often concerned simply with a single dimension of a person's social being, not with other attributes. They may not be concerned with their group characteristics at all: it may be their individual purchasing-power the analyst is interested in, not their clubs or trade unions, or their conflicts or other relationships with other classes. The analyst, that is, may be interested only in class as a category or set of individuals, not in its group aspects.

If we just want to tax income, then all we need is an estimate of income; we do not even need to know a person's job. Since ability to pay a given level of rent or mortgage depends on income, housing officials or hire-purchase firms can be satisfied with income, too. But the Registrar-General in Britain, or the Bureau of the Census in the U.S.A., need better indicators of the *totality* of a person's social attributes than income alone, because governments need to know about the characteristics of their population for a great *variety* of purposes, not just to tax them or house them, but for educational purposes, for transport policy, for military purposes, for health and social welfare purposes, and a hundred and one other reasons.

Simply to classify by income will probably give us a good indicator of class, for some limited purposes. Income depends more on occupation than anything else (except, mainly, for the very wealthy). But the income-bracket between, say, £1000 per annum and £1999 will in fact contain people of quite different occupations and therefore classes: some skilled workers, some small shopkeepers (independent proprietors), some managers of small firms and so on. Since these are very different occupations, this means that people from different social classes fall within the same income-bracket, for some will be independent, others employers, others the employed.

So income is not enough for many sociological purposes, because income-brackets constitute 'logical' classes, *categories* of people sharing some property in common, not a sociological picture of those collectivities that exist in society and not simply in the shape of sets of figures. A 'logical' class like an income-bracket may *reflect* social class, it does not constitute it.

The most commonly used indicator of social class used in both Britain and the U.S.A., is occupation. Over 30,000 officially-named different occupational titles are recognized by the Registrar-General in Britain, so the attempt is made to group sets of occupations together to form what are claimed to be 'social classes' (see Cole, 1955, p. 6). In the British Registrar-General's scheme of five social classes, Class I is not very satisfactory because, being based on occupation, it neglects wealth and ownership; the extremely wealthy and powerful are therefore lost to view amongst thousands of much less important 'directors' (and even 'university teachers', who are also Class I). Class II contains over half the minor administrative, professional and managerial occupations, as well as farmers, shopkeepers, and small employers. It thus mixes up groups which belong to quite *different* social classes: some belonging to what Mills describes as the 'old' middle classes, on the one hand, and others to the 'new' middle classes: the one-man shopkeeper, say, as against the departmental manager in a big firm. Class III, critics have remarked (Carr-Saunders *et al.*, 1958, p. 117), 'is too mixed ... to serve any useful classification', for it includes half the male population, mostly skilled manual workers but also a high proportion of 'lower middle class' occupations, as well as shop assistants, clerks, foremen and supervisors.

There is an equally unsatisfactory further grouping of occupations to form 'socio-economic groups', constructed sometimes by classifying occupations in the same *industry* together, sometimes by grouping occupations that *cut across* industrial divisions. Thus crane-drivers are lumped together, whether they work in the building-industry or on the docks; captains of ships, fishing-vessels, and planes are also grouped together.

The confusion is compounded because these classifications inevitably involve not just the listing, but the *ranking* of the differing occupations according to prestige, power, income-level, skill, or some such criterion.

Some occupations are ranked 'high' and some 'low'. The criteria used are remarkably inconsistent, nor is there any satisfactory explanation of the logic or practical procedures used. Thus, as well as simple occupation, we find that 'employment *status*' is used, that is, whether a person is an employer, or pursues an occupation in which he is *employed*, or is his own employer. Yet at other times, 'employment status' means the *level* of a job, for example, whether one is an apprentice, foreman or such like; 'farmers' are distinguished from 'agricultural workers'; 'employers' and 'managers' are divided into different sets according to the size of the enterprise.

Thus all sorts of inconsistent criteria are used, and this is in the nature of things, for no adequate analysis of social class can be developed simply on the basis of occupation. Even apparently 'objective' indices such as income or occupation, then, prove inadequate for sociological purposes (they may be perfectly adequate for governmental purposes). The inadequacy derives from trying to reduce the three dimensions of stratification – economic role, status, and position in the system of power – to one single indicator, and from trying to eliminate the subjective aspects. In the end, they are smuggled in: occupations are *evaluated* according to skill, prestige, power, etc. Since different people judge things in different ways, there can be no general agreement. In the United States, three different major occupational scales devised by different sociologists place farmers in social classes I, II and III respectively, and insurance agents likewise (Caplow, 1954, ch. 2).*

Putting whole groups into different categories can thus lead to radically-different pictures of the overall class structure.

Since purely 'objective' criteria, such as income, are inadequate for many sociological purposes, and since the 'subjective' prestige attaching to different kinds of jobs is obviously a crucial element in social class, some researchers have tried to develop models of 'social class' on a purely subjective basis. They have not tried to rank occupations so as to form classes at all: instead, they asked people to say what class *they* put themselves in, or asked a panel of informants what class they thought other people belonged to.

The problem here is that people's responses are affected by the jobs, people and statuses they know about, and by the categories you offer them (and by the categories you use to group their answers if you leave them free to answer in any terms they like to use), as well

* Caplow has shown how various attempts to classify occupations in the U.S.A. also use many different criteria: technical distinctions (such as between farming and non-farming); distinctions of level (some jobs are labelled 'professional' or 'executive'); a public/private distinction (policemen, soldiers, firemen are 'public' workers, not ranked with other workers who are classified as 'skilled', 'semi-skilled' or 'unskilled') and so on. And, he asks, how do we classify 'deviant' occupations – gamblers, prostitutes and so on (should they be 'skilled workers'?).

as by the situation at the time of the inquiry. Thus a famous Gallup inquiry of 1939 found that 88 per cent of a sample of the U.S. population classified themselves as 'middle class'. 'America is middle class', ran the headlines. But Gallup had only allowed people to rate themselves as 'upper', 'middle' or 'lower' class. Few evidently liked to call themselves 'lower', for when the survey was repeated shortly afterwards and the term 'working' class was introduced instead of 'lower', 51 per cent now described themselves as *working* class! Obviously, no revolution had taken place in people's self-images; it was just that different questions and different possible answers had been used. A purely subjective approach to social class thus leaves us with no firm conclusions.

Indeed, the answers people give will always be relative and situational. Their attitudes will be affected by national developments – by strikes, by the degree of national prosperity, by their personal degree of success or their experience of their own or other people's mobility, etc.

Class consciousness, then, is constantly shifting and people will think about class in quite different ways in different contexts. We can never hope, then, to get an *absolute* picture of social class in its totality, for there is no such uniformity in people's thinking or behaviour. What we can do is to develop usable indicators, which will help us predict and to work out how variables hang together (say, occupation and degree of colour prejudice). Though we cannot reach complete agreement about class, we are by no means prevented from discovering how it works or from developing quite useful ways of measuring it for our given purposes.

A purely subjective concept of class is certainly as unsatisfactory as objective ones which omit the subjective altogether, for underlying people's varying ideas are common experiences of real things happening in the world around them. Too many people in similar occupations think in similar terms for class to be simply an arbitrary matter of self-definition. Underlying these shared views of the world – and the conflict between vital models of class – are real inequalities of wealth, power and prestige. So common patterns of behaviour emerge amongst people in common life-situations and the range of variation is not likely to be very large on many matters.

The search for a model of class which can command the agreement of all is, in the end, an illusion, for in class-divided societies consensus about the social values which underly different perceptions and evaluations of class and status does not exist. There are only different views of the class structure held by different groups in that structure, and normally the views of the most powerful classes become the official cultural pattern, even though it may be constantly challenged by many of the less privileged. We should scarcely be surprised to find, then, that there is no consensus about the shape of the class system, or how it works, for this is exactly what we should expect to find in a class-divided society: different, even radically opposed models. The existence of many differing conceptions of the class system is naturally even more likely in rapidly-changing societies.

The complexity of conceptions of class, that is, reflects not only the different positions and interests of people in the system, but also the constant changes going on in society. The idea that class divisions used to be much simpler and more obvious in the nineteenth century is undoubtedly wrong. They are no more self-evident or simpler today. Few people think, for instance, of social class solely in terms of one single factor – whether it be income, educational level, residence-area, job or accent. They usually think of a *cluster* of related variables (Martin, 1954a, pp. 60–62). Most people accept, however, that these differences occur as a result of a prior division of labour – differences in the roles people play in the productive process and associated inequalities in the distribution of wealth. Most sociologists, too, would probably agree with this analysis. Though there is a lot more to Marxism, to this extent, we are all 'Marxists' today, and even the most capitalistic of advertising managers divides the population into income-brackets when carrying out his surveys of consumer habits; the Registrar-General divides the country up into social classes he has constructed mainly on the basis of occupation: and even the most conservative political parties break electoral constituencies down in terms of their class composition so that they can calculate where their main vote lies and where it is worth canvassing. The only other social attribute of such general importance (and therefore predictive power) is sex.

The basic economic inequality, it is often forgotten, is not that of *occupation* at all. It is the social relations of economic domination and subjection at work and in the market-place which result in inequality of *property*: possession of goods – capital, land, plant – which are themselves the sources of income which may be used for further acquisition. For there are wealthy people who do not work, or whose income from various kinds of property means that 'earned income' is not vital or the largest source of income, or who work because of the social value placed on work, or because they must do something. Often they work (e.g., as directors) in an occupation which is the source of their property – managing a farm they own, an enterprise they hold a key block of shares in, and so forth. Hence rich people often 'work' at such activities as politics and other forms of 'public service', too, such as running voluntary associations. Hence, too, the curious phenomenon we noticed of the disappearance of the extremely wealthy in census categories. Their *wealth* disappears because they are only classified by 'occupation' (their income, we saw, also disappears in taxation records). The great bulk of the population, conversely, owns little beyond their 'personal' property. This difference between personal property and property as a source of income means that the former is composed largely of houses on mortgage and cars on hire-purchase.

It follows that the reduction of general inequalities, in a class system based on private property, depends primarily on making changes in the distribution of property. Despite the elimination of extreme poverty, despite the mobility we have described, and despite the greater power of labour in an epoch of full employment, little redistribution of property has occurred. So the chances that those born into different social classes will stay in those classes are still very high.

Though there is a good deal of mobility, most of it is, in fact, very short-range mobility. The myths of 'long-distance' mobility – 'from log-cabin to President' – are, overwhelmingly, myths as far as the life-chances of the mass of the population are concerned. Though something like a third of the population moves upwards, if one compares the job they do with the one their father did, a further third also moves down, and these proportions remain remarkably constant for industrial capitalist countries such as the U.K., the U.S.A., W. Germany, France or Sweden which otherwise differ greatly in culture and in historical development. Much of this mobility is caused by migration from the countryside into the towns, much by the availability of new jobs and the displacement of others due to technological innovation. People change their social class, too, not solely by changing their job, but by changing their status in other ways. Thus Illsley and his colleagues found that 46 per cent of Aberdeen women with professional and managerial class origins married skilled-worker husbands, and 40 per cent of the wives of professionals and managers had fathers who were skilled workers (quoted in Lipset and Bendix, 1959, p. 46).

The two countries with the highest rates of long-range mobility are the U.S.S.R. and the U.S.A., precisely the most dynamically-expanding economies. Similarly, with all the horrors of the Industrial Revolution in nineteenth-century Britain, that too was an expanding economy capable of absorbing the population drawn to the cities. By contrast, in under-developed countries today, cities are expanding but industry, in most cases, is not, producing massive unemployment or under-employment and, in consequence, situations of explosive revolutionary potential.

In contrast to feudal or caste stratification, then, class membership within an individual's lifetime, in industrial society, is much more variable, due to changes of the types just mentioned, even if people do not move very far above or below their parents. Inter-generational upward and downward mobility are the consequences of these changes. Comparatively, too, the strata in a class system are more open. The sheer multiplication of occupations in modern societies, moreover, divides such vast categories as 'working class' into innumerable specialized occupations, many of which (like 'clobberer', plugger-up', 'poker-in', or 'roarer') we would not recognize even if we were told their (quite official) names.

Individual mobility is by no means the sole form of mobility, however, for corporate groups also use their organized strength to promote the interests of their members as a collectivity. This kind of collective mobility is the main kind for most people whose chances of improving their position are likely to depend on trade union action rather than on individual advancement. But there are other avenues, for individual mobility, too, for example, promotion, the acquisition of qualifications, etc.

Individual mobility in the lifetime of most people is not very impressive: it is usually restricted to one move across a class line. Most people know this, for their social aspirations do not usually aim very far. Skilled workers typically aim at higher education for their children, but not, usually, *university* education. They have more limited aspirations which are consonant with their industrial experience: they hope their children will go on to technological studies. The educational system is, of course, the single major new channel of social mobility available to the working class, and a quarter of the students at British universities today come from working-class homes. Only 2 per cent of them, however, had fathers who were semi-skilled or unskilled manual workers, nor has the proportion at university changed since before the Second World War.

The one group of working-class people which does have exceptionally high aspirations for its children is the new clerical strata, whose ambitions indeed exceed those of professional and executive parents (Martin, 1954b, p. 172). The education industry itself provides many jobs for intelligent and ambitious young working-class men and has done so since mass education began: in the 1930s, for example, working-class recruits typically became teachers who staffed the expanded secondary and primary school systems. One of them was D. H. Lawrence, whose biography is typical: not only the son of a miner, but also under the close influence of a mother who had married 'beneath her'.

His history of social mobility thus brings us to one of the most crucial social groups, membership of which profoundly affects one's prospects for mobility – the family. Though we do not often think of it as such, the family is, in fact, a unit of *social class*, not merely a private domestic arrangement. Thus the family may 'sponsor' a son's advancement, and families like Lawrence's, where the mother is more highly educated than the father, are likely to produce more ambitious and successful offspring than families where the father is the more educated of the two parents, the reason being that since the mother's relationship to the children is usually closer than that of the father, she influences them more. The family is the critical unit in the class system at the upper end of the class hierarchy, too. The kinship connexions of the British 'power élite' have been well-documented (Wilson and Lupton, 1959), and family connexions in business are, of course, often very important. The continuity of the privileged classes also depends upon another aspect of the family– the inheritance system. And more widely, the position of children and wives in most societies has been primarily dependent upon the father's and husband's place in it; they are 'dependent variables'. The family is also a central socializing agent through which children are prepared for their future roles. The role of the family as a unit of social class demonstrates, then, that it is far too simplistic to describe modern society as predominantly 'achievement-oriented'. There are indeed important areas open to individual achievement, but ascriptive considerations – the roles one is 'born into' or has allotted to one – remain very significant.

Marx's Theory of Class

It has been said that all modern sociology is a debate with the ghost of Marx. Certainly, much of it is, and a key element in Marx's sociology is the role he gives to class. For him class is the motor of social development. True, there was a period of primitive communism, according to Marx, and there will be classless society in the future, but most of hitherto recorded human history, as the Communist Manifesto declares in its opening lines, has been the history of class struggle. More fundamentally, class struggle itself is only one manifestation of change and conflict which are endemic in society. Society is continually undergoing development, and different groups of men have different interests at stake which they seek to promote and defend: the most important of such groups are those occupying a similar position in a system of production-classes.

Because they occupy different positions in the productive system, they come into conflict with each other. The class which owns the means of production is able to secure the surplus product and keep other classes in subordinate positions. The exploited class, however, does not inevitably resist, nor even question the ruling class's right to rule. In the earlier phases of development of a new productive system, too, they may even secure certain benefits by allying themselves with a dynamic new class which overthrows an older dominant class standing in the way of both of them.

Thus, despite this division of society into potentially-conflicting classes (since the surplus social product produced by the peasants or workers is appropriated by those who own the means of production –

the land, machines, capital), the antagonistic classes do not necessarily always come into open and direct conflict. The exploited do not, indeed, necessarily even become aware that they are a *class*. By virtue of their situation, then, men may be 'objectively' in conflict whilst, subjectively, they lack this 'consciousness of class'.

Marx, following quite orthodox classical economic theory, distinguished three major classes, each of which was characterized in its role in the productive system by the 'factor of production' it controlled – the land-owners, obviously, by their ownership of *land*; the capitalists ('bourgeoisie') by their ownership of *capital*; and the proletariat (working class) by their 'ownership' of their labour-power.

For classical economics, each of these classes was a necessary and economically creative component in the productive process, each performing a functionally useful role in providing the needed 'factors' of land, capital and labour. Marx, however, regarded the relationship between the classes not as one of functional complementarity, even less harmony, but as one of social inequality, economic exploitation and political domination of the workers by the bourgeoisie. Thus the return to the capitalist on his capital – profit – and the return to the landlord on his land – rent – were a different order from the return secured by the worker on the labour he expended. For the labourer was the only one of these three economic actors who was actually a *producer*: even the capital of the capitalist was not something the capitalist had produced. It was simply the past labour of worker-producers, 'congealed' or locked up in the form of capital. Since the worker produced *more* than he received back in the form of wages, this 'surplus value' went to the owner of the means of production. The capitalist's capital first came from this surplus extracted from the worker – hence the intrinsic conflict between them. The exploited class was not inevitably revolutionary. Industrial workers, in defending their interests by fighting for improvements in wages or working conditions, commonly restricted their demands to such narrow economic issues, and confined their interests to their particular trade, shop, factory or industry. They did not automatically associate and collaborate with other workers to form 'working-class' organizations even for strictly economic ends. Even less did they necessarily move beyond the economic issues to a wider concern with political ones.

They might thus have what Lenin was later to call a 'trade union consciousness', but not a 'political consciousness'. But the workers might not even possess a simple 'trade union consciousness' of themselves *as a class*, especially where they were working in small-scale workshops, under a master who controlled them personally and directly, whether by paternalistic or repressive methods. They might thus be a class in so far as they occupied a *common situation* in a productive system, but even though the observer could see that they were all in the same boat and similarly exploited, even though each man individually might feel or even understand that he was being exploited, they did not necessarily feel themselves to *be*, even less act *as*, a class. They were, in Marx's classic phrases, a 'class *in* themselves' but not yet a 'class *for* themselves'.

The *objective* situation of having a common position in the production system needed complementing by *subjective* class consciousness of their common interests before they could fully become a class. Marx's theory is thus not just 'economic determinism', as is often commonly assumed, nor is his theory an 'objective' theory of class, because for him, a class could never become fully a class without this interplay between their subjective consciousness and their objective life-circumstances which he called a 'dialectical' interplay. Subjective consciousness, then, was not an automatic concomitant of exploitation, for Marx: it is something that develops and emerges over time. Poor people, indeed, have been very passive throughout history. Class-consciousness develops in part because the antagonistic parties engage in struggle, and find themselves lining up with different allies on different sides. They come to know who is friend, and who enemy, in action. Yet men do think, too, and some have the training and leisure to do so more effectively: intellectual and political leadership is often given to the masses by 'intellectuals' whose role is to generate ideas, analysis and consciousness and to communicate these ideas to others.

As we have seen, economic power, for Marx, gave the wealthy the resources and the authoritative control over men which enabled them also to exercise *political* power, for if production was a highly co-operative social activity, appropriation of the surplus was a highly anti-social act, resulting from private ownership. Each class of people, further, tended to associate socially with its own kind and have its characteristic outlook and sets of ideas about the world. Class was therefore not simply an 'economic phenomenon', but a *social* one. It permeated all areas of social life. Power, wealth, religious and social prestige, and culturally distinctive ways of life tended to cohere and to form a different pattern – a 'culture of class' – for each social class. But the 'weight' of each of these various attributes was not equal, for it was the position of a person in a system of production that was the factor that Marx saw as under-pinning all his other relationships. The 'mode of production' in a society – the way it organizes labour and capital, men and instruments to produce goods – is the foundation or basis on which are built the other major institutions of social life.

The major institutions of society reflect the interests of the dominant social class. These institutions are congruent with, or at least do not endanger the interests of that minority which controls both economic production and society: the complex cultural life of a whole society thus reposes upon an economic foundation.

All these other spheres of life – the dominant ideas of the time, the family, religion, the law – 'reflect' or are shaped by relationships established in production – for example, in law, the importance of the *contract* reflects the basic relationship between employer and worker in capitalist society – the contract, under which the worker undertakes to work so many hours and the master to pay specified wages in return. Their relationship outside work was of no legal concern to either partner; the master had no responsibility for his worker's housing, for the health of his children, etc. The relationship was an economic one, in which each party contracted to perform certain services, and had no other social obligation towards the other. The contrast between this pattern of relationship, symbolized by the contract, which Marx thought to typify capitalist society, in which the only important relationship between man and man was a relationship established by what he called the 'cash nexus', and the pattern of relationship in, say, feudal society, is very marked, for in a feudal society a man owed his lord a whole variety of social obligations, and his lord owed him various services likewise. The relationship between the two, that is, was not simply a one-stranded economic relationship, but a much wider, even total, social relationship, albeit an exploitative one. The relationship of worker to employer under the law in capitalist society, however, appears to be one of two formally equal partners freely entering into an agreement.

In fact, Marx says, this equality is spurious and the workers' freedom illusory. The law formally seems to treat each party equally, but this is a deception. The law works to the advantage of the powerful, sometimes because the worker is directly deprived of legal rights (as when trade unions are proscribed), or, more obliquely, because in any case the worker can be dismissed, whilst he cannot similarly sanction his employer. Only by collective organization (trade unions, political parties) can the worker's position be strengthened; this strengthening of the workers' hand would lead eventually to revolution. Revolution would occur in the most developed capitalist countries where the social nature of production was most advanced since thousands of workers co-operated in producing a product, but where the owners still appropriated the surplus privately. Under such conditions of 'socialized' production, the private appropriator was clearly an anachronism. He would be swept away, and the surplus made available to society in general. Hence the term 'socialism'. Thenceforward, the already social production-system would proceed without the capitalist, but would be run instead by the producers in the general interests of the whole society.

The advanced capitalist industrial countries have indeed seen a great development of working-class institutions, notably trade unions and socialist and communist political parties. The working class, however, has also continued to give massive support to non-socialist parties (seven million voted Conservative in 1951, including 30 per cent of trade unionists). And the very power of the Labour movement has led to major improvements which seem to have muted the appeal of revolution rather than led the workers to move on to a revolutionary total challenge to capitalism and to its overthrow. Instead, the revolutionary countries of the twentieth century have been backward, mainly agrarian countries such as Russia, China and Cuba.

There has thus been no serious threat either to the continued social domination of the ruling classes, or even to capitalist ownership of industry on which the whole system clearly depends. This is not to say that the working class plays no part, exercises no power, or does not have its own institutions, even culture. It is to say, simply, that the working class does not *dominate* society. As we noted Marx's theory is essentially a theory of development. He saw history as a succession of historical epochs each with its characteristic and dominant mode of production: the ancient, Asiatic, feudal and capitalist epochs and – to come – the Communist. In each epoch, there was an early phase, when the owners of the decisive resources (in the feudal era, the owners of land; in the capitalist, the owners of capital) were real agents of expansion and progress – pushing production towards the limits given by the state of technology. Later, however, when the productive capacity of a given system came into contradiction with the interests of the owners, they became decelerating, regressive agents. This growing contradiction between the system of production and the relations of production does not lead the controllers to give up their grip on power, prestige and wealth easily; they are likely to resist being replaced, and so have to be removed by revolutionary violence.

For Marx, the relationship between economic power and political power was clear: the capitalists were not simply an *owning* class; they were a *ruling* class too. Their decisive control over the key type of property (capital) was the basis for control over the society's political life, whether parliamentary democracy existed or not.

Since technological advance leads to intensified competition, those with most capital tend to come out on top. As a result, the bourgeoisie grows smaller in numbers, and intermediate classes – the petty bourgeoisie (e.g., owners of small factories and businesses, shop keepers, etc.) and the independent professionals – suffer downward mobility towards the proletariat. The same spiral of competition increases the numbers, and the misery, of the working class. Differences of skill between the kinds of worker a developed industrial system needs also diminish: more and more people come to see their common interests and are drawn into the class struggle. They find, too, that they cannot make serious progress via personal, isolated actions. An understanding of what needs to be done, and appropriate machinery for doing it, are thus generated, that is, a 'scientific' socialist theory and the organizations through which the class struggle would be waged.

Marx, then, was not simply a determinist. But there are elements of determinism in Marxism. Engels responded to the failure of the revolutions of 1848, for instance, in part by insisting that inexorable economic processes would ultimately produce the collapse of capitalism, despite this temporary setback. At the same time, Marx and Engels also responded to this failure by emphasizing the need for organization and leadership: the revolution would not just 'happen', but had to be organized carefully and *made* to happen, when circumstances were right.

The conditions needed for revolution are thus twofold: an appropriate 'revolutionary situation' and an appropriate revolutionary agency (a party). It is always possible to emphasize one or the other. 'Deterministic' Marxists insist that one must wait until the situation matures, wait for the inevitable crisis, conflict and breakdown of capitalism (as with the mass 'institutionalized' electoral Communist parties of Italy and France). The 'voluntaristic' Marxists insist that the revolution must be created, notably the recent Marxisms which holds that the situation in the 'Third World' is everywhere a revolutionary one already (Guevara, Maoism, Debray) as well as the militant activistic Marxism of the 1968 Paris student revolt. Marxism can thus accommodate very different courses of action; it does not provide an unambiguous 'scientific guide' to action. There are parallel disputes amongst Marxists about just how much emphasis can be laid on the 'economic base', and how much 'autonomy' can be allowed to the 'superstructure' of social arrangements and ideas erected on that base. One emphasizes the 'inevitability of history', the other the importance of men, ideas, creativity, innovation, activity. Neither of these schools of Marxism, however, have provided very satisfactory explanations of why the revolution has not occurred in advanced capitalist countries. Some Marxists have explained capitalism's survival in terms of imperialism or war. But little attention has been given either to rises in real living standards or to increased social mobility.

Marx himself had noted that the ruling class might make its rule 'more solid and dangerous' by providing a selective avenue of individual upward mobility. He paid less attention to the possibility – which his enemies pointed out – that the working class might, by wresting concessions from the ruling class, take the edge off a potentially revolutionary militancy, so that group mobility of this kind might be a much more effective prophylactic against revolution than the merely individual mobility of a privileged few, or even such privileged minorities as the 'labour aristocrat', the skilled craft-worker.

The effect of newer avenues of mass upward mobility, such as the education system, were not foreseen, though Marx and Engels were aware that the new working-class parties, unions, and co-operatives themselves constituted sizeable new channels of mobility for ambitious working-class men, who became full-time bureaucrats with an interest not only in maintaining themselves in office, but also in not disturbing the wider social system in which they now occupied (however minor) a privileged position. These concessions to a rising and ever better-organized working-class movement were of course only possible in an expanding economy. The situation in underdeveloped countries today is one in which the ruling classes, even if they wished to (which is rarely the case), are not able to offer concessions to the demands of the mass of their populations, because the economies they dominate are stagnant. The possibility of making concessions is thus very much more limited than it was for the ruling classes of Great Britain in the nineteenth century.

The future of capitalism is thus not unproblematic. But there seems little evidence that any major breakdown of the internal functioning of the highly-developed and rich societies – including the U.S.S.R. – is likely, unless the era of comparative freedom from 'boom and slump' trade-cycle in the capitalist countries is challenged by the instability engendered by the disturbances in the world outside the capitalist 'West' (notably through revolution in the non-communist 'Third World'), as well as by the ever-growing competitive challenge of the communist countries. Neither is some kind of long-term 'co-existence' inconceivable – or the possibility of massive destruction.

Status

Let us turn now to the second dimension of social stratification – status. Apart from the word 'class', 'status' is the only other term quite so widely used in studies of social stratification, and in everyday speech too – and so is inevitably loaded with a variety of meanings. The term is often used interchangeably with 'class' in everyday usage, however, and some sociologists have compounded this confusion, but it is necessary to keep them analytically distinct. One use of the term, for example in law, refers to a *position* determined by statute or case-law; individuals occupying such positions are treated differentially according to the position they occupy. 'Status' here is thus used where others use 'role', in the sense of an 'office' in an organization or a position in a family. Thus a man may be a sergeant, an 'in-law', a manager, or a member of a congregation. Or you may have a status ascribed to you, not because you are part of an organized structure, but by virtue of belonging to some social category with particular social characteristics which others can observe: by being 'coloured', female, young or old. Such distinctions involve much more than simply classifying people; they involve allotting people different jobs in the social division of labour and these positions have different amounts of prestige and power attached to them and different rewards. Thus being a 'minor' or a 'pupil' means that one is treated in a special way, both within and outside the courts.

So when motor-car advertisements suggest that the car you have is a symbol of your *status*, 'status' here does not merely refer to the position a man occupies in a division of labour in which some do one job and others different ones. For the jobs are not just 'different', they are also ranked *hierarchically* in a system of inequalities of power and of material and other reward. They are further ranked as 'higher' or 'lower' in a hierarchical system of prestige: *esteem* is unequally distributed too. 'Status' in this second sense thus refers to the way in which prestige is differentially distributed, so that people on different levels of the social structure are marked off from those below them, and from their 'superiors' or 'inferiors' by a whole complex of ways of thinking, acting and feeling recognized by members and outsiders alike – what are normally called 'class distinctions' but which the sociologist usually labels 'status differences', reserving the term 'class' to refer primarily to a person's productive role with its correlates of property and power. Status, in the sense of prestige, is thus usually visible in a particular 'style of life', in a person's everyday behaviour at home as well as at work, and notably in the way he uses his income. One's ability to consume in a certain way and the models of behaviour one adopts are certainly affected by one's position in a system of production, but one can adopt models which are more usually appropriate to people whose occupations are very different. The basis of membership in a status-group is the possession of the appropriate status-characteristics. Such status-groups commonly turn themselves into classes: they monopolize opportunities and exert power over others. Thus in South Africa, Whites constitute a status-group membership of which can never be acquired by Africans: an African cannot become a White man. No matter how wealthy or skilled he may become, he can never acquire the crucial status-characteristic. Hence, status-groups often operate in ways that have little to do with maximizing efficiency or economic growth or with encouraging achievement, but rather with maintaining superiority.

Extremely inflexible status-groups may go so far as to ruin themselves rather than give up the exclusive position they prize so much.

In a strict class system, wealth, possession of capital, etc., provide the person who has it with the resources through which he can exercise both economic and political power. He usually also uses his wealth to buy his way into a superior status-group. Thus class and status come to coincide. But to become *socially* accepted into a status-group may be difficult, and highly status-conscious groups may keep the wealthy *parvenu* or *nouveau riche* at arm's length, since he lacks the cultural characteristics required. He may not be able to adapt his behaviour to that demanded by the status-group he aspires to join. But his wealth will usually enable him to buy his children the formal education and the instruction in 'proper' ways of behaviour called for, so that *they* will be accepted, a lag of a generation. So one's ability to be accepted does not simply 'go with the job' one does, and situations in which we experience contrary demands from different status-groups, common enough wherever a person is socially mobile, induce strains of 'cross-pressure' and 'status-anxiety'. Thus, though they commonly do overlap, a person's class position and the status he aspires to may not exactly coincide: he may have 'more respectability than means', he may be a 'social climber': wealthy, but lacking the social graces and therefore denied full equality by his (often poorer) 'superiors'.

A person's *self*-image, *his* conception of his status, may also differ from that which is more usually attached to his occupation; other people's definitions of your status may differ from your own, and have to be taken into account, for not to do so would be to have 'delusions of grandeur'. There are situations, of course, in which people glory in being of *low* status, as when people contrast 'honest' ordinary folks' standards with the 'artificial' pretentions of their so-called 'superiors'. Amongst unskilled workers, but especially among the 'lower classes' below the 'working classes' (Klein, V. 1965, Section 1) who lack stable jobs and have unstable family-lives, we find 'upside-downers', who reject the values of those who normally have the power to set the pattern for 'proper' behaviour. 'Upside-downers' rate doing a hard manual job or a socially valuable job highly. Thus they put nurses and agricultural labourers high in their scheme of things, and company directors low. Such ideas, of course, are not peculiar to the 'lower classes'. Socialist ideas include similar notions that people should be rewarded according to their usefulness to society, that labour is honourable, and that usurers, 'coupon-clippers', rentiers and capitalists in general are either functionally unnecessary or an actual negative force, a 'fetter on production' whose removal would help rationalize and humanize economic life and permit a 'social-ized' economy because industry would no longer be run for their private benefit, but in the interests of the mass of society.

Status, in the prestige sense, thus depends very much on *subjective* factors: ideas and feelings, both on the part of the social actor and those with whom he interacts, even though one's pretentions are also controlled by one's pocket. In general, because of this last consideration, people's status-aspirations are not likely to be very ambitious. Skilled or clerical workers may imitate lower middle-class models; they are scarcely likely to aim higher. Their 'reference-group', in sociological language, will not be very remote; their hopes of social mobility are fairly realistic. Indeed, if people are asked about their *expectations* as against their *aspirations* – what they *expect* to be, as against what they would ideally *like* to be – their expectations are usually much humbler than their aspirations. One's aspirations may, of course, be focussed not upon one's own career-possibilities, but, vicariously, upon those of one's children. Social mobility is thus by no means confined to *intra*-generational movements within a single person's lifetime; it can be *inter*-generational. We have seen that the family is itself a unit of social class. This is where people acquire much of their class behaviour, their ideas and feelings about classes and status-groups. Inevitably, too, their hopes of upwards mobility (or fears of downward mobility) are projected on to others in the family besides themselves.

These quite common divergences between a man's personal conception of his own status or his aspirations to higher status and the status ascribed to him by others makes for difficulties in classifying many people unambiguously as belonging to one social class or another, since there is great room for such differences of subjectivity, and social class is by no means just a matter of occupation, no matter how important this may be. People's ideas are a vital part of social class, too, and affect their behaviour deeply. Status considerations therefore have to be added to strict economic position in order to produce a rounded understanding of social class.

We have seen that many people who write about class, and devise models of class, are only concerned with showing how people from different class backgrounds behave, or predicting how they will behave. They are not concerned to explain the genesis or basis of class – how it comes into being, what it is caused by, what its significance is for society – for they are not engaged in that kind of sociological explanation.

We can easily classify people according to occupation. We can even rank occupations according to such objective criteria as amount of income so to form a table of 'higher' and 'lower' occupations. For many practical purposes, such as estimating likely political behaviour, these rough and ready divisions may be good enough. Scales or tables of this kind are often used in business, in politics, in census work, and so on, by people whose ideologies in general and ideas about class in particular may otherwise differ widely. But, plainly, they are only very crude divisions. Even these classifications usually take into account additional elements, usually status-distinction, however, as when 'non-manual' occupations are distinguished from 'manual' ones, for even though both categories may be wage-earners, ideas about status still often cause white-collar workers to behave in aggregate in somewhat more middle-class ways, in some areas of their lives, than their manual-worker colleagues. Similarly, clerical workers, or even 'affluent' well-paid manual workers, brought up to think of themselves as *working* class, may continue to behave in working-class ways.

There is thus no simple, neat overlap between class and status, and people may follow quite different models in different areas of their lives. Non-manual workers are now increasingly prepared to join trade unions, for so long the characteristic institutions mainly of manual workers. The new trade unions in Britain, growing fat in numbers, militancy and political power, are the distributive workers, the technicians, the air-line pilots, the supervisors, local government officials, welfare workers, bank clerks, now even teachers and managers, reflecting the mechanization and 'proletarianization' of jobs formerly regarded as middle-class occupations, the growth of 'service' and technical occupations in the 'tertiary' sector of the economy, and the decline of older manual occupations, of which mining is perhaps the most obvious case. These changes are reflected in the general shift of power within the trade union movement from the older 'proletarian' unions to these new unions.

If the contemporary analysis of social class derives mainly from the 'debate with the ghost of Marx', modern discussions of status derive from Max Weber's original formulation in the 1920s (Gerth and Mills, 1948, p. 7). A person's *class*, Weber recognizes, is 'unambiguously' a function of his position in the economic system. The worker, for example, is a worker because he sells his labour-power on the market. But – Weber goes on to say – we accept or reject people as social equals, inferiors or superiors, not just on the basis of their economic standing, but on the basis of their social standing as a whole. One's social standing may depend upon one's economic position, but the connexion is not necessarily always a direct one. In particular, people's ideas are not automatically the same just because they do the same job. A skilled engineer may be 'upwardly-mobile' and middle-class in his orientation; he may be a craft-conscious militant unionist; and he may be both together. Nor are his other social characteristics directly determined by his occupation. He may be Presbyterian, a Catholic, or religiously indifferent. These differences are of crucial importance: he will belong to, or seek membership of quite different social circles and be accepted or rejected. Membership of these status-groups, and exclusion from others, will have important consequences for his whole life, even for his work. Conception of status and actual membership of status-groups may well vary independently of his economic position and be as important in affecting his behaviour. Yet normally, even though we cannot predict for the individual engineer what his religion or politics will be, we can be pretty sure about the likely behaviour of engineers in general on particular issues. Indeed, there is normally a good degree of association between occupation and other characteristics, including some very important ones. Even religion, for instance, is likely to be very broadly linked with class, for though many people think of religious experience as a peculiarly personal thing, religion is usually transmitted via the family, like ideas about class. Historically, Nonconformist denominations like Methodism did recruit primarily amongst the working class and provided opportunities for working-class leadership; the Anglican Church in England, or the Episcopalian in the U.S.A., reserved leadership for the gentry class. And despite the fact that a third of trade unionists in Britain vote Conservative, a distinct relationship between class and party politics persists too:

Conservative Party	1951 vote	Labour Party	1951 vote
Entrepreneurial middle class	2,440,000	Entrepreneurial middle class	370,000
Managerial middle class	650,000	Managerial middle class	190,000
Professional middle class	1,480,000	Professional middle class	400,000
White-collar middle class	1,920,000	White-collar middle class	900,000
Working class	7,000,000	Working class	12,000,000
Totals	13,490,000		13,860,000

(After Anderson and Blackburn, 1965, p. 250.)

These figures, however, do show that the 'fit' between class and politics is by no means neat. This is not surprising in a society with a high degree of short-range social mobility at the lower levels, since people move away from parental influence, have different jobs from those of their parents, meet different people, and experience the world differently. Thus those growing up during the Depression of the inter-war period; those maturing during the Second World War; the children of the immediate post-war 'austerity' period; those of the 'affluent' fifties; the new youth of the sixties, have, without resorting to purely rhetorical language, really experienced significantly different worlds. Hence the much-discussed phenomenon of the 'generation gap', or, in the extreme, 'the war of generations' which is held to underly much of the contemporary revolt of youth.

In less mobile societies, the 'fit' between occupation and other social characteristics may be much closer. In the least mobile, such as caste societies, it is likely to be very close indeed. We have seen that in India there was thus a tight-knit 'clustering' or overlap of economic, religious, marital and other norms of behaviour, the whole forming a *system* which brought all the separate castes together in a complex, hierarchical order buttressed by religion.

Such a system exhibits unusual consistency in the extent to which status differences and class differences coincide (or are 'congruent'). It is because of this extreme congruence and because of the rigidity of the system until recent times, that a special label – caste – has been used to distinguish a system like this from more open systems of stratification. Yet even in caste societies, changes took place, as we saw, and though a person belongs to a caste whose very title may indicate a traditional occupation (such as 'Distiller') most lower-caste villagers are, in fact, peasants working the land, whatever their caste-title, and Brahmins are more likely to be wealthy landowners than full-time religious functionaries. This dissociation of caste and occupation is, of course, greatly intensified in modern urban life. Although Brahmins are predominant in the higher occupational reaches, and caste remains an important force in political life, one's caste and one's occupation are much more likely to vary independently these days. Moreover, new solidarities and oppositions emerge on the basis of occupation, displacing or at least rivalling traditional ties of occupation and caste. In the town, the *jatis* of the abandoned village become irrelevant and are replaced by new *class* relationships.

The traditional overlap of economic, religious and political positions resulted in one single overall hierarchy of prestige. The weaving-together and elaboration of all of these separate elements into one large cultural scheme may seem remote from the experience of those living in industrial societies. But, Weber points out, it is only the carrying to its logical conclusion of patterns of stratification found nearer home, for here, too, one's politics, religious denomination, family life, tastes in entertainment, place of residence, etc., are all likely to differ from different classes, and thus form broad 'clusters' similar to those found in more exaggerated form in caste society. So we can easily distinguish the different class-areas of a city's residential districts, or, by looking at his dress, can judge a person's social status. Even such apparently quite personal and private things as the age at which toilet-training is begun are very closely associated with class (Newsom and Newsom, 1963, pp. 196–7). So too is the kind of language we use (Bernstein, 1962). Since most people marry partners from similar backgrounds there is a degree of endogamy, too. We tend to marry those near and like ourselves, though since it is not obligatory to do so, and since only a category (a social class) is involved and it is usually one's family rather than any wider group (such as an Indian village *jati* with its own caste-council) which exercises pressure on us, we usually speak of *homogamy* – like marrying like – or 'assortative' mating rather than endogamy (marriage within the group) proper.

Social distance is maintained in class society as well as in caste society by delicate, though often rigidly observed, distinctions of etiquette, just as notions of pollution or defilement keep the Indian castes apart. Classes may be split internally by status-distinction; status-distinctions may overlap with class divisions. The division within the working class between the 'rough' and the 'respectable', or the wider gulf between the 'working classes' and the 'lower classes' are striking instances of the importance of these distinctions. Where such distinctions coincide with other divisions – say, religious or ethnic – where differences of class and status coincide, the one reinforces the other and the divisions are therefore deeper. Thus it is one thing in Britain for the stable, employed working class to resent the 'roughs' who float from job to job, lead irregular domestic lives, etc., but when this resentment is focussed upon 'rough' groups that also happen to be Irish, West Indian or Pakistani immigrants, the division is reinforced: it is based on more than one element, and the conflict is the more intense.

Power

We have seen that one of the implications of Weber's analysis is that though status and caste very often overlap, status-distinctions can cut *across* class-solidarity. Classes, then, need not progressively develop greater class-consciousness; in particular, the working class may not become more cohesive and revolutionary. Secondly, Weber reminds us that to speak of 'social class' is to use a very abstract concept indeed, for 'the working class' does not, in fact, exist in institutionalized form. The 'working class', in fact, is a *category*, not a *group*. True, there are institutions – in Britain, trade unions, the co-ops, the Labour Party – which claim to be 'working class' and undoubtedly are in the sense that they draw their membership primarily from this class and base their programme on policies designed to improve its lot (or even to make it predominant in society). It can further be argued – in a more historical (others would say 'metaphysical') way – that such organizations are 'working class' because they promote the interests of the working class, whether members of it belong to such institutions and believe in them in any numbers or not.

We saw earlier that social strata are different from natural strata. Again, class in the *socio*logical sense involves more than class simply in the logical sense. In logic, we can classify all red-headed people together; they form a logical class. But red-headed people are not a *social class*: they are a *category* rather than a collectivity that behaves similarly, becomes conscious of its own identity and separate interests and thereby gives rise to organized groups. Red-headed people do not organize themselves, let alone engage in struggle with the blonde or the dark-haired.

Social classes, by contrast, exhibit common patterns of behaviour. People within their ranks, and outsiders, become conscious of them as a collectivity; numbers of them create organizations of a more structured kind to represent the class's interests. In the process, what is only a *category* ('the working class') becomes a group (the organized working class) or, more exactly, a whole set of groups (trade unions, parties, co-ops, etc.) which not only see themselves as 'working class' but act in accordance with that notion. Other classes oppose them. (Yet recruitment may be far from complete, so that we can have the paradoxical position of micro-sects of revolutionaries claiming that they, and no one else, authentically speak in the name of the proletariat, or the situation where a movement composed overwhelmingly of peasants, as in China or Vietnam, claims to be 'proletarian'.)

Stratification, as we have seen, has three principal dimensions. Two of these we have already examined: *class* (arising out of differences in economic role), and stratification by *status* into inferior and superior groups with different styles of life and claims to prestige. We come now to the power dimension or, more exactly, the *political* power dimension: the stratification of society into ruler, ruled and intermediate groups. Economic power and the competitions of status-groups have already been discussed in part but we must examine also the inter-relationship of all of these kinds of power, the combinations of class, status and inequalities which constitute the total phenomenon: social stratification.

Parties and other groups are specially organized to mobilize and exert power on behalf of interest groups. Such groups may have only limited interests in common. A much wider basis for collective action is provided normally by religion or ethnicity. These may or may not coincide with economic interests in common. In Britain, the major factor uniting the supporters of the major political parties is not religion or ethnicity, but social class.*

But not all political parties are built upon class-interests, as Weber pointed out. They may be based upon status-identity. Thus mass parties of the Right have commonly appealed to workers on some other basis than that of their common economic interests as a *class*. They have been appealed to as status-groupings: Christian workers as against Jews, White men as against Blacks. Another type of appeal based on status is to those who may have humble jobs, but who prefer to think of themselves as 'middle-class' or 'respectable': the 'little man'. Such status-identifications cut across class-definitions based on occupational identity. A further source of support by work-ing-class people for their social superiors arises for quite opposite reasons – because, far from aspiring themselves to join the middle classes, they believe that the latter, and even more the upper classes, are so skilled and well-equipped to rule them that things are best left in their hands. This is the so-called 'deference vote'.

There are also other ties cutting across class ties based on occupa-

* Lipset shows, contrary to what is often believed, that class is a major de-terminant of voting behaviour in the U.S.A. also, though the two major parties are not linked to the class divisions in the nation as a whole in the same way in every part of the country: the association between class and political orien-tation is local or regional rather than national (Lipset, 1963, p. 9).

tion. Though class solidarities are engendered in production – particularly at what Marxists call the 'point of production' and others the 'work-situation' – other kinds of interests, even economic interests, may cut across these. Thus a worker may find his job threatened because other workers are on strike; he may find himself in conflict with fellow-workers even in the same shop, over demarcation problems: who is to do what job. The organizations of Labour – here the trade unions – may be involved in conflict with each other over such issues as well as in conflict with management. As a consumer, the worker may find that wage-increases in other industries to his fellow-workers mean dearer goods in the shop for him. Collectively, too, farmers and their farm-labourers – though one group are employers and the other their employees – often combine politically in the face of city interests that threaten them: agricultural machinery corporations, banks, organized labour, grain exchanges, railways, etc.

There are thus cross-cutting interests which divide classes internally as well as ties which link segments of one class with another. In addition, status-distinctions within a class also operate, often very fine distinctions invisible to the outsider. Thus groups severely discriminated against, like urban Africans in South Africa who are both a class (unskilled workers predominantly) and in part almost a caste (because virtually no social intercourse with Whites is allowed by law outside the work-situation), develop exquisite distinctions of status within their own ranks, as well as voluntary associations (like football teams) which have lots of officers and elaborate displays of status-symbols and thus provide a source of dignity and self-esteem to the deprived (Kuper, 1965, ch. 22). If there were not these cross-cutting ties between classes and divisions within them, all classes would evince 'instant solidarity', and overt class-warfare would be a constant phenomenon. The capitalist class, Weber points out, is similarly divided as between finance-capitalists and industrialists, by differences of interest between different branches of industry, or most fundamentally, because one firm competes with others on the market.

There are thus many ties which cut across class, and which more positively unite members of different classes via personal or local-level links, or even via national institutions which cut across class divisions. Dutch sociologists have called the latter phenomenon 'pillarization' or *verzuiling* in contrast to 'stratification', the former being the division of society into *vertical* 'pillars' as against division into horizontal 'strata'. Clearly, *verzuiling* is a very important phenomenon, for ethnic and religous divisions in particular may well cut across horizontal class divisions in the modern world. We will look at this phenomenon in underdeveloped countries later, but it is equally to be found in countries like Belgium, with its Walloon-Flemish division, in larger multi-national societies such as the U.S.S.R. or India, and in any country with immigrant populations or strong 'vertical' religious or ethnic divisions.

Though religion and class may coincide, we have noted, churches are status-groups (groups of believers) which very often cut across class lines, too. They commonly encourage their members to focus their attention on future salvation rather than 'this-worldly' concerns. They have often been ideologically hostile to any emphasis on class which might be a division factor within the body of the church. Today, however, in an era of secularization, and in a world where the gulf between the under-developed and the developed parts of the world is of such major importance, racial and ethnic vertical divisions are usually more important than religious ones. Racial divisions, like religious ones, can be horizontal as well as vertical, for the bulk of the population in both the new societies of the former colonial world as well as the immigrant population in advanced countries tend to be both poor and coloured. When racial divisions overlap with those of class, in this way, society threatens to split open. Ethnic, religious or other status-groups may thus constitute a stratum *or* a 'pillar'. There is a third (and very common) possibility: that of the 'plural' society in which there may be a common national government, an over-all economy, etc., but, where one group lives in one part of the country with its own culture and specialized economic role (say, coffee-growing), while another speaks a different language, lives in *its* own area, and engages in trade. These divisions are *vertical*, but they divide the society into separate compartments. Vertical 'pillars', on the other hand, *integrate* the society because their members are not confined to one level in the social structure in one area of the country but are to be found at every level. Pillars cut across strata; 'plural' units do not, even though they do interact (e.g., in the market place) with other communities and thus form part of a wider society. These ethnic communities are something like the segments of a worm:

together, they form a whole, but each segment is distinct and only linked weakly. In a subsistence economy, the segments would be liable to break away, but in an increasing market-economy, such groups cannot survive on their own economically, no matter how segregated the rest of their social life from that of other ethnic groups.

We may thus find a variety of institutions, showing one or the other of these patterns. In Britain, there are vertical 'pillars' with members widely-distributed at all horizontal levels in society. Thus there are Anglicans and Catholics at all social levels in Britain (even if the former are over-represented in the higher reaches of British society and the latter in the lower reaches of some cities in the North-West). The social category, Whites, too, is distributed at all social levels. Blacks, conversely, predominate only at low levels. The former constitute a 'pillar', the latter a stratum. And where depressed 'ghettoes' of coloured people occur, we have an instance of segmented form. Yet there are few real ghettoes in Britain, unlike, say, the U.S.A. The society generally (least, it is true, for coloured people), is characterized by 'cross-cutting' ties, as Gluckman has called them (Gluckman, 1956). The horizontal divisions of class are indeed very profound, but there are also innumerable ways in which institutions are brought into contact, consultation and interconnexion, even where they have opposed interests (e.g., trade union and employer representation on Government committees), because at another level they recognize a common interest: in keeping the system going so that there will be some cake to fight over. Such cross-cutting ties also operate importantly at the inter-personal level as when foreman and worker may belong to the same church, see each other in the local pub, support the same football team, etc.

Reformers, as well as reactionaries hoping to preserve existing divisions of power and wealth, have long dreamed of actually creating institutional 'pillars' which would create cross-cutting ties not between individuals but between the groups and organizations of the different classes, so as to counteract and reduce class-conflict. They have usually pinned their hopes on religious institutions, or – more recently – on industrial 'corporations' which would link all those engaged in the steel industry, say, from blast-furnace operatives through foremen and managers to the top directors, in one organization, where their representatives could thrash out problems of the industry together.

This idea has been canvassed from the time of Comte and Saint-Simon, in the work of Durkheim, and in the era of fascism (Mussolini actually did establish corporations of this kind and a national council linking them together into one 'corporative' state, but they remained in effect paper institutions).

The notions of co-operation, participation and the rational planning of production are important elements in socialist thinking, too – with one crucial difference; they postulate the prior removal of the capitalist and the establishment, not of class co-operation, but of social control by the working class, in forms ranging from state nationalization to 'workers' control. Attempts to institutionalize vertical ties have remained ineffective, however, in capitalist societies, though contemporary attempts to regulate strikes through legislation hinge upon similar notions of inter-class co-operation, mediated by government, in which all co-operate to achieve generally-agreed goals, though each plays a different functional role in the division of labour.

The increasing intervention and the wider area of activity of the State in capitalist societies, and the role of State and Party in communist ones, raises the question of how it is that order and continuity are maintained, a problem we will discuss more fully in Chapter 8. Plainly, differences of interest and of culture as extensive as those we have seen existing in class societies have to be contained or counterbalanced somehow, if society is not to fly apart into its constituent components.

Social stability can be achieved by enforcing conformity, or as the outcome of positive support for the government in power. In the latter case, the government is said to have *legitimacy*, because people think it has the *right* to be in power. Its ability to get its policies accepted depends on more than mere coercion through monopoly of the means of violence (arms). Such a government has authority, not just power, because it has both the means of force and legitimacy as bases for its operation. In between these situations, a population may simply put up with its government, not according it positive support, but having as little to do with politics as possible. Many variations upon these situations are possible. Where the conflicts in a society between different strata run deep, there is little room for the kind of compromise that is often called 'agreement to differ'; the 'balance of power', or as Rex calls it, the 'truce situation' can no longer be operated (Rex, 1961, ch. 7). Instead, the conflict becomes sharper and is resolved by a move towards one extreme solution or its opposite – increased reliance upon force by the dominant classes and the established government, or successful resort to force on the part of those challenging their rule. The former Rex labels 'the ruling class' situation; the latter the 'revolutionary'. These extremes of class polarization seem very different from the 'consensus' politics of Britain or the U.S.A., where parties defeated in elections by only a few percentage points, commanding some half of the nation's allegiance, refrain from using this undoubted power to resist the rule of their opponents, but allow them to take over the government, whilst they go into 'loyal opposition'. Because of the existence of ideas about the legitimacy of the political system, divisions which elsewhere would result in revolutionary confrontations here only produce the ins-and-outs of parliamentary party politics.

Class conflict in developed societies has not matured as Marx believed it would. Whilst there is a powerful Labour movement, not only are most workers quite un-revolutionary but they even fail to participate in working-class organizations. Many identify themselves with other classes, or at least are not greatly or generally hostile to them. Class-consciousness and class-militancy also vary over time, and with the issue and the level at which the issues arise.

A worker may be conscious of belonging to a working-class community; a localized status-group of this kind, composed of people of common economic position, may be very 'working class' (Hoggart, 1958). It is a kind of *communal* class-consciousness, however. Then there is what Lenin called 'trade union consciousness': the militant defence of wages and working conditions. Distinct from this again is *political* working-class consciousness. Most people in Britain only think about politics when the occasion calls for decisions to be made – say, during an election – and pay little attention to such matters in more normal times. A person may thus combine high 'working-class consciousness' over economic issues with a low interest in politics. This common situation reflects itself in widespread shop-steward agitation, and unofficial disputes at shop-floor level, combined with disinterest in official trade unionism at higher levels and even less in political Labour (or great interest in neighbourhood affairs, but none in local government).

These different kinds of class-consciousness, displayed at different levels in different situations, have been looked at in a slightly different way by David Lockwood who has argued, in his study of clerical workers, that the broad concept of 'class' is too crude, and that for more refined understanding we need to break it up into three subsidiary elements: work-situation, market-situation and status-situation. In the work-situation, for instance, in contrast with manual workers on the shop-floor, clerks have in the past tended to work alongside their employers in small offices. They were often drawn via personal links from middle-class families themselves, and this personal contact at work reinforced their tendency to emulate the life-style of their employers, as well as giving them a certain amount of 'reflected' status, despite their lack of real power. Though offices are now larger and more mechanized, and though clerks may now earn only as much as manual workers, most clerks still have closer contact with management than do manual workers. The result is the continuation of distinction between non-manual and manual employees. To manual workers, clerks are part of 'Them'.

In the past a shipping clerk could not move to a solicitor's office, so that standardized wages and a supply of interchangeable labour comparable to that for manual labour did not emerge. This situation naturally gave rise to a collective sense of exclusiveness on the part of clerks, and was reinforced by marked wage-differentials instituted by employers, so that unionization of clerical workers was limited (also discouraged) between the two World Wars. However, after the First World War, the clerical labour force increased in size and the work itself now took place within ever-larger units, whether in industry, commerce or government. The road to promotion became more formal and dependent on education, and the introduction of managerial trainees of higher educational level above the heads of clerks set limits to promotion opportunities. The market-situation of black-coated workers has declined, especially if one compares them to manual workers. Clerical jobs used to be singularly well-paid and secure, even during the depression. But with continuing full employment and overtime for manual workers, the superiority of non-manual jobs is by no means so clear-cut today. A growing proportion of clerks, too, are now drawn from manual workers' families.

Clerks are thus in a status predicament. Cross-cutting ties pull them in contrary directions. Changes in their work-situation have reduced the chances that their claim to middle-class status will be accepted by the middle classes, whilst changes in the over-all labour market, the effectiveness of the manual workers' trade unions, and wider access to secondary education, have narrowed the gap between them and the manual groups to whom they used to feel superior. The consequence is that the superior status the clerk lays claim to – at work or in his neighbourhood – is increasingly open to successful challenge. This changing class-situation reflects itself in the wide range of differences in the political identifications of clerical workers, for example: there is no clearcut commitment to either major party. The more successful, who see themselves as 'middle class', reveal a marked preference for the Conservative Party. But the tendency to identify with the middle classes varies between industries in which clerical workers are employed. Thus, the Railway Clerks' Association always had close industrial and political contact with organized Labour and its members evinced a relatively high degree of working-class consciousness and loyalty.

Today, many more clerks are no longer clearly middle class either in their own eyes or in the eyes of others. Black-coated workers are split between Labour and Conservative, and move towards one or the other party with the general political swings in the country. Growing numbers, even of bank clerks, join trade unions and take strike action. Similar processes are affecting nurses, teachers, local government officials and other occupations once resistant to unionism, and yet also underlie the parallel claims of such occupations to 'professional' status. Both unionization and professionalization, however, involve collective group mobility as distinct from purely personal advancement.

These problems are developed by Goldthorpe and his colleagues in their discussion of the thesis of the 'embourgeoisement' of the British working class and the notion that, far from disappearing, as Marx predicted, the middle classes are growing in size, as more and more manual occupations disappear, as new jobs in the tertiary sector grow in number, and as now-affluent manual workers merge with the lower middle class (Goldthorpe *et al.*, 1967).

It is indeed the case that the work-force employed in traditional extractive and heavy manufacturing industries has declined, whilst the consumer-goods industries, transportation and service occupations have grown. It is also argued that the incomes of non-manual workers are no longer so superior, and that increased geographical mobility has gone hand-in-hand with upwards social mobility, too, as people move to better jobs in the Midlands and the South East, or move from slum areas in the older parts of the city to the new estates in the suburbs. Thus many workers experiencing affluence also experience the loss or weakening of the family and neighbourhood milieux within which their working-class attitudes and values were formerly created and sustained. Working-class affluence has followed a consumption pattern similar in some respects to that pioneered by the middle class: the telly, the washing-machine, home decoration and perhaps a car.

This emphasis on consumer durables is held to represent a new shift towards the home for the working class, a shift towards family consumption goals and perhaps more joint family life, and away from the older pattern of life in a traditional working-class community such as a mining town.

Here coal-mining is the single major industry in the community, a man is bound to his workmates at work, and in the pub, by strong ties of solidarity that pull him away from his family and the home. But the miner's job is changing, and in any case he is a fast-disappearing species. The emergence of the affluent 'home-centred' family, and the decline in the class-conscious solidarity of the older proletarian occupations such as mining, some people have argued, spells not merely the social 'embourgeoisement' of the mass of the population, but the ultimate eclipse of socialist and other organizations based on the working class and oriented to the collective restructuring of society.

In criticizing this thesis, Goldthorpe and his colleagues examine the evidence under three headings: economic, normative and relational. Firstly, the economic evidence for 'embourgeoisement' of the workers is not impressive, for when one takes income over the whole working life, as opposed to weekly wages, the apparent levelling up as between manual and non-manual workers is not so apparent, for pensions, prospects of promotion, sustained earnings, job security, loans and 'perks' are important inequalities as between non-manual and manual occupations. Secondly, in normative terms, the extent to which the working class is in fact losing its traditional attitudes and values and acquiring those of the middle class has little serious basis in research-findings. And thirdly, there is little evidence to show that relational patterns have changed: that middle-class groups have relaxed their exclusiveness and begun to admit working-class occupational groups to social equality.

In order to fill in the gaps themselves, these authors undertook a study of Luton car-workers, because these workers were exactly the people amongst whom the changes postulated should have gone furthest: among the most affluent in the working class, many of them residentially mobile and usually younger. They found, in fact, that loyalty to class organizations such as the unions and the Labour Party have not been affected by affluence. Nor have they become more satisfied with their work-situations; the boring and repetitive nature of car assembly-line work meant a very high degree of alienation from the work-task. The dominant motive for taking up the work was strictly instrumental – high wages and opportunities for overtime. Alienation from work reflected itself in 'privatized' preoccupations with home and family, though a bitter strike subsequent to their study indicates that alienation might take more collective and activistic forms at work also. There was still a very high degree of commitment to class organizations (80 per cent voted Labour), but in contrast with the traditional solidarity of the working class their collectivism was much more 'instrumental': the union was just a means to an end, a way of getting better incomes through collective bargaining, industrial action and political change, rather than part of the 'communal' solidarity of the older mining-town. The overall picture was clear: there was little indication that this new working class was being assimilated into middle-class society or that they even aspired to be part of it. Simply because they purchased consumer durables did not mean that they were becoming middle class in out-look. As the authors put it, 'a washing machine is a washing machine is a washing machine'; using one was a way of washing clothes, not a way of turning onself into a middle-class person. Their life-chances, consumption-styles, attitudes and values remained substantially different from those of the middle classes.

The 'embourgeoisement' thesis is concerned with quite low levels of the stratification-system: the manual/non-manual dividing-line. Other theories which purported to show that Marxist conceptions of class were outmoded have concentrated on higher levels in the class system. They have questioned whether ownership does any longer carry with it decisive power in the running of industry (Nichols, 1969). Writers in the 1930s and 1940s noted that joint-stock companies were becoming a mass phenomenon, since many large corporations had hundreds of thousands of shareholders. Under these conditions, 'ownership' became almost a fiction; the really decisive people were no longer the share-owners but those who ran the corporation from day-to-day: these, the real decision-makers, were the managers or directors. The capitalist was, in fact, disappearing.

The Second World War saw the involvement of Labour in government, and the growing intervention of government in industry, including direct government ownership of many enterprises. One influential analysis of these developments was James Burnham's *The Managerial Revolution* (1941), in which he announced that not only capitalist but also communist society was in reality coming under control of the new managers.

Research has demonstrated in fact that not only have enormous inequalities of wealth persisted, but that despite the wide diffusion of share-holding, the wealthy still dominate the large corporations, because they still own decisive blocks of shares. Even if they are a minority of the total, these blocks still enable a few such large share-holders (often 'institutional' rather than individual shareholders – banks and insurance companies) to outvote the hundreds of thousands of inactive small shareholders and thus control huge corporations with numerous subsidiaries. Sargant Florence has shown, too, for the U.K., that managers are not a quite separate class from capitalists – they usually have sizeable holdings in the firm, and in any case, their social background and education is similar, as are their attitudes, and their career depends on the success of the company. And though some differences can be found, large corporations are as sensitive to the need to pay attractive dividends to their shareholders as smaller ones – which runs against the theory that the bigger corporations, being more manager-controlled, are therefore less profit-conscious. (In the more extreme versions of these theories, the giant corporations were seen as virtually 'socialist' enterprises: the thousands of workers, shareholders and managers were said to form a partnership and the health of the enterprise was said to come before any 'sectional' considerations such as profits and wages.)

But whatever the relative powers of manager and shareholders, the crucial phenomenon is the growing power of giant capitalist corporations in political as well as economic life, rather than the eclipse of capitalism.

Theories which postulate the irrelevance of ownership are in fact much more helpful in understanding communist rather than capitalist society. For here the ownership of private property has been eliminated. Only the State or some other State-supported social group (co-operatives, collectives, etc.) owns 'means of production'. So those who control these organizations control the economy and therefore the distribution of wealth. The decisive body, over-all, is the Communist Party, open to those who follow its basic political requirements. In one sense, then, the Party can be said to 'own' the whole economy and its leaders to constitute, collectively, a class which is in effect the owning class. The model here is virtually the obverse of Marx's picture of capitalism. In that picture political power was the outcome of economic power. The state was a 'committee of the ruling class'. In communist society, writers like Djilas (1957) have argued, it is the other way round: wealth is a function of political power. One becomes rich by becoming a politically powerful leading Party or government official. The 'New Class', which controls the Party and the State, is firstly a ruling class, and by virtue of its political power, becomes an economic class too.

Djilas' analysis drew considerably on earlier writing by Trotsky and other Marxists, of which Trotsky's remains by far the most powerful and the best-documented analysis (Trotsky, 1969). There are major differences, however, between his interpretation of the U.S.S.R. and Djilas', and between Trotsky's interpretation and that of other Marxists who have variously seen the U.S.S.R. as 'State' capitalism, 'degenerated communism' and so forth. These differences in analysis, of course, have led to very different conclusions over the conclusions to be drawn for practical political action, and have led to severe sectarian quarrels.

Djilas denounced the 'New Class', and the system they operated, as a new despotism, and a self-perpetuating one at that. Many theorists have seen the Soviet experience as a further demonstration that, even given a gigantic revolution, any complex society will always require an apparatus of social control and a division of social labour in which there will be rulers and ruled. The so-called 'élite' theorists, indeed, insist that ideas of classless societies or of participatory democracy, under conditions of large-scale industrialization, are simply idealistic delusions, which may be scorned or admired, but which are fundamentally non-scientific dreams. Thus, Vilfredo Pareto (1848–1923) built his sociology around the simple, unsensational division of society into those who exhibited qualities of excellence in their given sphere of activity – the élite – and the rest, the non-élite (Pareto, 1966). A governing élite was constituted by those with the best-developed skills at ruling others, whether by the use of force or fraud. The masses, by contrast, were incompetent and ineffectively organized. In any case, mass and majority rule, he held, were both impossible in reality. Pareto believed that changes of régime and government merely reflected the periodic transfer of power from one type of élite to another, not from one class to another. Such a theory is psychologistic rather than sociological, for it explains social change in terms of there being reservoirs of *individuals* with fixed characteristics rather than as the outcome of conflicts in institutional arrangements. The economic and political dominance of the élites is explained as the outcome of their personal characteristics. Other élite theorists, notably Gaetano Mosca, produced more sociological versions in which they do not postulate the existence of different types in this way, but simply observe that some people perform more effectively than others in any activity; that in changing societies new people are constantly being recruited into the various élites, that the political ruling class is the most important of these élites and that modern democracy therefore represents a way of retaining 'open-ness' of the élite (Bottomore, 1964). An open system actually *increases* the effectiveness of the ruling class because it preserves allegiance to the system on the part of the most ambitious amongst the non-élite who always hope to rise in the social hierarchy, and who otherwise, if frustrated, might constitute a dissident force. Democracy thus depended on having a reservoir of talented middle-class people, some of whom could be recruited into the élite; it was also a more stable and popular political system than more reactionary and less flexible ones.

The model of a society in which key political power is firmly in the hands of a *political* class whose power does not derive from their economic holdings, has also been used in analysing the situation in some of the newer and more backward 'neo-colonial' independent states. These are agrarian societies; the decisive power is held not by a bourgeoisie or a class of capitalist landowners but by a political class of 'new men' of no great substance who, by founding and dominating the party, and then the government, become a new ruling élite rather than a ruling class in the Marxist sense, but do not develop the country. It is significant that so many studies use the label 'new élites' for these countries rather than 'new ruling *classes*', for decisive economic power lies outside the country – with those who own the plantations and mines, control the financial institutions, and regulate world-market prices.

Classes are, of course, developing in all these countries, and in some are already well-developed, since most of the world's peasants have long been drawn into the money economy as cash-crop producers, virtually all as consumers, and many into urban industry or plantations as labourers. Indigenous capitalist enterprise also emerges or continues to develop after independence. Hence, social classes are indeed coming into existence. But the ruling élites are not classic ruling classes, and ethnic divisions (usually labelled 'regionalism', 'tribalism' or 'separatism') are strong, and for a time at least constitute a powerful counter-balance to weakly-developed consciousness of class, and even weaker organizations based on such consciousness.

In communist societies, where private property has been abolished, and in backward 'neo-colonial' societies where the ruling class is not the decisive property-owning class, élite theory thus seems useful and helps complement theories which emphasize the economic basis of class alone.

Much contemporary theorizing about the development of backward countries assumes that they must follow other European patterns because 'modernization' or industrialization inevitably involves creating similar social institutions. Thus some assume, wrongly, that adoption of a given technology will lead to the emergence of parallel developments in other areas of social life also. Again, some theorists assume that the middle classes are indispensable for achieving and maintaining progress. But in Communist countries the most striking success in development occurred under the leadership of the Communist Party, not the middle classes, and Japan and Germany achieved their modernization under a centralized and militarized State controlled by an alliance between a segment of the traditional agrarian ruling classes and powerful new industrial magnates. In many countries, in fact, the intermediate strata act as a block on development. In Brazil, for example, people with salaried jobs in private and governmental bureaucracy are the political dependents of the dominant landed, capital-owning and military interests, and do little more than attempt to enlarge their share of economic and social resources. They thus tend to support the enlargement of the state apparatus, which has done little to improve the social and economic position of the vast bulk of the population. Such middle strata are scarcely a force making for development.

Again, in some African states, the government, higher civil servants and upper salariat draw incomes based on those of the former expatriate colonial personnel. Economic and social differences between this 'salariat' and the ordinary people are marked, and the salariat, overwhelmingly urban-based, is oriented in its general attitudes and values to the town rather than to the countryside where the bulk of the population live. Small middle-class business (as distinct from this salaried middle class) is usually involved in minor middleman roles in importing foreign manufactured goods, and exporting raw materials, or in petty shopkeeping trade rather than any development of production, whether in agriculture or industry. The petty traders, the artisans working on their own account, and the small land-owners are very numerous in some countries, but the bulk of them are very tiny operators indeed. In countries like India, Nigeria and Ghana, they include some very wealthy men: not a petty bourgeoisie, but a full-blown bourgeoisie proper: owners of big businesses, plantations, bankers and industrialists.

Frantz Fanon has argued, however, that even this 'national bourgeoisie' is too weak to challenge foreign enterprise and that in most small independent states they are not a source of beneficial growth at all, since they have developed as hangers-on of colonial society and now act primarily as direct or indirect agents of foreign investment capital (Fanon, 1965). Since they are a highly-privileged and minute fraction of the population, mainly confined to the towns, often educated in Europe and usually wielding great political power, they tend to defend their own interests strongly and to close their ranks against threatening competitors. Judging from rates of inter-marriage, the development of distinctive consumption-styles, residential, social and educational exclusiveness, they also form a status-group which is almost, but not entirely, closed: it is barely possible to enter these circles via the educational system, for only very limited mobility is possible through higher education since schools and colleges are so few and far between that only a few hundreds out of millions can hope to enter them.

The class structure in such societies thus differs from developed capitalist society in that there is no rich bourgeoisie at the top, or one with only limited economic power. Governmental power is usually decisively in the hands of those in the capital who control the party or the army, but their capacity to decide is always qualified because the 'commanding heights' of the economy are in foreign hands.

Despite the growth of a money economy the chances of acquiring wealth via agriculture are very limited, owing to the structure of international prices, for the gap between the prices paid for manufactured goods and those paid for the raw materials the poor countries produce grows wider year by year. This economic 'non-development' leads to peasant discontent, because the peasantry is the hardest hit. The urban workers, because they are fewer, relatively-privileged, and under closer control, are less volatile than the peasants.

Marx saw the French peasantry in the nineteenth century as most unlikely to become a revolutionary force because of their physical dispersal and the backwardness of their social life generally. However, in the twentieth century as we noted earlier, in more backward countries it is precisely the peasantry which has been the backbone, flesh and blood of revolutionary socialist and nationalist movements. The other revolutionary stratum, Fanon suggests, is the so-called 'lumpen-proletariat': the unskilled, frequently unemployed poor, who Marx believed to be also incapable of developing a revolutionary class-consciousness. In contrast, the proletariat of the new states appear comparatively inert. Fanon attributes this to the relatively privileged positions of workers in steady employment who may well feel a sense of deprivation when they compare themselves to the new élite, the new middle classes, or even the White man, but who possess a very important piece of property – a job – which ten others would snap up readily if it were available. And some have argued that this mass of urban poor constitutes potentially revolutionary material not merely in colonial or underdeveloped societies. The revolt of racial minorities in the United States can be seen, too, as not only a racial protest but as the protest of those who are utterly poor and unskilled – the 'lumpen' proletariat – large sections of whom also happen to be non-White.

Social classes in the full Marxist sense, characterized by a sense of solidarity amongst their members, and by class organizations which express and articulate conflict against other classes over the radically unequal division of property are not yet very well-developed in many underdeveloped countries, and vertical divisions of ethnicity – tribal, regional and 'ethnic' differences – often divide classes and unite people as 'pillars' despite economic differences of position and wealth.

Divisions of class often coincide with racial, biological differences (e.g. of colour) in which case the conflicts are usually both more transparent and likely to be especially severe, since the further element of racial conflict is added to class-conflict. Usually, however, it is not just a *racial* difference (i.e. a biological difference such as skin-colour) that is involved. (Indeed, biologists have trouble classifying the human species into races, and the three major divisions they recognize – Negroid, Causasoid ('White'), and Mongoloid – only have remote relevance for the understanding of so-called racial conflicts.) Many 'racial' conflicts occur between populations which are physically quite closely related (e.g. Chinese and Indonesians, Cubans and Americans). Serious and large-scale conflicts do occur, of course, between groups whose majority of members also differ racially (e.g. between China and the U.S.S.R., or China and India), and there is little doubt that racial prejudices play some part in such quarrels. But the major differences in these cases are political. Within a given country, they tend to be economic (e.g. White versus Black in South Africa). The exploited class is also racially different from the exploiters. And globally, Fanon points out, the 'Whites', by and large, are the wealthy, and the non-Whites are the 'wretched of the earth'.

These differences do not just arise because of the fact of physical differences, then. Physical differences often do mark off social groups which are also dominated, exploited or in rivalry with others. But these physical differences are only part of the differences between them; there are usually whole clusters of cultural differences also: of language, religion, dress, etc., and of different 'ways of life'. Such differences in culture, when they coincide with group physical differences are usually called 'ethnic', not just 'racial' differences. And there can be conflict between cultural communities which have *no* physical or racial differences, such as between Catholics and Protestants in Northern Ireland or Irish immigrants and indigenous British in the U.K., or in the ordinary conflict of classes within the indigenous British population.

There are thus many different and important lines of division. Such divisions are relevant for sociology in two ways: firstly, at the level of organization, because they form bases for social groups (and also for more spontaneous and unorganized 'social movements' or 'race riots'), and secondly, at the level of motivation, because social actors are moved by the ideas they have concerning the various groups and categories of their fellow-men. We could scarely understand the modern world if we thought that class was the only factor that mattered to people. Clearly, people go to war over religion or over political boundaries, and racial prejudice exists as a major independent factor. A man who believes in solidarity with his fellow trade-unionists does not necessarily believe in solidarity with his Black fellow-workers and fellow-citizens. Such alignments therefore very often cut across class-divisions. But often they reinforce them, and the so-called 'race war', internationally, overlaps with political and economic conflicts. Though at one level the major conflicts may be regarded as political and economic in the end, at the level of both individual motivation and of institutionalized ideology more people have probably been killed in the name of religion, and of national and ethnic-racial superiority, than from all other reasons taken together, and class war has been much less significant.

Such antagonisms may thus impede the development of 'class' revolutions of the traditional kind. But 'ethnic', national and economic alignments coincide all too commonly, and therefore provide an especially explosive propellant for revolutionary movements. These movements, like non-revolutionary political organizations, recruit across classes and often appeal to many other things than class. Indeed, revolutionary 'cadres', almost by definition, are likely to be made up of people whose position in the stratification-system *as a whole* has been upset, whether through economic misfortune (losing their land or their job) or through changes of status (becoming educated or converted) or through suffering from changes of political régime (e.g. experiencing occupation by foreign troops). But whatever the reasons why people become revolutionary, and whatever kinds of people readily join revolutionary movements, their organization is the more easily achieved because modern communications make available ready-made ideologies and programmes and there are organized parties ready to tell them what needs to be done. Given ideas, courses of action, and the social machinery (the party) which seem to promise to answer their needs, formerly passive peasants can be co-ordinated and energized to form a revolutionary force. The existence of parties of this kind thus emphasizes again that political institutions constitute an independent variable. Even though appropriate conditions have to exist, different responses can be induced by different leaderships. Much depends on the programmes and organizations available, and these do not 'inevitably' emerge in a given situation.

Chapter 8
The Problem of Order

To say that the problem of social order concerns asking whether and how social organization is possible may seem perverse, for obviously social life does exist. But it is by no means obvious as to how and why this persistence of organized social life comes about. Nor do we get much help in our efforts to solve this problem if we try to use many commonly-held beliefs about man and human nature – whether they be popular beliefs or some of those held and developed by major thinkers. For these theories, if carried through to their logical conclusions, would lead us to believe social life can never exist!

In one kind of theory, the individual is depicted as a basically egotistical being, entirely absorbed with his own objectives, indifferent to the consequences which his single-minded pursuit of his own private ends might have for his fellows, and resistant to any attempt to impose limitations upon his self-seeking. Society, on the other hand, is seen as consisting of rules which the individual must accept and respect, and which limit his freedom to pursue certain ends or to employ certain means in achieving those ends. These social rules, moreover, require the individual to subordinate his personal self-interest to the common good, and to consider his fellow man, with whom he has to live and with whom he must co-operate.

If such conceptions were true, society would run against the very grain of human nature, for social life is represented as the antithesis of everything in man – an essentially individualistic creature. Logically, then, there ought to be no such thing as society, for society could never have arisen spontaneously out of this kind of 'Human Nature'. Indeed, this is precisely what philosophers like Hobbes have argued. Society, they say, does exist; but since men are basically individualistic, society must have come into existence, and is only maintained in existence, through being imposed upon Man. Society can only survive through the constant suppression of these natural individualistic and anti-social inclinations. According to this view, therefore, the maintenance of society is inherently difficult, since it involves the constant suppression of the individual's impulses and an equal and opposite constant resistance and evasion on his part. This unwillingness of the individual members of society to remain within the confines of society would lead to its dissolution and disintegration were it not that power is constantly exercised to control this dissidence.

Sociologists would no longer accept such conceptions of either the individual or of society, and would certainly not accept any model in which 'the individual' is seen as something quite independent of, or opposed to, 'society', for, as we have seen, because human beings live within society, human individuals are inseparable from social organization. The animal that would develop 'outside' society would be very different from the individual described above. (He would be a 'wolf-child', not a 'human being'.) But though sociologists find such arguments unacceptable, the major problems these arguments raise (as distinct from the specific answers they offer) cannot be dismissed. Since there are, in any existing social order, forces which work toward the destruction of society, how are they contained and inhibited?

It is not a simple matter to explain just how societies do manage to 'work', to remain in existence for any period of time, and to cohere throughout that period. For societies are complex organizations of human activities, involving many different kinds of activity and kinds of person, all of which have to be concerted and co-ordinated in delicate patterns of co-operation; the existence of these different activities and different sets of people naturally makes for differences of interest. At the very least, it would seem at first glance, societies ought to break up along the lines of specialization which divide off one group of people with similar characteristics from another. It would then collapse into internal confusion, because the co-ordination needed to fit those diverse and separate units and activities together to form a co-operating whole could only be brought about by creating very complex machinery, which none of the conflicting and warring factions would accept.

There are many social theories which stress these divisive features of social life. Few of them provide any explanation of that fact that these tendencies do not always work themselves out and lead to social collapse. In most social organizations, there is some measure of stability and cohesion, the sources of which are not explained by such theories. It is at this point that the problem of social order arises; at this, the problem of explaining the integration and continuity of social structures.

Many critics are prepared to argue that to take this problem as one's focus of attention is to lead oneself, perhaps without being aware of it, into a politically conservative and theoretically naïve position. For a concern with 'order' is held to result in the neglect and underestimation of the role of force, fraud and conflict in social life, in favour of an emphasis upon, and approval of, the harmonious and co-operative aspects of social life.

It can, however, be argued that although these criticisms may justly be made of one or another 'order theorist', a concern with the problem of order does not *necessarily* result in conservatism and in a refusal to recognize that conflict, coercion and deception play an important role in social life. We can go further and say that those who have been interested in the problem of order have often been only too aware of the fragile and tenuous nature of social order, and of the frequency with which force and fraud enter into the relationships between men. The problem of order arises, in the view of these theorists, because they find the facts of conflict and division, and the sources of these conflicts and divisions only too apparent; what *is* obscure is the nature and sources of those forces which contain and limit the use of coercion, and thereby provide some solidarity, continuity and cohesion in society.

What is surprising, then, is not the fact that violence and cunning are often used but, rather, that they are not more often resorted to than they are; after all, it would seem that they are as efficient as any other means which men can use to obtain their ends. We find, however, that even in those situations in which men engage in the most large-scale violence – warfare – there are relationships between men which rest on things other than the simple coercion or deception of each man by others: although there may be no restriction upon the kind of atrocity which men may practise upon their 'enemy', there are very powerful restrictions upon the use of violence against members of their own side. In other words, although the only relationship *between* the armies is expressed through force, each army is internally organized through relationships based upon trust, co-operation, friendship, loyalty, authority and so on.

The point is not that force and fraud are not important, but that they, alone, cannot account for social life; no matter how widespread conflict may be in a society, we will always find that some members of the society are related to one another in other ways. Logically, this must be so if we are to speak of a society at all, for social life cannot 'work' through force *alone:* if we were to assume that it could, we would be caught up in an infinite regression, for we would have to argue that each member was forced to act as he did by someone else, who was in turn forced to do as he did by someone else, who . . . and so on, *ad infinitum*.

A concern with the problem of order need not lead to any lack of awareness of conflict, change and compulsion, for these are only, after all, the reverse side of the coin we are considering. If our explanation of the cohesion and stability of society is a good one, then it is also an explanation of conflict and change, for in specifying the conditions under which societies persist we are also saying that if those circumstances do not prevail, the society will change. It may thus be convenient and useful to begin by considering harmonious aspects of social life but we could equally begin the other way round: in starting with a consideration of order, then, we are simply taking a convenient point of entry which ought to lead us, eventually, towards the examination of the less harmonious characteristics of social life.

In stating our problem, we have used many terms as if they were interchangeable; harmony, integration, solidarity, cohesion and so on. They are not, of course, identical terms, and there are significant differences between them, differences which we shall not inspect here but which reflect different facets of the problem of order. The 'problem of order', in fact, is a very complex set of issues rather than a single, clearly-defined question, for there are many different dimensions and levels in the operation of social organization. Some of these issues we indicated above: the co-ordination of activities; limitations upon the use of force; the containment of conflicts; and the unification of diverse activities.

Since we cannot deal with everything relevant to the problem of social order – for there are far too many issues – we have chosen to pay special attention to three problem-areas which seem to us to be the most important and fruitful, and which also involve different levels of analysis.

Firstly, there is the problem of *meaning*, which we raised in Chapter 1: the ways in which men came to experience the world as an orderly place and are able to communicate with others about it. If one is to be able to communicate with others about it, if one is to be able to co-ordinate one's activities with those of someone else, one must be able to signal one's intentions, desires, commands and refusals to him, and, in return, be able to understand his. A communication process, therefore, is a basic precondition of co-operative and concerted social activity.

Next we shall take up the problem of *social control*: how are the activities of different individuals brought together into stable and enduring patterns? How can their activities be fitted together so that the behaviour of one person produces appropriate responses in another? How is it that when one individual initiates a particular line of action he finds that others respond to it in ways that he considers appropriate, act as he expects them to? Thirdly, we shall examine the way in which many different kinds of activities and groups are held together within common social boundaries, as part of wider social groups within which divisions and conflict have to be contained. The *unity of social life* is our problem here.

The division of the discussion into these three parts also involves a division in terms of the levels of social organization being examined. The 'problem of meaning' will analyse the social experience of the individual and the ways in which he encounters his world, whilst our discussion of 'social control' will involve an analysis, firstly, of the workings of small groups, and then of larger social organizations and groups. The total society will be the object of our attention in the third section, the unity of social life.

It should, however, be stressed that these divisions are not hard and fast: there is considerable overlap between the various sections of the analysis. The problems of meaning, social control, and unity, moreover, can be raised for each level of the social structure. We make these distinctions for purposes of simplification, then, and do not see them as lines which mark off separate areas of social life in such a way that only one kind of problem arises for each area.

The Problem of Meaning

Men experience the worlds in which they live as sensible and meaning-ful places; the things that happen to them, the people and objects that confront them, are recognizable and behave in more or less expected ways. Men feel with some confidence that they know about their world, that they can account for it and deal with it, that the things they have done in the past will contrive to produce the same results that they have previously done, now and in the future.

For most of the time men take it for granted that they know the world, feeling that there is nothing either problematical or curious about that fact. If they keep their eyes and ears open and their wits about them they cannot fail to understand what is going on about them for they need do no more than recognize the obvious; anyone else in their situation would see the world in exactly the same way that they do.

They think of themselves, in many ways, as passively registering experience, seeing the world in the way they do because that is how it is; things in the world simply present themselves and are seen. But a naked eyeball, passively observing, will not serve us as a model for human perception. Although men often regard themselves as doing no more than recognizing what takes place under their eyes, they are also, on other occasions, capable of recognizing that the world is not quite so transparently self-evident. Thus, although we may assert that 'anyone' ought to be able to see certain things because they are obvious, we nevertheless exclude children and strangers from the category 'anyone', and treat them with special patience and tolerance because we classify them as people who have not yet learned how to see the world the way we see it. We thus implicitly recognize that seeing the world this way is *not* obvious, but has to be learned.

As we insisted at the outset, the world is not 'given' to men, some-thing which is simply seen through wide open eyes. What is seen is as much a function of who is looking, how he is looking, and what he is looking for, as it is of what is 'out there'. We may, after all, see the 'same' thing as several quite 'different' things, now as this, now as that:

In the course of my professional work for a fire insurance company . . . I undertook the task of analysing many hundreds of reports of the circumstances surrounding the start of fires, and in some cases, of explosions. My analysis was directed towards purely physical conditions, such as defective wiring, presence or lack of air spaces between metal flues and woodwork, etc., and the results were presented in these terms. . . . Indeed it was under-taken with no thought that any other significances would or could be revealed. But in due course it became evident that not only a physical situation *qua* physics, but the meaning of that situation to people, was sometimes a factor, through the behaviour of the people, in the start of the fire. . . . Thus, around a storage of what are called 'gasoline drums', behaviour will tend to a certain type, that is, great care will be exercised; while around a storage of what are called 'empty gasoline drums', it will tend to be different – careless, with little repression of smoking or of tossing cigarette stubs about. Yet the 'empty' drums are perhaps the more dangerous, since they contain explosive vapor (Whorf, 1964, p. 135).

Whether the same gasoline drums are to be seen as 'full' or 'empty' is not dependent upon the drums themselves for they can be seen as *either* one or the other; how we shall see them depends upon the yard-stick that we are using to evaluate them; whether we are assessing them in terms of the amount of gasoline or the amount of gas that they contain. The yardstick that we will choose to employ as a measure will relate to the interests, purposes and knowledge that we have. If we are *interested* in the storage, distribution and sale of gasoline it is the amount of gasoline in the drums that will concern us, whilst it will be the vapour content of them that we will want to know about if it is our job to investigate and prevent fires. If we are storage-workers, we are likely to see the 'empty' drums as being 'safe', because we do not have much technical knowledge of fire hazards and thus do not realize that these drums are in fact more dangerous than the 'full' ones which we treat much more circumspectly. We are unlikely to discover this danger because our work role does not involve our having access to the information the insurance investigator has available to him, nor does our job require us to meditate upon the possible causes of explosions.

Thus the way in which something is seen depends upon the interests that we have, and upon the knowledge, information and opportunity available to us. We look upon the world selectively, looking for the things that matter to us, and ignoring things which are not relevant to what we want to do. We therefore acquire the knowledge and skill to be able to see whatever it is that we want to see, and there are others who help us to see the world in special ways, as we see with the trainee policeman:

As he walks through the beat with a mature officer, persons who to him appear legit are cast in the light of the illegal activities in which they are engaged. . . . The lovely young lady alighting from a cab is now observable as a call-girl arriving for a session. The novice is shown how to see the streets as, so to speak, scenes from pornographic films (Buckner, 1967, p. 64).

This selective perception of the world around us, then, affects our view of both the social world and the physical world, our view of gasoline drums as well as our view of people's actions. Sociologists have therefore spoken of the 'social construction' of reality (Berger and Luckmann, 1966). They do not mean that the world does not exist apart from our perceptions of it, but rather that the way men see the world is conditioned by their active engagement in it, including their efforts to achieve the ends they desire and their efforts to make sense of their experience.

Now people do not normally think of themselves as making constructions of their world, for the term implies methodical and deliberate work, and most of us usually make sense of things in a routine, automatic and habitual way. None the less, no matter how routine and unselfconscious, these interpretations of experience do entail a process of organizing one's experience. When, for example, we meet a new acquaintance we find out what kind of a person he is by observing his behaviour and by listening to the talk and gossip of others about him, putting together what we see and hear into a consistent picture of him as a particular type of person, a conception which we test against his conduct, perhaps modifying our conception of him after we have seen him 'in action'. We do not make a deliberate project of finding out about him, the way his biographer might, but we do, even so, gather and organize information about him.

Indeed we have to organize, even routinize, the way we go about making sense of our experience, because very often we need to size up situations with a glance and trust our impressions.

We have no time to do elaborate studies. If we were to be overly deliberate and methodical in deciding what it was that we were seeing, life would become too complex for us to handle. Take, for instance, the long streams of witnesses called over many days in a court of law to establish a few facts about a person or situation, facts which even then may be regarded as very dubious and debatable. To be able to decide what is going on about us in everyday life, by contrast, we must be able to do so quickly; we must trust our judgement and assume that what we see is a matter of patent and obvious fact that requires no further questioning, because it is indubitably so, for unless we make such assumptions we cannot act at all. In categorizing situations as being of one kind rather than another we are not carrying out an academic exercise, disinterestedly sorting out the phenomena that we observe: we have a deep practical interest in 'defining our situation', in recognizing the things that confront us, for we act towards and upon the world that we see. In identifying something we are indicating to ourselves what can happen in the future – that is, how that thing will behave – and, reciprocally, the kind of responses that we can make, the lines of action that are open to us. The case of the gasoline drums discussed above provides us with an example of the way in which our conduct is directed towards the situation that we perceive: if we see the drums as 'empty' and 'safe', we feel secure in their presence: we feel free to smoke because we do not expect these drums to explode or catch fire in the way that the 'full' and 'dangerous' ones might. Just as the establishment of a definition of the situation allows us to act, so the failure to establish such a definition inhibits our capacity to do anything; if we find ourselves in an ambiguous or confusing situation where we do not know 'what is going on' or if we decide that we do know, take action, and then discover that we were in error, we experience confusion, distress and uncertainty and cannot decide what to do next. At such times all that we can do is attempt to make some sense out of the situation.

This kind of situation can arise in even the most mundane and everyday settings, even within the game of chess. One sociologist, when it came his turn to move in chess, would

change the pieces around on the board so that, although the overall positions are not changed, different pieces occupy the squares – and then move. On the several occasions on which I did this, my opponents were disconcerted, tried to stop me, demanded an explanation of what I was up to, were uncertain about the legality (but wanted to assert its illegality none the less), made it clear that I was spoiling the game for them, and at the next round of play made me promise I would 'not do anything' this time (Garfinkel, 1963, p. 199).

This player's opponents do not know what he is doing and feel unable to continue the game until they have found out what is going on, what he is 'playing at'; one cannot play chess if one's opponent does unusual, unexpected and apparently meaningless things. In the same way, one cannot act in other social situations if it is unclear what is going on, if one does not know in what capacity the others are acting and so on; an individual's conduct cannot be related to that of other individuals unless he knows what they are doing.

So far, we have been arguing as if the construction of the social world were an idiosyncratic process, carried out on the basis of the individual's peculiar concerns and capacities. This is not the case, for complex social and cultural processes are involved; the equipment which the individual uses to order his experience into meaningful patterns is derived from the culture of the social groups of which he is a member, and the use he makes of this equipment depends upon the changing situations he finds himself in.

Our ability to make sense of the world, and to act towards it, is based upon our ability to name things, for to name something is to say what it is, and what it will do and how we may act towards it. The ability to name things is possible only through the use of language.

All things can be seen as unique, as if no two events are exactly alike, no two moments precisely the same. Yet we do not experience them in this way; if we did, we would live in a shapeless, everchanging world in which nothing would be like anything else. We could not understand or handle such a world. We would never be able to employ methods which had worked in like situations in the past, for there would be no like situations in the past. But the categories of language allow us to make abstractions, to ignore the peculiarities and uniqueness of things, and to notice the similarities and resemblances between them. In classifying this situation under the same name as that one, we are pointing out to ourselves the fact that the two situations are in some crucial respects the same, and that in these situations certain typical things may be expected to happen and may be done.

The use of language, then, is more than the learning of a long list of words; to use a language is to use it the proper way and on the right occasion as part of a wider process of communication. The use of language thus involves the use of non-verbal communications as well as words, for in order to apply the words of a language properly we must be able to 'read the signs'. We recognize things by seeing, hearing, feeling, touching and tasting them, by learning to recognize their properties: sights, sounds, odours and textures. In knowing, for example, what another person is we rely on the many non-verbal signs that he gives to us. We 'read off' from his appearance, dress, gesture, skin colour and ornamentation his character and the capacities in which he can act. The kind of dress which someone wears tells us about their ethnic background, their social status and their occupation; the uniform of the policeman, the nurse and the clergyman are highly visible signs of the craft that they practise, the casual dress which they adopt around the house indicates that they are in a relaxed and leisurely mood off duty. Even the ornaments which adorn the body and the markings of the body itself tell us about people; wedding rings signify marital status, expensive pearls indicate wealth. The significance of non-verbal signs is well shown in this description by a sociologist of his research into drug use and distribution:

I spent much time with people involved in heroin use and distribution, in their natural habitats; on rooftops, in apartments, in tenement hallways, on stoops, in the street, in automobiles, in parks and taverns. . . . On the one hand I did not dress as I usually do (suit, shirt and tie) because that way of dressing in the world I was investigating would have made it impossible for many of my informants to talk to me, e.g. would have made them worry about being seen with me because others might assume I represented the law. But on the other hand I took care always to wear a short-sleeved shirt or T-shirt and an expensive wristwatch, both of which let any newcomer who walked up know immediately that I wasn't a junkie (Polsky, 1967, p. 34).

Here we see a social actor deliberately manipulating the non-verbal clues which he gives to others in order to convey certain things about himself; through these clues he tries to convey to the users and peddlers of drugs that he is not connected with the law and can be trusted. To the policemen of the drug squad, he is signalling that even though he is in the company of addicts he is not himself an addict. The very use of space which someone makes, and the location in which he is to be found, suggest that he is a particular kind of person; addicts and pushers gather in open places where their transactions cannot easily be overlooked by the casual or deliberate observer, and where they can themselves observe what anyone else in the neighbourhood is doing. Then there is dress; those involved in the use of drugs see anyone who is wearing a suit as likely to be involved in some way with the law. The short-sleeved shirt serves to reveal that the author's arm is not scarred by needle punctures, a marking on the body associated with drug use, and that he wears an expensive wristwatch, something which an addict would sell to buy drugs. A man is known, too, by the company that he keeps; to be seen talking to somebody who looks like a law man is to become suspect oneself.

As with the whole process of interpretation of the world and its meaning, our reading of such non-verbal signs is much affected by the beliefs which we hold. As members of groups we acquire many beliefs which we do not even regard as beliefs but simply as 'facts' which are 'common sense' and which we are convinced any reasonable, sane and capable member of society would recognize as such. The policeman 'knows' for example, that anyone found in certain places, who keeps company with known criminals and has a history of offences himself is the sort of person that gets into trouble with the police, breaks laws and is likely to tell lies to anyone. It is in the light of these beliefs that he views situations: in encounters with people who fit his conception of a 'no-good' he will be suspicious and will refuse to accept or believe whatever he is told because he 'knows' that people like that can't be trusted. In the same way, he knows that drug addicts frequent certain places, that their addiction makes them steal and sell their valuables, etc.

This 'commonsense' thought, found in all social groups, is a loosely organized collection of beliefs, assumptions, rules and methods. The individual accepts these as being, without question, true and shared by everyone. He draws upon them to make sense of the events that he encounters, to transform these events into meaningful social situations and patterns of behaviour. He may, in addition, draw upon more complex and organized bodies of thought to order his experience, upon sets of beliefs which organize experience into a more systematic pattern.

Commonsense thought is dominated by practical concerns; the individual can make sense of his ordinary experience and get done the things that he wants done. We do not, however, live from moment to moment, interpreting each event as it unfolds, and treating each one with equal equanimity. We all attempt, to one degree or another, to organize our lives, to lay down plans and projects, and to see the whole of our experience as forming some meaningful patterns.

We prefer some experiences to others, regarding them as more satisfying, pleasing and gratifying. We evaluate our experience in the light of values which lead us to regard some things more highly than others, and the fact that we do have values gives rise to a problem of meaning on a different level:

If a friend is killed in an automobile accident the 'how' is usually fairly clear in a scientifically satisfying sense. It is true that our knowledge of the physiology of death is by no means complete – and the friend is not likely to be in possession of more than a fragment of that knowledge. But this is not what is problematical to him. It is rather the 'why' in a sense relative to a system of values. The question is, what purpose of value could his death serve? In this sense such an occurrence is apt to be particularly meaningless (Parsons, 1961, p. 667).

We tried to show, above, that the 'how' of events is by no means so clear cut as the author of this passage would have it, that complex processes are involved in ordinary, mundane experience. We have not yet, however, discussed the problem he raises of meaning 'relative to a system of values'.

In so far as we do evaluate experiences and prefer some of them to others, we present ourselves with the problem of the distribution of good and bad fortune. If the things that happen to us are unpleasant, cause us pain and distress, we raise the question as to why these things befall us? Why should we, out of all the people in the world, be subject to disasters, debacles and discomforts? Why do these things not happen to someone else, especially to people who do not lead 'good' lives? Could it perhaps be that we have done something to deserve these misfortunes? And even the possession of good fortune gives rise to similar questions; why are we, of all people, so fortunate and happy? Is it not because we are deserving of such good fortune? Is is not a result of our good, honest and upright conduct?

The fortunate is seldom satisfied with the fact of being fortunate. Beyond this, he needs to know that he has a *right* to his good fortune. He wants to be convinced that he 'deserves' it, and above all, that he deserves it in comparison with others. He wishes to be allowed the belief that the less fortunate also merely experiences his due. Good fortune thus wants to be 'legitimate' fortune (Weber, 1961, p. 271).

Such a need for explanation will not be satisfied by a mere description of the events which lead to good and ill fortune, for what is at stake here are not matters of fact but the question of the moral significance of the facts.

In response to this need for 'meaning' there have emerged bodies of beliefs which are more systematically organized than those of commonsense thought and which account for the nature of the world, man's situation within it, the significance of human life and the distribution of fortune among men.

Perhaps the most obvious example of such 'belief systems' are those of religion; they show that this world exists in some kind of relationship to a supernatural world and that the fate of men depends in part upon the forces or beings which inhabit the supernatural realm. The distribution of fortune is seen within the context of this relationship, its allocation to individuals and groups being seen as a consequence of the degree to which their conduct conforms to the moral standards sanctioned by the supernatural world. Thus good fortune may be seen as a reward given by God to those who have conducted their life in close conformity with the moral rules that he has given to men, suffering as a result of the continued violation of this moral code, i.e., 'sinfulness'.

Such beliefs transform the moral significance of events which occur in the everyday world; what happens to men is not simply an outcome of cause and effect relationships obtaining between events but, rather, a consequence of 'destiny' or the approval of the gods. The poor, the dirty and the diseased, within the framework of religious belief, may come to be seen as 'God's children', of far greater moment and significance in the eyes of God than those who have wealth and power in this life. Suffering, for them, in this life is without significance, for this life is brief and transient and all the pain of earthly existence will be more than compensated for in the next life or after the Day of Judgement:

Between the close of the eleventh century and the first half of the sixteenth century it repeatedly happened that the desire of the poor to improve the material conditions of their lives became transfused with phantasies of a new Paradise on earth, a world purged of suffering and sin, a Kingdom of the Saints. . . . Generation after generation was seized at least intermittently by a tense expectation of some sudden miraculous event in which the world would be utterly transformed, some prodigious final struggle between the hosts of Christ and the hosts of Antichrist through which history would attain its fulfilment and justification (Cohn, 1957, p. 13).

The relationship of religious beliefs to the world of daily life is more complex than these simple examples show, there are many ways in which religious beliefs give 'meaning' to life. We may, for example, classify such belief as 'this-worldly' and 'other-worldly': the former kind of beliefs stress the involvement of the individual in the activities of the secular world, that what happens in it has great significance and that a man's moral worth and the meaning of his life are to be found in the extent to which he fulfills the duties imposed on him there, or upon the extent to which he struggles to bring the conditions prevailing in this world into line with those demanded by God. 'This-worldly' beliefs, then, may be further classified in terms of the extent to which they encourage the believer to accept or reject the existing order of society. In contrast, 'other-worldly' belief-systems direct those who accept them to regard the things that happen in this life as a matter of mere indifference; ideally, a man's social status on earth has no significance and says nothing about his moral worth. What matters is his relationship with the supernatural, and he should devote himself to the cultivation of this relationship. The ideal, for him, is withdrawal from active involvement in daily life and dedication to a life of prayer and meditation – a monastic existence; for those that cannot meet this ideal, secular responsibilities should be accepted and fulfilled but should not displace a concern with salvation.

We do not suggest that these beliefs necessarily have the consequences which they are intended to have, that those beliefs which stress indifference to the things of this world lead to a withdrawal, for they may well have unintended consequences, results neither intended nor desired by those that preach them. Max Weber has shown how, for example, the Protestant teachings of Calvin which stressed indifference to worldly pleasures in favour of the realization of God's will on earth contributed to the growth of the avaricious, profit-seeking and quite worldly spirit of the capitalist entrepreneur (Weber, 1952).

We are not, here, concerned to pursue the question as to how such beliefs affect social life nor even with the specific kinds of social conditions which lead to the emergence of one or other kind of belief system. We have not even tried to discuss the problem of religion in any general way; we have simply used religious beliefs as examples which illustrate a general point, a point that could equally well have been made through the use of some secular beliefs, say, political doctrines or philosophical systems. What we have tried to show is that there is a problem of 'meaning' which members of society face, that they have a 'need' to see the events of daily life as fitting within some broader framework, as part of some grand design and that they find the significance of their own life within this design. We should further note a point that will become of some significance later in the discussion; these belief-systems provide a framework within which a set of moral prescriptions are 'legitimated' or ratified. The case of religion shows this: a man's worth is to be judged in terms of a set of moral rules but the moral rules in terms of which he is judged derive their significance from the fact that they are espoused and approved by the prophets and the gods.

Like commonsense thought and language, belief-systems are not the products of individuals. They are the outcomes of collective existence. A language is, above all, the property of a social group:

Any group of people that has any permanence develops a 'special language', a lingo or jargon, which represents its way of identifying those objects important for group action. Waitresses classify types of customers and other workers in the restaurant, give shorthand names to foods, and have special signs and gestures standing for important activities. So do criminals; and even ministers are not immune from the necessity of classifying their clientele and colleagues, otherwise how could they organize activity in an orderly and sensible manner? (Strauss, 1959, p. 325)

Language develops in social groups; the categories it contains discriminate most finely in those areas which matter most to the members of the group: the language of the medical profession is a mixture of both technical and slang terms for diseases and illnesses, that of the drug addict is an elaborate argot referring to the many different kinds of drugs and combinations of drugs. We are not suggesting that non-members of these groups could not make these distinctions, but that because they use different language they do not make these distinctions in the fine-grained and routine way that habitual users of these terminologies do.

Language is also a collective phenomenon, in the sense that the use of a language is its use within a language community; proper use of a tongue is use in such ways as would be ratified by other native speakers.

Commonsense thought, too, is a property of particular social groupings. Our knowledge of the social world is not gained from our own immediate experience of the situations that we know about: 'The first rule for understanding the human condition is that men live in second hand worlds. They are aware of much more than they have personally experienced. The quality of their lives is determined by meanings they have received from others' (Mills, 1959b, p. 405). We acquire our knowledge and beliefs from those who share the world with us; we learn by observation of what they do, from listening to their talk, to the advice and the lessons that they give, the stories they tell, the jokes they make and so on. We come to share with others the beliefs that we have learned from them.

Belief-systems are developed to appeal to categories and groups of people; they aim at persuading certain kinds of people in certain situations. They are carried, too, by social groupings; they become the property of churches, parties, classes, status groups and the like.

Interests, purposes and knowledge which the individual brings to bear on his interpretation of his experience also derive from his membership of social groupings; we get the goals that we pursue, the tasks that we have to do, and the knowledge that we use in doing them, from the groups to which we belong. We desire the things approved of by other members of the group; we do the things normally demanded within the group or commanded by those in authority; and we draw our knowledge from a common stock available to and current among the other members.

Even in taking decisions as to what has happened on a specific occasion we are involved in a complex social process. We find ourselves in the midst of a constant flow of information to and from other persons and, in reconstructing the events which have occurred, draw upon conversations with others, eye-witness evidence, expert advice and the files and records of organizations. In some cases, even the decision-making process is collectively organized; committees and juries, for example, find it necessary to establish a common definition of events, a shared conception of what happened. Consider, for example, the problem of reaching a decision as to whether or not someone has committed suicide. Common sense tells us that people who commit suicide usually leave notes, and that they resort to suicide because they are unhappy and in trouble, or because 'the balance of their mind is disturbed'. We look, therefore, for evidence in line with the common sense assumption: for notes stating suicidal intent, for evidence of difficulties in the suicide's family, sexual, financial or work life, and for evidence of 'odd', 'strange' or 'peculiar' behaviour in the recent past. Such information is drawn from the kin and friends of the deceased, from those who worked with him and those who handled his affairs, as well as from experts in medicine and pathology. The decision as to whether or not it is suicide is finally made by a coroner at an inquest (cf. Douglas, 1967).

Our decision making is influenced in yet another respect by an involvement in social organization; we make our decisions with regard to other people. In attempting to establish a definition of the situation, we wish to establish one which others will accept and share in; in advancing one conception of 'what happened' rather than another we are initiating lines of action in which others must become engaged. If, for example, we decide that this death is a 'suicide', the consequences are quite different from what they would have been if we had decided it was 'murder'. The latter categorization of the death would have set in motion a search for a killer, would have involved the police, the press, the public, etc. We need to establish definitions which are in line with those held by others because if we share a common conception of the situation we are able to fit our actions together much more easily. We know what is appropriate and expected of both of us, whereas if we work with different understandings of the situation we initiate lines of action which will lead sooner or later to conflict and disagreement.

The possession of a common language, or common body of belief and set of shared meanings, enables the members of society to live in a common world, to have the 'same' experiences as one another and to communicate with one another about their world and experience. These shared meanings are at once derived *from* society and are also a precondition *of* it; the meanings develop within ~~particular~~ particular groupings and organizations and the indivi~~dual~~ the meanings through participating in such grouping~~s~~ sharing common understanding in this way, groups wou~~ld~~ able to operate. If men did not live in a common world a~~nd~~ experiences, they would not be able to communicate with one a~~nother~~ nor to concert their actions towards commonly defined object~~s~~ ~~and~~ situations.

Our emphasis has been upon the way in which men make sense of the world and the connexion between their understanding of the world and their mastery of it. They interpret the world and give it meaning so that they may act upon it, control their situation and destiny, and thereby achieve the ends that they desire. We do not suggest that men never find their world 'meaningless' and 'chaotic'; disasters, in particular, are often experienced in this way, as a meaningless jumble of happenings, for in disasters normal channels of communication break down, authority-structures collapse, those involved lack experience of similar situations. Even here, however, shared understandings rapidly develop. Rumours find fertile ground because:

Rumour is a substitute of news: in fact, it *is* news that does not develop in institutional channels. . . . When activity is interrupted for want of adequate information frustrated men must piece together some kind of definition of the situation and rumour is the collective transaction through which they try to fill the gap (Shibutani, 1966, p. 62).

Confronted by situations which they find shapeless and chaotic, men immediately set out to discover sense and significance in them.

Social Control

In the previous section we examined the ways in which men transform their experience into a meaningful, orderly and predictable social world, and establish effective expectations about the behaviour of the things that populate the world. We must now turn to the problem of why these expectations are effective, why the world behaves in accord, more or less, with our expectations.

This is not too difficult to understand as far as relationships to mate objects are concerned, for our expectations about them are reasonably well-founded generalizations based upon their past behaviour. The social world presents, however, some slightly different problems, for here we are concerned with human individuals and they, it may be argued, surely have minds and wills which render their behaviour unpredictable? If so, we can have no expectations about their behaviour, because they can make and carry out decisions on the basis of impulse and inclination.

We do not deny that individuals have minds, or that they make decisions; we do not agree that this renders their conduct inexplicable and irregular. That men have these characteristics does mean that their conduct must be explained differently from that of the inanimate world, but it does not mean that no explanation at all can be given.

Men do make decisions and choices and carry them out, not in a random and idiosyncratic way, however, but within the context of rules which they share with other individuals. It is the fact that they act in terms of rules that makes men's conduct predictable, and it is the fact that these rules are shared that makes one man's conduct predictable to another.

In playing a game of chess, for example, the players have a choice as to which moves they will make. They cannot, however, make *any* moves, but only those which are allowed within the rules of chess; one can move a pawn, on the first move, either one or two squares forward, but one cannot move it backwards.

If we observe a number of the moves that either player makes (assuming that he is playing chess and not just shoving the pieces about), we can often calculate the strategy that he is playing with and can thus predict what his next moves are likely to be. We know which particular rules of play he is following at any one moment, and these rules of play limit the successive steps that can be made and the way in which counter-strategies can be devised. Because a player's moves follow an intelligible sequence, a rule, it does not mean that he is not making choices, but, rather, that he has chosen to play this particular strategy rather than another.

Within the context of the chess game, then, what can and cannot be done is regulated by the rules of chess, although the players have the choice of which particular moves they will make and, even, of whether or not they will remain within the rules or not. In playing chess, one need not, of course, only make those moves that are legal – one can, as the player in our example did (p. 345), move the chess pieces in all sorts of ways – but if one does not abide by the rules, then the game is spoiled: it ceases to be 'chess'. This does not mean that the conduct of a player who breaks the rules in this way becomes 'unintelligible'; it means, rather, that his behaviour has to be seen within some other framework of interpretation: instead of playing chess he is 'making jokes' or 'losing his temper'.

Rules *constitute* the activities in which people are engaged. The movement of a chess piece from one square to another can only *mean* 'checkmate' *within* the rules of chess; if one does not know the rules of chess then it is impossible to say what those who are playing the game are doing: one sees movements, but not the tactics involved in a game of chess.

Although we have been using as our example, a game, chess, which is governed by explicit and clearly stated rules it should not be thought that when we speak of 'rules' we mean only those which can be found in rule-books, manuals, contracts, statutes, charters and the like. Most social activities are governed by rules which are implicit and unstated, rules which participants often could not articulate even if they tried to do so. The most explicit rules always rest upon a further set of rules which are not explicated; Emile Durkheim pointed out, long ago, that the explicit rules stated in a contract always presuppose that the parties to the contract accept the rule, not stated in the contract itself, that the terms of the contract will be binding upon them (Durkheim, 1964). Furthermore, people are often unable to say what the rules which they are following are; when we speak a language we follow the rules of grammar, that is produce grammatical utterances but most of us cannot say what these rules of grammar are.

One of the reasons why we do not think of ourselves, in very many situations, as following or obeying rules is because we have, through the process of socialization, 'internalized' the rules, made them a part of ourselves; we learn things in such a way that they become habits, skills, beliefs and convictions of our own, just as our speaking of a tongue is thought of simply as an ability that we have. This is, too, one of the prime reasons why we obey rules and conform to them. All our activity is governed by *some* rule or other but we are always faced with the option of breaking out of any particular set of rules; thus, if we are losing at a game we might simply 'spoil' it or refuse to continue playing. We remain within the confines of a particular set of rules, however, partly because we have internalized them, because we have learned to do things *this* way and cannot imagine doing them in any other way or because, even though we know of other ways of doing things we feel, very strongly and deeply, that our way is the right and moral way.

Internalization is not the only thing which keeps us conforming to rules; we often feel a temptation to break the rules but refrain from doing so because we fear the consequences which a violation will have for us, fear the ways in which others will react to our misdemeanour. The rules which we learn, we learn through the process of socialization; we learn them *from* others and therefore can be said to share the rules with them. We know, then, not only that certain things are 'right' but, also, that others believe them to be 'right' and that if we fail to do the right thing, the others will respond by doing things which we find punishing.

Other people *sanction* our conduct; when we act in ways of which they approve they show us that they approve and they reward us, but when we fail to act as they desire they manifest their disapproval and punish us. There are, then, two kinds of sanction, the positive (or rewarding) and negative (or punishing) sanction.

The most obvious sanctions are, of course, the negative, coercive ones; we may be punished through being deprived of life, liberty, physical comfort and well-being. Economic sanctions are also important; the ability to give and take away valued goods and services is a powerful control over people's conduct. These physical and economic sanctions are very important but they are not the only, nor, indeed, the most important; *approval* itself is very basic. We are very sensitive to the opinions that others have about us, are gratified when they show us that they approve of our actions, distressed and disturbed when they manifest their disapproval. That we can gain valued social positions and symbols of merit which express the love, respect and admiration which others have for us is a strong inducement to continue to behave in ways of which they approve whilst fear of the mockery, public insult, degradation and exclusion, which expresses the disgust and distaste of others for us, makes us hesitate to do those things of which they disapprove. Consider the agony of embarrassment experienced when we do the 'wrong thing' in public and the way in which this indicates the intense sensitivity that we have to the evaluations others make of us.

Conforming conduct, then, is to be understood within the context of collective life; we learn the rules through socialization and we learn them *from* others; we share the rules *with* others. When tempted to depart from the rules we are constrained by the fact that others value them and are prepared to back up their beliefs about what is right with sanctions.

These observations can enable us to obtain some understanding of the processes which operate to create and maintain stable and enduring social relationships.

It is because rules are shared that the activities of many individuals can be 'fitted' together and brought into an organized pattern. When we talk of 'shared' rules we do not wish to imply that everyone behaves in the same way, for of course they do not. In a game, the players are governed by the same rules, but these rules make provision for the various players to do different things within the game and, in fact, regulate the relationships between the players. Thus the rules of cricket specify what the players may do *vis-à-vis* each other – one cannot be a batsman without a bowler to play against, and to be a batsman involves acting in a certain way towards the bowler, in trying to get runs off him. The game 'works' because the rules ensure that the activities of the various players complement each other.

It is thus through the existence of shared rules supported by sanctions that stable patterns of social interaction arise and are maintained. Shared rules governing the conduct of the members makes for mutual predictability of their actions and, thus, for the 'fitting' together of their activities. The fact that the rules are morally binding and supported by sanctions means that the patterns of behaviour prescribed by the rules will be repeated and that tendencies to change these patterns of behaviour will be inhibited.

These arguments apply to social life in general. We can look at any kind of social organization as being divided up into a set of 'positions', which we term 'roles'. The conduct of the individuals in the various positions is governed by a set of rules which prescribes what they can and cannot do; these rules we term 'role-expectations'. The activities of the individuals are also related to one another in that they are complementary; they behave in appropriate ways towards individuals occupying related roles: the 'teacher', for example, gives lessons and instructions to which his 'pupil' attends. The complementarity of roles operates through shared rules, in that the actors know both how they ought to behave when occupying a given role towards the occupant of another related role and how, in turn, the other ought to behave towards them.

A study of a small work group may illustrate the operation of these processes. Researchers found that among a group of workers in a manufacturing plant there developed a rule which specified the amount of work that each of the workers ought to do in a day. If anyone did work too fast or too slowly he was called abusive names – a 'rate-buster' in the former case, 'a chiseler' in the latter – and he was 'binged', given a warning thump on the arm. The application of sanctions by other workers to those who broke their rule meant that the rate of production in that group varied very little from day to day (Homans, 1951, pp. 48–156).

The term 'social control' designates those processes within social groups which operate to prevent the violation of social rules; 'deviance' is the concept used to describe such violations. Within social groupings, there operate processes of social control that inhibit deviations from the rules of the group and thus maintain the established rules.

This does not imply that the rules are never broken, nor that patterns of deviant activities do not become established or that the rules do not change. For although there are processes which tend to maintain the social order and the rules which tend to inhibit deviance, it is always possible for deviant activities to be stronger than these social control mechanisms. Indeed, the control processes may themselves contribute to their own defeat (a process which has been called 'deviance amplification'), in the following way: a violation of the rules may be responded to by punitive sanctions which the deviant feels have been unjustly applied to him. His feelings of injustice and resentment lead him to feel less respect for and attachment to the rules and thus to violate them again. This results in further sanctioning of his behaviour which, in turn, increases his resentment . . . and so on. We can see such processes at work in the school, for instance, where new pupils accept the rules of the school and wish to attain the goals approved by the school, notably academic success. But failure in examinations shows them that they have failed within the framework of the school rules regarding 'hard work' etc. Such failure leads to a loss of interest in academic success by some of the pupils and this in turn causes them to be punished for laziness. They then feel even less attachment to the school's rules and values and begin to flaunt these rules quite deliberately, showing they have rejected the school and the rules in terms of which it evaluates them as 'failures', and eventually even come to form a distinct 'anti-culture':

... a boy who does badly academically is predisposed to criticize, reject or even sabotage the system where he can, since it places him in an inferior position. A boy showing the extreme development of this phenomenon may subscribe to values which are actually the inverted values of the school. For example, he obtains prestige from cheeking a teacher, playing truant, not doing homework, smoking, drinking and even stealing. As it develops, the antigroup produces its own impetus. A boy who takes refuge in such a group because his work is poor finds that the group commits him to a behaviour pattern which means that his work will stay poor and in fact often gets progressively worse (Lacey, 1966, p. 253).

These simple ideas which we have sketched out enable us to understand the ways in which stability is produced in face-to-face relationships, in small groups and in simple organizations; they are useful in the analysis of stable patterns of behaviour in work groups and of deviant behaviour patterns among schoolboys. Can they be extended and applied to more complex problems, such as the analysis of deviance within the wider society? Can they enable us to understand how order is created in society itself?

Obviously we cannot extend these ideas directly to these more complex problems. It is reasonable to assume that all the members of a relatively simple organization like a school act with reference to the same rules but such an assumption cannot reasonably be made about a complex and differentiated society. Such a society is composed of many different kinds of people engaging in different kinds of activities in different groups and organizations; since, as we have already argued, each activity is governed by distinctive rules we cannot argue that the diverse activities which compose a society are 'fitted' together by common rules.

Some sociologists argue that although we cannot assume that all the members of society are governed by the same rules, we can and must assume that all the members of society subscribe to the same values. The assumption of a 'value *consensus*' enables us to account for stability in a complex society.

'Values' are general conceptions of 'the good', ideas about the kind of ends that people should pursue throughout their lives and throughout the many different activities in which they engage. They are relatively diffuse conceptions of the ends that men should pursue in that they can be pursued in many different contexts and situations and realized in a whole range of specific ends. Thus it is often argued that in America the dominant value is 'success'; it is easy to see how one can be successful in a whole range of quite different ways: one can be successful at school, in work, at sport etc.

These values arise in response to the need for 'meaning' to which we referred in the preceding section. There we discussed the ways in which religions, and other, similar belief systems, placed people within a meaningful context, and showed them that their lives, society, even the cosmos itself fit into a coherent pattern. People do not only want to see that there is a pattern in the world, they also wish to know where they are going and how to get there; such belief systems provide them with directives, state the sort of values that they should pursue throughout the course of their worldly existence – thus Protestant beliefs stress that man should be industrious, and abstemious in this life.

These values hold society together, it is argued, because they are shared in common. They *legitimate* the rules which govern specific activities; the rules are accepted as rules which ought to be followed because they express the values which everybody accepts. Americans are exhorted to believe that the capitalist organization of industry is best because it allows people to seek success, encourages them to do so and rewards them for doing so.

The fact that the values are shared, further, produces some kind of compatibility between different sets of rules. Since people seek the same *kinds* of ends through all the different spheres of life in which they are involved, they try to modify the rules to facilitate this pursuit and, as new activities emerge, they create rules in the light of their beliefs about what is 'good' and 'right'.

Finally, common values give rise to feelings of solidarity and unity among people. We tend to prefer to associate with those who think as we do, who value the same kind of things that we do; we like them better than those whose preferences and values conflict with ours. The sharing of values, therefore, means that the members of society feel an attachment to one another which will tend to override conflicts that may arise between them.

The *sense* of solidarity with others is conveyed to men through their rituals. The Coronation service is said to be

a series of ritual affirmations of the moral values necessary to a well-governed and good society. The key to the Coronation service is the Queen's promise to abide by the moral standards of society. The whole service reiterates their supremacy above the personality of the Sovereign. In her assurance that she will observe the canons of mercy, charity, justice and protective affection, she acknowledges and submits to their power. When she does this she symbolically proclaims her unity with her subjects who, in the ritual – and in the wider audience outside the Abbey – commit themselves to obedience within the society constituted by the moral values which she has agreed to uphold (Shils and Young, 1953, p. 224).

Through ritual the members of the society are reminded of the values to which they subscribe (but which they tend to take for granted in their daily lives) by seeing them explicated and enumerated. Their participation in the ritual with others reminds them that they are members of a moral community. Their awareness of the values, their commitment to them and their sense of solidarity with others are thus renewed and revitalized.

These arguments can now be summed up in a model of the perfectly integrated and stable society. Such a society would be one in which all members had internalized the values and the rules and acted in conformity with the rules in pursuit of these values, and any tendency towards deviation being effectively countered by the operation of social control mechanisms.

No one is, of course, arguing that such a society exists or that it has ever existed; no existing society can ever be perfectly integrated for there will always be contradictory or ambiguous rules, there will always be people who have not been properly socialized and there will always be weaknesses and breakdowns in the operation of social control. These factors, however, hardly seem sufficient to account for the amount of deviance that does occur in society – does the consensus model in fact provide a completely satisfactory account of deviance in society?

Robert K. Merton (1957, chs 4 and 5) has argued that this model can show how deviance is *systematically* created in the society; at least, it can account for the ways in which deviance arises in American society. He argues that we can see the values of a society as specifying the ends which people shall pursue, and the rules as specifying the means by which they may be *legitimately* pursued. Deviance occurs when people adopt illegitimate means to realize these ends and arises from a dissociation between ends and means.

In American society overwhelming emphasis is placed upon the value of financial success, and the legitimate means for its attainment are hard work and industry. All Americans are encouraged to seek financial success but the means to its achievement are not equally available to everyone; if one is very poor, illiterate and has no skills then it does not really matter how hard one works, one will never make a future by 'honest' means. There are many members of American society who find themselves in a situation of 'anomie' – they have internalized the value of pecuniary success but they do not have access to *legitimate* means by which they can attain it. They must resolve this problem, make some adaptation to the situation. The majority of people will be 'conformist', pursuing success by the prescribed means even though the task is hopeless, but some members of society will not – they will engage in deviant activities; they will either abandon the goal of success or will seek it by prohibited means.

Members of the American lower classes, Merton argues, are the ones most likely to 'innovate' – to seek success by resorting to illegitimate, 'dishonest' means. The pressure to do so is greatest upon them because the only legitimate avenues open are manual occupations and there is only a minute possibility that one can get on the road to the top through those occupations. Members of the lower middle classes are more likely to become 'ritualist', to abandon the pursuit of success as fruitless and yet to insist on adhering to the prescribed means; they 'go through the motions' in their occupation and fulfil its demands meticulously but they do not seek to advance themselves within it. They make this response to the situation because they have been socialized into regarding the rules as sacred. Thus when they lower their aspirations and no longer expect success, they find themselves unable to break out of their commitment to the rules.

Others 'retreat' from the society; they refuse to pursue wealth either by legitimate or illegitimate means and refuse, also, to lead a 'conventional' life:

Sociologically, these constitute the true aliens. Not sharing the common frame of values they can be included as members of the *society* (in distinction from the *population*) only in a fictional sense. ... In this category fall some of the adaptive activities of psychotics, autists, pariahs, outcasts, vagrants, vagabonds, tramps, chronic drunkards and drug addicts (Merton, 1957, p. 135).

This withdrawal from society is the response of those who have been unable to succeed by either legitimate or illegitimate means; they are unable to obtain success 'honestly', but have internalized a prohibition upon resort to dishonest means which they cannot break; the solution to their dilemma is to 'drop out' of society.

This is one response open to those who reject both ends and means. Another is to reject the prevailing order and to engage also in efforts to replace that order, to substitute new ends and means for those that exist; in short, to rebel.

Merton's argument that deviance is the result of a disjunction between the ends desired and the means available to attain them brings together many different activities within a single framework of analysis. It explains why people deviate and why their deviation takes the form it does, why some become rigid and inflexible bureaucrats (the ritualists) and why others become drug addicts (the retreatists).

These simple principles do appear to account for a wide range of facts. The question is whether or not Merton simplifies too much or whether he adequately accounts for the facts available?

In classifying together as 'deviant' a wide variety of activities, he disregards the different attitudes held towards these activities by the members of society. His 'ritualist', for example, is not likely to be regarded as a deviant by others, nor is he likely to be punished by them for his deviation (he might even be esteemed for his honesty and uprightness), whilst the rebel is likely to be severely sanctioned for his activities, losing his liberty and, possibly, his life. Merton does not consider the fact that the members of society themselves employ the concept 'deviant' in a different way in their daily lives and use it to categorize people. He attempts, rather, to define deviance 'objectively' in relationship to the norms and values that he postulates as being those of American society.

Many people feel that it is the business of scientists to develop a technical terminology, and that scientists must move beyond mere 'commonsense' thought and 'everyday language' in order to obtain the refinement and discrimination of thought they need in their work. We would suggest that while this argument *might* hold good for other sciences it does not do so for sociology. Since as we tried to show in the preceding section, common sense and ordinary language are *used in* society, the sociologist *cannot* simply cut himself off from these uses: rather the concepts and theories which the members of society themselves develop must be built into the sociologist's models. For if we are going to consider the problem of deviance we must recognize that members of society have conceptions of what is deviant. We must consider who and what *they* see as deviant, and how they come to see things this way.

Merton classifies together activities which he considers deviant in the light of his 'anomie theory', because these activities depart from the norms and values which he postulates as *the* legitimate norms and values of American society. Merton's category of 'deviance' only partly overlaps with the category of 'deviance' which Americans themselves use; he includes some activities which do not seem to be regarded by most Americans as particularly reprehensible, whilst excluding other practices – such as child-molesting, rape and homosexuality – which would be regarded with revulsion by most people. He also attempts to explain why the deviant practices which concern him occur, but he does not tell us why all of these departures from 'the American way' are responded to by people in very different ways; some of his 'deviant' activities are not negatively sanctioned whilst others are savagely punished. Nor does he explain to us why, even though the rules and values of American society remain unchanged, there is continual change in the pattern of activities which people regard as deviant – prohibition, for example, meant that for only a short period of time drinking was, in the eyes of the law, a deviant activity.

Some sociologists have argued that it is more useful to focus upon the 'societal reaction' to deviance, to ask how it happens that the members of society come to see certain activities as deviant and come to identify particular people as 'deviants', sanctioning them by placing them 'outside' the moral community. Howard S. Becker proposes a 'labelling' theory of deviance – societies

... *create deviance by making those rules whose infraction constitutes deviance* and by applying those rules to particular people and labelling them as outsiders. From this point of view, deviance is *not* a quality of the act the person commits, but rather a consequence of the application by others of rules and sanctions to an 'offender'. The deviant is the 'offender'. The deviant is one to whom that label has successfully been applied; deviant behaviour is behaviour that people so label (Becker, 1963, p. 91).

In approaching the problem in this way a shift in the focus of attention is involved. Merton's model assumes that people accept the legitimacy of the rules and will conform to them *unless* there is some kind of 'pressure' upon them which pushes them to deviate; the individual must break a rule which he accepts and must be motivated to do so. The sociologist's task, therefore, is that of identifying the special kinds of motivation which characterize the deviant. The 'labelling' approach does not concern itself so much with the motivation of deviant conduct for it assumes that *some* people who are labelled 'deviant' come to be labelled in this way as a result of engaging in activities which are, to them, quite ordinary, everyday and routine. It does not ask why the individual is motivated to engage in deviant activity but asks, rather, why certain activities and persons come to be seen as deviant.

Those who adopt the kind of view advanced by Merton assume that once the rules have been internalized the individual has no problem in applying them – as if he were simply an actor performing on the basis of a carefully prepared and detailed script. Conformity is not problematical to the sociologist, it is a result of socialization; what is problematical to him is the fact that people who have been socialized do deviate. The views which underlie the 'labelling' theory, however, encourage the sociologist to regard conformity itself as a problem. The individual may wish to conform but the rules themselves may be vague or ambiguous, the situation to which they are to be applied may be confused, or it may be new and unfamiliar; the individual has to work out his own solution, make decisions, use his judgement and try to act in such a way that his behaviour is conforming. In such a situation the individual may, from the point of view of those who enforce the rules, make the wrong decision or misjudge the situation and find himself being labelled as deviant even though he was *trying* to conform.

If we ask the question 'How are people labelled as deviants?' then we realize that there is a good deal of disagreement amongst the members of the society about who shall be considered a deviant. Some people are judged to be deviant by others but refuse to accept this judgement, declaring that they do not subscribe to the rules in terms of which they have been condemned. Others accept that they have broken a rule which is legitimate but argue that they only did so because they were obeying some other rule which has equal legitimacy and equal claim to be respected. On the other side of the fence we find people complaining that there are things going on which ought to be sanctioned but which are not, that some people are getting away with murder and so on.

Given such extensive disagreement about what is deviant it is wisest to dispense with Merton's assumption of common norms and values:

... it is theoretically conceivable that there are or have been societies in which values learned in childhood, taught as a pattern, and reinforced by structured controls, serve to predict the bulk of the everyday behaviour of members and to account for prevailing conformity to norms. However, it is easier to describe the model than it is to discover societies which make a good fit with the model (Lemert, 1967, p. 7).

Instead of assuming that society has a set of shared values it is best to assume that there is a 'plurality' of norms and values – in American society at least. There the population is heterogeneous, divided by ethnic, religious and regional differences as well as by those of social class; in such a context what is considered to be 'right' varies from group to group and from area to area.

With such an emphasis on the diversity of values and rules it is possible to introduce considerations of power. In a society composed of many different groups it is likely that some of them will have more power than others and will be able to impose their definitions of what is deviant upon other groups. Rule-making and rule-enforcement are political processes in that people attempt to have that which they believe to be right accepted by, or imposed upon, others who do not necessarily agree with them about what is right. If one group has more power than others it can effectively make rules for, and impose them upon other groups; this is the case in the U.S.A. where legislative power is largely in the hands of White Anglo-Saxon Protestants. It is the members of this ethnic group who are in a position to be rule-makers in political, economic and other fields and it is they who decide what activities shall be lawful for Blacks, Italians, Mexicans, Puerto-Ricans and other minority groups. Since the members of these groups have rules which are quite different, in some respects at least, from those of the Whites it is hardly surprising that there are higher recorded rates of crime for the lower classes since these strata are composed, in large part, of non-Whites.

The rules that are current in any society must be enforced and applied to particular persons in particular places. If we wish to understand how rules work, and how people come to be labelled as deviant we cannot, as Merton does, define deviance in relationship to the rules themselves, as if these were seen in the same way by everyone, but must look at the way in which they are applied to people, in order to see how decisions are made as to whether or not the rules have been broken.

Sociologists often assume that there is nothing problematical in recognizing deviance and that anyone can tell that a rule has been broken. We tried to show above when we discussed the problem of 'meaning' that it is always problematical for a social actor to decide 'what happened'. In attempting to enforce rules people are constantly confronted with situations which are more than usually problematical and they are constantly uncertain as to whether they are confronted by a clear-cut case of rule violation or merely by something which 'looks like' an offence but is, in fact, something else entirely, something which should not be taken seriously like a 'joke' or a 'trick' or something which was not intended, such as an accident.

If a policeman comes upon a fight, say, he is often uncertain as to what is going on; he does not know, at first glance, if it is a 'real' fight or simply friends playing about. If he intervenes in the fight and tried to find out what is really going on, he finds that he is offered different accounts, one of the participants claiming that it wasn't serious, the other claiming that it was. If he tries to decide who started it, who is to blame, he finds that again he is offered different stories, that each blames the other and gives a different description of the way the fight started.

In order to decide what has happened, the policeman must gather what facts he can, summon up his commonsense knowledge about how fights occur and use his judgement to decide what 'did happen'. If one of the combatants is a Black youth from a broken home in the slum, known to run with gangs, and who has a history of delinquent activities, then the policeman is likely to see whatever the boy does as malicious and delinquent because he 'knows' that children from 'bad' environments turn delinquent. He will not believe whatever excuses, justifications and explanation the boy offers to him and will suspect that he is lying. Whatever the boy has actually done he is likely to find himself being charged with an offence, sent through the courts and on to probation or reformatory. If, however, the fighters are White boys from 'good' middle-class homes then there is much less chance that they will be charged and processed by the courts, for the policeman is much more willing to believe that these are 'basically good' boys, and he will accept their explanation that it was just 'high spirits' and let them go with an apology and a promise not to do it again.

There is much evidence that there is a bias in law enforcement practices against the lower classes. Edwin H. Sutherland, in a classic study of *White Collar Crime* (1961) showed that many of the major American corporations systematically engaged in trading practices which could be considered as defying the law, but legal proceedings were seldom, if ever, undertaken against them.

Law enforcement practices are also shaped by the organization of the enforcement agency itself. In modern society, the task of rule enforcement is often in the hands of specialized and differentiated agencies. Social control is not exercised by those who are subject to the rules (as it is among a group of workers) but by those whose occupational task is that of enforcing rules upon others; policemen, lawyers, judges, government inspectors, the military and the like maintain public order and impose the law upon the citizenry. That the enforcement process is differentiated in this way has important consequences for the manner of its operation.

The situation of the enforcement agency in society and its relationships with other groups affects the diligence with which it applies itself to the task of enforcement, and the ways in which it applies itself. That law enforcement in the U.S.A., for example, is controlled by elected officials ensures that it will be very sensitive to public opinion and political pressure. When the public conscience is outraged by scandals the officials will be inclined to press for a drive against the activity which is attracting attention, even though the police normally tolerate it and do not interfere. Thus a scandal involving prostitution will lead to a drive against soliciting and brothels although in 'normal' times the police allow soliciting to occur as long as it does not lead to disturbances in public order.

The fact that enforcement becomes an occupation also serves to shape its organization. Policemen have a job to do; they have to show that they are effective and solve the cases that they are given to handle. The detective builds up a network of informants upon whom he relies for information in his work and he will ignore the fact that his informant is himself engaged in law-breaking activities. The division of the detective force into specialized squads is also reflected in the way use is made of informants; a detective from the vice-squad, for example, will use as an informant a drug-user or peddler and pay no attention to his offences because they are not his concern but are, rather, the province of the narcotics detail. Too, the fact that the policeman works in shifts shapes law enforcement; he will, if possible, let off an offender with a warning rather than make an arrest if he is near the end of his shift since the paper-work involved in an arrest may keep him at work long beyond the end of his working day.

The process of labelling itself, and the very existence of social control agencies themselves give rise to deviant activities, for the fact that someone is processed by these agencies and stigmatized as a deviant may compel him to go on practising the activities for which he was labelled a deviant in the first place. The individual who is arrested, tried and convicted for theft often finds, after his release from prison, that he cannot find a job because no one wants to employ an ex-convict; in such a case, often the only way in which he can keep himself alive and earn a living, is by resort to theft, particularly if, during his time in prison, he has been compelled to associate with other thieves who have become his friends and have taught him the arts and crafts of professional theft.

In the light of such considerations we should regard 'official statistics' with more than a good deal of suspicion, rather than as a source of data about social activities such as deviance. Sociologists have long known that official statistics on crime are unreliable because, for example, there are many crimes which are not known to the police or crimes that are never reported; nonetheless sociologists have been prepared to use them as evidence for their theories. Merton does this, admitting that crime statistics are not reliable, but claiming, however, that they support his theory since they show higher crime rates in the lower classes. In reality we do not know what crime statistics do measure, since we do not know how many 'crimes' go unreported nor how many of the 'crimes' in the statistics were in fact 'crimes'. It would seem that there is, at the very least, a systematic bias against the lower classes in the collection of these statistics; the commonsense knowledge of the policeman about the 'kind of people that commit crimes' and so forth shapes the way in which he 'reads' the evidence that is presented to him, and his theories about crime are such that he is always more likely to ascribe criminal guilt to members of the lower classes, as opposed to members of the middle classes.

These arguments should also persuade us that the 'labelling' approach to deviance is the most useful of the two presented here. We do not know whether, 'objectively', people who are labelled 'deviant' are, in fact, guilty of the offence for which they have been ostracized; all we know is that they have been judged guilty, that those who enforce the rules have decided that they did the things of which they were accused.

Although we have been concerned largely with issues relating to law enforcement it should be obvious that the same kinds of arguments apply to all kinds of rule enforcement and not just to the legal process; the labelling process operates in the same way in ordinary day to day relationships between people.

The purpose of the foregoing discussion has been to demonstrate that there are indeed situations to which our simple model of core values, shared norms, and mechanisms of social control applies well enough, perhaps best of all to small groups or organizations where the internal system of social control is a normal part of the routine activities of the organization. There is no guarantee that this model applies to every kind of situation. In particular the argument would seem to apply not at all well to complex differentiated societies, where there are specialized agencies of social control. Here, in order to account better for more of the facts of deviance, we need a model of social organization which allows for a plurality of values and norms, and an unequal distribution of power. We have tried to show how both of these models rest upon and employ a number of assumptions that were developed and elaborated in the discussion of the problem of meaning. We have moved from a discussion of the way in which conflict is handled in interpersonal relations to a more complex discussion of the ways in which deviance is handled within a society, though showing the connexions between them. We have seen repeatedly that the operation of social control varies considerably depending on such considerations as where political power rests, for power can be used to impose norms and pressurize agencies of social control. But the power context itself has been treated as though it were not a problem. We must now consider the problem of order, and the significance of political power in the total society.

The Unity of Society

In the preceding section we began to analyse the problem of order at the level of the total society by introducing a simple 'value-consensus' model of societal integration. We examined the applicability of that model to a specific problem, that of deviance, and showed that it had a number of shortcomings, that the problem could be more usefully considered on the basis of an assumpton of a plurality of values in society. We cannot, however, terminate our discussion of the value-consensus theory at this point for we have, thus far, presented only a very crude and simplified version of it: the theory is, in fact, much more complex and elaborate than it would seem from the sketch that we have given. It has been offered as a general theory for sociology and its application to the problem of the unity of society has been worked out in some considerable detail.

The claim that consensus theorizing is adequate for a general sociological theory has not gone unchallenged; many sociologists have criticized the theory, many of them arguing that a 'conflict' model of society provides a much more satisfactory basis for a general theory in sociology. The last decade in sociology has been dominated by the arguments between the proponents of conflict and consensus view-points – although, of course, the origins of each of these views can be traced far back into the history of social thought (see Further Reading, p. 409).

In this section we will present and compare these two competing models of society. The views, as we shall present them, will be formulated as if they were completely antithetical, in order that the differences between them might be seen more clearly and sharply. To do this we shall make composites of the thought of a good many writers who would, in important respects, disagree with one another. Although the major disagreements have been between members of the conflict and consensus camps it should not be thought that there is complete coincidence of opinion within each of these camps, that consensus and conflict theorists are not critical of each other's formulations. It should also be remembered that there are areas of agreement between these opposed positions and that some of the disagreement between them is a result of misunderstanding rather than of genuine differences in opinion.

Both the two approaches are concerned with the problem of social unity, both seek to answer the question 'Under what conditions do societies remain stable and unified and under what conditions do they change and/or disintegrate?'

The differences in the answers which they give to this question begin with assumptions which they make about the nature of man and society, assumptions from which their more specifically sociological views follow.

The consensus view stresses the essentially social nature of the human animal, the fact that the individual only becomes truly human through socialization and through membership in society. They stress the essentially co-operative nature of society itself; through the organization of a great many men into patterns of activity, tasks can be performed which would never be possible for individual human 'animals'. Co-operation not only makes possible the completion of complex and elaborate tasks, it is itself rewarding; men appreciate the company of others, their approval, and want to participate with them in common enterprises.

The unity of society arises 'naturally' from the relations among men and is a consequence of the operation of the same principles as govern face-to-face relationships; through interaction men work out sets of rules and values which they come to share with one another and which stabilize their relationships: the unity of society derives, just as does the solidarity of a work or friendship group, from commonly held beliefs and sentiments. The exercise of social control which sustains this solidarity and maintains stability of relationships is an expression of the moral outrage of the *whole* community, the response of the whole united group against the individual who violates its shared rules.

The conflict view is also founded upon the assumption that man is an essentially social creature but it does not assume that every society is equally suited to the realization of man's human nature. Some forms of social organization, particularly those divided into oppressors and oppressed, prevent some human beings from fully realizing their human capacities, from deriving full benefit from their membership in society. It may be that co-operation does allow for great achievements but in itself it is not virtuous; there is little value in collaboration between men if some people exploit an advantageous position within the co-operative process for their own benefit and at the expense of others. Differences of *interest* are just as important as agreements upon rules and values. Most societies are so organized that a given arrangement of relationships which benefits some will deprive and discomfort others; people placed in different positions in society, therefore, develop quite different interests, for any action or policy intended for the benefit of one group or category will threaten the well-being of others. Upon the basis of different locations within society, different interests and, consequently, different experiences, it is more than likely that quite different sets of values and quite divergent outlooks on the world will develop. The unity of any particular society is, therefore, to be seen as an outcome of the struggle by those with an interest in the *status quo* to maintain their advantage against those whose interests lead them to desire change. The exercise of social control, then, does not express the will of the whole community, its moral unity, but, instead, the wish of one group to keep society in its present condition, despite the desire of others for change, even though it may be necessary for them to resort to the use of naked force to maintain their position.

Such divergent assumptions must lead to quite different views about the way in which society 'works', about the relationships which obtain between its various parts. Let us look at some of the sociological arguments which follow from these basic assumptions.

A consensus view of society lays stress on the reciprocity which characterizes the relationships between one part of society and another. Society is seen as a system in which the various institutions, organizations and groups specialize in some activity. Such specialization means that no group is self-sufficient, no group is able to meet all its own needs and those of its members from its own resources. If it is to continue in operation the group must, therefore, exchange the products of its own activity for that of other groups. The group's survival now depends upon the fact that other groups will continue to produce those things that it needs but which it does not produce itself. Groups exchange the 'output' of their activities with one another but their relationship becomes more than a simple exchange relationship, it becomes a relationship of dependence. Each group now depends, if it is to continue with its normal activities, upon other groups continuing in theirs; since, however, all groups are specialized they are all in the same situation, each group being dependent on other groups; the relationships between them are not relationships of dependence but, rather, of *inter*dependence.

These patterns of exchange and interdependence can most easily be observed in economic life; there the specialization of people in one particular productive activity means that they are dependent, for their very survival, upon being able to exchange the goods which they manufacture for the goods which others produce. These processes, however, can also be observed at work in other kinds of activity than the purely economic; the relationship between the politician and his public can be conceptualized as an exchange relationship. The politician can be seen as exchanging his promises and his attempts to fulfil these promises for the votes and support of the electors; the politician 'produces' the 'goods' which people desire in the form of legislative and executive decisions, the people being willing to give in return, their continued support to and compliance with the politician's commands.

The conflict perspective recognizes the existence of exchange and interdependence but does not regard 'reciprocity' in quite the same light. Although parties do exchange with each other there is no necessary equality in such exchange; it may be either that there is *exploitation* in the relationship or that the relationship is unilateral. Exploitation operates in relationships in the sense that one party may, because of an advantageous position, be able to get greater value than he gives. The classic conception of exploitation is, of course, Marx's: he saw the economic enterprise as one not characterized by an equal exchange of pecuniary reward for labour-power, for the labourer does not receive the full worth of his labour, only such rewards as enable him to keep himself alive and at work: the share of the value of the products of his work above and beyond the minimum necessary to keep him alive, is appropriated by his employer.

A unilateral relationship is characterized by one-sided dependence. The subordinate party in such a relationship is dependent upon those above him for his livelihood, promotion and increases in income, but has little control over these and other things that matter to him. When unilateral relationships exist in this way it is usual for the exchange process to give rise to power because if one has no other resources to give in exchange for what is received, one can only offer oneself in return, comply with the demands of the more powerful party, and do whatever he asks.

The consensus view is more concerned with the way in which society operates as a whole; with the way in which a society encounters the problems that it faces *as a society*. If a society is to exist at all it must meet certain requirements – what are called 'functional prerequisites' – which ensure its survival: it must 'produce' members to fill the roles that are available within society or there would be no members, no society. Each society, then, must have some economic organization to produce food, clothing and shelter for its members, some kind of family system to produce new members and to socialize them, and so on.

Those who adopt the conflict view tend to take it for granted that there must be some kind of economic organization, that there must be some members in the society, etc. This must obviously be so or else there would be nothing for the sociologist to study, but it is not very interesting to observe that societies need members. It is much more interesting, they feel, to look at the *ways* in which these 'functional prerequisites' are met and to consider how the benefits derived from a 'solution' are distributed since the same 'problem' can be 'solved' in many different ways – there can be many different kinds of family system – and each 'solution' has quite different consequences for the different members of society.

It is no use, they continue, speaking of problems as ones that 'society' must solve since the members of society are by no means univocal: society is a confederation of groups which have different and, usually, conflicting interests. A 'solution' which is in line with the interests of one group and satisfactory to the group's members may be thoroughly damaging to the interests of another group and very costly to its members; the solutions at which 'society' arrives are more likely than not to be those which are favoured by the ruling group within the society and which enhance its interests.

Let us illustrate these two perspectives on 'society' and 'its' problems by looking at the way they view the role of social stratification. The 'functional theory of stratification', developed by sociologists who hold a consensus viewpoint, attempts to assess the role of stratification in enabling the society to 'adapt' itself for survival. They argue that stratification must always be a feature of social organization, that inequalities of power and wealth are inevitable, because they enhance the adaptive capacity of the society. If a society is to survive it must, to a greater or lesser extent, develop specialized institutions and, within them, specialized social roles – a social division of labour. Specialized roles require specialized skills, and some roles require skills which are more complex and difficult to master than others. Greater rewards must therefore be provided for those members of society who have to subject themselves to the deprivations involved in extended periods of training needed for them to acquire the skills necessary to carry out these more difficult, demanding and responsible tasks. The complexity of these skills, and the extended period of training associated with them, ensure that there will be few people in the society who possess the skills; the scarcity of personnel who can fill these roles means that such roles will be highly rewarded to encourage those with the requisite skills to occupy them. Further, some roles are more important than others, notably those which are crucial to holding the society together. If these important roles are to be filled they must be attractive, to ensure that a supply of occupants for them will be forthcoming.

The functional theory of stratification argues that stratification is an inevitable characteristic of social organization because it is the means by which every society resolves the problem of 'role allocation', of getting people to fill available social roles. The unequal distribution of rewards is necessary because social roles are of differential importance and require differential levels of skill; the assignment of higher rewards to key roles provides an incentive to people to fill them.

Rather than viewing stratification as necessary to the continuity and survival of society, the conflict theorist is more likely to see it as one of the basic sources of division and conflict in society. He is also often doubtful that it is, in any sense, 'necessary'. The fact that rewards are unequally distributed in society ensures that groups will struggle and manoeuvre, some to obtain redistribution in their favour, others to maintain a distribution which already favours them. Those arguments advanced by the functional theorists are much the same as those often offered by the members of ruling groups to justify their dominance; they attribute their wealth and power to the contribution which they make to the well-being of the society. Such arguments, the conflict theorist will counter, are justifications rather than explanations; the true explanation for the power of ruling groups is to be found in their monopolization of some valued resource or in their monopolization of power itself.

Consensus theorists argue that the powerful do try to justify their power but point out that these justifications are not empty verbiage. In order to provide justifications the powerful appeal to beliefs and values about what is 'right', and about who is 'deserving' – beliefs and values which they *share in common* with those that they dominate. There is, they continue, no discontent and opposition in society if the power of the powerful is accepted as legitimate; the poor, the underprivileged will accept an unequal distribution of resources if they believe that some people have a *right* to a greater share in these resources. Discontent occurs when the actions of ruling groups go against the values and beliefs of those they dominate; if the powerful do not act in accordance with the values held by the masses then the legitimacy of their rule becomes questionable and will be challenged.

The conflict school of thought does not deny that beliefs may be widespread in a society and shared by the majority of its members, but they do not regard such beliefs as 'really' shared nor as spontaneous developments. The dominant beliefs in society are those of the politically dominant group: they are expressed on behalf of that group by the major institutions of the society which are staffed by people who, if they are not actually from the dominant group, are in some way bound to it. The fact that such beliefs become accepted by persons outside the power group is not surprising: those who possess power over society possess power also over the machinery for the creation and dissemination of their ideas, and are thus able to ensure that ideas which are acceptable to them are communicated to other members of society. If members of society do, then, 'share' beliefs, this is to be accounted for in terms of the distribution of power; the beliefs which are shared usually serving to legitimize the position of those in power and to further their interests. Shared beliefs are thus seen as just one more device which the ruling group employ to gain compliance with their wishes on the part of other members of society.

Political institutions are, of course, very important sets of institutions for both schools of thought. For the first school – consensus theory – such institutions exercise power within society on the basis of a mandate from the members of society to implement the collective goals of the society. It has been suggested that we view power as a lubricant which smoothes the running of the society since through the use of power people are mobilized and directed towards collective goals. The political institutions, that is, seek to realize the goals of all the members of the society, acting within the broad framework of common values; to achieve this, these political institutions must command special use of some of the societies' resources – time, labour, wealth and so on – in order that they may organize activities in pursuit of these goals, enjoin participation upon recalcitrant members of the society, and control deviants. The capacity to mobilize social resources and to engage the support of the unwilling requires the granting of power to political institutions.

Often this line of thinking sees the power of political institutions as being only *one* kind of power within the society. Power is to be found at all levels of society and is possessed by groups and institutions other than the formal political ones. Such dispersion of power serves as a control over the specialized political institutions and ensures that they remain within the broad framework of shared values. The decentralized power units (in a society like our own, such groups as trade unions, voluntary associations, industrialists' associations, professional associations, pressure groups and so on) are able to exert pressure on the government in order to prevent the promotion of policies unacceptable to them and to encourage the adoption of more acceptable ones. Power, here, is a matter of degree: each group in society has power, but some have more and some less than others, governmental organizations having, in our own time, the greater share.

How does this school cope with the problem of apparent political conflict in the form, in our society, of a two-party system? This kind of conflict between two parties is seen as confirming the view of the consensus theory. The fact that society contains two organized mass political parties which recommend different policies, but that little political violence occurs, is said to show that there must be an underlying consensus for the two parties disagree within a framework of common values. Both bodies accept these values; they disagree only over the means by which such values are to be realized for the society as a whole. There is also consensus over the rules of political operation: the parties accept that elections are binding, that they require a mandate from the people to take and hold power, and that if the mandate is withdrawn, they must cede power to the other party and go into opposition without adopting violent means to retain or regain power.

The conflict school do not see the workings of democracy, the distribution of power, nor the role of political institutions in the same way. Political institutions like Parliament and the Civil Service basically work for the ruling group: it is their task to enact and implement legislation which furthers and protects the interests of the ruling group, and the political bodies are largely staffed by and deeply involved with and dependent on members of the ruling group. This school, too, stresses the fact that political institutions are subject to power which exists outside them. Such power is not seen as flowing directly from the large mass of the public through organized public opinion or secondary associations: instead, this crucial power is exercised by those in the 'command posts' of the other major institutions in society. Each set of institutions – religious, financial, industrial, etc. – has its internal hierarchy of power, and it is those at the top of these hierarchies who exercise pressure upon the political institutions through friendship, kinship, common association, control of resources and, to some extent, coercion. C. Wright Mills, a major representative of the conflict school, argues that the three dominant institutional spheres in American society are the political, the military and the industrial, and that these three spheres are becoming increasingly interdependent with each other because they face common problems and have common interests. The government is, of course, becoming more and more the major consumer of the products of the military and industrial sectors, and thus there is massive interdependence between them in that, although the politicians depend on the military and upon industrialists for their support, the latter are equally dependent upon governments as their major and most profitable client. Equally, with the increasing technicization and mechanization of warfare, the military and industrial complexes become more and more entangled with each other, and the military must obtain their equipment from the industrialists. This interdependence is reinforced by the fact that the top staff of each sector are drawn from common social and educational backgrounds and are often connected by kinship and marriage. Top-level personnel, too, circulate through the higher ranks of each sector. The United States, Mills concludes, is dominated by a single power élite staffing these three institutional spheres (Mills, 1956).

In this argument, it can be seen that the political institutions are subject to pressure from and dominance by the military/industrial complex. Such pressure derives not from support rooted in mass and popular consensus, but in the power of the different élites. 'Public opinion' does back the decisions of the powerful but it is not the spontaneous voice of the people themselves: it is to be seen rather, as a product of the mass media and their opinion forming activities.

Power, here, is conceived much more in terms of a division between the 'haves' and 'have nots': there is a limited supply of power in society, and this is largely monopolized by the élites: there *is* power outside the political sphere, but this is in the hands of a limited segment of the population at best: the mass of the people have little power compared with the power monopolized by the élite. What, then is left of traditional notions about democracy?

The existence of political parties and political competition is seen as a formality which serves, in greatest part, to mask the political realities and grant to the people an illusory share in power. The fact that there are competing parties is recognized, but the similarity of their programmes both in terms of the values they pursue as well as the means they use to achieve such values, is stressed. These facts indicate that the parties are limited and constrained by the realities of power distribution. Because of the power of these interest-groups, the parties themselves are pressed to develop programmes which further the ends of the powerful: should they fail to do so, then, on taking power, they will find themselves deprived of co-operation and support from the other major power-centres and will be unable to achieve anything at all. The parties therefore modify their policies so as to ensure the co-operation of the powerful.

Mass political parties are seen as important devices for 'incorporating' dissident groups within the existing social order; they do this by modifying the desires of such groups for radical change and by persuading them to confine their opposition to peaceful and, ultimately ineffective methods. Such parties attract the leaders of potentially revolutionary groups and turn them into 'successes' within the existing social order; in the course of becoming successful these men are socialized into the life-style and values of the dominant institutions and their enthusiasm for radical politics and rapid change in the basic social order gradually abates. The leaders of dissident groups thus come to accept the legitimacy of dominant values, and they use their position of leadership to get their followers to accept these same convictions and to adopt policies which will not lead to any significant change in the institutional structure of society.

For the conflict theorist, consensus is a temporary state: conflict is endemic in society because of deep-rooted differences of interest among the various groups and because of the unequal distribution of resources. If there is consensus this is merely a result of the successful inculcation of the ideas of the ruling group to the ruled. The stresses and strains of social life, and the conflicts inherent in the social structure will eventually disrupt this fragile agreement, and the issues that are critical will rise to the surface again; conflict will re-emerge, and eventually a revolution or internal war will lead to the establishment of a new balance of power and the emergence of a new ruling group.

The consensus theorist, on the other hand, feels that this makes far too much of conflict. There will, of course, be conflict in any society because no real society can meet the conditions of the ideal model; every empirically existing society will be imperfectly integrated, will have some rules and values which conflict with one another, members who are not fully socialized and so on. It is, however, misleading to say that conflict is 'endemic' in society itself since many of the most important conflicts have their origin *outside* the society – either in the physical or technological environment of the society or in its relationships with other societies – or are a product of temporary disturbances and changes which affect the 'balance' of the society. Conflict is not *rooted* in the society but occurs because of 'readjustments' which the society undergoes as a result of radical technical changes; for example, the industrializing process will produce many conflicts in society as social relationships have to be adapted to new economic relationships.

The question of social change has been one of the central issues between the two perspectives which we are discussing. Those who promote conflict theory argue that its greatest advantage is its ability to account for social change. Consensus theory, they continue, is incapable of dealing with problems of change in any effective way and the most crucial and pressing problem which we face today is precisely this problem of change.

There is some substance in this accusation, for consensus theory has concentrated the greater part of its effort on accounting for stability and persistence in social structures; it has given relatively little attention to the problem of change, except to remark that no society is perfectly integrated and that there are always sources of change in the inadequate socialization of some of society's members and in the conflict of rules and values. They have, however, paid a good deal of attention to the long-term patterns of change which characterize social structures and have been particularly concerned with patterns of 'progressive social differentiation'.

This notion of 'progressive social differentiation' does not so much *explain* social change but describes a continuing tendency which has been present, particularly in the social structures of Western societies, a tendency towards increasing specialization on the part of social institutions. In pre-industrial societies there is little separation of social functions; within such societies kinship is the institution through which religious, political, economic, familial and other roles are organized.

In contrast an industrialized society is characterized by the separation of these activities and the performance of each of them by an institution which specializes in that task; thus work is now separate from the home, the socialization of children is in the hands of schools and educators. The transition between the two types of society involves the separation of functions from one another and their allocation to specialized agencies; it does not mean that new *functions* are being perfected – for the number of functions which society must meet remains the same – but only that more institutions are involved in handling them. The process is 'adaptive' for the society since the differentiation of activities in this way allows much more complex patterns of social organization to develop; the great bureaucracies of modern society could not operate as they do if economic and occupational relationships were still carried on through kinship ties, for the personal bonds of kinship would interfere with the impersonal relationships which characterize bureaucracies.

The process of differentiation does produce strains and conflicts in the society. The development of the Lancashire cotton industry in the eighteenth and nineteenth centuries, for example, involved the separation of economic productive activities from family and kinship relations. In the early stages of the process of industrialization the family often moved *en bloc* into the mills and worked there as a team, but

the enlargement of mules and the introduction of power-looms threatened to separate the labour of children from that of adults (often parents). These technological pressures, while long in the maturing, reached a critical point in the mid-1820s. For the family economy of the factory operatives, the pressures represented a serious dissatisfaction. . . . The worker and his family could no longer work on the old basis which fused the family economy with other, more general family functions. If the worker refused to accept the new conditions of employment, he could no longer support his family satisfactorily; if he accepted labour on the new basis, certain non-economic relations in his family – particularly the rearing of children – might suffer. These pressures, magnified by an appeal to independence and personal responsibility as a family value, pressed for a thoroughgoing reorganization of family relationships.

The factory operatives, especially the adult male spinners, reacted immediately and fiercely to this pressure in a number of disturbed social movements . . . a series of vigorous but unsuccessful strikes to resist the new machinery; a commitment to the ten-hour agitation of the 1830s, one effect of which would have been to preserve the old work-structure; a prolonged attempt to subvert the Factory Act of 1833, which threatened to separate the labour of adult and child even further; and a brief though intensive flirtation with the Utopian co-operative movement (Smelser, 1959, p. 406).

The conflict and violence involved in the process of industrialization are to be seen as responses to disturbances in the society, disturbances created by the readjustment of relationships between family and economy. These conflicts, however, were 'handled and channelled' by social control mechanisms which prevented them from disrupting the social fabric too greatly and society was 'reintegrated' around a new, more differentiated, structure of relationships. Social control prevents the emerging pattern of relationships from moving too far out of line with already established and unchanging structures and directs the patterns of change along routes which will make the new relationships compatible with other parts of the social structure and with the values of the society.

The consensus theorist, therefore, can handle social change but there is some substance to the criticisms which are made of him; although his model does deal with long-term trends quite well and can provide some account of conflict it does not really account very well for processes of radical and rapid or revolutionary change.

Conflict theory claims a much greater capacity to handle change, change of both the gradual kind and of the rapid and revolutionary kind. It does not begin, as does consensus theory from the assumption that societies tend towards stability but, rather, begins with the idea that the natural state of society is change, that social structures are inherently unstable and will tend to change unless such tendencies can be stayed by the exercise of power. Consensus theory has to appeal to rather feeble notions such as 'inadequate socialization' or to factors outside the society in order to account for change, but conflict theory emphasizes the *inherent* pressures towards change in the society, particularly the role of conflict groups struggling for advantage; much social change is an outcome of shifts in the relationships between such groups.

Consensus theory regards structural changes as occurring within the framework of a given set of values, which, with their associated mechanisms of social control, articulate and limit the directions of development; since these values are shared, there can be no real basis within the society for the emergence of distinctively new values. Consensus theory is not, therefore, well equipped to explain those fundamental changes which involve the alteration of society's basic values; conflict theory, however, is in a position to do so.

For conflict theory, the dominant values of the society are the *politically* dominant values, the values of the ruling group: alternative values do exist, being carried by politically subordinate groups. There is, then, no problem in accounting for changes in the basic values of society, since overthrow of the ruling group will result in the introduction of new value-systems.

We said, at the beginning of this presentation, that we would describe these two theories as extreme positions. This we have done, outlining the core themes which preoccupy the members of each 'school' of thought and showing how these themes are related, one to another.

These perspectives each rest upon a basic set of assumptions about the relationship of men to one another and are, in this respect, 'visions' of society which lead those who adopt them to look only for those facts which will confirm them in their beliefs; if, for example, conflict is seen as an intrinsic and basic feature of social life, then the arguments of the consensus theorist are not to be taken seriously. Each view discourages its proponents from looking at evidence which contradicts its basic assumptions or when such evidence is encountered – encourages them to treat it as a 'mere' irrelevance or to reinterpret it so that it fits within their scheme of thought. But if we can bear both of these visions in mind when thinking about social organization, we can treat them as heuristic devices – ways of looking at social organization – so that we will be unlikely to simply and arbitrarily decide to emphasize the elements of conflict in society over against those of consensus – or to do the reverse. In practice, there is perhaps not so much difference between the two perspectives as we have hitherto argued.

Conflict theorists do not usually adopt the extreme position of refusing to recognize the existence of any consensus whatsoever in society. Most of them, though they regard *society* as being divided by conflict *groups*, are fully aware that for these groups to function as agents in a conflict it is necessary that there be consensus among the group's members and that they have a sense of solidarity with one another. In Marx's thought, whilst conflict was seen as endemic and as permeating the whole of society, a vital step in the understanding of social change was the analysis of the emergence of consensus within conflict-groups; notably, the development of class-consciousness – the recognition on the part of members of a class of their common situation and interests, and the adoption of a common plan of action to realize those interests. The emergence of this common consciousness was thus crucial to the solidarity of the group. This heightening of solidarity within classes, at the same time, presaged intensified conflict between classes. Thus Marx, often depicted as a typical conflict theorist, was vitally concerned with aspects of consensus too.

Nor need conflict always be seen as disruptive. It may be viewed in the light of the contribution which it makes to the continuity, unity and solidarity of society for, in many ways, conflict can promote unity; it may, for example, bring into the open discontents and disagreements which are present in the society but which have not previously been recognized and allow them to be alleviated, it may lead to the dissolution of relationships which have been a source of tension and lead to the formation of new relationships.

There is not, then, total disagreement between the two positions for each accepts that there are elements of both solidarity and opposition present in society. Furthermore, both accept the truth of the proposition 'consensus promotes solidarity and unity'; the issue between them is the question of whether or not this principle is adequate to serve as a basis for analysing complex societies?

Consensus theorists feel that it is, that in such societies there are very marked consensual features; they point to the stability of advanced industrial societies and to the fact that the promised proletarian revolution has not occurred. There is nothing wrong, they feel, in treating the social conflicts which do occur as the results of maladjustment in a basically stable society; after all these conflicts have tended to be mild, insignificant and of short duration, failing to produce changes of anything like the same importance as those which arise from, say, technological developments. They have also emphasized the affluence of the developed societies and have argued that although there are still significant differences in wealth and power, it is within the capacity of these societies to provide all their members with secure and decent lives.

Conflict theorists do not accept that such an analysis of industrial societies is adequate; they would assert that 'consensus promotes solidarity and unity but the unity of society can also be gained through the use of force'. It is true that industrial societies have been stable, but conflicts commonly occur within them, and there are fundamental disagreements about matters of value within them. Furthermore stability has been maintained through more frequent resort to force than consensus theorists allow. Consensus theorists also neglect the extent to which stability in industrial societies has been purchased at the expense of the countries of the Third World, and ignore the fact that the advanced industrial societies are no longer closed systems but are, instead, members of a worldwide social order which can hardly be described as consensual or conflict-free.

There is no way in which one can choose between these viewpoints since each can provide evidence to support its own case. The fact that there is evidence for each view, but also evidence against it, shows that neither adequately accounts for the facts. One can, alternatively, recognize that both have their uses, that for some purposes it is best to use one perspective and for other purposes to use the other perspective; each allows us some understanding of any problem and in some cases one allows us a deeper understanding than does the other. Most importantly, however, one should recognize that while both have their virtues, neither has a monopoly of truth and that there is room for a more comprehensive theory which will encompass both the phenomenon of conflict and that of consensus.

In this chapter we have provided an introduction to some of the work that has been done on the problem of social order, have outlined some of the most general of sociological theories, and sketched some of the developments that follow from these theories.

The organization of the interpersonal traffic which constitutes everyday life requires a significant measure of consensus for its successful operation. Without shared and sanctioned rules held in common, actors would be unable to communicate with one another and would be unable to concert and co-ordinate their actions. Society, without doubt, involves some moral order. But what is an open question is how much consensus is necessary for more complex forms of social life to operate?

In the discussion, we have outlined three models of society which differ in the emphasis that they place upon value consensus. The *consensus* model sees a set of dominant values as a precondition of social order and regards any society which is not torn by civil war as being characterized by such a consensus. They recognize that, of course, consensus is never universal in society and that in certain areas the commitment of some members to the core values become attenuated; there one finds deviance and dissaffection.

The *conflict* perspective stresses the diversity of values present in society and regards such diversity as either a consequence or a cause of conflicts of interest: the existence of diverse values is correlated with the existence of conflict-groups. A value consensus holds the conflict-group together and is one of the bases upon which the groups are mobilized for conflict; the heightening of conflict between groups often intensifies the consensus within them. The society itself is not held together by consensus but, *primarily* by the use of power and force; dominant groups may try to promote consensus but only do do so to improve their position of domination.

The *pluralist* model stresses the diversity of values within society and emphasizes the fact that these values are associated with distinctive groupings – often ethnic groups – but does not assume that diverse values necessarily mean conflicting values. It may be that conflicting values develop and social conflicts occur, but quite distinctive values might well be compatible with one another, or, if incompatible, might not give rise to conflict because they are segregated from one another by social and geographical distance. The society is not held together by any single principle; some elements of shared values will operate together with coercion, manipulation and purely calculative interest, as well as intricate mechanisms of social control and adjustment which limit the possibilities of friction and conflict arising from diversity. Indeed, to some extent the society is not 'integrated' at all, in so far as each of the groups which compose it lives within its own world and leads its life independently of, and without reference to, the other groups.

We have tried to suggest that no single one of these models can account for all the facts about society but we wish to stress that each of them does have its uses and enables us to obtain some understanding of some problems.

We shall not attempt to pull together the various strands of our argument in order to provide a misleadingly systematic portrait of the state of sociological theory. We have tried, more than anything else, to show in this chapter that sociology is currently diversified and divided and that it faces many problems. Our discussion of deviance, for example, was intended to show that great difficulties are involved in relating very general theories about the workings of complex society to the everyday activities and situations which constitute that society, but that a failure to make this connexion weakens and undermines the usefulness of the theory. Sociologists have yet to solve the problem of relating these two levels of analysis together, but this is only one of many problems which theory faces. There are interesting problems to solve; much constructive work needs to be done.

Sociology thus has a great variety of tasks ahead of it, and difficult theoretical problems to resolve. Throughout this book, we have seen that there is an extraordinary diversity of approaches to the study of society. Indeed, we have to some extent deliberately underemphasized the fact that some approaches are not only different, but see themselves as in rivalry to other 'schools'. Most sociologists are fairly eclectic; even though they try to systematize their thinking, they draw their ideas from a variety of sources. Some of these are, however, attempts to construct consistent 'world-views' or theoretical systems which lay claim to be *the* way of looking at the world. Some of these visions are political ideologies, such as Marxism, and hence carry a special attractiveness to some because they are backed by institutional loyalties and invested with social ideals; others are more academic 'schools' of sociological thinking, some of them with appalling names like 'symbolic interactionism' and 'ethnomethodology' Rather than frighten off the gentle reader, we reserved the shock of confrontation with these polysyllabic monsters for the back of the book.

Yet in fact he has been reading about their ideas all the way through, in less austere language. If he now goes on to read the originals, he will have been at least exposed to an initial awareness of the kinds of problems and approaches to those problems these schools of thought represent. He will not necessarily find them easy to master, but then thinking about anything problematic is not easy; that is why we have to do some work in order to become better at it. As for finding one's way between the rival schools, that, in the end, is the reader's own job. We cannot pontificate about what are ultimately matters of judgement necessarily affected by the kinds of values one holds. We have tried, in this book, to give the reader the basic tools with which to make his own judgements in a more informed and better-equipped way, and have tried to draw a map for him. We hope that he has enjoyed his intellectual journey so far, and that he will continue to enjoy it, as we have enjoyed ours – or, more exactly, have enjoyed ours *so far*, for there is only one thing certain about intellectual journeys: that though we do get somewhere, the journey itself never ends.

References

Anderson, P., and Blackburn, R. (eds.) (1965), *Towards Socialism*, Fontana.
Arensberg, C. M., and Kimball, S. T. (1940), *Family and Community in Ireland*, Harvard University Press.
Aubert, V. (1965), 'The sociology of sleep', in *The Hidden Society*, Bedminster.

Baldamus, W. (1967), *Efficiency and Effort*, Tavistock.
Banks, J. A. (1954), *Prosperity and Parenthood: A Study of Family Planning among the Victorian Middle Classes*, Routledge & Kegan Paul.
Banks, O. (1968), *The Sociology of Education*, Batsford.
Banton, M. (1965), *Roles*, Tavistock.
Beauvoir, S. de (1953), *The Second Sex*, Four Square.
Becker, H. S. (1963), *Outsiders: Studies in the Sociology of Deviance*, Free Press.
Becker, H., S., Geer, B., Hughes, E. C., and Strauss, A. L. (1963), *Boys in White*, Chicago University Press.
Bell, N. W., and Vogel, E. F. (eds.) (1960), *A Modern Introduction to the Family*, Free Press.
Berger, P. (1963), *Invitation to Sociology*, Doubleday; Penguin, 1967.
Berger, P. (ed.) (1964), *The Human Shape of Work*, Macmillan.
Berger, P., and Luckmann, T. (1966), *The Social Construction of Reality: A Treatise on the Sociology of Knowledge*, Doubleday.
Bernstein, B. (1961), 'Social class and linguistic development: a theory of social learning', in A. H. Halsey, J. Floud and A. C. Anderson (eds.), *Education, Economy and Society*, Free Press, pp. 288–314.
Bernstein, B. (1965), 'A socio-linguistic approach to social learning', in J. Gould (ed.), *Penguin Survey of the Social Sciences*, Penguin Books.
Black, M. (ed.) (1961), *The Social Theories of Talcott Parsons: A Critical Examination*, Prentice-Hall.
Blau, P. M. (1963), *The Dynamics of Bureaucracy*, 2nd edn, University of Chicago Press.
Blau, P. M., and Scott, W. R. (1963), *Formal Organizations: A Comparative Approach*, Routledge & Kegan Paul.
Bott, E. (1957), *Family and Social Network*, Tavistock.
Bottomore, T. B. (1954), 'Social stratification in voluntary organizations', in D. V. Glass (ed.), *Social Mobility in Britain*, Routledge & Kegan Paul, pp. 349–82.

Bottomore, T. B. (1964), *Elites and Society*, Watts.

Briggs, A. (1960), 'The language of class in early nineteenth-century England', in *Essays in Labour History*, Macmillan.

Briggs, A. (1962), *The Age of Improvement, 1783–1867*, Longmans.

Buckner, H. T. (1967), *The Police: The Culture of a Social Control Agency*, unpublished Ph.D. dissertation, University of California.

Burnham, J. (1941), *The Managerial Revolution*, Putnam; Penguin, 1945.

Burns, T. (1955), 'The reference of conduct in small groups: cliques and cabals in occupational milieux', *Human Relations*, vol. 8, pp. 467–86, Bobbs-Merrill.

Burns, T., and Stalker, G. M. (1961), *The Management of Innovation*, Tavistock.

Caplow, T. (1954), *The Sociology of Work*, University of Minnesota Press.

Carr-Saunders, A. M., Caradog Jones, D., and Moser, C. A. (1958), *A Survey of Social Conditions in England and Wales*, Clarendon Press.

Chapin, F. S. (1947), *Experimental Designs in Sociological Research*, Harper.

Chombart de Lauwe, P. H., Antoine, S., Couvreur, L., and Gauthier, J. (1952), *Paris et l'agglomération Parisienne*, Presses Universitaires de France, Paris.

Church of England (1965), *Facts and Figures about the Church of England*, no. 3, Church Information Office.

Cicourel A. V. (1968), *The Social Organization of Juvenile Justice*, Wiley.

Clinard, M. B. (ed.) (1964), *Anomie and Deviant Behaviour*, Free Press.

Cloward, R. A., and Ohlin, L. E. (1960), *Delinquency and Opportunity*, Routledge & Kegan Paul.

Cockburn, A., and Blackburn, R. (eds.) (1969), *Student Power*, Penguin.

Cohen, P. S. (1968), *Modern Social Theory*, Heinemann.

Cohn, N. (1957), *The Pursuit of the Millennium: Revolutionary Messianism in Medieval and Reformation Europe and its Bearings on Modern Totalitarianism*, Heinemann.

Cole, G. D. H. (1955), *Studies in Class Structure*, Routledge & Kegan Paul.

Coleman, J. S. (1964), *Introduction to Mathematical Sociology*, Collier-Macmillan.

Cooley, C. H. (1964), 'Primary groups', in L. A. Coser and B. Rosenberg (eds.), *Sociological Theory*, Collier-Macmillan, pp. 311–14. (Reprinted from C. H. Cooley, *Social Organizations*, Scribner's, 1909, pp. 23–8.)

Coser, L. (1956), *The Functions of Social Conflict*, Routledge & Kegan Paul.

Cunnison, S. (1966), *Wages and Work Allocation*, Tavistock.

Dahrendorf, R. (1968), 'Out of Utopia', *Essays in the Theory of Society*, Routledge & Kegan Paul.

Dennis, N., Henriques, F., and Slaughter, C. (1956), *Coal is Our Life*, Eyre & Spottiswoode.

Djilas, M. (1957), *The New Class*, Thames & Hudson.

Douglas, J. D. (1967), *The Social Meanings of Suicide*, Princeton University Press.

Douglas, J. W. B. (1966), *The Home and the School*, MacGibbon & Kee.

Drucker, P. F. (1962), 'The educational revolution', in A. H. Halsey, J. Floud and A. C. Anderson (eds.), *Education, Economy and Society*, Free Press, pp. 15–21.

Dubin, R. J. (1956), 'Industrial workers' worlds: a study of the "central life interests" of industrial workers', *Social Problems*, vol. 3, pp. 131–42.

Durkheim, E. (1952), *Suicide: A Study in Sociology*, Routledge & Kegan Paul. (First published in French in 1897.)

Durkheim, E. (1964), *The Division of Labor in Society*, Free Press. (First published in French in 1893.)

Emmett, I. (1964), *A North Wales Village*, Routledge & Kegan Paul.

Engels, F. (1953), 'The condition of the working-class in England', in *Marx–Engels on Britain*, Foreign Languages Publishing House, Moscow. (First published in 1845.)

Ensor, R. C. K. (1960), *England, 1870–1914*, Clarendon Press.

Etzioni, A. (1961), *A Comparative Analysis of Complex Organizations*, Free Press.

Etzioni, A. (1964), *Modern Organizations*, Prentice-Hall.

Fanon, F. (1965), *The Wretched of the Earth*, MacGibbon & Kee; Penguin, 1967.

Festinger, L., Riecken, H. W., and Schachter, S. (1966), *When Prophecy Fails*, Harper & Row.

Finer, S. E. (1962), *The Man on Horseback*, Pall Mall.

Fletcher, R. (1962), *The Family and Marriage in Britain*, Penguin.

Fortes, M., and Evans-Pritchard, E. E. (1940), *African Political Systems*, Oxford University Press.

Frankenberg, R. (1957), *Village on the Border*, Cohen & West.

Garfinkel, H. (1963), 'A conception of, and experiments with, "Trust" as a condition of stable concerted actions', in O. J. Harvey (ed.), *Motivation and Social Interaction*, Ronald Press, pp. 187–238.

Garfinkel, H. (1967), *Studies in Ethnomethodology*, Prentice-Hall.

Geddes, D. P. (1954), *An Analysis of the Kinsey Reports*, Mentor.

Gerth, H. H., and Mills, C. W. (eds.) (1948), *From Max Weber: Essays in Sociology*, Routledge & Kegan Paul.

Giddens, A. (1968), '"Power" in the recent writings of Talcott Parsons', *Sociology*, vol. 2, pp. 257–72.

Glass, D. V. (ed.) (1954), *Social Mobility in Britain*, Routledge & Kegan Paul.

Gluckman, M. (1950), 'Kinship and marriage among the Lozi of Northern Rhodesia and the Zulu of Natal', in A. R. Radcliffe-Brown and D. Forde (eds.), *African Systems of Kinship and Marriage*, Oxford University Press, pp. 166–206.

Gluckman, M. (1956), *Custom and Conflict in Africa*, Blackwell.

Goffman, E. (1961), 'On the characteristics of total institutions', in *Asylums*, Doubleday, pp. 1–24; Penguin, 1968.

Goldthorpe, J. H. (1964), 'Social stratification in industrial societies', in *The Development of Industrial Societies, Sociological Review*, Monograph no. 4, Keele, pp. 97–122.

Goldthorpe, J. H., Lockwood, D., Bechhofer, F., and Platt, J. (1967), 'The affluent worker and the thesis of embourgeoisement', *Sociology*, vol. 1, no. 1, pp. 11–31.

Goldthorpe, J. H., Lockwood, D., Bechhofer, F., and Platt, J. (1968), *The Affluent Worker: Industrial Attitudes and Behaviour*, Cambridge University Press.

Gorer, G. (1955), *Exploring English Characters*, Cresset Press.

Gough, E. K. (1960), 'Is the family universal? – the Nayar case', in N. W. Bell and E. F. Vogel (eds.), *A Modern Introduction to the Family*, Free Press, pp. 80–96.

Gould, J. (ed.) (1965), *Penguin Survey of the Social Sciences*, Penguin.

Gouldner, A. W. (1955), *Patterns of Industrial Bureaucracy*, Routledge & Kegan Paul.

Gouldner, A. W. (1959), 'Reciprocity and autonomy in functional theory', in L. Gross (ed.), *Symposium on Sociological Theory*, Harper.

Greenfield, S. M. (1961), 'Industrialization and the family in sociological theory', *American Journal of Sociology*, vol. 67, pp. 312–22.

Gunther, J. (1947), *Inside USA*, Hamilton.

Hillery, G. A. (1955), 'Definitions of community: areas of agreement', *Rural Sociology*, vol. 20, pp. 111–23.

Hillery, G. A. (1968), *Communal Organizations*, University of Chicago Press.

Hinton, W. (1966), *Fanshen: A Documentary of Revolution in a Chinese Village*, Monthly Review Press.

Hoggart, R. (1958), *The Uses of Literacy*, Penguin.

Homans, G. C. (1951), *The Human Group*, Routledge.

Jackson, B., and Marsden, D. (1962), *Education and the Working Class*, Routledge & Kegan Paul; Penguin, 1966.

Janowitz, M. (ed.) (1964), *The New Military: Changing Patterns of Organization*, Russell Sage.

Kapferer, B. (1969), 'Norms and the manipulation of relationships in a work context', in J. C. Mitchell (ed.), *Social Networks in Urban Situations*, Manchester University Press, pp. 181–244.

Kerner Commission (1968), *Report of the National Advisory Commission on Civil Disorders*, Bantam.

Kerr, C., Dunlop, J. T., Harbison, F. H., and Myers, C. A. (1962), *Industrialism and Industrial Man*, Heinemann.

Klein, J. (1965), *Samples from English Cultures*, Routledge & Kegan Paul.

Klein, V. (1965), *Britain's Married Women Workers*, Routledge & Kegan Paul.

König, R. (1968), *The Community*, Routledge. (First published in German in 1958.)

Kozol, J. (1968), *Death at an Early Age*, Penguin.

Kuhn, T. S. (1962), *The Structure of Scientific Revolutions*, University of Chicago Press.

Kuper, L. (1965), *An African Bourgeoisie*, Yale University Press.

Lacey, C. (1966), 'Some sociological concomitants of academic streaming in a grammar school', *British Journal of Sociology*, vol. 17, no. 3, pp. 245–62.

Lacey, C. (1970), *Hightown Grammar*, Manchester University Press.

Laslett, P. (1965), *The World We Have Lost*, Methuen.

Leach, E. (1968), 'Ignoble savages', *New York Review of Books*, vol. 10, no. 8, pp. 24–9.

Lemert, E. M. (1967), *Human Deviance, Social Problems and Social Control*, Prentice-Hall.

Lenski, G. (1961), *The Religious Factor*, Doubleday.

Liebow, E. (1967), *Tally's Corner*, Routledge & Kegan Paul.

Linton, R. (1963), *The Study of Man*, Appleton-Century-Crofts.

Lipset, S. M. (1963), *The First New Nation: The United States in Historical and Comparative Perspective*, Basic Books.

Lipset, S. M., and Bendix, R. (1959), *Social Mobility in Industrial Society*, Heinemann.

Lockwood, D. (1956), 'Some remarks on "The Social System"', *British Journal of Sociology*, vol. 7, pp. 134–45.

Lockwood, D. (1958), *The Blackcoated Worker*, Allen & Unwin.

Long, N. (1961), 'The local community as an ecology of games', in O. P. Williams and C. Press (eds.), *Democracy in Urban America*, University of Chicago Press. (First published in the *American Journal of Sociology*, vol. 64, 1958.)

Loomis, C. P. (1955), Translator's Introduction to F. Tönnies, *Community and Association*, Routledge & Kegan Paul.

Lupton, T. (1963), *On the Shop Floor: Two Studies on Workshop Organization and Output*, Pergamon Press.

Lupton, T., and Wilson, C. S. (1959), 'The social background and connexions of "top decision makers"', *Manchester School of Economic and Social Studies*, vol. 27, pp. 30–52.

Lynd, R. S. and Lynd, H. M. (1929), *Middletown*, Harcourt, Brace & World.

Lynd, R. S., and Lynd, H. M. (1937), *Middletown in Transition*, Harcourt, Brace & World.

McGregor, O. R. (1957), *Divorce in England*, Heinemann.

MacIver, R. M. (1937), *Society*, Macmillan. (Also in the revised edition of R. M. MacIver and C. H. Page, *Society*, Macmillan, 1961.)

Malinowski, B. (1922), *Argonauts of the Western Pacific*, Routledge & Kegan Paul.

Malinowski, B. (1944), *A Scientific Theory of Culture*, University of North Carolina Press.

Mannheim, K. (1948), *Ideology and Utopia*, Routledge & Kegan Paul.

Markley, O. W. (1967), 'A simulation of the SIVA model of organizational behaviour', *American Journal of Sociology*, vol. 73, pp. 345–69.

Marshall, T. H. (1950), *Citizenship and Social Class*, Cambridge University Press.

Martin, F. M. (1954a), 'Some subjective aspects of social stratification', in D. V. Glass (ed.), *Social Mobility in Britain*, Routledge & Kegan Paul, pp. 57–75.

Martin, F. M. (1954b), 'An inquiry into parents' preferences in secondary education', in D. V. Glass (ed.), *Social Mobility in Britain*, Routledge & Kegan Paul, pp. 160–74.

Marx, K. (1942), *Capital*, vol. 1, Everyman. (First published in 1867.)

Mead, M. (1964), *Sex and Temperament in Three Primitive Societies*, Routledge & Kegan Paul. (First published in 1935.)

Mencher, J. P. (1965), 'The Nayars of South Malabar', in M. F. Nimkoff (ed.), *Comparative Family Systems*, Houghton Mifflin, pp. 163–91.

Merton, R. K. (1957), *Social Theory and Social Structure*, rev. edn, Free Press.

Merton, R. K., Gray, A. P., Hockey, B., and **Selvin, H. C.** (eds.) (1952), *Reader in Bureaucracy*, Free Press.

Merton, R. K., Reader, G. G., and **Kendall, P. L.** (eds.) (1957), *The Student Physician*, Harvard University Press.

Mills, C. W. (1956), *The Power Elite*, Oxford University Press.

Mills, C. W. (1959a), *The Sociological Imagination*, Oxford University Press.

Mills, C. W. (1959b), 'The cultural apparatus', in I. L. Horowitz (ed.), *Power, Politics and People: The Collected Essays of C. Wright Mills*, Ballantine, pp. 405–22.

Miner, H. (1963), *St Denis – A French-Canadian Parish*, Phoenix. (First published in 1939.)

Mitchell, J. C. (1966), 'Theoretical orientations in African urban studies', in M. Banton (ed.), *The Social Anthropology of Complex Societies*, A.S.A. monograph no. 4, Tavistock.

Mitchell, J. C. (ed.) (1969), *Social Networks in Urban Situations*, Manchester University Press.

Mitchell, W. C. (1967), *Sociological Analysis and Politics: The Theories of Talcott Parsons*, Prentice-Hall.

Mitford, M. R. (1951), *Our Village*, Dent. (First published in 1824.)

Moser, C. A. (1958), *Survey Methods in Social Investigation*, Heinemann.

Murdock, G. P. (1949), *Social Structure*, Macmillan.

Newson, J. and E. (1963), *Patterns of Infant Care in an Urban Community*, Penguin.

Nichols, T. (1969), *Ownership, Control and Ideology*, Allen & Unwin.

Nimkoff, M. F. (ed.) (1965), *Comparative Family Systems*, Houghton Mifflin.

Nordhoff, C. (1961), *The Communist Societies of the United States*, Hilary House. (First published in 1875.)

Packard, V. (1957), *The Hidden Persuaders*, McKay; Penguin, 1960.

Pareto, V. (1966), S. E. Finer (ed.), *Sociological Writings*, Pall Mall.

Parker, S. R., Brown, R. K., Child, J., and Smith, M. A. (1967), *The Sociology of Industry*, Allen & Unwin.

Parsons, T. (1961), *The Structure of Social Action: A Study in Social Theory with Special Reference to a Group of Recent European Writers*, Free Press. (First published in 1937.)

Parsons, T. (1962), 'The school class as a social system: some of its functions in American society', in A. H. Halsey, J. Floud and A. C. Anderson (eds.), *Education, Economy and Society*, Free Press, pp. 434–55.

Parsons, T., and Bales, R. F. (1956), *Family, Socialization and Interaction Process*, Routledge & Kegan Paul.

Perrucci, R. (1967), 'Education, stratification and mobility', in D. A. Hanson and J. E. Gerstl (eds.), *On Education – Sociological Perspectives*, Wiley.

Peters, E. L. (1965), 'Aspects of the family among the Bedouin of Cyrenaica', in M. F. Nimkoff (ed.), *Comparative Family Systems*, Houghton Mifflin, pp. 12–146.

Polsky, N. (1967), *Hustlers, Beats and Others*, Aldine.

Presthus, R. (1962), *The Organizational Society*, Knopf.

Pugh, D. S., Hickson, D. J., and Hinings, C. R. (1964), *Writers on Organizations*, Hutchinson.

Radcliffe-Brown, A. R. (1952), *Structure and Function in Primitive Society*, Cohen & West.

Radcliffe-Brown, A. R., and Forde, D. (eds.) (1950), *African Systems of Kinship and Marriage*, Oxford University Press.

Redfield, R. (1955), *The Little Community: Viewpoints for the Study of a Human Whole*, University of Chicago Press, Phoenix.

Reissman, L. (1964), *The Urban Process*, Free Press.

Reitzes, D. (1960), 'The role of organizational structures: union versus neighborhood in a tension situation', in S. M. Lipset and N. J. Smelser (eds.), *Sociology: The Progress of a Decade*, Prentice-Hall, pp. 516–21. (First published in *Journal of Social Issues*, vol 9.)

Rex, J. (1961), *Key Problems of Sociological Theory*, Routledge & Kegan Paul.

Rex, J., and Moore, R. (1967), *Race, Community and Conflict*, Oxford University Press for Institute of Race Relations.

Riesman, D. (1953), *The Lonely Crowd*, Doubleday.

Robbins Report (1963), Report of the Committee on Higher Education, H.M.S.O.

Roethlisberger, F. J., and Dickson, W. J. (1964), *Management and the Worker*, Wiley. (First published in 1939.)

Routh, G. (1965), *Occupation and Pay in Great Brtiain 1906–1960*, Cambridge University Press.

Rudé, G. (1959), *The Crowd in the French Revolution*, Clarendon Press.

Runciman, W. G. (1966), *Relative Deprivation and Social Justice*, Routledge & Kegan Paul.

Salisbury, R. F. (1962), *Structures of Custodial Care*, University of California Press.

Sampson, A. (1965), *Anatomy of Britain Today*, Hodder & Stoughton.

Schnore, L. F. (1967), 'Community', in N. J. Smelser (ed.), *Sociology: An Introduction*, Wiley, pp. 79–150.

Schofield, M. (1965), *The Sexual Behaviour of Young People*, Longmans; Penguin, 1968.

Seeley, J. R., Sim, R. A., and Loosley, E. W. (1963), *Crestwood Heights: A Study of the Culture of Suburban Life*, Wiley.

Sheth, N. R. (1968), *The Social Framework of an Indian Factory*, Manchester University Press.

Shibutani, T. (1966), *Improvised News: A Sociological Study of Rumour*, Bobbs-Merrill.

Shils, E., and Young, M. (1953), 'The meaning of the coronation', *Sociological Review*, vol. 1, pp. 63–81. (Reprinted in S. M. Lipset and N. J. Smelser (eds.), *Sociology: The Progress of a Decade*, Prentice-Hall, 1961.)

Simmel, G. (1950), K. A. Wolff (ed.), *The Sociology of Georg Simmel*, Free Press.

Smelser, N. J. (1959), *Social Change in the Industrial Revolution: An Application of Theory to the Lancashire Cotton Industry 1770–1840*, Routledge & Kegan Paul.

Smith, A. (1950), *An Inquiry into the Nature and Causes of the Wealth of Nations*, Dent, Everyman's Library. (First published 1776–8.)

Sorokin, P. (1955), Foreword to F. Tönnies, *Community and Association*, Routledge & Kegan Paul.

Spiro, M. E. (1960), 'Is the family universal – the Israeli case', in N. W. Bell and E. F. Vogel (eds.), *A Modern Introduction to the Family*, Free Press, pp. 64–75.

Stacey, M. (1960), *Tradition and Change: A Study of Banbury*, Oxford University Press.

Stafford-Clark, D. (1952), *Psychiatry Today*, Penguin.

Statistics of Education (1962), vol. 1, 1961, H.M.S.O.

Statistics of Education (1968), vol. 1, 1967, H.M.S.O.

Stein, M. R. (1960), *The Eclipse of Community*, Princeton University Press.

Storr, A. (1968), *Human Aggression*, Atheneum, Allen Lane The Penguin Press.

Strauss, A. (1959), 'Language and identity', reprinted in J. G. Manis and B. N. Meltzer (eds.), *Symbolic Interaction: A Reader in Social Psychology*, Allyn & Bacon, 1967.

Strauss, A. (1964) (ed.), *George Herbert Mead on Social Psychology*, rev. edn, University of Chicago Press.

Sudnow, D. (1967), *Passing On*, Prentice-Hall.

Sutherland, E. H. (1961), *White Collar Crime*, Holt, Rinehart & Winston. (First published in 1949.)

Talmon, Y. (1965), 'The family in a revolutionary movement: the case of the Kibbutz in Israel', in M. F. Nimkoff (ed.), *Comparative Family Systems*, Houghton Mifflin, pp. 259–86.
Thompson, E. P. (1967), 'Time, work-discipline and industrial capitalism', *Past and Present*, vol. 38, pp. 56–97.
Titmuss, R. M. (1958), *Essays on the 'Welfare State'*, Allen & Unwin.
Titmuss, R. M. (1962), *Income Distribution and Social Change*, Allen & Unwin.
Tönnies, F. (1955), *Community and Association*, Routledge & Kegan Paul. (First published in German in 1877.)
Trotsky, L. (1969), *The Revolution Betrayed*, New Park Publications. (First published in 1937.)
Turner, V. W. (1957), *Schism and Continuity in an African Society*, Manchester University Press.

UNESCO (1965), *Educational Priority Projects for Development: Guatemala*, UNESCO, Paris.
U.S. Bureau of the Census (1967), J. K. Folger and C. B. Nam, *Education of the American Population*, a 1960 census monograph, U.S. Government Printing Office, Washington, D.C.

Warner, W. L., Meeker, M., and Eells, K. (1949), *Social Class in America*, Harper & Row.
Warner, W. L., and Low, J. G. (1947), *The Social System of the Modern Factory*, Yale University Press.
Warner ,W. L., and Lunt, P. S. (1941), *The Social Life of a Modern Community*, Yale University Press.
Watson, J. (1968), *The Double Helix*, Weidenfeld & Nicolson.
Webber, M. M., Dyckman, J. W., Foley, D. L., Guttenberg, A. Z., Wheaton, W. L. C., and Wurster, C. B. (1964), *Explorations into Urban Structure*, University of Pennsylvania Press.
Weber, M. (1952), *The Protestant Ethic and the Spirit of Capitalism*, Allen & Unwin. (First published 1904–5.)
Weber, M. (1961), 'The social psychology of the world religions', in H. H. Gerth and C. W. Mills (eds.), *From Max Weber: Essays in Sociology*, Routledge & Kegan Paul. (First published 1922–3.)
Weber, M. (1964), *The Theory of Social and Economic Organization*, Free Press. (First published in 1925.)
Whorf, B. L. (1964), 'The relation of habitual thought and behaviour to language', in J. B. Carrol (ed.), *Language, Thought and Reality: The Selected Writings of Benjamin Lee Whorf*, M.I.T. Press. (First published in 1941.)
Whyte, W. F. (1948), *Human Relations in the Restaurant Industry*, McGraw-Hill.
Whyte, W. F. (1954), *Street Corner Society*, Chicago University Press.

Whyte, W. H., Jr (1957), *The Organization Man*, Cape; Penguin, 1960.

Williams, R. (1958), *Culture and Society 1780–1950*, Penguin.

Wimperis, V. (1960), *The Unmarried Mother and Her Child*, Allen & Unwin.

Winch, P. (1958), *The Idea of a Social Science and Its Relation to Philosophy*, Routledge.

Wirth, L. (1963), 'Urbanism as a way of life', in P. K. Hatt and A. J. Reiss (eds.), *Cities in Society*, Free Press, pp. 46–63. (First published in *American Journal of Sociology*, 1934–5, vol. 44.)

Woodward, J. (1965), *Industrial Organization: Theory and Practice*, Oxford University Press.

Worsley, P. (1967), *The Third World*, Weidenfeld & Nicolson.

Young, M., and Willmott, P. (1957a), *Family and Kinship in East London*, Routledge & Kegan Paul; Penguin, 1962.

Young, M., and Willmott, P. (1957b), 'Social grading by manual workers', *British Journal of Sociology*, vol. 7, pp. 337–45.

Further Reading

Chapter 1

An excellent discussion of the way in which man's animal characteristics affect his social arrangements is Anthony Barnett's *The Human Species* (Penguin, 1957). Peter Berger's *Invitation to Sociology* (Penguin, 1966) is a delightful and thought-provoking discussion of the social, philosophical and ethical implications of sociology. Thomas Kuhn's *The Structure of Scientific Revolutions* (University of Chicago Press, 1962) is a masterly and lucid examination of how science progresses, while Philip E. Hammond's *Sociologists at Work* (Basic Books, 1964) shows the gap between conventional theories of scientific procedure and the reality.

The work of Erving Goffman has introduced new dimensions into sociology, and is eminently readable. The extent to which we are determined by society, and our resistances to those constraints, are typically examined in *Interaction Ritual* (Doubleday, 1967). C. Wright Mills' *The Sociological Imagination* (Oxford University Press, 1959) remains the most challenging general discussion of the moral implications of sociology, and Irving Louis Horowitz has edited a set of essays on an extremely controversial social research project: *The Rise and Fall of Project Camelot* (M.I.T. Press, 1967) in which all these issues came to a head. An excellent reader on sociological theory is Lewis A. Coser and Bernard Rosenberg's *Sociological Theory* (Macmillan, 1969) while *The Discovery of Grounded Theory*, by Barney G. Glaser and Anselm L. Strauss (Weidenfeld & Nicolson, 1968) opens up new conceptions of theory. Finally, H. S. Hughes' *Consciousness and Society* (MacGibbon & Kee, 1959) sets the emergence of modern sociology in the context of the general ideas which shaped European social thought between 1890 and 1930; it is not an elementary work, but is very lucid.

Chapter 2

A detailed study of the logic of inquiry could lead eventually to fundamental problems of philosophy or complex problems of mathematical statistics. For the purposes of the ordinary student of sociology the problems of epistemology set out by Ernest Nagel in *The Structure of Science* (Routledge, 1961), by Abraham Kaplan in *The Conduct of Inquiry* (Chandler, 1964), by Peter Winch in *The Idea of a Social Science* (Routledge, 1958) or by Quentin Gibson in *The Logic of Social Enquiry* (Routledge, 1960) are probably adequate. The more advanced reader will find Cicourel's *Method and Measurement in Sociology* (Free Press, 1964) a useful examination of the epistemological foundations of common research procedures. As far as statistical procedures are concerned there are many elementary textbooks for the beginners in general. The books by Hubert Blalock, *Social Statistics* (McGraw-Hill, 1960), however, and the older one by Margaret Hagood and Daniel Price, *Statistics for Sociologists* (Holt, Rinehart & Winston, 1952), address themselves specifically to the needs of sociologists.

There are several books dealing with research methods in general. Margaret Stacey's *Methods of Social Research* (Pergamon, 1969) is a clear and relatively simple account of the basic procedures suitable for a British public. W. Goode and P. Hatt's *Methods in Social Research* (McGraw-Hill, 1952) has been a stand-by for many years. J. Madge's *The Tools of Social Science*, (Longmans, Green, 1953) provides a British equivalent. The book by C. Sellitz, M. Jahoda, M. Deutsch and S. W. Cook, *Research Methods in Social Relations* (Methuen, 1965) is probably the most comprehensive of this sort of book. The paper by Lazarsfeld on 'Interpretation of statistical relations as a research operation' in P. Lazarsfeld and M. Rosenberg, *The Language of Social Research* (Free Press, 1955) further developed by H. Hyman in *Survey Design and Analysis* (Free Press, 1955) provides a useful statement of the problem of ordering variables in research.

Chapter 3

General and comparative works on the family

There are several good readers and collections of articles which contain a wide variety of comparative material. The following is particularly useful in this respect: N. W. Bell and E. F. Vogel (eds.), *A Modern Introduction to the Family* (Free Press, 1960). The articles or extracts by Murdock, Spiro (on the kibbutz) and Gough (on the Nayar) are directly relevant to this chapter. R. L. Coser, *The Family: its Structure and Functions* (St. Martin's Press, 1964) is an unusual collection which stresses the functional approach. Readers with an anthropological interest will find several interesting and detailed studies in A. R. Radcliffe-Brown and D. Forde (eds.), *African Systems of Kinship and Marriage* (Oxford University Press, 1950). The introduction by Radcliffe-Brown is especially useful. Reference has already been made to the collection of articles edited by Nimkoff; the reader is referred especially to the essays by Peters on the Bedouin, Mencher on the Nayar and Talmon on the kibbutz.

The family in Britain

The reader is referred to the works by Fletcher and Klein. There are a large number of community studies which deal directly or indirectly with the family in modern Britain. In addition to those by Bott and Young and Willmott; C. Rosser and C. Harris, *The Family and Social Change* (Routledge, 1965) is particularly interesting. We would mention also P. Townsend, *The Family Life of Old People* (Routledge, 1957, Penguin, 1963), which contains a useful postscript dealing with some wider issues; and N. Dennis, F. Henriques and C. Slaughter, *Coal is Our Life* (Eyre & Spottiswoode, 1956). A more general account of British community studies can be found in R. Frankenberg, *Communities in Britain* (Penguin, 1966), and J. Klein, *Samples from English Cultures* (Routledge, 1965). Both these books contain a large amount of material about the variety of family situations to be found in modern Britain.

Functionalism

We have already referred to the works by Malinowski, Radcliffe-

Brown and Merton. There are useful sections in L. A. Coser and B. Rosenberg, *Sociological Theory: A Book of Readings* (Macmillan, 1969, 3rd edn).

Chapter 4

A reader can obtain an overview of current interests and research in the sociology of education from the articles in A. H. Halsey, J. Floud and A. C. Anderson, *Education, Economy and Society* (Free Press, 1962). The most recent comprehensive examination of the field is provided in Olive Banks, *The Sociology of Education* (Batsford, 1968). An interesting summary of the impact of social factors on education is available in the article by Robert Perrucci, 'Education, stratification and mobility', in D. A. Hansen and J. E. Gerstl, *On Education – Sociological Perspectives* (Wiley, 1967). In contrast to these general introductions to the field are a series of perceptive case-studies of particular aspects of education. Brian Jackson and Dennis Marsden's *Education and the Working Class* (Routledge, 1962, Penguin, 1966) is a constant source of insight into the effects of social background over the whole period of a child's education. Jonathan Kozol in his *Death at an Early Age* (Penguin, 1968) provides descriptive, and often polemical, material on the workings of a school system, focussing on the administrators and teaching staff. A detailed study of the importance of the social relationships formed within a school for a child's educational progress is given by Colin Lacey in his article on 'Some sociological concomitants of academic streaming in a grammar school'. Lacey shows the way in which the internal social organization of an educational institution affects the learning process. In higher education, a similar focus on the internal dynamics of an organization, as an independent factor affecting learning, is given by Howard Becker and his co-authors in their study of a medical school, *Boys in White* (Chicago University Press, 1963).

Chapter 5

The work by S. R. Parker *et al.* (Allen & Unwin, 1967) already referred to deals largely with British material. William A. Faunce has edited an excellent reader concentrating on American material called *Readings in Industrial Sociology* (Appleton-Century-Crofts, 1967). Readers with an anthropological interest will find a fascinating collection of articles in E. E. LeClair Jr and H. K. Schneider, *Economic Anthropology* (Holt, Rinehart & Winston, 1968).

The theme of alienation is discussed to some extent in the work by J. H. Goldthorpe *et al.* (1968) already cited. A more extensive treatment, referring to four specific work-situations, can be found in R. Blauner, *Alienation and Freedom* (University of Chicago Press, 1964).

Reference has already been made to the works by Merton and by Banton on roles. A more detailed collection of articles on this topic is found in B. J. Biddle and E. J. Thomas (eds.), *Role Theory – Concepts and Research* (Wiley, 1966).

The reader has already been referred to case-studies by Blau (1963), Cunnison (1966), Dennis *et al.* (1956), Goldthorpe *et al.* (1967), Gouldner, Lockwood and Whyte in the text of chapter 5. Another useful study, this time looking at occupants of managerial and professional roles, is provided by T. Burns and G. M. Stalker, *The Management of Innovation* (Tavistock, 1961).

The main comparative studies of organizations have been referred to in the text. For a critical summary of Etzioni's thesis, see 'Sociological approaches to organizations' in S. R. Parker, R. K. Brown, J. Child and M. A. Smith, *The Sociology of Industry* (Allen & Unwin, 1967, ch. 7). Weber's discussion of bureaucracy is to be found in H. H. Gerth and C. W. Mills (eds.), *From Max Weber* (Routledge, 1948, and in Merton *et al.*, *Reader in Bureaucracy* (Free Press, 1952), an excellent collection of writings on all aspects of bureaucracy in many different types of organization. Another useful collection of articles on the structure and functioning of large organizations is A. Etzioni (ed.), *Complex Organizations: A Sociological Reader* (Holt, Rinehart & Winston, 1969, 2nd edn).

There are, of course, numerous studies analysing individual organizations. As well as those mentioned in the text, the following may be recommended: G. Sykes, *The Society of Captives* (Princeton University Press, 1958) and T. Mathieson, *The Defences of the Weak* (Tavistock, 1965) (prisons); S. H. Stanton and M. S. Schwarz, *The Mental Hospital* (Basic Books, 1954), and W. Caudill, *The Psychiatric Hospital as a Small Society* (Harvard University Press, 1958); J. Lofland,

Doomsday Cult (Prentice-Hall, 1966) (a religious sect); P. Selznick, *TVA and the Grass Roots* (University of California Press, 1949) (a development organization); S. M. Lipset, M. A. Trow and J. S. Coleman, *Union Democracy* (Doubleday, 1962) (a trade union); R. Michels, *Political Parties* (Free Press, 1949).

On the concept of network, J. C. Mitchell (ed.), *Social Networks in Urban Situations* (Manchester University Press 1969), is recommended.

Chapter 6

A most useful collection of readings on urban sociology is provided by P. K. Hatt and A. J. Reiss (eds.), *Cities and Society: The Revised Reader in Urban Sociology* (Free Press, 1957), particularly the essays by C. D. Harris and E. L. Ullman on 'The nature of cities', H. Miner's 'The folk-urban continuum', and R. D. Mackenzie's 'The rise of metropolitan communities'.

R. E. Pahl's *Readings in Urban Sociology* (Pergamon, 1968) contains more British material, including N. Dennis' interesting article on 'The popularity of the neighbourhood community idea' (originally published in the *Sociological Review*, vol. 6, no. 2, 1958).

Maurice Stein's *The Eclipse of Community* (Princeton University Press, 1960) (especially parts 1 and 2) needs no further recommendation. Herbert J. Gans' *The Urban Villagers* (Free Press, 1962) is an excellent study of city community life, whilst A. L. Epstein's 'Urbanization and social change in Africa' (original in *Current Anthropology*, vol. 8, no. 4, 1967) takes us out of the developed world, as do all the contributors to G. Breese (ed.), *The City in Newly Developing Countries* (Princeton University Press, 1969).

Chapter 7

An excellent reader on social stratification is André Béteille's *Social Inequality* (Penguin, 1969). A larger, now classic compendium is Lipset and Bendix's *Class, Status and Power* (Routledge, 1967, 2nd edn). The author's introductions to the various parts of *Structured Social Inequality*, by Celia S. Heller (Free Press, 1969) are valuable overviews. Otherwise, the reader can follow up the topics dealt with in the chapter by consulting the works cited in the text. G. D. H.

Cole's *Studies in Class Structure* remains relevant for analysis of British Census data, but P. Anderson and R. Blackburn (eds.), *Towards Socialism* (Fontana, 1965) is a much more imaginative and challenging analysis of the whole class-system; Westergaard's contribution is particularly valuable. And it is always rewarding to read Marx and Weber. Bernstein's (1962) previously cited work on language and social class is an exciting modern development.

Chapter 8

The best short guide to the issues discussed in this chapter and to many other relevant and related issues is P. S. Cohen's *Modern Social Theory* (Heinemann, 1968).

The major discussions of the problem of order from a consensus viewpoint are to be found in the work of Emile Durkheim – particularly his *The Division of Labour in Society* (Free Press, 1964) – and Talcott Parsons. Parsons' writings are extraordinarily difficult and best approached through an introductory text such as William C. Mitchell's *Sociological Analysis and Politics* (Prentice-Hall, 1967) or through the papers in Max Black (ed.), *The Social Theories of Talcott Parsons* (Prentice-Hall, 1961).

Critical discussion of consensus theorizing – and of Parsons' work in particular – together with statements of a conflict perspective, can be found in John Rex's *Key Problems of Sociological Theory* (Routledge, 1961), Ralf Dahrendorf's 'Out of Utopia' (Routledge, 1968), David Lockwood's 'Some remarks on "The Social System"', (1956), and Anthony Giddens' '"Power" in the recent writings of Talcott Parsons' (*Sociology*, vol 2, 1968).

Merton develops his anomie theory of deviance in the two essays 'Social structure and anomie' and 'Continuities in the theory of social structure and anomie', both contained in his *Social Theory and Social Structure* (Free Press, 1957). Marshall B. Clinard (ed.), *Anomie and Deviant Behaviour* (Free Press, 1964) consists of a series of papers criticising, revising and extending Merton's formulation. Criticism and alternative views of deviance can be found in Howard S. Becker *Outsiders: Studies in the Sociology of Deviance* (Free Press, 1963), Edwin M. Lemert, *Human Deviance, Social Problems and Social Control* (Prentice-Hall, 1967), and Aaron V.

Cicourel, *The Social Organization of Juvenile Justice* (Wiley, 1968).

Discussion of the problem of meaning in social life and of the role of common understanding can be found in Peter Winch's *The Idea of a Social Science and its Relation to Philosophy* (Routledge, 1958) and Harold Garfinkel's *Studies in Ethnomethodology* (Prentice-Hall 1967) although each of these books is, in its way, difficult.

Author Index

Subject Index

Abstraction, 109
Age-set societies, 284–6
Aggregate psychology, 108
Aggression, 22, 25, 32
Alienation, 208–9, 225, 245, 327
Alternation, 62
Analysis
  primary, 74
  secondary, 74
Anomie, 245, 364
Anthropology and sociology, 30–31
Anticipatory socialization, 154
Anti-school culture, 186, 361
'Applied' research, 51, 59
Area sampling, 87
Achieved roles, 126
Ascribed roles, 126

Behaviour, 25, 32, 44, 47
Belief-systems, 350–53, 362, 379–80
Biology and culture, 21–8, 32, 117–21
Boundary-maintenance, in education, 181
Bureaucracy
  and authority, 224, 228
  and community, 248
  and impersonality, 226
  and rationality, 225
  and rigidity, 225–6
  and routine, 229
  and uncertainty/change, 226–8
  definition of, 224, 228
Bureaucratization, 267ff.

Capitalism, 202, 304–8
Case-studies, 109, 111
Caste societies, 284, 286–7, 315–16
Class, 284, 287–9, 301–8
  and affluence, 325–6, 327
  and education, 168–9, 182, 184, 299–300
  and property, 287–8, 303
  and religion, 320–21
  and revolution, 291, 302, 305–6, 332–4, 335–6
  and voting patterns, 305, 314, 318
  and work situation, 324–5, 327
  conflict, 301, 321–3
  consciousness of, 288, 296, 302–3, 310–12, 323–4

indicators of, 287, 288, 292–7, 312
Coding, 98–9
Commonsense thought, 348, 353
Community
  'communities within community', 252
  contrast-conceptions of, 255ff, 269
  communities of interest, 271, 274, 278–9
Contract, 304–5
Concepts, 49, 73
Conflict, 255, 374–6, 379ff.
  in industry, 202
Conformity, 358–9, 364, 367
Consciousness, 44, 58, 65–6
Consensus, 362, 373ff.
Consequences, intended and unintended, 194–5
Consumption, social, 198–200
Content analysis, 81–2
Correlations and causal connexions, 103
Correlation coefficient, 103
Cross-pressures, 310
Culture
  accumulation of, 23
  and biology, 22–8, 117–21
  anti-school, 186
  definition of, 24
  discontinuities of, 26

Dependent variables, 102
Deprivation, relative, 290, 333–4
Descent, 120, 131
Determinism, 27, 57–8, 64–6, 306–7
Developing countries
  and education, 173, 192–5
Development
  social and economic, 172–3, 192–5
Deviance, 360ff.
Differentiation
  social, 155
  structure, 384–6
Division of labour
  at work, 200, 219–22, 224
  between sexes, 132–3, 140, 142, 146–7, 201, 205
  classical view, 200
  in the home, 132–3, 140, 142, 146–7, 201

Penguin Education

CRR

~~£1 50~~

Sap

Introducing Sociology

Peter Worsley

Roy Fitzhenry, J. Clyde Mitchell,
D. H. J. Morgan, Valdo Pons, Bryan Roberts,
W. W. Sharrock, Robin Ward